HISTORY

OF THE

2nd KING EDWARD'S OWN GOORKHAS

(The Sirmoor Rifle Regiment)

VOL. II

1911–1921

Sketch by I.W.S.]　　　　　　　　　　　　　　　　　　　　　　[Frontispiece

SANTAUR DEVI TEMPLE NEAR DEHRA.
GREATLY VENERATED BY OUR GOORKHAS.

[*For private circulation only.*]

HISTORY

of the

2nd King Edward's Own Goorkhas

(The Sirmoor Rifle Regiment)

VOL. II.
1911–1921.

By

Colonel L. W. SHAKESPEAR, C.B., C.I.E.
(Late 2nd K.E.O. Goorkhas)

GALE & POLDEN, LTD.
Wellington Works, Aldershot
Also at London & Portsmouth

TO THE MEMORY OF MY OLD COMRADES, BRITISH AND GOORKHA, WITH WHOM I SERVED MANY HAPPY YEARS, AND OF THOSE WHO GALLANTLY LOST THEIR LIVES IN THE GREAT WAR, 1914 TO 1918.

"Not fearing death nor shrinking from distress
But always resolute in most extremes."

PREFACE

In the autumn of 1921 an honour was paid me in a request from my old Regiment to continue its History through all the stress of the Great War, bringing it as near as possible up to date from the point where my earlier volume left off. This was undertaken with some misgivings as to capability in dealing with so large and complicated a subject, seeing I was not present with the Regiment in any of its operations, my humble share in the war having been three years in Mesopotamia on Divisional Staffs.

The work of compilation from masses of brief and often meagre war diaries, a few letters of officers, three private diaries, and other information collected from despatches, etc., at the War Record Office in London, has not been of the easiest though full of deep interest : but if the result hoped for, viz. to perpetuate the gallant actions of our comrades who made the final sacrifice and to recall in the hereafter our days of strenuous services in widely different lands is attained, my efforts will have been amply repaid.

My hearty thanks are due to Major Wyrall and other officials at the War Record Office, for kindly assistance in hunting out any documents, maps, etc., bearing on the subject as well as for providing other bits of information, and to Colonel J. E. Merewether, C.I.E., and the Secretary of State for India, who kindly allowed me to make use of the valuable "History of the Indian Corps in France," in connection with the tactical reasons prefacing certain of the leading operations in which the Regiment bore its share. I would also record my gratitude to Colonel Sweet who very kindly read through, checked, and corrected the whole work, and to Colonel Mackinnon and Major McCleverty, who assisted with corrections in certain portions. In the matter of illustrations I am further most grateful to W. Martin-Hurst, Esq., Director of the "Exclusive News Agency," who most kindly allowed me to reproduce from his collection, free of copyright fees, all the pictures relating to Persia and some of Baghdad, as until meeting him I had been unable to get any of those localities with which to embellish the History. Of the sketch plans which came with the War Diaries those of actions in France are by Major Corse Scott, assisted, I understand, by a friend of his, the others I have arranged from various sources.

It may be added that compilation of casualties has not been easy and may even be slightly incorrect here and there, the reason being that Battalion, Brigade, Divisional and private War Diaries differed frequently as to numbers, in some cases giving two separate and different statements for the same action, and using the term " slight " instead of numbers sometimes. Enquiry was made at the War Record Office if any official list of actions and casualties existed. As there was none, and many other officers similarly employed there were equally perplexed, I had to do the best under the conditions.

1924. L. W. S.

CONTENTS

PART I.—FRANCE, EGYPT, NORTH-WEST FRONTIER, INDIA.

CHAPTER I.
March to December, 1911. (*Sketch I.*)

Dehra and the Abor Expedition—1st Battalion at Kobo—Advance of Ledum Column to Mishing ... ...
PAGE 1—8

CHAPTER II.
December, 1911, to August, 1914. (*Sketch I.*)

Abor Expedition—Rohtang—Kekyar Monying—Surveys—Casualties and Rewards—Return to Dehra—Dehra Items and Pāni Pattia Depot—Centenary Arrangements—Infantry Polo Tournament Cup won by Regimental Team ... ... 9—15

CHAPTER III.
August, 1914, to October 29th, 1914. (*Sketches IX, II.*)

Departure of 2nd Battalion for France—Arrival at Marseilles—Composition of Meerut Division—Orleans—Entry into Zone of Operations—Description of Locality near Neuve Chapelle—General Situation in October, 1914 ... ... 16—23

CHAPTER IV.
October 29th to November 3rd, 1914. (*Sketches IX, II.*)

France—Work in Trenches—Opening of Action November 2nd, 1914—Account of Action—Losses ... ... 24—29

CHAPTER V.
November 3rd to December 17th, 1914. (*Sketches IX, IV, V, III.*)

France—In Billets—Fatigue Parties in Front Line—Captain Duff killed—Lord Roberts' Visit—2nd Battalion attached Garhwal Brigade—Billets—Frostbite Trouble—D.C. Title changed to Company—Quiet in Front Trenches and Work—New Officers and Draft join us—2nd Battalion rejoins Dehra Brigade—La Quinque Rue—State of Trenches—Places for Fresh Operations—Need for Rest and Refitting—Visits of H.M. the King and of the Prince of Wales ... ... 30—35

CHAPTER VI.
December 18th to 23rd, 1914. (*Sketch III.*)

Disposition of Indian Corps—Heavy Bombardment of our Trenches at La Quinque Rue—Account of Action December 20th, 1914—German Success—Our Losses—Gallant Conduct—Further Fighting on December 22nd ... ... 36—40

CONTENTS

CHAPTER VII.

DECEMBER 23RD, 1914, TO MARCH 9TH, 1915. (*Sketches IX, IV, V.*)

Indian Corps in Billets—Battalion at Croix Marmuse for Christmas; then at Floringhem—Account of unofficial Armistice at Christmas—Princess Mary's Gift—Plague of Lice—Colonel Norie leaves us—Brigade Commanders changed—Military Police Draft with Major Nicolay and Captain Dallas Smith—Billets—In Rue du Bois Redoubts—Water-logged Trenches—Billets at La Couture—Military Police Draft with Captains Mullay and Cruickshank—Flooded Trenches in Front Line—Clothing—60th Rifles' Gift—Preparations for Big Offensive—Battalion returns to Front ... ... 41—47

CHAPTER VIII.

MARCH 10TH TO 12TH, 1915. (*Sketches IX, VI.*)

Position of British Line in this Area—Intentions *re* Offensive—Neuve Chapelle and Locality—Objectives in Attack—Arrangements—Battle of Neuve Chapelle—Battalion attacks the Bois du Biez—Major Nicolay missing—Gallantry—Battalion withdrawn from Wood—Attack renewed on 11th—Major Watt wounded—Attack checked—Battalion's Losses—German Massed Attack—Fresh Attack on March 12th checked—Results of Battle—Strength of Germans at Neuve Chapelle ... ... 48—56

CHAPTER IX.

MARCH 13TH TO MAY 10TH, 1915. (*Sketches IX, VII.*)

Billets—Military Police Draft—Battalion in Front Line North of Neuve Chapelle—Finding of Captain Becher's and Captain Barton's bodies—Flooded Trenches—Billets—Sir John French's Inspection—Battalion in Front Line South of Neuve Chapelle—Our Missing and Prisoners of War—First Use of Gas and Precautions—Honours—From Billets to "Port Arthur"—Fresh Offensive—General Situation and Intentions—Orders for Attack—Our Advance held up—Heavy Losses—Fresh Advance checked—Major Rooke, Captains Mathew, Park, and Mullay killed—Our Casualties—Failure of Offensive ... ... 57—66

CHAPTER X.

MAY 10TH TO SEPTEMBER 24TH, 1915. (*Sketches IX, IV, V, VIII.*)

France—Billets—Depletion of Battalion—Battalion in Front Trenches near the Ferme du Bois Front—Major Sweet's narrow Escape—Good Shooting by Lance-Naik Jitman Gurung—Readjustment of Indian Corps Front—Battalion in Trenches facing Cour Ferme d'Avoué—Trench Work—Billets at Les Lobes—News *re* our Prisoners with the Germans—Draft from Dehra—La Couture Billets shelled—"Chocolate Menier" Corner—Farm Corner—Intelligence Report—Battalion in La Quinque Rue Front, and Patrolling—Regrouping of Indian Corps Units—Calonne Billets—Leave to England—Draft from Dehra—Amusements—Brigade Grenadier Company formed—La Gorgue Billets—Platoons of New Army attached to old Units—Battalion at Front North of Neuve Chapelle—The "Duck's Bill" Salient—Trenches flooded again—Draft 7th Goorkha Rifles attached to Battalion—First Moves of Indian Units from France—New Army Officers attached to us to learn trench work—Badinage between opposing Troops—Riez Bailleul Billets—Battalion at Moated Grange—Changes in High Commands—Colvin Trenches—The coming Offensive—Gas to be used—Arrangements of Moated Grange section of Front—Detachment joins 4th Goorkha Rifles for Gallipoli ... ... 67—76

CHAPTER XI.

SEPTEMBER 24TH TO NOVEMBER 9TH, 1915. (*Sketches IX, VIII.*)

General Position in this Area of Front—Plans for fresh Offensive—Indian Corps Objectives—Battle of Loos—Our Gas fails—Dehra Brigade advances—No. 2 Company only in Action—Its Casualties—Failure of Offensive—Rugby Road Billets—Major Sweet transferred to 2/8th Goorkha Rifles—Battalion sent South to Givenchy—Disposition of Battalion and Work—Festubert—Battalion's last Casualty—Move to Lansdowne Post—March to La Pannerie for the King's Inspection—His Accident—Unfit men sent to Nieppe Forest wood-cutting—Dassera Festival—Withdrawal of Indian Corps from France, and reasons—Battalion's last time in Front Trenches—Entrains for Marseilles—Embarkation ... 77—83

CHAPTER XII.

NOVEMBER 9TH, 1915, TO MARCH 3RD, 1916. (*Sketch X.*)

Arrival in Egypt—Kantāra—Situation on the Canal—Kantāra Camp—Reconnaissances—Battalion's First Outing in Desert—Inspection by Sir Herbert Cox—With Movable Column to El Katia—Detachment from Gallipoli rejoins—Christmas at Hill 70—Move to Suez—Ayun Musa—Inspection by Corps Commander—Military Police with Battalion to be sent to 1st Battalion in Mesopotamia—Battalion leaves Egypt and embarks for India—Arrives Karachi—Greetings—Arrival at Dehra and Home-coming ... ... 84—89

CHAPTER XIII.

MARCH 3RD, 1916, TO END 1920. (*Sketch XI.*)

Dehra—Manœuvres—Nepalese Contingent—New Goorkha Battalions formed—Battalion ordered to Burhan—Colonel Boileau leaves us—Brigade Training—Rewat—Training of I.A.R. Officers—Move to Tank—200 Rifles sent to Manipur for the Kukie Operations—Marri Expedition—News of General Fulton's Death in France—Return to Tank—Inspection by Sir Arthur Barrett—3rd Afghan War—Battalion at Murtaza, Jandola, Manzai, and minor Actions—Battalion moved to Hyderabad (Scinde) and Karachi—"Mentions" for Good Service—Lieut.-Col. Wigram to command Battalion—Return to Dehra ... ... 90—97

PART II.—MESOPOTAMIA AND NORTH PERSIA.

CHAPTER XIV.

OCTOBER, 1914, TO APRIL, 1916. (*Sketches XII, XV, XIII.*)

Changes and Occurrences in Cantonments—Draft for Gallipoli—Mobilization—Departure of 1/2nd Goorkhas for Karachi—Battalion strength—Arrival at Basra—Formation of 37th Brigade—The Country—Campaign prior to our arrival—Russian Action—Battalion reaches Tigris Front—Attack on Dujailah Redoubt and failure—Our Casualties—Senna and Twin Canal Camps—Co-operation with Left Bank Offensive—Abu Roman and Battalion Casualties—Lieut.-Colonel Sweet and Major Bruce join—Casualties near Twin Pimples—Beit Aiessa attack and casualties—Bombing accident—Fall of Kût ... ... 101—116

CHAPTER XV.

MAY 1ST, 1916, TO FEBRUARY 21ST, 1917 (*Sketches XII, XIII.*)

Sheikh Saad : Work : Cholera—Draft—Arab thieves—Supply Difficulties—Cossacks reach Ali Gharbi—Turks abandon Es Sinn Position—Turkish Air superiority—New 14th Division formed—Scurvy—Battalion in Es Sinn Area—War Comforts—Work on Pentagon Post—Active Operations cease during Hot Weather—Sickness—Railway pushed forward to Front—Looting of Stores—Leave to India

CONTENTS

CHAPTER XV.—(continued.)

opened—General Gorringe leaves—Draft—Interchange of wounded Prisoners—Better Aeroplanes arrive—General Maude to command the Force—General Improvements—Plans—New Officers join—Scurvy and sickness increases—Railway reaches Front—Bands arrive—15th Division on Euphrates—Major Ridgeway joins—Turkish strength—Machine Gun companies formed—Battalion at Magasis Fort—Draft—Scouting work—Position of opposing Forces—Winter Operations—Aeroplane success—37th Brigade crosses the Hai River—Capture of Kāla Haji Fahān—Demonstration towards Shumrān—Christmas—Battalion in Picquet Line—Battalion enters Offensive and supports Sikh attack—Our Casualties—Major Bruce and Captain Marsh killed—Battalion and Devons attack—Trenches captured—Casualties—Liquorice Factory occupied—Turkish Losses—Salvage Work—37th Brigade reconstituted ... ... 117—134

CHAPTER XVI.

FEBRUARY 22ND TO MARCH 26TH, 1917. (*Sketches XV, XIII, XIV.*)

Arrangements for crossing the Tigris—The Crossing—Major Ridgeway killed—Toogood's and Rowbotham's action—Attack of Dahra Position—Casualties—Sannayat assaulted—Turks retreat—Pursuit—Passage of Diāla River—Baghdad occupied—Battalion at Diāla Village—Salvage Work—Rewards—Our men visit Baghdad—Description of City—Battalion at Hanaidi—Reasons for further Operations ... ... 135—147

CHAPTER XVII.

MARCH 27TH TO APRIL 30TH, 1917. (*Sketch XV.*)

Battalion marches to Baquba—To Deltāwa—Battalion reinforces Cavalry Division near Deli Abbas—Joins Division at Dishdāri—Draft—Advance and action—Casualties—Battalion sent to General Marshall's Force on the Shatt el Adhaim—Attack on Band i Adhaim ... ... 148—152

CHAPTER XVIII.

MAY 1ST TO DECEMBER 31ST, 1917. (*Sketch XV.*)

Successes on Tigris—Operations cease during hot weather—Battalion holds Posts on Tigris—Decorations—Battalion marches to Beled Rūz—Reconnaissances—Railway pushed beyond Baquba—Turkish Strength in Upper Diāla Area—Honours and Rewards—Our Band arrives from Dehra—Battalion moves to Mendali—General MacLachlan's Column—Operations against Kizil Robāt—General Maude's Death—Changes in High Commands—Operations resumed towards Kizil Robāt and Kifri—Meeting with and Impressions of Russian Troops—Advance successful—Turks retreat—Battalion at Kardarra Crossing—Christmas—Battalion Strength and Casualties ... ... 153—158

CHAPTER XIX.

JANUARY 1ST TO CHRISTMAS, 1918. (*Sketch XVII, XV.*)

Battalion at Mirjāna—Russian Disorganization owing to Revolution—14th Hussars enter Persia—Severe Weather—Kardarra Defence Works—"Dunster Force"—Reasons, Object, Composition—Jason Camp—Detachment sent to 2/11th Goorkha Rifles—Rewards—Battalion despatches 600 Rifles to Persia—Draft—Rest of Battalion marches for Kermanshah—Description of country and route—Famine—First Action at Menzil—Captain McCleverty at Resht—Casualties—Battalion at Kermanshah and Posts—Move to Hamadān—Refugees—Hamadān and Posts—Captain McCleverty's Detachment at Zinjān—Tabriz Reconnaissance—Battalion marches to Zinjān—Tabriz Column retires, reinforced by Captain McCleverty—Stand on Kuflon Kūh Range—Casualties—Detachments from Resht and Kāsvin arrive at Zinjān—Move to Sarim Sāgli—Captain Dallas Smith's Column to Akhnagar—Draft—Armistice—Two Companies sent again to Resht and Kāsvin—Honours and Rewards—Distribution of 36th Brigade—Decorations—Total Casualties to close of 1918 ... ... 159—172

CONTENTS xiii

CHAPTER XX.

CHRISTMAS, 1918, TO MAY 31ST, 1920. (*Sketches XVI, XVII.*)

Detachments to Shiah Dehan—Irregularity of Mails—Death of Captain Chenoy, I.M.S.—Lieut.-Colonel Sweet and Captain McCleverty to England—Indian Peace Contingent—Battalion marches to Kāsvin—Bolshevik Troubles—Draft—Escort duty towards Tabriz—Lieut.-Colonel Sweet rejoins and takes a Column to Enzeli—Arrival of Denikin's Fleet—Fleet interned, Ships disarmed—Protection measures of Enzeli—Bolshevik Fleet shells Enzeli—Armistice arranged, but disregarded by Bolsheviks—Landings—Fighting—More Landings and highroad blocked—Bolshevik Terms accepted and Troops withdraw to Resht—Hopeless Situation in Persia ... ... 173—182

CHAPTER XXI.

JUNE 1ST, 1920, TO JUNE 19TH, 1921. (*Sketch XVII.*)

Resht evacuated—Lieut.-Colonel Sweet's Column at Menzil—Move to Loshān—Persian Cossack Force to retake Gilan Province—Two Companies reinforce Menzil—Bolsheviks attack Menzil—Sortie by Captain Johnson and Lieutenant Warhurst—Casualties—Menzil and Loshān vacated—Troops withdraw to Kāsvin—Cossacks retake Resht, but defeated at Enzeli—Subadar-Major Sarabjit Gurung—Reconnaissances—Menzil reoccupied—Delhi Day—Battalion strength—General Ironside succeeds General Champain—Persian Official's attitude—Captain Dallas Smith commands Menzil Column—Cossacks retire—Various small Actions north of Menzil—Lieut.-Colonel Sweet and Captain Dallas Smith leave for India—North Persian Force broken up—Battalion leaves Persia and Mesopotamia—Arrival at Dehra ... ... 183—191

CHAPTER XXII.

THE 3/2ND GOORKHAS.

JUNE 12TH, 1917, TO OCTOBER 31ST, 1920. (*Sketch XI.*)

Raising of new Goorkha Units—Our 3rd Battalion formed—Colonel Grant commands—Battalion moved to Peshawur—Major Arbuthnot succeeds Colonel Grant—Lieutenant Newman's gallantry—3rd Afghan War—Battalion's duties at Peshawur—Picquet attacked at Narai Khwar—Battalion returns to Dehra—Disbandment ... ... 192—195

APPENDICES.

A. LIST OF OFFICERS AND MEN RECOMMENDED FOR REWARDS FOR SERVICES IN FRANCE, 1914-15, AND "MENTIONS" IN DESPATCHES ... ... 198—209

B. CASUALTY LIST IN ACTION IN FRANCE, EGYPT, WAZIRISTHAN, MESOPOTAMIA, AND NORTH PERSIA FROM OCTOBER, 1914, TO JUNE, 1921 210

C. DECORATIONS AWARDED FOR SERVICES IN FRANCE, EGYPT, WAZIRISTHAN, MESOPOTAMIA, AND NORTH PERSIA, 1914-1920 211

D. MESSAGES OF CONGRATULATION DURING THEIR SERVICES IN FRANCE AND THE NORTH-WEST FRONTIER OF INDIA, 1914-1920 ... ... 212—223

E. LIST OF COMMANDING OFFICERS FROM 1911 TO 1920, AND THEIR SERVICES DURING THE GREAT WAR ... ... 224—226

F. SERVICES OF OFFICERS WHO WERE DETACHED FROM THE REGIMENT DURING THE WAR ... ... 227—229

APPENDICES—(*continued*).

		PAGE
G.	The Regiment's Charter	230—232
H.	List of Actions and Casualties sustained from 1911 to 1921	233—234
I.	List of Indian Army Reserve Officers Attached during the War, 1914 to 1921	235
J.	The Regimental Ram	236
K.	List of Polo Tournaments and Football Matches for which the Regiment entered Teams, and their Results	237—242
L.	"Fire"—Translation from "Lille War Gazette," March 3rd, 1915	243—244
M.	Note on the Abor Expedition, 1911-1912	245—246

LIST OF ILLUSTRATIONS

Santaur Devi Temple, near Dehra, greatly venerated by our Goorkhas. (*Sketch by L. W. S.*)	*Frontispiece*
	FACING PAGE
Typical Abors with Wooden Helmets	4
Clearing Forest for Camp Ground in the Abor Country—Native Cane Bridge of the Abor and Mishmi Countries	8
Janakmukh Post and Distant Abor Hills—Mishing Stockade, Leaf and Bamboo Shelters for our Men, Abor Country—Convoy Crossing a Stream in the Abor Country	10
2nd K.E.O. Goorkhas' Centenary Arch at Dehra Doon	14
Centenary Centrepiece in the Officers' Mess, Dehra Doon	16
France, January, 1915: Group of Officers with Names	40
Group of Goorkha Officers, 2/2nd K.E.O. Goorkhas, France, July, 1915	52
Group of Officers, 2/2nd K.E.O. Goorkhas, France, August, 1915, and Names	74
Indian Contingent Cemetery at Gorre, near Festubert, in which many of 2/2nd K.E.O. Goorkhas are buried	83
Defensive Post, 2/2nd Goorkhas, near Ayun Musa, Suez—2/2nd Goorkhas Camp on the Suez Canal	86
British Residency, Manipur	90
Typical Hill Country in the Manipur State	92
Goorkhas Halting at a River in Manipur	93
Subadar-Major Sarabjit Gurung: Presentation of King's Commission by H.R.H. the Prince of Wales	101
Ashar Creek, Basra	104
A Sternwheeler on the Tigris	105
Country Boat and Small "Mashoof" near Amāra. (*Sketch by L. W. S.*)	108
Turkish Prisoners Marching into Amāra	110
Country and Trenches near Beit Aiessa	114
The Tigris below Kurna	115
Trenches in Es Sinn Area and Light Railway to the Front	122
Bivouac on the Tigris Bank: Early Breakfast	134
Camp at Bāwi	142
Baghdad: A Typical Kelek on the Tigris—General View from the Barracks	143
Camp on Tigris at Hanaidi, near Baghdad. (*Sketch by L. W. S.*)	146
The Leaning Minaret in Baghdad	148

LIST OF ILLUSTRATIONS

FACING PAGE

The "Mejidieh" River Steamer lying off Baghdad—The Bridge of Boats at Baghdad	149
Corner in Baghdad City. (Sketch by L. W. S.)	152
Camps and Trenches near Baquba	154
Road Difficulties in the Ranges between Khānākin and Kermanshah	162
Resht, where serious Fighting occurred in late June, 1918—Mahidasht, near Kermanshah, where the 1/2nd Goorkhas held a Post in 1918—British Consulate at Resht saved by Captain McCleverty and his Detachment in late June, 1918—Kangavār, between Kermanshah and Hamadān, where the 1/2nd Goorkhas held a Post in 1918	163
Persia—Kerind, the First Place of Importance in the Persian Hills beyond Khānākin—Kermanshah, General View—Ancient Stone Bridge about ten miles North of Kangavār	168
Shows the "Jebel Hamrin" Range and Country in the Neighbourhood of Kizil Robat—The Russian Road through the Elburz Mountains between Imām Zādeh Hachem and Enzeli	169
On the Road near Menjil—The Ancient Fortress of Kāsvin, just Outside the Town	184
The "Goorkha Post" in the middle distance near Imām Zādeh Hachem beyond the Naglebar Ridge, and held by the 1/2nd Goorkhas in 1920	188
Unveiling King Edward's Memorial at Delhi, 1922	189
Brass Memorial Tablet in Dehra Church to Officers 2nd Goorkhas who Fell in the Great War	194

LIST OF SKETCHES

SKETCH NO.		FACING PAGE
I.	Sketch to illustrate the Area of General Bowers' Operations in the Abor Hills in N.E.F., India	12
II.	Sketch to show Events of November 2nd, 1914, near Neuve Chapelle	28
III.	2nd Goorkha Trenches at La Quinque Rue, December 10th to 21st, 1914	38
IV.	(1) 36th S.W. Sheet 3. Trench System South of Neuve Chapelle	46
V.	(2) 36th S.W. Sheet 3. Trench System opposite the Ferme Cour d'Avoué	46
VI.	Battle of Neuve Chapelle, March 10th, 1915	54
VII.	To illustrate Attack of the Dehra Doon Brigade, May 10th, 1915	66
VIII.	Rough Plan showing the Meerut Division in the Battle of Loos, September 25th, 1915	80
IX.	Plan of Area in France where the Meerut Division operated from October 29th, 1914, to November 6th, 1915	82
X.	Sketch to show our Positions on the Suez Canal	88
XI.	Shows Areas on the N.W.F., India, operated in by the 2/2nd Goorkhas from January, 1918, to January, 1920	96
XII.	Sketch showing Area operated over by the 1/2nd Goorkhas between March 5th, 1916, and February 25th, 1917	130
XIII.	Sketch to show Operations of the 1/2nd Goorkhas near the Liquorice Factory from January 28th, 1917, to their Assault on February 3rd, 1917	132
XIV.	Sketch showing Position of the Ferries for the Crossing on February 23rd, 1917, and Turkish Position at Dahra taken on February 24th, 1917	140
XV.	Sketch of Area of the Mesopotamia Campaign, 1914-18	158
XVI.	Sketch of the Enzeli-Kazian Positions, May 18th, 1920	182
XVII.	Sketch showing Area in Persia in which the 1/2nd Goorkhas operated, June 27th, 1918, to May 25th, 1921	190

BOOKS OF REFERENCE.

Battalion War Diaries for France, Egypt, North-West Frontier, Mesopotamia, and Persia.

Letters and some private diaries of officers.

" The Long Road to Baghdad," by E. Candler.

" History of the Indian Contingent in France," by Colonel Merewether.

" The 'Dunster' Force," by General Dunsterville.

Brigade and Divisional despatches seen at the War Record Office.

Colonel A. B. Lindsay's pamphlet on the Abor Expedition.

Regimental Records of the Marri and Waziristan Operations, 1918-19.

Regimental account of the 3/2nd Goorkhas.

PART I.
FRANCE, EGYPT, NORTH-WEST FRONTIER, INDIA.

HISTORY

OF THE

2nd K.E.O. GOORKHAS

(The Sirmoor Rifle Regiment)

"The mere battle day when every glowing feeling of the soldier and the gentleman is called into action will ever be encountered nobly where British armies are engaged; but it is in the privations, difficulties, and endless toils of war that the trial of an army consists, and it is these that denote its metal and the material of which it is formed."—(*From a speech by Lord Gough.*)

CHAPTER I

MARCH TO DECEMBER, 1911. (*Sketch I.*)

THE first volume of this History brings the life of the 2nd King Edward's Own Goorkhas from the year in which it was raised up to early 1911. In this second volume the Regiment, after various interesting incidents in peace time, will be seen on active service again in the wild, unknown region of the North-Eastern Frontier of India, to be followed by its unforgettable experiences in the varied theatres of the Great War, full of valiant deeds, hard fighting under hitherto unknown conditions in countries where climate, language, and people were strange to our men, and full, too, of irreparable losses in most gallant officers and men.

In the end of March, 1911, my tenure of command of the 2nd Battalion having come to its end, I was succeeded by Lieutenant-Colonel C. de M. Norie, D.S.O., Colonel J. Fisher being then in command of our 1st Battalion; and in this spring the former Battalion succeeded in winning the Cawnpore Woollen Mills Cup at the Annual Meeting of the B.P.R.A. at Meerut. The 1st Battalion football team also won the Garhwal Brigade Cup by 4 goals to 0 from the 2/8th Goorkha Rifles, and the Goorkha Brigade Cup by 2 goals to 0 from the 2/6th Goorkha Rifles. The Regiment also had the honour of being detailed to send a small party, viz., Subadar-Major

Narbahadur Gurung, Subadar Man Sing Borah, with two Riflemen, to England to attend the Coronation ceremonies of H.M. King George V.

The winter 1911-12 saw Their Majesties visiting India, and the 2nd Battalion, with the Truncheon party under Captain Hill, left Dehra in November for Delhi to take part in the Royal Durbar and Review held at that historic city. Guards of Honour were furnished on several occasions, and the Truncheon party, together with the Colour parties of the other King Edward's Own Regiments, was on duty at the laying, by His Majesty, of the foundation stone of King Edward's Memorial on the Champs de Mars, facing Delhi Fort. Later Their Majesties graciously presented their portraits to the Officers' Mess.

In the meantime active service conditions had arisen, and the 1st Battalion under Colonel J. Fisher, was detailed for field service on the far north-east borders of India—in a country and amongst a people very different in every way to those of the north-west border, where most of **Abor Expedition,** our activities had been exercised. A spell of some twelve **1911-12.** years' peace was broken by the order to mobilize and join the Abor Expeditionary Force forming in the extreme corner of Upper Assam, under command of Major-General H. Bowers, C.B.

The reason for the visit of a force into those wild, unknown hill regions was to punish the Minyong Abor clan for their treacherous murders in March, 1911, of Mr. Noel Williamson, the political officer of the Sadiya district, and Dr. Gregorson, together with a number of their native followers. They were on a friendly visit into the hills with a view to exploring **Reasons for** the unknown and had reached the village of Komsing, **the Expedition.** some 35 miles beyond the border, when the tribesmen fell upon and cut them up. This act of hostility by a tribe always a turbulent one, against whom in the past several futile expeditions had been sent, could not be allowed to go unpunished; hence orders were issued by the Government of India for military operations to be undertaken against the offending tribesmen as soon as climatic conditions would permit. This could not be till the long, rainy season of generally seven months was over—that forest-clad, mountainous region being about the wettest in the Empire, thus giving only an open season of five months (November to March) for operations. It proved, however, a far wetter winter than usual, only one and a half months out of the five being anything like dry, which increased the many other local difficulties in a country where every yard of path had to be cut, every halting place had to be laboriously cleared of heavy forest before camps could be formed, and where malaria was extremely prevalent.

The troops detailed to rendezvous at Kobo at the junction of the Dihang and Lohit Rivers, and which from its position in regard to the Abors was to form the main base, were as follows :—

Composition of Force.
The Maxim Gun Detachment Assam Valley Light Horse.
No. 1 Company Sappers and Miners.
Brigade Section No. 31 Divisional Signalling Company.
32nd Sikh Pioneers.
1/2nd Goorkhas.
1/8th Goorkha Rifles.
The Lakhimpur Military Police Battalion (Goorkhas).

The artillery consisted of two 7-pounder guns manned by detachments of the 8th Goorkha Rifles, and carried by Nepalese coolies, while the Sappers had two useful little howitzers.

Owing to the absence of paths passable for pack animals, coolies were employed for transport purposes, 3,000 Nagas being concentrated at Kobo early in October and 2,000 Nepalese as porters, divided into corps of 600 each, these units being in charge of officers of the S. and T. Corps. The force thus totalled 80 British officers—2,987 fighting ranks—5,000 transport coolies.

Arrival of Battalion at Kobo, 6/10/11. A Wing and Headquarters, 1/2nd Goorkhas, with which went 3 Goorkha officers and 100 Riflemen of the 2nd Battalion, left Dehra in late September, 1911, the other Wing following shortly after; and travelling by rail, and river steamer up the Brahmaputra River, duly reached the base at Kobo on October 6th and remained there a fortnight, being employed with other troops in arranging the big camp, in road making, and in various reconnaissances. The British officers present with the Battalion on this expedition were the following :—

Colonel J. Fisher (Commandant).
Major W. Beynon, D.S.O., who rejoined in the field from leave in England and was then appointed to the Brigade Staff.
Major A. B. Lindsay, D.C.C., who rejoined from the Quetta Staff College.
Major E. H. Sweet, D.C.C.
Major N. Macpherson, D.C.C.
Captain B. R. Nicholl, D.C.C. (2nd Battalion).
Captain H. G. Becher, Provost-Marshal, rejoined from Commander-in-Chief's Staff.
Captain H. C. Nicolay, in charge of the Machine Gun Detachment.

Lieutenant A. J. H. Chope (Adjutant).
Lieutenant A. H. R. Saunders (Quartermaster).
Lieutenant G. M. McCleverty (Signalling Officer).
Lieutenant H. F. Marsh (Scouts Officer).
Major F. Davidson, I.M.S., in medical charge.

The scale of kit to be carried for officers and men when once in the hills was 60 lbs. for the former, 10 lbs. for the latter.

In a country as yet unexplored and unmapped—nothing was practically known beyond the border here some 23 miles north of Kobo—the difficulties confronting the force were unusual and considerable. From the Brahmaputra River dense impenetrable forest is the one feature of the country to the border at Pasighat, where the foothills of the Eastern Himalayas are met and the Dihang River breaks out of the mountains into the Assam Valley.

Description of Abor Country.

This part of the country is flat and much intersected by streams which in the rainy season overflow, converting the locality into a vast morass. From the border onwards the hills rise equally densely jungle covered, enormous trees with thick undergrowth flourishing up to 8,000 feet. The mountains rise sharply, their sides stretching down in precipitous "khuds" to a network of rocky ravines below. From the summits of the highest points no view can be had without felling the surrounding trees at considerable labour and time, and the hillsides are only clear of jungle in the immediate neighbourhood of villages where cultivation exists. Rivers force their way for miles through rocky gorges, and navigation is impossible owing to the frequent presence of dangerous rapids. Roads did not exist, three rough tracks only led from the plains up to Kebang (*Sketch I*), the chief village for punishment, viz.—taking them in order from east to west—via Pasighat up the right bank of the Dihang—via Balek and Kālik villages—via Ledum and Mishing, and these were blocked by the Abors directly they knew their country was to be entered by us. These, like all hill tracks, run straight from point to point over and down ridges, so that in a distance of six miles at least three ascents and descents each averaging 1,000 feet, were not unusual. There being no paths beyond what were mere goat-tracks these had to be cut and roughly graded as the force advanced ; and as often as not these, as soon as made, were rendered almost impassable by rain.

No supplies being obtainable in the hills every scrap of food had to be carried, entailing long lines of transport coolies and endless convoy escorts. Climatic conditions and inability to obtain fresh meat, caused much sickness, so much so that six weeks after the operations started returns showed 50 per

TYPICAL ABORS WITH WOODEN HELMETS.

cent. of the British officers and 30 per cent. of the men in the force as being incapacitated through dysentery or malaria. Our Goorkhas, however, managed to supplement their rations here and there with mushrooms, edible ferns and fungi, sweet potatoes, and other indigenous vegetables. Shikar was also good in this country and where possible meat was thus obtained. On one occasion two of our men were out shikaring with their rifles when turning into a narrow jungle track they came on a deer being stalked by a tiger. One man shot the deer while the tiger fell to the other's rifle. When in the neighbourhood of rivers fish were fairly plentiful.

The armament of the Abors, as with all tribes on this frontier, was primitive, consisting of bows with poisoned arrows, spears, swords, and a few old-fashioned muskets. Their tactics were known to be those of the "guerilla" kind, for which their country was eminently suited, such tactics consisting in harrying convoys, in relying on stockades or obstacles to check an advancing force, and while so checked to fall on its flanks and rear from skilfully prepared ambuscades, or by rolling down rocks collected high up the hillsides to form rock "shoots." Picqueting the hills and the use of flanking parties was impossible, as without many hours of cutting the jungle was impenetrable; so troops had to move in single file, rarely seeing farther than five yards on either side. Their stockades over which they spent great labour, were anything from a couple of hundred yards long to a quarter of a mile, built of thick, sharp pointed stakes, 12 to 14 feet high, in a double row with earth and stones in between, and were loop-holed and located mostly at the top of steep ascents or where the flanks could easily be turned. Their rock "shoots," well concealed, were made of stout bamboo hurdles built out from the hillsides, on which heavy rocks were laid, the inner edge of the hurdle resting on the slopes, the outer edge supported by two stout canes which were easily slashed through to release the load. The search by our men for these booby traps was continuous and laborious.

Abor Tactics and Weapons.

The object of General Bowers' force was to reduce the Abor clans to submission—the murderers of Williamson and Gregorson to be given up—and to establish political relations with the tribes. Survey work was to be undertaken and opportunity availed of to extend our knowledge of this unknown country and to improve communications in it.

Object of Operations.

By the middle of October all arrangements having been completed, the advance from Kobo started on the 20th in two columns (*Sketch I*)—the main column*, under the immediate command of General Bowers, was to advance via Pasighat along the right bank of the Dihang River on Kebang. The other, called the Ledum Column†, under command of Colonel J. Fisher, 2nd Goorkhas, was to move on Ledum via Onyuk, 8 miles off toward the foot hills, to build a post there, to visit such villages as were within reach but not to sleep out of the post; and generally to cover the left flank of the main column, the attitude of the Gālong tribe being doubtful. The rest of the force was employed in convoy escorts and holding the various posts on line of communications as the forward move lengthened out.

Start of Column, 20/10/11.

After a reconnaissance by Major Lindsay to the border through Onyuk, the Ledum Column left Kobo, its progress necessarily slow, as most of the route had to be hacked through the forest, and one transport corps only was available to lift 28 days supplies. Our advanced party reached Ledum (20 miles) on the 23rd, which was found lying in low hills and deserted. As signalling to Kobo was found impossible from here a party under Lieutenant Chope pushed farther into the hills on the 26th to the deserted village of Mishing, 7 miles farther (*Sketch I*), which being found to answer requirements, the column concentrated there. This advanced party was the first to have contact with the Abors in surprising and dispersing a hostile picquet, and a little later that day Chope was able to punish with the Maxim gun a body of some 50 Abors spotted for a few moments crossing a "jhoom" (cultivation patch). His party was ordered to bivouac there and to try to picquet the hills for the advance of the column. By October 29th Colonel Fisher's force was assembled here.

Mishing, 26/10/11.

Knowing that the best way to protect the flank of the main column slowly moving up the Dihang Valley, was by an active and rapid offensive in all directions, plans were formulated for a systematic clearance of the enemy from the neighbouring country, to be followed by wider moves afield; but the General Officer-in-Command's orders *re* having to return to camp each night precluded the possibility of going sufficient distances out, and limited the sphere of action for a time.

On the 30th a strong patrol pushed over the 3,000 feet ascent north of Mishing, down into the head of the Sirong Valley, a few miles distant; but

---

* *Main Column.*—One 7-pr. gun; Maxim gun detachment, A.V.L.H.; No. 1 Coy. S. and M.; No. 31 Signal Coy.; two companies 32nd Sikh Pioneers; one company 2nd Goorkhas; 8th Goorkha Rifles.

† *Ledum Column.*—One 7-pr. gun; two companies 2nd Goorkhas; detachment 32nd Pioneers; three companies Military Police; Signallers.

save for a few rock " shoots," and the track being blocked for a considerable distance, no enemy was seen until returning to camp, when this and another patrol, working in another direction, were fired on from ambuscades, fortunately without casualties among our men. On the two following days hostile ambuscade parties were surprised and two of their camps destroyed. These "scraps" induced the Abors to retire from our immediate vicinity, enabling us to get farther out. On November 5th 100 rifles, 1/2nd Goorkhas, made an attempt to reconnoitre Kāking village, some 6 miles across the hills south of Mishing, but owing to limited radius of action did not get beyond Doshing (4½ miles). The country being extremely difficult without any track, and rapidity of movement being essential, precautions usual in jungle warfare were dispensed with. After six hours scrambling up and down ravines and "khuds," our scouts came up against a strong stockade admirably sited at the top of a steep ascent and invisible through the jungle 10 yards off. The advanced guard came under a heavy fire of arrows and rocks from all directions, some ten rock " shoots " being let down simultaneously from above the left of the stockade, sweeping two officers and several men down the hillside. The position was instantly rushed by Captain Nicolay with his men, who shot an Abor in the act of releasing another large " shoot." Several of the enemy were killed inside and a number wounded, some of whom with the rest of the defenders managed to escape into the jungle. These were followed up and Doshing village, a mile beyond, was burnt. While this was being effected a picquet under Lieutenant McCleverty was sturdily rushed by a body of Abors, who were driven off with some loss. Our casualties this day were 2 Goorkhas wounded, and 2 officers and a number of men incapacitated by bad contusions from rocks, one officer being Major Lindsay. Later on it was found the fall had strained his heart which caused him to be invalided to England, and from which he eventually died.

Doshing Stockade, 5/11/11.

At last welcome orders were received in mid November from the G.O.C. relaxing the instructions as to all sleeping in Mishing post at night; consequently Colonel Fisher's sphere of activity widened. This was at once taken advantage of in the despatch of two columns which included all the 1/2nd Goorkhas at Mishing, one via Ledum, the other via Doshing, to co-operate against Kharan, 2 miles west of Kāking, a large village of the Gālongs. whose men had fought us at the Doshing stockade alongside of the Kebang men. Kharan (*Sketch I*) was surrounded at night and destroyed, the resisting Gālongs receiving a severe lesson. Our casualties here were slight,

Kharan, mid Nov., 1911.

1 Rifleman killed, and a few wounded by " pānji " stakes. This affair had the best results, for representatives of several other Gālong villages who had declined overtures came in at once, protesting friendship and stating they would take no further part with the Minyong Abors.

Till the end of November Colonel Fisher had detachments out scouring the hills on a wide and distant front, extending from the Sidè River, some 10 miles north of Mishing to Kāking on the south. To permit of this and to improve communications so as to facilitate the anticipated co-operation with the main column against Kebang, detachments of 100 rifles each were sent to the Sidè River and towards Kālek village about 9 miles off, and to render this mobility possible, the troops had to be called on to do the work of porters, as only 80 Naga coolies were available for hospital and other purposes, and all responded with fine spirit. But the weather had broken and it rained steadily for a fortnight, which with this severe extra work produced a considerable amount of sickness by the end of the month.

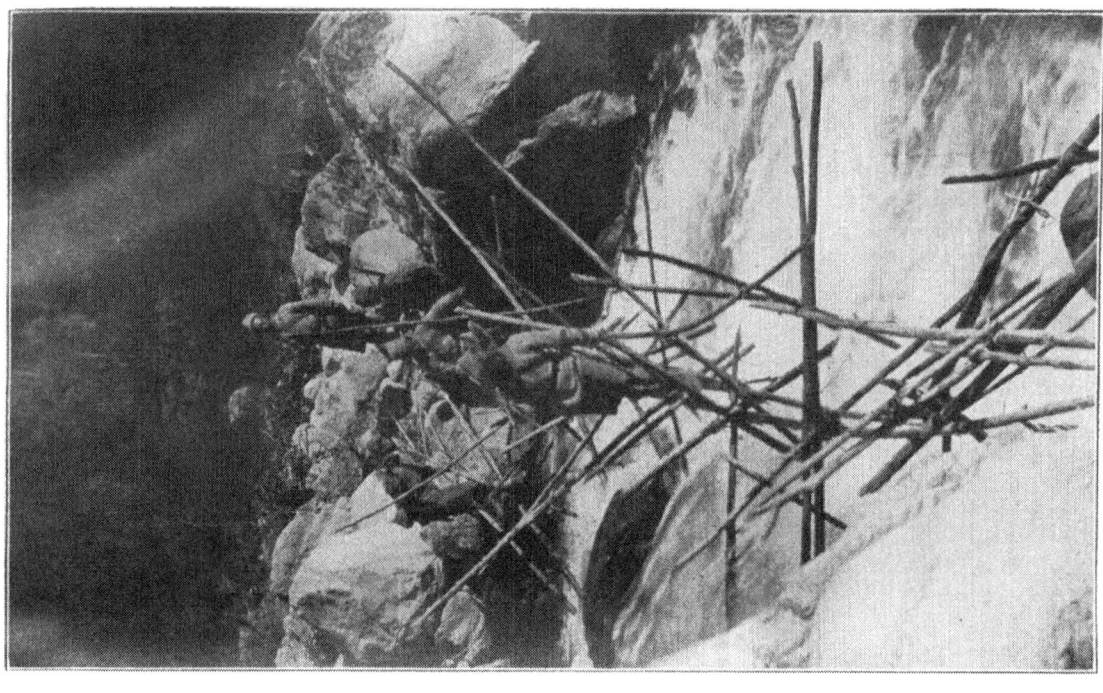

NATIVE CANE BRIDGE OF THE ABOR AND MISHMI COUNTRIES.

CLEARING FOREST FOR CAMP GROUND IN THE ABOR COUNTRY.

CHAPTER II

December, 1911, to August, 1914. (*Sketch 1.*)

Main Column's Movements.
As the rest of the 1/2nd Goorkhas were with the main column, we will now follow General Bowers' movements, who, leaving Kobo on October 22nd, concentrated at Pasighat at the foot of the hills three days later, a distance of only 25 miles on the flat, but rain had converted the track into a bog along which progress was made little faster than a mile an hour.

From October 26th to November 2nd the days were spent in building stockades for Line of Communication troops here, and at Janakmukh Camp, 5 miles farther up the Dihang Valley. Supplies were also sent forward from Kobo, while reconnoitring parties pushed into the hills. From Janakmukh onwards the hills were entered, and now steep ascents and descents added to the labours of the force.

A further advance to Roi of 3 miles was made on the 3rd, the Sirpo River being reached 9 miles on, by November 6th. Up to this no active opposition had been met with, due to the activities of the Ledum Column in advance of Mishing, which had inoculated the Abors with a disinclination to leave their big stockades at and beyond Rohtang for distant operations. On November 7th a strong reconnoitring party of the 1/8th Goorkha Rifles and 1/2nd Goorkhas gained contact with the tribesmen,

Sirpo River Action, 7/11/11.
who on this and the following day suffered considerably, and in which the main column's casualties were Captain Hutchinson, A.V.L.H., severely wounded in the thigh by a poisoned arrow, 2 Goorkhas killed, and several slightly wounded.

Incessant rain falling made the movements more than ever difficult, as loads naturally became heavier and carriers going up and down slippery hill-sides took three times as long as they would ordinarily have taken. The 32nd Pioneers and 1st Sappers and Miners did remarkably good work under most trying conditions, the latter being usually with the advanced guard employed in road cutting, bridging, etc., the former following, converted the roughly cut track into a bridle path. Of the 1/2nd Goorkhas (less the Ledum Column) five companies were distributed on the Line of Communication holding important posts and doing convoy escorts, one company moving with the main column.

On November 19th General Bowers approached Rohtang some 40 miles from Kobo (*Sketch I*), when it was found the large stockade believed to be at that village was really 2½ miles south of it, defending the crossing of the Egar River from the top of a steep hill-side. As the advanced guard neared it the Abors cut loose a number of rock "shoots" high above the track, narrowly missing the General and knocking Captain Becher down the "khud," and also opened fire with muskets and arrows, one of the latter hitting General Bowers slightly in the hand. As it was impossible to shell the stockade or take it from the front, the advanced guard, strengthened, held the defenders in front, while two Goorkha companies climbed up through the jungle outflanking the position which was then rushed and taken. Our casualties were small—1 Goorkha wounded by a musket ball, and several hurt by rock contusions and "pānji" stakes.

Egar River Action, 19/11/11.

The next ten days were spent in concentrating the force at Rohtang, in bringing up supplies, in road making, and reconnaissances. On various occasions parties of Goorkhas encountered the enemy, killing a number, notably near Kālek, previously destroyed by a detachment of the Ledum Column, and where they made a short stand. From Rohtang reconnoitring parties located a very large stockade some 3 miles up the Dihang at Kekyar Monying, the name for a precipitous rock face 500 yards long sloping down to the river, across the face of which the track to Kebang ran. The rock face was very high, and above it towered the steep, wooded spur dividing the Sirong from the Sidè River. Unlike other stockades, this one could be seen running down to the water, while beyond it was a large Abor camp. To them it must have seemed strong, and it was here the force hoped to inflict a severe blow before the chief village was reached (*Sketch I*).

Kekyar Monying Stockade.

The main column now being abreast of Mishing and the services of the Ledum Column being no longer required on that side, it was broken up, orders being sent to Colonel Fisher to leave two companies of the Military Police Battalion at Mishing, one company at Balek, and to push across the hills to join the main force with the remainder. These reached Rohtang three days later after a trying march in heavy rain, many deserted rock "shoots" were found, but save for a slight scrap with a hostile picquet no enemy was met.

Plan for Attack of Stockade.

The plan for capturing the Kekyar Monying stockade was as follows:—To throw a force across the Dihang River north of Rohtang by night, which was to move up the left bank into a concealed position opposite to and within

JANAKMUKH POST, DIHANG RIVER, AND DISTANT ABOR HILLS.

MISHING STOCKADE—LEAF AND BAMBOO SHELTERS FOR OUR MEN—ABOR COUNTRY.

CONVOY CROSSING A STREAM IN THE ABOR COUNTRY.

effective range of the position. This force to consist of one company 1/2nd Goorkhas with a Maxim gun and three companies 1/8th Goorkha Rifles—a flanking column of two companies 1/8th Goorkha Rifles to ascend the steep hill above and south of the stockade, and having gained this point to move down into the Sidè Valley to cut off the Abors' retreat—the frontal attack to consist of the two 7-pounder guns, three Maxims, one company 1/2nd Goorkhas, and four of the 1/8th Goorkha Rifles, who were to move along the track across the rock face, capture the position, and pursue as far as possible towards Kebang, 8 miles beyond.

After many unsuccessful attempts the Sappers succeeded on December 3rd in getting a hawser across the Dihang, here rapid and broad; and the right flank force was across by 11 p.m. Its move, however, was detected by the tribesmen, who ambuscaded and charged the column as it was crawling through the jungle in the dark, two Riflemen of the 1/2nd Goorkhas being killed. When at midday on the 4th the left flank detachment had nearly reached the hill-top above the position, the front attack opened and the stockade was taken shortly after. This frontal attack, unfortunately, started prematurely or the Abors would have been heavily punished; as it was, they bolted after the first few shots. A few were killed inside the stockade and some more in the pursuit, during which the village of Bābuk, 4 miles on, was burnt. It being found impossible to get laden coolies across or over the Kekyar Monying rock cliff in its present condition, a few days' halt were necessary for road making, and it was not till December 9th that an advance was made on Kebang, 8 miles off, when this reputed stronghold was found deserted, and was destroyed. The following day a column visited Yemsing, 6 miles south-west of Kebang, cutting its way through the forest instead of using the village track, with the result that it surprised and destroyed the place inflicting heavy loss on the enemy.

Action at Kekyar Monying Stockade, 4/12/11.

Kebang reached 9/12/11.

With the punishment of these villages of the Minyong Abors, the first phase of the expedition was ended. This tribe had during the advance carried on " guerilla " fighting, attacking convoys, cutting the telegraph wire, etc., and the companies of the 1/2nd Goorkhas had been kept busy on the Lines of Communication, daily parties being sent out from the posts to scour ravines and hill-sides to either side of the road, in which numerous small raiding parties were met and dispersed with loss. Other detachments from the front diligently searching the country in the neighbourhood of Kebang, Bābuk, and Sissin, to which latter place Major Sweet with three companies of our

Battalion was sent from Rohtang, succeeded in capturing quantities of grain, many cattle, and recovered some of Mr. Williamson's property.

Komsing village where the tragedy took place was now visited, but only fined, as it had been found out the murders, though they occurred in and near it, were effected by Kebang and Rohtang men, and not by those of Komsing (*Sketch I*).

With villages destroyed, numbers killed and wounded, their food supplies confiscated or destroyed, by the end of December the Abors had had enough.

End of Expedition, early January, 1912. Early in January, 1912, they began sending in to Headquarters representatives from all tribal sections seeking peace. The terms of Government having been explained to them were speedily complied with, the murderers of Mr. Williamson and Dr. Gregorson were given up and political relations through chiefs were opened with other sections farther afield, with a view to the exploration and survey work to follow the military operations, which were now concluded.

This next work was conducted with three columns of 100 rifles each—the first with Mr. Bentinck, Assistant Political Officer and detachment 1/8th Goorkha Rifles, proceeded up the Dihang Valley, but got no farther than Singin owing to various difficulties and sickness among the transport coolies—

Surveys and Exploration, January to April, 1912. the second under Colonel Macintyre with a detachment 1/2nd Goorkhas and some Pioneers went up the Yamne Valley, crossed the high range between that river and the Dihang, visited Geku, the largest village of the Panghi Abors, and by hard marching and living more or less on the country, were able to cover a great distance and survey the whole area. When this was over Colonel Macintyre with another company 1/2nd Goorkhas under Major Sweet, with Lieutenant Oakes, Royal Engineers, again crossed the Dihang at Pasighat, and proceeded through the hills till the left bank of the Yamne high up was struck, whence Damroh the chief village of the Padam Abors was reached. Every village in this area was visited and the country thoroughly surveyed in spite of many difficulties and most inclement weather. Thus from mid January to April, 1912, the Abor country was explored and mapped in all directions, and although it was not found possible to get as far afield as originally desired, very valuable geographical work was accomplished.

With late April the force was broken up and units began returning to their stations, the 1/2nd Goorkhas reaching Dehra in early May, 1912.

Rewards falling to the Regiment in this expedition were:—Colonel

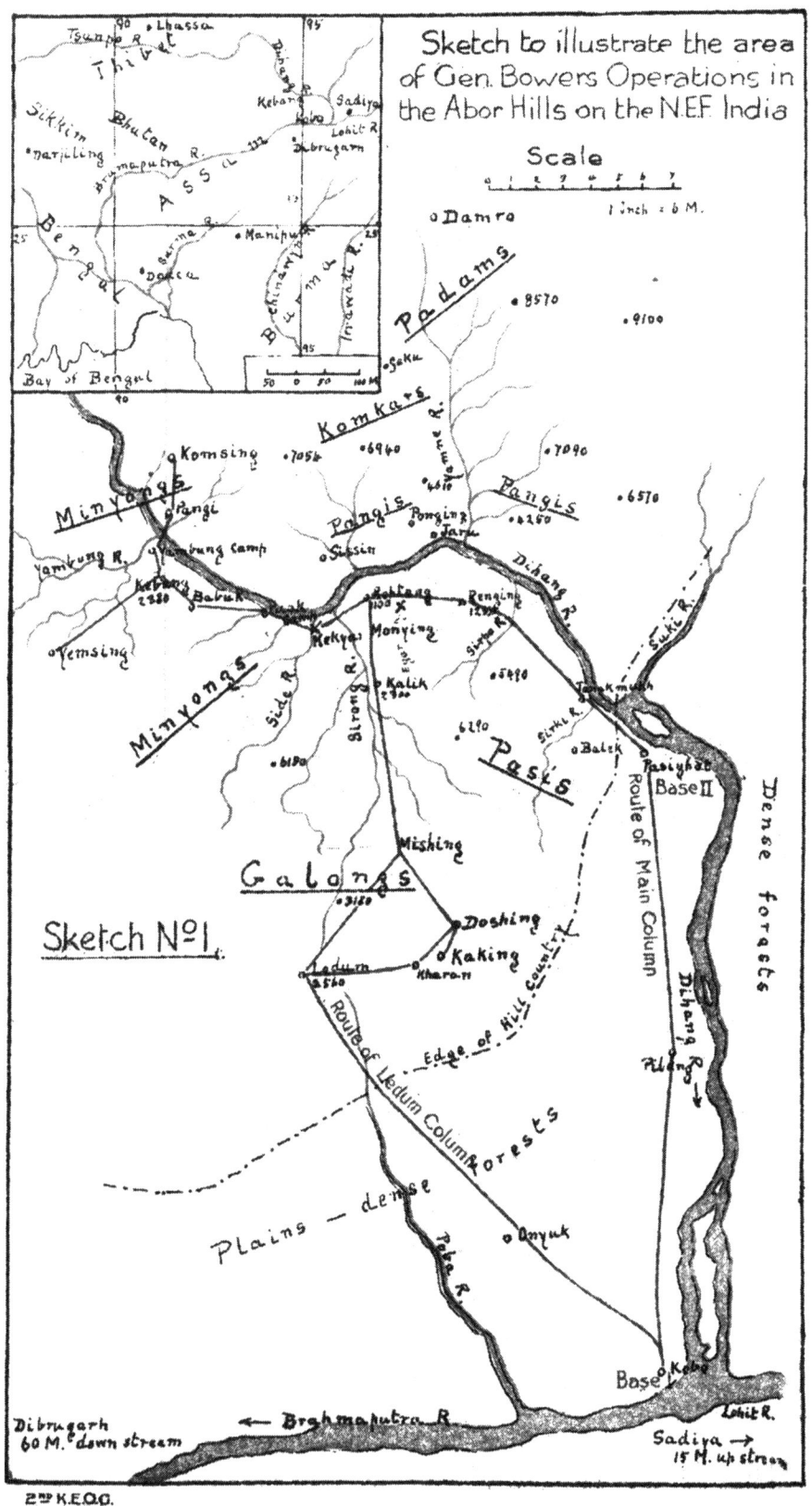

J. Fisher gazetted to a C.B. ; Major A. B. Lindsay was promoted to a Brevet Lieutenant-Colonelcy ; Major Davidson, I.M.S., received the D.S.O. ; while Major Sweet, Captains Becher and Chope, Lieutenant Marsh, **Honours and Awards.** Subadar-Major Dalman Ale, Subadar Tegbahadur, 2912 Havildar Sirilal Thapa, and 3280 Rifleman Budhiman Gurung were " mentioned " in despatches. 4144 Rifleman Deosar Thapa gained the Indian Order of Merit, 3rd Class, for conspicuous gallantry in having on the night of December 3rd-4th, 1911, whilst under fire, gone to the assistance of Rifleman Dewan Sing Gurung who had been wounded and had fallen 50 feet down the hill-side, and in remaining with him until the enemy was driven off and assistance was forthcoming.

General Bowers, C.B., recorded in his despatches dated May 23rd, 1912, that " the 1/2nd Goorkhas well maintained its reputation for efficiency both on the Ledum Column and in guarding the Lines of Communication. An excellent spirit pervades the Regiment."

We came lightly out of this bit of field service with **Casualties.** a total of only 3 men killed and 7 wounded ; several died later of disease due to exposure and malaria.

In the autumn of 1912 Colonel J. Fisher, C.B., vacated the 1st Battalion command, being succeeded by Lieutenant-Colonel W. G. L. Beynon, D.S.O., and both Battalions took part in the manœuvres held in the area Delhi–Loni–Bhāgpat during November and December.

The year 1913 was uneventful save for the winning of the Army Cup Race at Lucknow by Captain E. W. C. Ridgeway, who had the good fortune to carry off the coveted trophy with his grey Arab gelding " Rajbahadur " In November the 2nd Battalion attended manœuvres near Roorki, being brigaded with both Battalions 9th Goorkha Rifles and the 3/60th Rifles.

It was in the latter part of this year that trouble first arose in regard to the religious aspect of Goorkhas crossing the sea to visit England, though all who had done so had on return gone through a brief ceremony with the Regimental Pandit in order to regain caste. On Subadar-Major Santbir Gurung's retirement and going to Nepal (he had been to England as one of the King's orderlies) the Durbar took exception to the regimental procedure for regaining caste, and considered him as still outcasted. This led to much correspondence with Simla, which ended in an agreement **Establishment of** that the Nepal Durbar should maintain a specially selected **the Pāni Pattia** Pandit in India to conduct the required ceremonial, by **Depot at Dehra.** means of which all could regain their caste when necessary. This agreement coincided more or less with the commencement of the Great War, and Army Headquarters ordered a "Pāni Pattia" Depot to be established at Dehra Doon as being central, where this Pandit should reside and to which all Goorkhas of every unit were to be sent for the ceremony on return to India from overseas. Each year of the war naturally saw hundreds of Goorkhas thus collected at Dehra, and it would have been far less expensive to Government had the Pandit been directed to visit all Goorkha Regiments in turn at certain times instead of sending large numbers of men from port to Dehra first, and then having to pay all their rail fares back to distant stations like Quetta or Myitkhyina in Upper Burma. But such action recommended proved a bit of high finance beyond the powers of Olympus to comprehend! The ceremony can be completed in three days and if a Goorkha goes to Nepal without having performed the required ceremonies he is liable to arrest and punishment there.

The following year (February, 1914) opened with the winning of the Infantry Polo Cup, played at Bareilly, by the Regimental team consisting of Major G. F. C. Ross (back), Lieutenant H. C. M. Lucas (3), Captain K. Wigram (2), and Captain A. J. H. Chope (1). They defeated the team of the 2nd Rifle Brigade after extra time, and with widened goals, and it was the first time this cup had been won by other than a British infantry team.

About 1912 it was decided to hold a Centenary Commemoration in 1915, and a beginning was made in a large masonry archway at the entrance to the 1st Battalion lines, which was completed in the winter of 1913-14. The war, however, put a stop to any further proceedings in connection with the commemoration. This archway is adorned on either sides with plaques setting forth actions in which the Regiment took part between 1816 and 1914 and the names and numbers of those killed. A bronze medallion of King Edward VII, the work of Sir G. Frampton, also adorns the structure.

After the Armistice the Battalions were still so separated that nothing could be done towards the Centenary celebration, but it was decided to rearrange and increase the size of the Mess table centre-piece to include the other medals and battle honours won since the late Captain C. Judge's conception of it, and in this way to mark the historic occasion. This work is now (1923) in the hands of the Goldsmiths and Silversmiths Company, will be in bronze as more durable than ebony, and with lettering and scroll work in silver. At the four corners of the base will stand silver statuettes of an Officer and a Sepoy in the old uniforms of 1827 and an Officer and a Rifleman in those of the present day. The whole will stand nearly three feet high, will support as before the Queen's Truncheon on state occasions, and will form both an ornament to

2nd K.E.O. GOORKHA CENTENARY ARCH AT DEHRA DOON.

the Mess and a fitting memento of the hundred years' life and services of the 2nd King Edward's Own Goorkha Rifles. (See photograph facing page 16.)

While on the subject of memorials it may be mentioned that Colonel C. de M. Norie, D.S.O., when in command of the 2nd Battalion had intended erecting a small obelisk or pillar on the top of Kalunga Hill in memory of the serious fighting that took place there in October, 1814, at the opening of the Nepal War, and also of that of the Nepalese wounded recovered in our hospital and prisoners taken who joined the British service forming one might say, the nucleus of our Regiment. As with many other projects this was upset by the Great War, but one may hope that possibly some future Commanding Officer may find it desirable to carry out Colonel Norie's idea.

CHAPTER III

August, 1914, to October 29th, 1914. (*Sketches IX, II.*)

WE now arrive at the period immediately preceding events and experiences which tried the metal of the Regiment far higher than ever before. All eyes were turned towards Europe, and with comparatively little warning the Great War was upon us. When the call to India came it was responded to with enthusiasm by all units of its army and its Indian Princes, and by none more so than by its Goorkha ranks.

In late July and early August rumours were rife that two Divisions would be sent from India either to relieve other troops from Egypt or to reinforce the Home Expeditionary Force; consequently our 2nd Battalion as being one next for active service, began to prepare for the anticipated order, a medical inspection being held on the August 4th to gauge how many were fit to complete field service strength. Previous to this, viz., on the 2nd, an issue of the new Mark III S.L.E. rifle had been made to the Battalion, which raised everyones' hopes; then on the 8th came orders to recall all furlough men, and at 4 a.m. on August 9th instructions to mobilize on Scale A were received, winter scale with one blanket being stated. Deficiencies in war strength were now made up from the 1st Battalion, viz., 165 rifles with Subadars Tegbahadur Gurung, Sarabjit Gurung, and Jemadar Karakbahadur Gurung; the whole including 73 men as first reinforcement. Captain McCleverty and Lieutenant Reid were transferred from the 1st to the 2nd Battalion, the former as Signalling Officer, while Major Becher at home on leave, who would ordinarily have returned to the 1st Battalion, was directed to join at Port Said. Captain Barton was detailed as Staff Officer to the Deputy Director Railway Transport with grade as D.A.Q.M.G. to leave Bombay on the 15th, and with him went Lieutenant Lucas. Lieutenant Walcott left for Roorki at once to collect the field service clothing for the Battalion, which was received on the 14th. Colonel Norie, D.S.O., rejoined from leave, and Captain O'Brien, I.M.S., came to us as Medical Officer. On August 17th a telegram was despatched to the 7th (Meerut) Division to the effect that mobilization was complete, and on the 21st orders came for the 2nd Battalion to entrain for Bombay on September 1st. In the meantime Captain Mathew had rejoined from duty with the Assam Military Police, but for a time was left at the Depot, and Captain Chope, 1st Battalion, was ordered to join the Bikanir Camel

Marginal note: Mobilization Orders, 9/8/14.

THE 2nd K.E.O. GOORKHA CENTENARY CENTREPIECE IN
THE OFFICERS' MESS, DEHRA DOON.

Corps and to proceed with them to Suez. At this time the Regiment had four officers, viz., Captains Nicolay, Dallas Smith, Cruickshank, and Mullaly, absent with the Assam and Burma Military Police forces, and who some months later were released to join the Battalion in France with reinforcements; also Lieutenant Newall absent with the Air Force. The British officers to leave Dehra at the start were as noted below.*

Battalion leaves Dehra, 1/9/14. On the afternoon of September 1st the 2nd Battalion left Dehra in two trains, reaching Bombay on the morning of the 4th, where it was housed along with the 1/9th Goorkha Rifles in the large Carnac Bunder goods shed, the embarkation and railway staffs having made every arrangement for cooking, washing, and sanitation. Two British officers were told off daily to live with the men, and were accommodated in a saloon carriage beside the goods shed. The s.s. *Angora*, in which the Battalion and a Wing of the 9th Goorkha Rifles was due to sail, was not yet in port, and when she did arrive needed fitting up, causing a ten days' stay in Bombay, which was varied by route marches through the city, drills, sightseeing, and sea bathing, this latter a new experience for our men. Hardly any of them ever having seen the sea took soap to wash with, and were immensely surprised to find the water salt and soap useless. The Bombay inhabitants having rarely seen Goorkha troops, it was amusing to find they mistook them for Japanese.

Embarkation at Bombay, 14/9/14. The *Angora* being ready by the 13th, embarkation took place next day in pouring rain, and she moved out of the dock to anchor in the Bay till the whole convoy was ready, which owing to heavy weather did not occur till the 20th. Early that day the convoy of 32 ships, escorted by H.M.S. *Swiftsure*, H.M.S. *Fox*, H.M.S. *Dartmouth*, and R.I.M. ships *Dufferin* and *Hardinge*, started in fine weather, though a heavy swell naturally upset many men and animals. The day before leaving port a large consignment of comforts and cigarettes for the Indian troops from the kindly people of Bombay had been made over to us, and a wire had also been received notifying to the regret of all the death of Lieutenant-Colonel Lindsay in England from heart disease, which had been brought on by contusion and strain in the Abor Expedition and aggravated by pressure of work at the War Office.

The usual troopship life went on daily; on the 23rd the convoy was joined by another from Karachi of ten ships, and at Aden the *Dufferin* and

---

* Colonel Norie, D.S.O.; Major Macpherson, Major Ross, Captain McCleverty, Captain Corse Scott (Adjutant), Lieutenant Innes, Lieutenant Scoones (Quartermaster), Lieutenant Reid, Lieutenant Walcott, Captain O'Brien, I.M.S.

Hardinge returned to Bombay. The heat in the Red Sea being great, drills, etc., were excused, and half-way up it the *Angora*, with three others, were directed to steam forward in order to coal quickly at Port Said. At Ismailia, where a short halt was made, the 1/1st and 1/4th Goorkhas were met, their Brigade (9th) having been dropped by the 3rd (Lahore) Division to protect the canal, as Egypt was in a doubtful condition and danger not unlikely from Palestine, although the Turks had not yet definitely joined in with the Germans. At Port Said Major Becher joined, and we heard that Captain Barton and Lieutenant Lucas had been sent on to France.

A point of interest may here be noted regarding the secrecy attending the objective of the two Indian divisions, both starting without any definite knowledge as to their ultimate destination. The 3rd (Lahore) Division left first, from Karachi, and while at sea a wireless message was received announcing the naval victory off Heligoland, and also giving Lord Kitchener's statement in the House of Lords that two Indian divisions were *en route* to France, and thus the troops became aware of their destination.

Port Said was left on October 6th by 18 of the fastest ships of the convoy escorted by the French battleship *Jaurè Guiberry*, and after bad weather for two days Marseilles was reached on the 12th. Early that morning the *Angora* went into the docks, disembarkation at once began, and orders came to leave five companies there for fatigue work, while the other three companies, with tents, equipment, and stores, were to march to Camp Valentine, 8 miles away. The day was a very busy one for, in addition to the landing of stores, etc., all rifles, machine guns, and ammunition had to be handed in to the Ordnance Department, where at once new pattern weapons were issued. While here Major F. Norie (late 6th Goorkha Rifles), brother of our Colonel, joined the Battalion as Interpreter.

Arrival at Marseilles, 12/10/14.

The reception accorded to the Meerut Division by the French people vied with that given to the Lahore Division, which had landed three weeks earlier, in warmth of welcome and kindness. The Press, both English and French, were eloquent in praise of the Indian troops, but unfortunately filled their columns with exaggerations giving totally absurd ideas as to numbers and the part the contingent would play in the great struggle—a part (according to them) which would have been beyond the capability of human beings to accomplish. This led naturally to impossibly high expectations, so that many imputed failure to the Indian troops when they left France, forgetful of the new conditions of warfare, the appalling winter, and equally appalling losses with which our men were confronted, and which were met and sustained

GOORKHAS (THE SIRMOOR RIFLE REGIMENT)

with a heroism to which all the highest authorities on the spot recorded their deepest appreciation. Later views showed the contingent to have entered the arena and saved the situation for the Allies at a most critical period, when the British forces were seriously outnumbered, were exhausted with constant fighting, and had then no trained reserves to draw upon, these being still in the making.

Camp Valentine, on open hayfields close to a village, was reached in the evening, and with the arrival next day of the dockyard companies all camp arrangements were completed. Owing to shortage of transport it was necessary to reduce the scale of kit, consequently increasing the load on the man, who from now on had to carry with his greatcoat, a sweater, balaclava cap, and an extra blanket. Here we were given the services of two French interpreters, MM. Bellefonds and Gantés.

Camp Valentine, Marseilles.

On the 14th notice was received of a visit next day by the Governor of Marseilles and the G.O.C. Indian Army Corps (General Sir James Willcocks), but bad weather setting in this was cancelled; the G.O.C. later did come out to see us and at once took exception to our black greatcoats, which had to be changed.

Until the 17th most of the time was taken up in obtaining and issuing British warm coats and other kit as available, and at noon that day the Battalion marched into Marseilles to entrain for Orleans, which was reached on the 20th and camp formed at Champs des Groves, 2 miles from the city, where the 7th Division was to assemble. The journey being through highly cultivated country, impressed our men greatly with its remarkable fertility. Here more warm kit and entrenching tools were issued, and the G.O.C. addressed British and Goorkha officers on a few matters, chiefly impressing the undesirability of officers exposing themselves except in the actual assault. The rifle range at La Cercotte was placed at our disposal, where practice was obtained by all in the new rifle, and while here Captain Barton and Lieutenant Lucas rejoined us from Staff duty. On October 24th the first intimation of the near approach of our move into the actual war area came, in an order for a billeting party under Lieutenant Reid with Jemadar Dan Sing Lama to proceed northward. During our stay at Champs des Groves many books and standing orders were received, dealing with the composition of the various armies in the field, tactical circulars in connection with machine guns, the holding of trenches, street fighting, scouts, etc., and general experiences so far gained in the war.

Orleans, 20/10/14.

The units of which the 7th (Meerut) Division were composed were as follows:—

Dehra Doon Brigade:

Composition of Meerut Division.

Commander—Brigadier-General C. E. Johnson.
1st Seaforth Highlanders..
1/9th Goorkha Rifles.
2/2nd Goorkhas.
6th Jāt Light Infantry.

Garhwal Brigade:

Commander—Major-General H. d'U. Keary, C.B., D.S.O.
2nd Leicestershire Regiment.
2/3rd Goorkhas.
1/39th Garhwal Rifles.
2/39th Garhwal Rifles.

Bareilly Brigade:

Commander—Major-General F. Macbean, C.B., C.V.O.
2nd Black Watch.
41st Dogras.
58th Vaughan's Rifles.
2/8th Goorkha Rifles.

Divisional Troops:

4th Cavalry.
No. 3 Company Sappers and Miners.
No. 4 Company Sappers and Miners.
Signal Company.
107th Pioneers.
Headquarters Divisional Engineers.

Artillery Units:

Headquarters Divisional Artillery.
4th Brigade R.F.A. and Ammunition Column.
9th Brigade R.F.A. and Ammunition Column.
13th Brigade R.F.A. and Ammunition Column.
110th Heavy Battery.

Orleans was left by train on October 26th, and travelling via Calais, the Battalion detrained at St. Thiennes at 4 a.m. on the 28th, pushing on 8 miles to Merville, which was reached at 9.40 a.m., where the men

Merville, 28/10/14. were billeted in two factories with officers in small cottages near by. We were now well into the zone of operations, guns could be plainly heard in the distance, hostile and friendly aeroplanes frequently passed overhead, and all wondered how and when they would make their début into the stirring scenes going on in the front. We were not kept wondering long, for at 5 p.m. the 2/2nd Goorkhas received orders to march at once for Vieille Chapelle along with the Seaforths, and by 8 p.m. both were well *en route* experiencing much trouble with the transport which got blocked and lost its way in the dark. We arrived at Vieille Chapelle at midnight, when Colonel Norie went off to report to G.S.O. 3rd Division, who explained to him the enemy's position at Neuve Chapelle and the possible points to which he might have to march to reinforce a section of that Division's line. In the morning of the 29th the Battalion was ordered to take over certain trenches from the Northumberland Fusiliers immediately north-north-east of Neuve Chapelle village, so the four Double

Battalion enters Company Commanders went ahead to take over their
Trenches, 29/10/14. sections and at 11 p.m. we marched to Pont Logy via Croix Barbée—Pont du Hem—Rouge Croix. Here, after
First Casualties, distributing ammunition and entrenching tools, our Double
30/10/14. Companies moved out to their positions in the front line (*Sketch II*) and while so advancing came under fire, causing our first casualties in 4 men and a mule wounded.

Getting into our advanced trenches, which formed the most forward part of a salient in the line between Neuve Chapelle and the Ferme Vanbésien or Moated Grange (*Sketch IX*) was no easy matter, it being an isolated and exposed locality with trenches scarcely dug and few traverses, this bit of the line having only been occupied by the 5th Fusiliers the previous night; also much fighting had taken place here, more was expected, and parapets (such as they were) were much battered. It was dawn before our occupation was completed, and all day was taken up improving the trenches under desultory bursts of fire which caused a few casualties, 2 men being killed, 7 wounded, and to the regret of all our first officer to fall Major Macpherson, who was in command of the companies in the front trenches, shot through the head in No. 1 double company trench.

Some description of the locality in which our Battalion found itself is now necessary (*Sketch IX*). It may well be spoken of as a forlorn desolate country as we found it in winter, being a low lying area stretching out flat for miles, dotted with a few small villages, orchards, and farms, standing in a sea of mud, interspersed with pools of water formed by flooded shell holes. The chief points catching the eye in front were the nearer houses of Neuve Chapelle, the village of Mauquissart, a corner of the Bois du Biez a little to the south-east, and the low, distant Aubers Ridge, all in German hands. Water being so near the surface here made the digging of deep trenches very difficult, and often impossible, as they soon became waterlogged. Heavy rains had turned these trenches into a series of muddy excavations. No revetting material was available, and parapets were often so weak that men were sometimes shot through them. Troops stood and moved about all day, frequently knee deep in mud and water, into which often if a wounded man fell he was drowned before he could be got out. Dug-outs were frail and continually blown to bits by shells, even billets some distance in rear were unsafe. Life under these conditions was one of utter discomfort, wallowing in mud and filth, continually digging or bailing out water.

Locality and Trenches.

The situation into which the Meerut Division entered stood somewhat thus. The 2nd Corps, under General Sir H. Smith-Dorrien, of which the two Indian Divisions were now to form a part, was on October 19th on a line from Givenchy near the La Bassée Canal, through Violaine to near Radinghem (*Sketch IX*) where it linked with the French cavalry under General Conneau, beyond whom again were General Allenby's cavalry corps and the 3rd Corps under General Pulteney. The Germans were attacking from Lille towards Béthune, La Bassée having been taken by the Crown Prince of Bavaria's Army Corps which also held the Lille—La Bassée Canal and country to its south and east. Our object was to attack the La Bassée—Lille line and cut off the former place, but the Germans forestalling this move, made their first attack on a large scale on October 22nd, the result of which was to push us out of Violaine, where their efforts were arrested. As it was evident from the strength of this attack that the 3rd Division (the 2nd Corps having only two divisions, the 3rd and 5th) continuing the line to the left could not hold its ground, the line was drawn back to run just east of Givenchy in front of Neuve Chapelle to a point near Fauquissart, whence it turned towards Laventie.

General Situation, October, 1914.

The Germans again attacked vigorously on the 24th, but were beaten off only to resume the heavy fighting on October 27th and 28th, which lost Neuve Chapelle to us, the line now being withdrawn to run from Givenchy —Richebourg l'Avoué—west of Neuve Chapelle—Fauquissart. From this date our line had been subjected to constant attacks and bombardment, all units having a hard and anxious time, which was not lessened by the knowledge that the British were out-numbered and out-gunned, being also without such munitions as bombs, grenades, searchlights, etc., which apparently the enemy had in profusion. The only bombs we had for a considerable time were such as could be improvised out of empty jam tins!

Germans take Neuve Chapelle, 28/10/14.

The situation was grave, our front which was too extended for the numbers of men available, was now owing to heavy casualties too thinly held, and adequate reserves were lacking. The arrival, therefore, of the Indian Contingent was most opportune.

CHAPTER IV

October 29th to November 3rd, 1914. (*Sketches IX, II.*)

The Indian Contingent was now ordered to relieve the 2nd Corps and take over its portion of the line which was carried out on October 29th in heavy rain, turning the countryside into a worse bog than ever, and all reached their positions soaked through and plastered with mud. Owing to absence of communicating trenches in those early days the front line had to be gained by crawling over the open or along any existing ditches.

The order of the three brigades of the Meerut Division on taking up their sections west and north of Neuve Chapelle was from right to left (*i.e.*, south to north) the Bareilly, Garhwal, Dehra ; then came four British Regiments left by the 2nd Corps, and beyond these the Jullunder Brigade of the Lahore Division. Severe fighting had taken place on the Bareilly Brigade front, between the night 29th-30th and 31st, in which their losses were heavy, involving their front trenches, some of which they succeeded, however, in regaining.

Returning to the 2/2nd Goorkhas—during October 30th our men had their first experience of high explosive shells, and this and the following two days were busily employed in improving front trenches, digging communicating ones, and connecting up with units on either flank. A slight bombardment and desultory firing went on, causing us 10 men wounded on 31st, and 4 more next day, and this bombardment tended to become more pronounced. Opposite us the German trenches were as close as 30 to 40 yards on our right front, though the greater part of their line on our left was from 100 to 150 yards off, in one case they practically flanked our right. During November 1st they began using a mortar firing a large shell with high explosive, and the enemy could be heard working away like moles as earth was continually seen being thrown up though no men were visible. It was also rumoured that a big attack on our line in this area would probably take place before long under the personal direction of the Kaiser.

Work in trenches and Position of Opposing Lines, October, 1914.

The morning of November 2nd opened with a perfect tornado of high explosive shells directed on to the trenches of the 2/2nd Goorkhas, on whose right and left were respectively the 9th Goorkha Rifles and the Connaught Rangers, the latter belonging to the 2nd Corps, but temporarily attached to the Indian Corps (*Sketch II*). As stated before, the Germans had captured

Opening of Action of 2/11/14.

Neuve Chapelle a few days earlier, and our trenches formed a dangerous salient in the general line which the existence of a spinney, an orchard, and later some burning houses in our rear did not improve. Communication between front and rear was rendered difficult and slow owing to the telephone lines being so often cut, and the enemy had also driven saps close to our parapet.

About 9 a.m. the hostile fire was concentrated on to No. 1 Double Company under Lieutenant Lucas, violent explosions soon obliterating the trench and parapet, blowing many men high in the air and burying others. Human endurance being limited and finding it impossible to hold out longer, some of the survivors joined No. 2 Double Company on their left, others seeking cover in a ditch slightly in rear—all save one non-commissioned officer, Naik Padamdhoj Gurung who remained behind keeping up a rapid fire until compelled to retire as the Germans swarmed into the battered trench. For this act of gallantry he was later awarded the Indian Order of Merit, 2nd Class.

The enemy's fire next concentrated on No. 2 Double Company in a series of terrific explosions which wrecking everything soon rendered this trench untenable. One shell blew four men into the air, killing Lieutenant Lucas who was rallying his men, and destroying a machine gun. Subadars Chet Sing Thapa and Tegbahadur Gurung had held on to the trench as long as possible awaiting orders, but under the hail of explosives were compelled to evacuate it and hold the ditch in rear together with a rough breastwork on the south side of the road.

Our Trenches heavily bombarded.

Major Becher, commanding No. 2 Double Company, finding his trench congested with the men crowding in from No. 1, and being himself now the target of the bombardment moved back to occupy a newly dug communication trench. While doing so his losses were great and he was killed.

It was now that Major Ross seeing the serious state of affairs led a party of his No. 3 Double Company with Subadar-Major Man Sing Bohra in a fine effort to retrieve the situation and charged the Germans now completely occupying the trenches of No. 1 and 2 Double Companies. A stiff hand-to-hand fight ensued, in which the enemy were driven out, but overwhelmed us again. Major Ross, the Subadar-Major, and most of the men with them were killed, and the survivors a mere handful of eight or ten, had to draw off and regain their trench.

Captain Barton, commanding No. 4 Double Company, just before this had been shot dead in his trench, and the command devolved on Lieutenant Reid, this Double Company holding the left of our front line Being heavily shelled and seeing the condition of No. 3, he sent a message to the Connaught Rangers on his left asking for help, and going to the Double Company on his right took command, rallying the men, encouraging them to hold on as reinforcements were coming up, and managed somehow to stem the enemy's advance just here. He then returned to his own Double Company, under heavy fire, met the detachment of the Connaught Rangers and was guiding them to No. 3 trench where both he and the Sergeant in command were killed.

Connaught Detachment arrives to assist.

Meanwhile Lieutenant Walcott, of No. 2 Double Company, with Lieutenant Innes, machine gun officer, one of whose guns had been destroyed, collected as many of their men as they could and made a most gallant counter-attack; they were also joined by a party of a dozen men under Naik Rampershad Thapa, who were still holding on desperately in a corner of the front line. With fine bravery they charged the Germans but to no effect for both officers lost their lives in the effort, and with them Subadars Tegbahadur Gurung and Gopal Sing Rawat. The force of the charge being expended and the enemy coming on in strength, the survivors under Subadar Chet Sing fell back, this Goorkha officer being killed in the retirement. Naik Rampershad was decorated with the Indian Distinguished Service Medal for his gallantry just mentioned.

Counter-attack by Lieuts. Walcott and Innes.

More small parties under Goorkha officers and non-commissioned officers had managed to retire from the front trenches to the rear, where they were collected by Lieutenant Scoones, who was behind with the first line transport, and joined the reserve (*Sketch II*).

There now only remained in the front line No. 4 Double Company with Subadars Fateh Sing Newar, Dalbahadur Rana, and Jemadar Suba Sing Gurung, together with stray men of other companies and the detachment of the Connaughts totalling some 150 men, and these faced the enemy, still grimly holding on to their bit of the front. Superior numbers of the enemy, however, forced them out and Subadar Fateh Sing Newar ordered a retirement to a communicating trench some way in rear, but before reaching this they had to traverse a stretch of trench down which the enemy had trained a machine gun and the passage was blocked with dead and wounded to such an extent that those in rear of this block could not pass, so they turned and faced it out. Their desperate condition was intensified by the Germans in the orchard at the time, so that they were fired at from two sides until

Subadar Fateh Sing Newar and No. 4 Company.

reinforced by a company of the Connaughts under an officer and their situation improved. When it was dark enough this officer told Subadar Fateh Sing Newar to retire from the trench which he and Subadar Dalbahadur Rana, with the remains of their units duly accomplished, joining the reserves some 400 yards in rear. A certain number of their men not hearing the order to retire stayed with the Connaught men through the night, rejoining their units in the morning. The coolness and gallantry with which Subadar Fateh Sing Newar commanded his men after the British officers had fallen and the way he behaved generally under most serious and bewildering circumstances was later rewarded with the Order of British India, 2nd Class.

We may now turn and see how the Reserve had been occupied during this heavy fighting, for they had played their part admirably. This Reserve of one and a half companies made up of men spared from the front line, under Subadar Karan Sing Rana, was stationed about 400 yards in rear of the right of our line in front and to east of a road. Here were also Colonel Norie, D.S.O., Captain McCleverty, Captain Corse Scott (Adjutant), and Major Norie (Interpreter). About 8.30 a.m. the Reserve moved forward, led by Colonel Norie to endeavour to help in the general trend of the action, and to succour the hard hit defenders in the front trenches. They advanced towards the right of No. 1 Double Company, working their way forward to the road running past the left flank of the 9th Goorkha Rifles, and succeeded in locating a German mortar playing havoc with our men and silenced it, causing its removal (*Sketch II*). Finding our own trenches now could not be best helped from this flank they retired, replenished ammunition, and reinforced by two dismounted squadrons of the 34th Poona Horse under Colonel Swanston, moved forward again towards the left trenches of the Battalion. Here, however, they found the enemy occupying part of the front in great strength, and were brought to a standstill within 150 yards of the front by a deluge of rifle and machine-gun fire, causing many casualties, including Colonel Swanston killed. They managed to hold their position till about 2.30 p.m., when a concentration of high explosive shells compelled the Reserve to retire to a position 200 yards back, which they held till nightfall. In the evening that portion of the line now held by the 2/2nd Goorkhas and 9th Goorkha Rifles was reinforced as follows :—Behind the 9th Goorkha Rifles three squadrons 7th Dragoon Guards and one company 6th Jāt Light Infantry, and behind the 2/2nd Goorkhas the Royal Scots Fusiliers and a composite Battalion of Indian infantry. The 34th Poona Horse also remained, all being directed to report to ColonelNorie. About 5 p.m. or so, just after dusk, a number of men were seen coming from the direction of the front trenches who turned out to be Subadars Fateh Sing Newar and Dalbahadur Rana with the survivors of No. 4 Double Company.

At 5.30 p.m. Colonel Norie decided to attack the right trenches of our old line with the Reserve, a company Royal Scots Fusiliers, some of the 7th Dragoon Guards, and the 6th Jāt Light Infantry in support. Captain McCleverty was directed to move forward at 6 p.m. with the Reserve to the south-east corner of the orchard (*Sketch II*) from where after reconnoitring and receiving fresh instructions they were to attack the old trenches held originally by No. 1 Double Company. Colonel Norie and Captain Corse Scott with the rest were to move up the road to Neuve Chapelle and attack in that direction, Major Norie also accompanying them (*Sketch II*). The Reserve reached the far side of the orchard and halted to reconnoitre, Captain McCleverty going across to Colonel Norie on the left for further instructions. Captain Corse Scott and Major Norie here had then gone forward up a ditch on the left of the road to ascertain if the Germans were still actually holding the old trenches. As Captain McCleverty reached the Royal Scots Fusiliers, fire was opened on them, and both officers came back reporting the Germans' presence, on which Colonel Norie shouted " charge," and all rushed forward up the road and the ditch just as a machine gun started firing down it. After going a short distance the four officers crossed the road into a half-dug communicating trench near the breast work, but heavy rifle fire opening and finding themselves alone, the rest it was thought having missed their way in the dark, the officers emptied their revolvers into the Germans now 20 yards off, and retired as quietly as they could. Major Norie and Captain McCleverty were both badly wounded, the former being lost in the dark. It now transpired that at the first outburst of the machine gun the officer and a number of men of the Royal Scots Fusiliers had been killed. The assaulting parties, including our Reserve, finding further advance impossible in face of increasingly heavy fire, withdrew. Captain R. Ross, brother of our Major G. F. C. Ross, with a company of 6th Jāt Light Infantry, had now come up in close support, and later he and his men reconnoitring forward found the enemy had vacated the trenches and they brought in Major Norie, who was found lying wounded.

It now being night, Colonel Norie redisposed the troops on his front, withdrawing the 2/2nd Goorkhas and 6th Jāt Light Infantry units, sending the Cavalry to their own headquarters, and filling the gap left between the 9th Goorkha Rifles and the Connaught Rangers with the Royal Scots Fusiliers. This disposition was approved by the Brigadier-General, and at dawn our Battalion received orders to retire and refit.

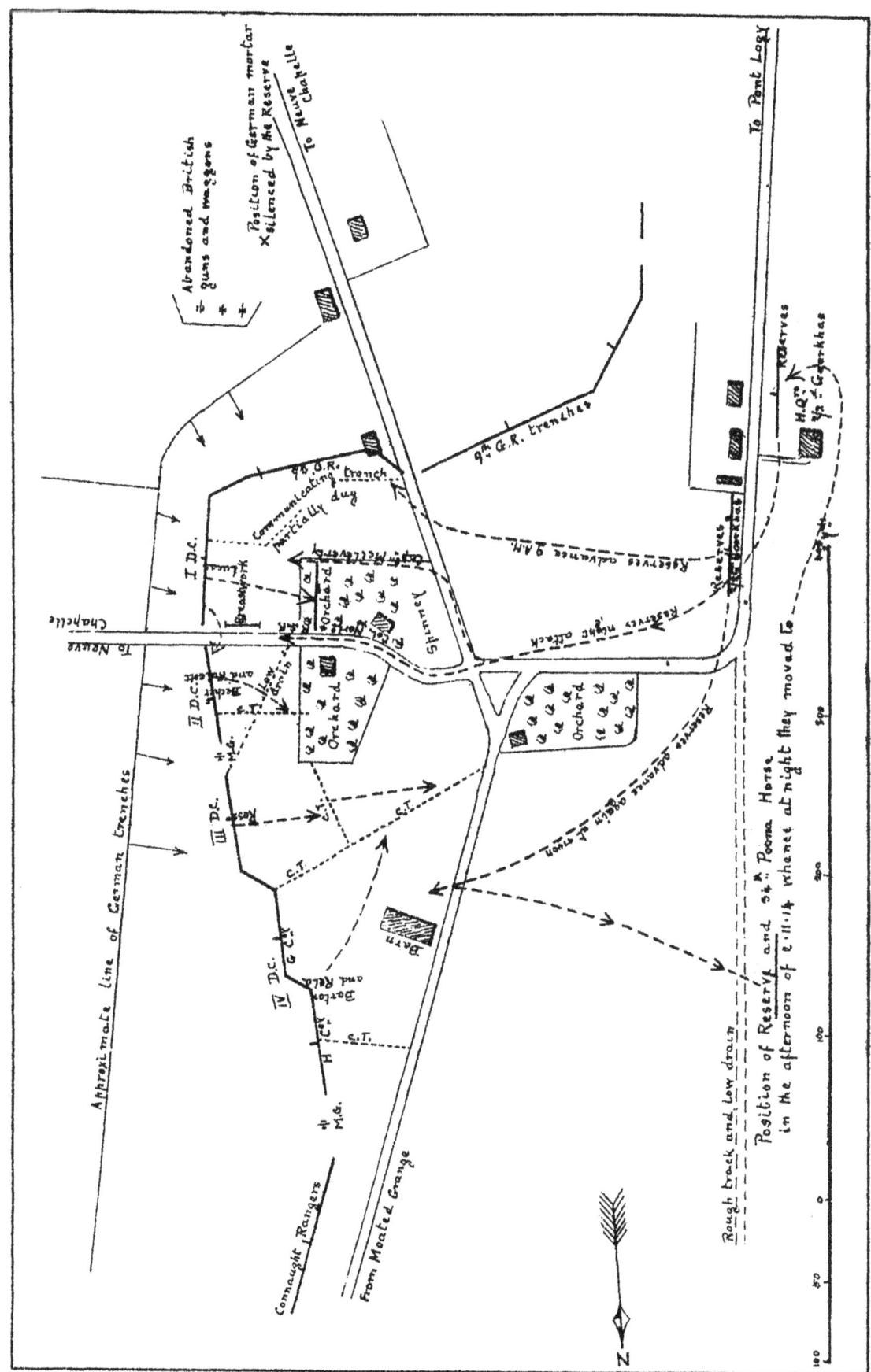

So ended for us a disastrous but gallantly fought action against superior numbers far better provided with the modern machinery of war than we were. Although this portion of the line was taken for a time one result was good, for it appeared the stubbornness of our opposition, together with his own heavy losses, inclined the enemy to nervousness in regard to his new position, which caused him to withdraw again to his own trenches during the night.

The historians of the Indian Corps in France record concerning this action that "the heroism of the British officers has seldom been more brilliantly demonstrated than on this occasion. Not a single British officer of the 2nd Goorkhas in the front trenches got back alive, several being killed while leading attacks against vastly superior numbers. The bravery displayed by all ranks fully sustained the great reputation of this Regiment."

Casualties during Action, 2/11/14.

An official diary notes "the 2nd Goorkhas did magnificently, losing 8 officers and a large number of men. The heavy mortar shells caused the trenches to fall in, burying many alive."

Our losses in this day's action were deplorably heavy, viz. :—

	Killed.	Wounded.	Missing.
British officers	7	1	0
Goorkha Officers	4	3	0
Other ranks	31	64	37

or a total of 147. Our fighting strength this day was 9 British officers, 13 Goorkha officers, 507 men. Of those shown as "missing" a great number must have been buried in the trenches ruined by the furious bombardment.

For this action Brigadier-General Johnson recommended for "mention in despatches" Colonel Norie, D.S.O., Major Norie, Captain McCleverty, Lieutenant Corse Scott, and Lieutenant Scoones, while the following were specially recommended by Colonel Norie for having held out till the last and for having fought exceptionally well:—Subadars Fateh Sing Newar and Dalbahadur Gurung, Jemadars Karakbahadur Gurung, Tirthe Gurung (wounded), Bahadur Ghale, and Suba Sing Gurung.

CHAPTER V.

NOVEMBER 3RD TO DECEMBER 17TH, 1914. (*Sketches IX, IV, V, III.*)

THE 2/2nd Goorkhas reached Pont du Hem (Brigade Headquarters) and were disposed in billets by 8 a.m. on November 3rd, when the work of refitting and reorganizing began at once, occupying the next few days, while the men had a rest broken by calls now and then to send supports to the Seaforths and the 9th Goorkha Rifles. Captain W. B. Bailey rejoined the Battalion here from Staff duty taking command of No. 1 Double Company, while Captain Duff, 1/1st Goorkhas (son of the Commander-in-Chief in India) sent us to fill a vacancy, was given command of No. 2. The equipment of our troops now received a welcome addition in the shape of both rifle and hand grenades though not in sufficient quantity, the lack of which had been so badly felt, and instruction in their use went on apace.

<small>In first Billets, 3/11/14.</small>

In the afternoon of the 6th orders came to support the Seaforths now in trenches south-west of Neuve Chapelle, close to what later became known as "Port Arthur," and Colonel Norie with No. 1 and No. 3 Double Companies, proceeded to the front and opened a line of trenches in rear of the Seaforths' right flank, intending eventually to connect up with the 39th Garhwalis. He was, however, recalled next day with three companies, Captain Duff being left with "B" Company to stiffen the Seaforths' right. During the 7th the three trenches were heavily attacked, the Germans using a new trench mortar with a range of 600 yards, one shell, it is recorded, made a hole 15 feet wide and 8 feet deep, burying a sergeant and several men. The attack being pressed home, Captain Duff pushed his men forward to reinforce, and while steadying all and helping to direct their fire, was shot through the head and killed. A few Germans got into his trench but were bayoneted, and the attack was repulsed, our casualties being 3 killed and 6 wounded.

<small>"B" Company in Action, 7/11/14.</small>

<small>Capt. Duff killed, 7/11/14.</small>

The succeeding three days were spent in billets, Captain Bailey's Double Company being with the Seaforths in front, but we were soon sent out again in support of certain reconnaissances prior to a probable local offensive, and at dusk Lieutenant Scoones with No. 4 Double Company was sent to support the 9th Goorkha Rifles. During the night of November 10th two double companies, with three squadrons 7th Dragoon Guards, received orders to move out in support of an artillery concentration on Neuve Chapelle, the object of which was to demolish the houses in front of the Seaforths and to search the ground in rear of the village. No offensive movement against our line took place as had been expected, the Germans only replying with desultory firing. Our companies were then withdrawn at daylight and employed in trench digging in a raging hail storm.

The visit by Lord Roberts to the Indian Contingent at the front was one to cause a very deep impression on the force. His name inspired even Indian soldiers who had not served under him, while the reverence felt for him by those left who had so served is well known. Representative detachments of all Indian units in France were sent to the château at Hinges, where he inspected them, making a short but stirring speech. The severity of the climate, however, told upon the aged Field-Marshal, who fell ill, and three days later he died in sound of the guns, leaving a feeling of personal loss to all in the corps.

Lord Roberts' Visit, Nov., 1914.

Our strength in British officers was now increased by the transfer to us of Captain H. T. Molloy and Lieutenant E. P. Hay Webb from the 5th Goorkha Rifles, and Captain L. A. Bethell from the 10th Goorkha Rifles.

November 13th we moved to Le Touret and two days later Nos. 1 and 3 Double Companies were sent to dig trenches in rear of the 2/39th Garhwalis and support them. The following day our Battalion relieved this unit, and was temporarily attached to the Garhwal Brigade then holding a section of the front line on the Rue du Bois, 1800 yards south of Neuve Chapelle.

Battalion attached to Garhwal Brigade, 14/11/14.

Major E. H. P. Boileau, 1/2nd Goorkhas, had now arrived, and was posted as Second-in-Command, while Major Rooke, 10th Goorkha Rifles, joined us as a Double Company Commander.

Our days with the new brigade were almost entirely occupied in trench digging, making splinter proofs, improving trenches in rear, and connecting up with either flank, all of which was done in bitter weather and cases of frost-bite began to occur. For a short period two of our Double Companies were in the front trenches, where they had 3 men killed and 4 wounded. A few collisions between opposing patrols took place, and Captain Bailey was slightly wounded on the head by a shrapnel bullet.

Work on the Rue du Bois Section, Nov., 1914.

Two Germans gave themselves up to one of our patrols, unable to endure their situation longer; they had been hiding in a cellar of one of the nearest houses of Neuve Chapelle for days ever since the last fighting, and had been living on a dead cow. In the same house our patrol found numbers of the enemy's dead and brought away their rifles, equipment, etc. During a slight action on the 21st both our machine guns became useless, the water in their jackets having frozen during an interval, and they were eventually put into working order by means of applying hot bricks. The same day was made memorable as that on which H.R.H. The Prince of Wales arrived at the Indian Corps' line, visiting as many of the trenches as were possible—a visit hailed with most loyal appreciation by all ranks.

Prince of Wales's Visit, 22/11/14.

Snow having fallen, Lieutenant Hay Webb, in charge of our scouts, fitted his men with white clothing, enabling them to creep close up to the hostile line without being observed, and bringing back often valuable information. We were now treated for the first time to a bombardment of "crumps," one of which destroyed one of our machine guns, and a stack of rifles near it. As it burst in the trench it was marvellous no men were hurt. The evening of the 23rd we returned to our old billets at Le Touret on being relieved by the 59th Rifles, whose Colonel was killed during the process, and the relief of the Meerut Division by that of Lahore was completed.

Billets at Le Touret, 23/11/14.

Because our Battalion had not been seriously engaged since the fatal November 2nd, it must not be imagined all was quiet on this part of the Indian Corps' front. On the contrary, other parts of the line held by it had been concerned in warding off desperate assaults, while others again had been engaged in local attacks. In all of which Indian regiments added fresh laurels to their names in the fighting near Festubert and Givenchy, to the south of where the Battalion was, and in spite of the weakness of the line it was never broken.

Frost-bite proved an unpleasant foe to contend with under the severe climatic conditions to which the men were exposed; in the last ten days of trench life 32 men had to be evacuated owing to severe frost-bite. Not nearly enough vaseline had been supplied us, but at Le Touret arrangements were made to give each man three pairs of socks—two to be worn and one spare. Our stay at Le Touret was uneventful; we were only called out on November 29th to support the 47th Sikhs and 59th Rifles in the left section of the same front, viz., on the Rue du Bois, and later detaching two Double Companies in support of the right section; nothing occurring, we returned to billets with nine more cases of frost-bite (*Sketch IX*).

Frost-bite Trouble.

It was on December 1st that His Majesty the King paid the Indian Corps at the front the honour of a visit. This was a surprise only first heard of the night before, when the various officers and detachments were told off for the inspection parade. The deep interest in and concern His Majesty held for the welfare of all ranks, was abundantly shown in his conversations with officers and his constant queries to the men. Susceptible as all our Indian soldiery are to the personal influence of their "Bādshah," the visit was a hearty stimulus to all and a treasured memory to those who were fortunate in seeing him.

H.M. the King's Visit, 1/12/14.

Orders had been received on November 30th that we should relieve the 47th Sikhs in the trenches on the night of December 2nd-3rd, which was duly carried out, Nos. 1, 2, and 3 Companies (the new title for the old Double Company) in front line, No. 4 in support. This new line was on the immediate right of those we had dug and held with the Seaforths a fortnight earlier, the Battalion still being with the Garhwal Brigade, the 2/39th Garhwalis being on its left, the 2/3rd Goorkhas on its right. Here at last a proper supply of sandbags, viz., 3,000, was made over to us; these had been badly needed but difficult to obtain.

Battalion relieves 47th Sikhs in Front Trenches, 3/12/14.

This tour of trench duty was comparatively quiet as far as the enemy were concerned, who occasionally peppered our No. 3 parapet. Our whole time was occupied in cutting "caponiers" on both sides of the ditch leading to the picquet post, in blinding loopholes, in improving splinter proofs and the trenches in general. Lieutenant Hay Webb, with our scouts, was busy locating and dispersing snipers, and on one or two occasions was able to approach the hostile trenches, where quiet reigned for a time. The left picquet post was gradually developed into a strong redoubt and "Port Arthur" (*Sketch IX*) was enlarged to contain the machine guns. On December 6th the weather changed, heavy rain coming on which seemed to stir the enemy to some activity, for a lot of rifle fire was expended on the right of our line, but without much effect, and on the night of the 8th the 1/39th Garhwalis moved up, relieving the 2/2nd Goorkhas, who went into billets in the Rue de l'Epinette, where a welcome reinforcement was found in Captain A. M. Graham, 5th Goorkha Rifles, Lieutenant L. C. Rogers, 7th Goorkha Rifles, Subadar Sarabjit Gurung, Jemadar Guman Sing Gurung, and 131

Work in Trenches, till 8/12/14.

Billets in the Rue de l'Epinette, 8/12/14.

Draft arrives, 8/12/14.

D

men from Dehra. Our casualties since December 2nd had been very slight—1 man killed, and 4 wounded.

As mentioned before, the enemy was equipped in profusion with various modern munitions of war in which our forces were badly lacking. With some of these deficiencies the Sappers did all they could to cope, and early this month they had evolved searchlights out of motor-car headlights, to which electric bulbs were attached, power being arranged for from machinery in rear. They also cleverly improvised a form of catapult for bomb throwing, which with fair accuracy could land its missile up to 300 yards, both contrivances being of great use in coming actions.

After a couple of days in billets the Battalion moved out to the front trenches at La Quinque Rue (*Sketches IX, III*) on December 10th to relieve the Leicesters, and information came to hand that the French had made a short but successful advance south-south-east of Béthune, across the La Bassée Canal, good news to hear. The new trenches we occupied now were fairly good, but owing to shocking weather the communications were in a bad state, and much spadework had to be done, during which we had 2 men killed and 1 wounded. The 6th Jāt Light Infantry (for we had now rejoined the Dehra Brigade) continued the line to the left, the Seaforths to the right, while the trench mortars in this section were operated by men of the Leicesters, between whom and the Germans a continuous duel went on, with advantage for once in a way on our side.

Battalion moved to La Quinque Rue Front Line, 10/12/14.

Battalion rejoins the Dehra Brigade, early Dec., 1914.

On December 12th a reconnaissance was made of the enemy's saps, two having been pushed out 50 yards from the south face of the "Orchard" in our front line, and our Sappers burrowing towards these points had laid a mine with intent to blow up both sapheads. The actual front trenches of the "Orchard" had been badly dug and planned by an earlier regiment, and consisted of a deep, narrow trench entirely covered in like a tunnel, defended with loopholes so badly placed close up to the roof that it was almost impossible to get a clear view through them. The Leicesters, whom we relieved, had therefore dug a fresh trench in rear across the "Orchard," cutting off the south-east angle, and this we now occupied, together with Trench "E" (*Sketch III*), holding the old front line with picquets only. View here, however, was restricted, the whole area was most difficult to hold and defend, and was constantly under heavy shell fire. It also lay in

Condition of Trenches at La Quinque Rue.

a slight depression, more or less dominated by the German front, while a low culvert under the road behind the "Orchard," knee-deep in thick mud and water, interfered with direct movement to either flank.

On December 14th the Germans evidently brought up reinforcements opposite our front, as considerably more movement was apparent, men in new uniforms being seen here and there, while our line was treated to rather more bombing, causing us 5 casualties. On the 17th they exploded a mine in front of our right section, which damaged the wire entanglement. Lieutenant Hay Webb and Captain Corse Scott were both wounded by the same bullet, the former seriously, while they were reconnoitring the hostile front from a haystack. Lieutenant Hay Webb had done excellent work with our scouts, and his loss was much felt.

Germans, reinforced, attack La Quinque Rue.

The middle of this month being deemed a fitting time in which to assist General Smith-Dorrien's big attack on Messines by local operations from our portion of the line so as to contain the enemy in this area, the Indian Corps was directed to carry this out. On the 16th, therefore, the Ferozepore Brigade (Lahore Division) opened operations to the north-west of Givenchy, where furious fighting took place not altogether in our favour in spite of most gallant efforts. The following day further orders directed the Corps to carry out a demonstration along its entire front, seizing every opportunity which might offer to capture any hostile trenches, thus also assisting the French, who were operating to the south in the neighbourhood of Arras.

Plans for Fresh Operations, 16/12/14.

Now the line held by the Indian Corps had become through heavy casualties extremely thin, making it no easy task to defend a long line and to deliver an offensive effectively. All were also feeling the strain of seven weeks of incessant trench warfare in most trying weather, when it was almost impossible to so apportion the day that men got a fair distribution of working and rest hours. Generally it was endeavoured to divide the day into eight hours of guards and sentries, eight hours of work, and eight for rest; but what with ration, wood, ammunition, and various other incidental carrying duties, plus the depleted state of the ranks, it was not possible to adhere to such daily arrangements, hence men got overworked with frequently scant leisure for meals. This had been reported to Sir John French with a view to a period of complete rest and refitting being given. This need was fully recognized, but the exigencies of the time precluded the possibility of carrying it out, so the corps had had to extend its already attenuated line to include Givenchy—always a locality causing much anxiety.

CHAPTER VI.

DECEMBER 18TH TO 23RD, 1914. (*Sketch III.*)

THE Indian Corps was now disposed as follows :—The Meerut Division held the left half of the line with the Garhwal Brigade occupying the section from the cross-roads just south of Neuve Chapelle (*Sketch IX*) village to the cross-roads on the Rue du Bois opposite Richebourg-l'Avoué, whence the Dehra Doon Brigade carried on the line round the " Orchard," north-east of the cross-roads at La Quinque Rue to the cross-roads half a mile south, not far from which point was the " Picquet House," held by the Seaforths. The Bareilly Brigade was in reserve. From here the Lahore Division continued south with an indentation towards the west and Festubert, whence it rounded the north-east of Givenchy, the French carrying on the line from the La Bassée Canal southwards.

Disposition of Indian Corps, mid Dec., 1914.

It was decided to open operations with the Meerut Division, of which the Garhwal Brigade would be the first to attack the German line, to be followed by the Dehra Doon Brigade directly the first was successful.

To return to our Battalion. The earlier instructions *re* endeavouring to contain the enemy on this front and thus aid the French " push," appeared to have borne good fruit. The Leicesters on our left front had captured some 300 yards of hostile trenches, but had retired unable to hold what they had gained. The explosion of our mine under the U-shaped German sapheads (*Sketch III*) close to the " Orchard " south face having been put off, was still further postponed until the attack on our left had developed.

About noon on December 19th, and while the relief of our No. 1 Company by No. 4 was in progress, a terrific bombardment started on the " Orchard " defences by " Minenwerfer," the whole of our parapet was blown in, the east and south faces being almost obliterated, so that the " Orchard " front of the section had to be evacuated temporarily (*Sketch III*). It was a sudden and severe handling in which we lost a number of men. A new line in rear was now formed by turning a communicating trench into a fire one, but this was weak and open to enfilade at several points though it was the best that could be done at the time. Two companies of the 9th Goorkha Rifles came up to support us and they with ours were digging

First Bombardment at La Quinque Rue, 19/12/14.

all night in heavy rain, which frequently washed down the walls of the trenches, smothering the rifles in mud. No further action having taken place from the German side in the night beyond a few stray shells, at dawn on December 20th all stood to arms, the 9th Goorkha Rifles returning to billets. Thereafter followed heavy fighting for us, the various accounts of which differ and are somewhat complicated, from which this narrative is framed.

At 8.50 a.m. on December 20th Colonel Norie was summoned to a conference at Brigade Headquarters, and before going he sent Majors Boileau and Watt, who had been in the front trenches, back to Battalion Headquarters for rest and food. Our front was held as follows:—

The Action at La Quinque Rue, 20/12/14. Captain Graham, of No. 3 Company, on the right, with Captain Molloy as Company Commander, Major Watt with Captain Bethell and No. 4 Company holding the centre, Major Rooke with No. 2 on the left, linking up with the 6th Jāts, Major Boileau with No. 1 in reserve. Our two machine guns were disposed, one on Major Rooke's right, the other with Captain Graham's company, both being under Captain Molloy.

Battalion's Disposition, 20/12/14. At 9.30 a.m. the whole place was shaken by the explosion of a large German mine under the "Orchard" parapet, with which our own mine under their western saphead went up; in the centre and right trenches the walls and parapets in many places falling in. This was instantly followed by a deluge of concentrated shrapnel, high explosives, and machine-gun fire for a few minutes, ending with a rush of the enemy into the "Orchard" and trenches south of it.

Germans gain the "Orchard" Position. Captain Bethell forced out of the "Orchard" and Trench "B," retired before the mass of the enemy on to Trench "C." This he found useless on account of its depth, so they fought their way to the "Strand," where Majors Boileau and Watt, with Lieutenant Corse Scott who had come forward with the Reserve, were met. These then made a rear-guard action, fighting from traverse to traverse, back to Trench "F," where a final stand was made, the enemy pressing on across the open to points H, M, G, and placing machine guns there. These were the farthest points to which their assault reached, and they were not there long. On the west of Trench "F" was a wooded hamlet, where a picquet of 25 rifles was at once posted as it formed a covered approach to Major Boileau's right. No. 2 Company under Major Rooke, who was wounded, fortunately had been able to stem the German attack on his front and having barricaded the right end of his trench was able to hold on where he was, though

Action of the Battalion Reserve, 20/12/14.

for a short time the enemy were both on his front and rear (*Sketch III*). On our right No. 3 Company and the machine gun found a good target at first as the Germans issued from their west saphead, but folds in the ground favoured their rush into the " Orchard," and on to Captain Graham's front.

Captain Graham killed.
Heavy fighting took place here and on the Seaforths' left front, Captain Graham was killed, the machine gun with exception of some spare parts was captured, and we had no bombs with which to reply to the Germans, whose attack was chiefly made with those missiles. Captain Molloy, now in command of No. 3, was forced back to the south portion of Trench " C," a move also rendered necessary as the explosion of the German mine and our own had completely wrecked the left of No. 3 front Trench " D ," about " Charing Cross," burying many men, while the entry of the enemy into the " Orchard " exposed our left flank of which they took immediate advantage. In Trench " C " Molloy and his men managed to hold on successfully, though separated from the Battalion, keeping touch with the Seaforths through a strong picquet at point *U*, and barricading the north end of the trench at the Rue des Cailloux. In this position he withstood the German assault across the open on his front, and the Seaforths' left, and during the evening of the 20th the 58th Rifles coming up relieved his picquet, and moving to Molloy's left established themselves about point *P*, filling that gap. Captain Molloy's company held

Captain Molloy's stand helps the Seaforths, 20/12/14.
this line steadily till the morning of December 22nd, when the Royal Sussex arrived to relieve them, and they were able to rejoin the Battalion. It is certain that but for the dogged hold on this bit of the line by No. 3 Company on our extreme right the Seaforths would have fared far worse, and perhaps have been unable to regain their left trenches which they had lost in the earlier stages of the fighting.

Returning to affairs on our left, Colonel Norie had returned from Brigade Headquarters during the morning, heavy firing was still going on, and Colonel Widdicombe with the 9th Goorkha Rifles arrived with orders to support

9th Goorkha Rifles reinforces the Battalion, 20/12/14.
the 6th Jāts. However, placing one of his wings behind their line, he moved the other wing to help Major Boileau, sending forward one company under Captain Mackinnon to occupy Trench " Q.R.," and who managed to barricade the " Strand " on his right—a move which caused the Germans to fall back a little. Colonel Norie now went to the 6th Jāts, where with Colonel Roche and Lieutenant Trevor, Royal Engineers, he arranged a plan to bomb the enemy out of our old trenches north of the " Orchard ";

Sketch No. III

2nd Goorkha Trenches at La Quinque Rue Dec. 10th to 21st 1914

Scale: 0–300 yds

Labels on the sketch:
- German Trenches
- To Festubert
- Seaforths
- Pond
- U Picquet of No III
- Redoubt
- Molloy's stand No III
- Major Graham / Capt. Molloy No III
- M.G. Trench D
- Charing Cross
- German Mines
- German
- To la Tourelle
- The Orchard
- Capt. Bethell
- Ruined Houses
- Road
- Tunnel
- Pall Mall
- Trench B
- 58th Rifles advance
- Rue des Caillous
- Trench C
- Hd. Qrs. Dug-out
- Trench E
- Major Watt No IV
- Old Leicester Hd. Qrs.
- Final Position held
- Trench P
- M.G. S
- Left of 2nd G.R. Position
- Major Rooke No II
- Road
- H
- The Strand
- Barricade
- 1 Coy 9th G.R.
- The Salient
- T M G
- From Chocolate Menier Corner
- 6th Jats
- N
- German Trenches
- K
- Trench F
- Boileau's & Watt's stand
- Picquet
- Hedge
- S
- O
- From Richebourg L'Avoué
- 2nd G's. Hd. Qrs. Reserve No I, Major Boileau (The Indian Village)

2ND K.E.O.G.

GOORKHAS (THE SIRMOOR RIFLE REGIMENT)

the plan, however, had to be given up as those trenches were found to be too narrow with no traverses and with long stretches of overhead cover. Later in the day Colonel Ritchie, Officer Commanding Seaforths, reported he had been able to regain his lost trenches and a small portion of ours by bombing, and by evening German efforts had almost ceased, that night being employed in improving our present positions. The rest of the 1/9th Goorkha Rifles had prolonged Captain Mackinnon's line to the right forming a new front, and a wing of the Black Watch and the 41st Dogras came up during the evening to prevent any further attempt to break our line, also a British brigade we were informed would arrive next morning.

Further reinforcements arrive.

During the night of December 20th-21st much firing took place, chiefly between the enemy and the 58th Rifles, while our guns shelled the " Orchard " and trenches in German hands, but the latter attempted no further advance. Early on the 21st it was decided to give up the salient $Q\ S\ T$, hitherto gallantly held by our No. 2 Company and one of the 6th Jāts, which was, therefore, demolished and evacuated. All day our guns shelled the " Orchard," and its neighbourhood, which the enemy vigorously replied to, and a haystack in rear of our line being set on fire by a German shell, a beacon was given them, which caused us further loss. That night the 1/9th Goorkha Rifles relieved most of our companies in the front for a time.

The 2/2nd Goorkhas greatly exhausted and having suffered in many killed and wounded, were finally relieved during the night of December 22nd-23rd by the Royal Sussex Regiment, and withdrawn into billets at Vieille Chapelle. In this last fighting our casualties were :—

Battalion relieved, 23/12/14.

Casualties at La Quinque Rue.

	British Officers.	Goorkha Officers.	Other Ranks.	Total.
Killed	1	0	29	30
Wounded	2	4	34	40
Missing	0	2	60	62
				132

while in addition 70 men were suffering from frost-bite of whom 24 had to be evacuated, including Major Boileau and Captain Molloy.

Major Boileau in his account of the fighting on the 20th records an act of gallantry on the part of Lance Naik Tula Gurung who, when a large minenwerfer shell wrecked a portion of the front, causing a gap in the trench and pinning down a Goorkha under the debris, went out at imminent risk, being fully exposed to

Gallantry recorded.

the enemy and succeeded in releasing the man. He also mentions an act of devotion to duty when Captain Bethell had to retire in the early stages of the action, in two of our signallers, Sula Sing Lama and Ranbir Sahi, who, when the fighting in the "Strand" was in progress, were found standing at their post completely isolated. They had not retired as they considered it their duty to remain at their telephone till orders reached them.

Although the activities of our Battalion in the front line now ceased for a time, it may be mentioned that owing to the worn-out state of the Indian troops through incessant trench life and warfare, General Sir Douglas Haig's 1st Corps was sent forward, of which the 2nd Brigade, 1st Division came up **Further Fighting at La Quinque Rue, during 22-23/12/14.** to support the Dehra Doon Brigade during the night of December 21st, when a British Brigade consisting of the Loyal North Lancs and Northamptons, with the King's Royal Rifles in support, carried out an attack. Part of the "Orchard" front was regained, but the old 2nd Goorkha trenches there were found so completely obliterated by German shells, mines, and bombs, that they could not be occupied—a proof of the severe handling our Battalion had undergone. Early on the 23rd the Loyal North Lancs, after a stiff struggle, were bombed back again with heavy losses, while the Northamptons almost ceased to exist, **Indian Corps relieved by the 1st Corps, 23/12/14.** nearly 800 men, one account states, being killed, wounded, and captured. On this date at midday the 1st Corps took over the entire line held by the Indian troops, though certain units of the Meerut Division were not completely relieved till the 27th, when the whole corps was in much needed rest in billets.

In regard to these last days of fighting General Sir John French records how "the Indian troops have fought with the greatest gallantry and steadfastness whenever called upon."

It is a coincidence worth noting that both on November 2nd and December 20th, 1914, the Germans seemed to pay the section of the line held by us their fullest attention, delivering violent and overwhelming assaults on our trenches, and being thoroughly well provided with bombs and mortars, lacking in our line, they gained temporary successes which the utmost effort and gallantry on our part could not entirely deny them.

FRANCE, JANUARY, 1915.

Captain Corse Scott (*Adjutant*). Major Watt. Captain Macintyre. M. Gantes (*Interpreter*).

CHAPTER VII.

December 23rd, 1914, to March 9th, 1915. (*Sketches IX, IV, V.*)

Indian Corps in Rest Billets, Dec.-Jan., 1914-15.

The Indian Corps having well earned a change and rest, were now distributed in various billets well in rear of the actual zone of fighting, where they remained practically a month, during which time refitting in clothes and equipment went on, also instruction in new pattern of trenches, in bomb throwing, etc. Route marching was practised, for men's feet had become soft and easily got sore after long weeks of standing and moving about in waterlogged trenches.

Battalion in Floringhem Billets.

To follow the doings of our Battalion at this period we find they were in three different billets, viz., Vieille Chapelle, Croix Marmuse, and Robecq before they finally settled down at Floringhem on December 27th. Christmas Day, which seems to have been observed in some parts of the front by a cessation of firing, greetings on both sides, and an unofficial armistice to admit of burying the dead, was spent quietly by the Battalion at Croix Marmuse, which is recorded by our officers as having been the most comfortable and hospitable locality they had yet been in.

Christmas Day Fraternization of Troops, 1914.

Some accounts of this " unofficial armistice " on the first Christmas Day of the war are curious. An officer of an English regiment told the writer how he was in his dug-out that morning when one of his sergeants came in with a beaming face, saluted, and said : " Sir, the war's all over." On the officer telling him not to be a qualified idiot, the Sergeant still beaming, replied : " Well, Sir, just you come up and see." He did so, no guns or rifles were active ; all was quiet save for a multitude of voices. On climbing over the parapet he beheld the extraordinary spectacle of " No Man's Land " covered with the soldiery of both opposing forces walking about and fraternizing with each other. He found it impossible at the moment to collect his men and get them back, and while trying to do this he was greeted by a German officer who insisted on the British officer coming and joining them at a meal. After going back to fetch his rations, with which to help out his hosts in their meal, the officer joined his hostile friends, and later they showed him round their trenches, where he saw a machine gun which a day or two before he and some of his men had tried to locate when crawling out in the mud reconnoitring.

This amazing scene went on nearly all day though officers were trying to get their men back to their respective lines. A senior German officer came up to my friend saying excitedly : " Mein freund, dis is to be shtopping ! " but nothing seemed to avail at the time. Later in the day orders were issued, it was said, on both sides that if the men did not separate at a certain hour German and English guns would open on to " No Man's Land," the ground was then cleared, and scenes ended which were never after repeated. The Garhwal Rifles in their history record a slighter but somewhat similar outburst of fraternization near Givenchy.

Floringhem is described as being none too good in the matter of quarters, and many farmers were unwilling to afford our men any help in matters like firewood for instance. Here three Goorkha officers had to be evacuated for frost-bite, leaving only seven for duty ; owing to the recent heavy casualties men got promotion rapidly, but the Goorkha officer was difficult to replace. It was just after Christmas that the consignment of Princess Mary's kindly gift to the troops arrived—a pipe, some tobacco, and cigarettes for each soldier, which was much appreciated by our men.

Confined life in the trenches for long spells, the dirt, and inability to wash themselves or their clothes had produced another discomfort, viz., a plague of lice, which now had to be contended **Lice Plague.** with. The men had no fresh underclothing, but a rough sort of laundry was established and as many irons as possible were collected, so that after repeated washings the plague for the time being was got rid of.

On December 29th Colonel Norie, D.S.O., left the Battalion on appointment as G.S.O. 1, Meerut Division, and went on leave before joining the Staff, Captains Bethell and O'Brien, I.M.S., and Lieutenant **Colonel Norie leaves** Corse Scott going with him. The officiating command of **us, 29/12/14.** the Battalion now fell to Major Watt. During early January, 1915, the 2/2nd Goorkhas marched to Permes, 468 strong out of 531 present in France, for inspection by the General Officer Commanding Indian Corps, and we were joined by Subadar Dalpati Thapa with a small draft of 20 men, also by Captain Macintyre of ours, and Lieutenant Clifford, I.A.R.O., the former taking over the machine guns, of which we were shortly to have six instead of two, thus necessitating the training of more gun teams. A change of Brigade Commanders took place this month, when Brigadier-General Johnson was succeeded by Colonel Jacob.

On January 7th the Commander-in-Chief, General Sir John French, inspected the Dehra Brigade, when he congratulated the Battalion on its behaviour throughout the operations so far. Bad weather again set in, greatly impeding the various instructional works in progress; still, much was accomplished during our stay at Floringhem. Parties of recovered sick and wounded now began returning to us, for on January 16th 52 men arrived from hospitals in Rouen and England; also we were joined by Major Sweet who had been on duty elsewhere. Two days later Major Nicolay and Captain Dallas Smith, both of ours, arrived from India with drafts of 43 men of the Lushai Hills Military Police Battalion (now 1st Assam Rifles), under Subadar Mansur Rai, and 23 of our own men from Dehra. The former were a fine lot of men, and all had volunteered. These formed a welcome addition, for duties heavy at the front, were by no means light in billets. Our strength at this time totalled 720 Goorkha ranks—practically up to full strength again, and we only wanted two more British officers.

Inspection by Sir John French, 7/1/15.

Military Police Draft arrives with Major Nicolay and Captain Dallas Smith, 18/1/15.

The period in billets ended with January 25th, when the Dehra Brigade moved to Calonne, each unit travelling half the way in motor buses and marching the remaining 13 miles. Here orders met us that our Brigade was to be in support to that of Garhwal, now moving into the front trenches near Richebourg l'Avoué. The weather still bad caused some sickness, necessitating the evacuation of Subadars Fateh Sing Newar and Arjun Rana—the former with bad neuritis, the latter with dysentery, both a great loss. Only one Goorkha officer now remained of all who left India with the Battalion, but fortunately we had excellent ones from the 1st Battalion at Dehra. Vieille Chapelle was reached on the 26th, and we were once more in sound of heavy firing on right and left and were soon employed, the right Wing under Major Sweet, being sent almost at once to the Garhwal Brigade front to build redoubts behind the Rue du Bois (*Sketch IV*) as a second line of defence, and were relieved in the evening by Major Nicolay with the Left Wing. Most of the trenches being under water, the main line of defence was the road and redoubts to its front, the actual front trenches being lightly held by picquets. The next line of defence was formed by the works around

Battalion returns to Front, 25/1/15.

Richebourg St. Vaast and the whole section appeared a strong one. These digging and building works occupied us till January 29th, when we moved from Vieille Chapelle to the front, relieving the 1/39th Garhwalis as a support to the Garhwal Brigade. Better arrangements were now made for meals while front trench life and operations were going on, the former number of men for cooking was doubled and bread or biscuits issued, as the men found " atta " unsuitable for trench life.

Battalion relieves 1/39th Garhwalis near Richebourg l'Avoué, 29/1/15.

Nothing of importance occurred during the next three days, the enemy being fairly quiet on our front, during which our time was occupied in manning certain redoubts, in digging fatigues, and in reinforcing the left section of the line on the Rue du Bois. This section only was an unquiet corner just now, being subjected to some shelling, but it was plainly noticeable that we had superiority in guns over the Germans—a very different state of affairs to what was formerly the case.

Captain O'Brien, I.M.S., was at this time transferred to the Meerut Divisional Hospital, at Boulogne, his place with us being taken by Captain W. B. Cullen, I.M.S.

February 1st saw our Battalion move up into the firing line in relief of the 6th Jāts and part of the Seaforths, the front fire trench in which was some 3 feet of water, only being lightly held by picquets of 1 non-commissioned officer and 6 men each. The main line of resistance was the Rue du Bois (*Sketch IV*), and the long breastwork in front which, being hardly bullet-proof, required a lot of strengthening; and the companies were mostly billeted in houses left standing along the Rue du Bois.

In Trenches along Rue du Bois, 1/2/15.

On our right we linked with the 4th Suffolks; on the left with our old friends, the 9th Goorkha Rifles, and the machine guns of the 4th Seaforths, and the 107th Pioneers were located in our section of the front line. This tour of front-trench duty was a short and comparatively quiet one, the enemy only shelling parts of the line spasmodically, causing us one man seriously wounded, and this shelling appeared to come from a field gun which was so cleverly concealed it could not be located by our gunners. The wounded man was carrying a " degchi " of meat when hit, and when he recovered consciousness his first words were to the amusement of those helping him: " What *has* become of that meat ? "

The stream between picquets and breastwork would have proved a considerable difficulty in an advance, but early on the 4th we received from the Sappers a number of bridges ready made up which were soon placed in position behind each picquet, and at nightfall we were relieved by the 2/3rd Goorkhas.

Our Battalion marched to the La Couture billeting area at first, thence on the 8th to Le Cornet Malo, where we got the cheering news of the successful attack of the Guards Brigade supported by the guns of the Indian Corps at Cuinchy, south of Givenchy, just across the canal, and on the 10th we moved to Robecq, where a stay was made till orders were issued to return to La Couture (*Sketch IX*) on the 22nd. This period as usual was filled with drills, route marches, special instruction for the new military police drafts, issue of fresh clothing, cutting of brushwood for fascines at the front, and so on; all under happier weather conditions. While at Robecq we had received a further draft of Burma Military Police, viz., 1 Goorkha officer and 25 men, and with them came Captains Cruickshank and Mullaly, who had been doing good work on the far-off North-East Frontier of India—welcome additions being our own officers.

Battalion in Billets at Robecq and La Couture, 8–23/2/15.

Military Police Draft arrives, 18/2/15.

On February 23rd the 2/2nd Goorkhas were ordered up to the front line and took over the centre sub-section of the Indian Corps' northern section from the Jullunder Brigade, consisting of some 800 yards of front more or less in the old locality, about $1\frac{1}{2}$ miles south of Neuve Chapelle. Two companies were in the firing line having for defence a breastwork revetted with hurdles 3 feet 6 inches in height, with a shallow trench in rear and running 40 yards in front of the Rue du Bois. The old trenches, mostly full of water, about 350 yards to the front, were held by picquets in posts dug into the parapet; the rest of the Battalion were in two farms on the right of Edward Road, near the factory, and reliefs were carried out at nightfall. The hostile trenches were only 150 yards from our picquets, and as the nights were bright moonlight and weather clear and frosty, patrolling had to be discontinued, as the Germans regularly took toll of the patrols.

Battalion relieves Part of Jullunder Brigade, 23/2/15.

A certain amount of hostile shelling went on daily and much spadework had to be put in over communicating trenches, and snow falling on the night of February 25th–26th, scouts were able to move out to reconnoitre the German trenches and obstacles. They reported high wire entanglement continuous along their front and *chevaux de frise* with gaps here and there, breastworks 3 to 4 feet high in which large numbers of sandbags were used. Our No. 3 picquet was heavily fired on during the 26th, having its parapet knocked to pieces and 1 man killed and another wounded. Shelling continued during the next three days causing us 8 more casualties, and the **Flooded Trenches.** scouts were busy reporting on the depth of water in all trenches in our area. This water presented a great difficulty, as all trenches had an average depth of 3 feet some being brimful of water to the top, and on the 26th when heavy rain fell it rose still more. From the scouts reporting sounds of pumping from the enemy's trenches it seemed they were in similar discomfort. Considerable movement was also observed in the German trenches, and they could be seen shifting machine guns it seemed towards the Seaforths' front on our right.

March 1st, 1915, saw the Battalion in billets at Richebourg St. Vaast, having left certain fatigue parties behind for work at the front, and next day it moved to La Couture (*Sketch IX*), Bareilly having **Battalion in Billets** now relieved the Dehra Doon Brigade. Frequent snow-**at La Couture,** storms set in with high, cold winds, which our men said **1/3/15.** they felt far more than any cold in the Himalayas, the long periods of damp cold being particularly trying for all Asiatics.

While here the matter of clothing was gone into with a view to seeing what would be required for summer wear. During the winter the men had worn the following :—

	Woollen undervest (thick)	2 pairs socks
	Woollen drawers (thick)	Woollen muffler
	Flannel Shirt	Woollen gloves
Clothing.	Sweater	Greatcoat
	Serge jacket	Putties
	Serge trousers	Felt hat
	Balaclava cap.	

and each carried a waterproof sheet, blanket, 1 pair of socks, towel, soap. In the train was an extra blanket and flannel shirt for each man. In addition to these, short sheepskin jackets had been issued in December, 1914, which were much appreciated for actual trench life, but could not be worn under accoutrements, belts not being long enough.

When in the trenches as a precaution against frost-bite at night men wore a sandbag full of straw on each foot and leg, and whale oil well rubbed in was also found efficacious. It was decided for summer wear to ask for a serge jacket and trousers, flannel shirt, cotton vest and drawers, and that as Government did not provide the two last-named articles, to ask the Indian

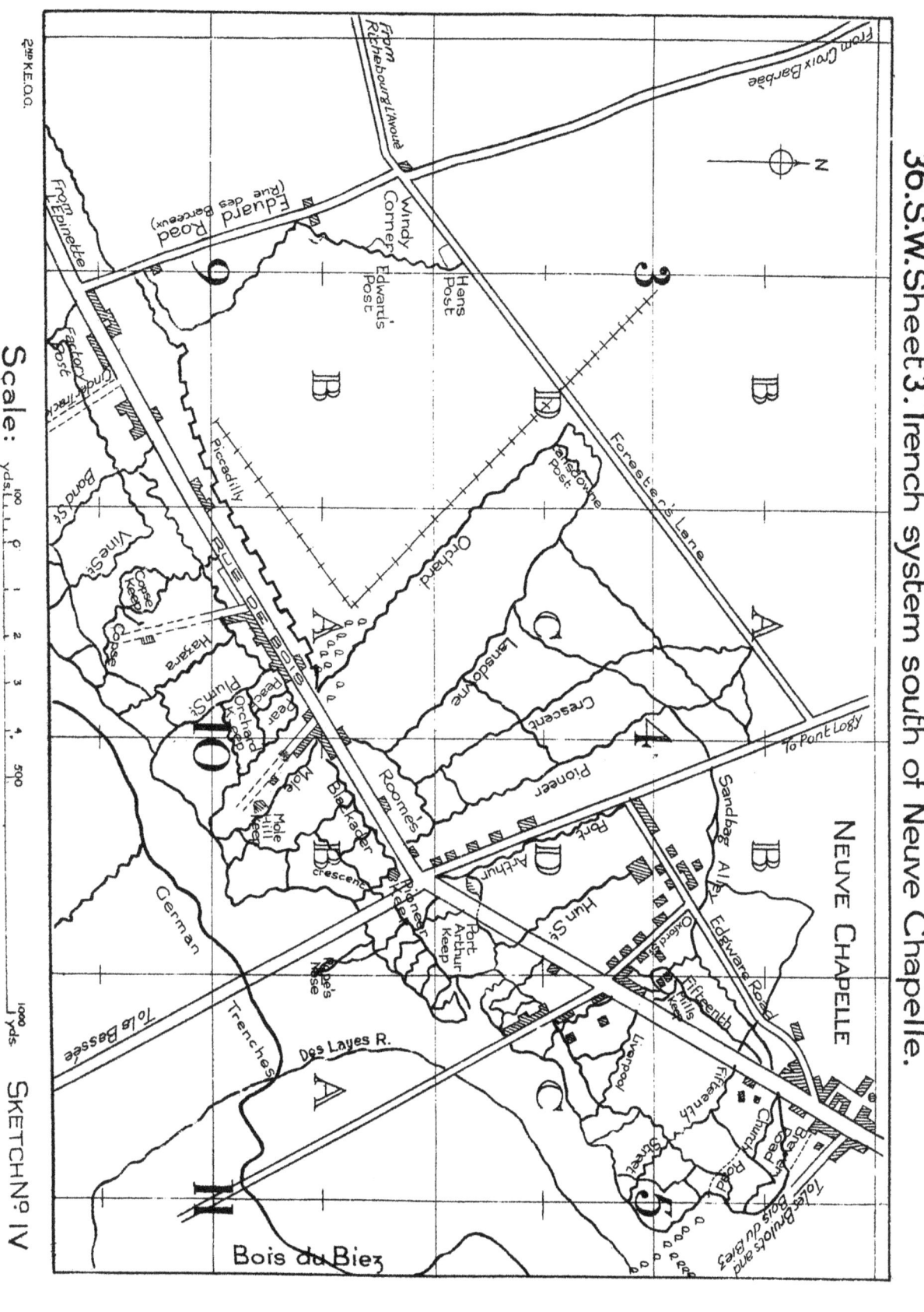

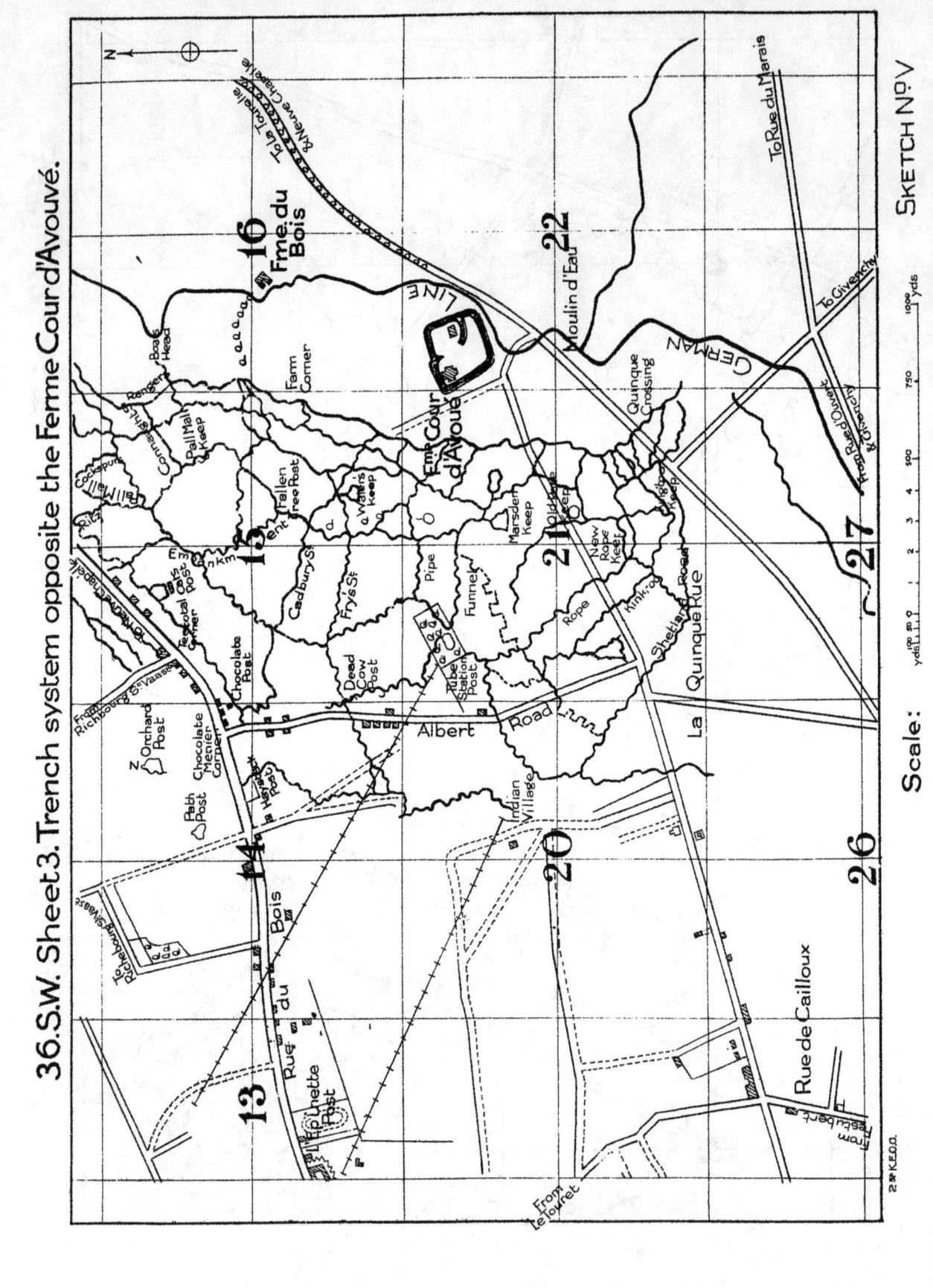

Soldiers' Fund to provide them. The waterproof sheet and extra shirt would be carried in the train, and the remaining items would not be required in summer.

In late February we had become the recipients of a most kindly and generous token of the friendship existing since 1857 between the 60th Rifles (King's Royal Rifle Corps) and the 2nd Goorkhas, of the valued gift by the former regiment of £100 towards ameliorating any distress which had fallen to our men and their families. As all will know, this friendship was cemented during the stirring times of the Indian Mutiny when both Regiments fought side by side during the siege and capture of Delhi, after which we were honoured by being made a Rifle Regiment, and the 60th Rifles asked that we might be allowed to wear their uniform, a request which was duly sanctioned. This further proof of the strong bond of friendship between the two regiments could not but be an extra incentive to our efforts in the cause for which the British Army was fighting. The correspondence on the subject will be found in Appendix *D*.

60th Rifles' gift to Battalion, 19/2/15.

The Battalion was not to be in billets long this time, for on March 7th secret orders came heralding a big offensive in which the Meerut Division was to lead, the Garhwal Brigade opening the attack supported by that of Dehra Doon.

On this Major Boileau with the Adjutant went to the front to see the ground we should occupy and paid a visit to the trench works known as "Port Arthur," now an important point in our line, where our guns were shelling the German breastworks and doing considerable damage to them. The following day company commanders similarly visited the front to acquaint themselves with the ground and trenches over which the Battalion was likely to move in the coming offensive.

Preparations for Fresh Offensive, 7/3/15.

Subadars Kasiram Gharti and Dalpati Thapa had unfortunately to be invalided owing to ill-health and left here for India and eventual discharge on pension, and Subadar Karakbahadur Gurung rejoined for duty from hospital.

Confidential orders arrived on the 9th that the Garhwal Brigade would start its attack against the enemy's line at the south corner of Neuve Chapelle at 8.5 a.m. next day, that that village was to be taken by the 8th British Division and that the Dehra Doon Brigade would then pass through the Garhwal Brigade and attack the Bois du Biez. The 2nd Goorkhas were to march for the front at 3 a.m. on the 10th, so all fatigue works ceased and preparations for the advance went apace, all stimulated by the feeling that a really important effort evidently on a large scale was near.

Battalion returns to Front, 10/3/15.

CHAPTER VIII.

March 10th to 12th, 1915. (*Sketches IX, VI.*)

Our Battalion being now about to enter a fresh and successful phase of the great struggle, we will see how the British and French line stood in this area where we were concerned in early March, 1915. The position briefly was that the right of the Indian Corps at Givenchy linked with the French Tenth Army across the La Bassée Canal, its left joined with the 4th Corps under General Rawlinson, to the north-west of Neuve Chapelle, while beyond this again was General Pulteney's 3rd Corps, opposite Armentières.

Position of British Line in this Area, March, 1915.

The French successes in Champagne to the south of our line and favourable conditions consequent thereon, together with the belief that the Germans had somewhat depleted their line about here both to oppose the French advance and to strengthen General Hindenburg facing the Russians, who were also achieving success, now induced Sir John French to arrange for a vigorous offensive along our part of the line, viz., from Givenchy to Armentières, with particular attention to Neuve Chapelle, its re-capture, and the seizure if possible of the Aubers Ridge (*Sketch IX*) which to a certain extent dominated the city of Lille, no great distance beyond. Success here it was hoped would cut off that portion of the German troops holding their line from Neuve Chapelle to La Bassée.

Intentions for fresh Offensive.

A readjustment of our line ordered on February 28th had been carried out, and the Meerut Division occupied the front from "Chocolate Menier Corner," about 1¼ miles south of Neuve Chapelle, through "Port Arthur" to a point on the Estaire—La Bassée road (*Sketch IX*), the Lahore Division being in Corps Reserve first at Calonne and Robecq, then later moved forward.

Meerut Division's Front.

The results of the earlier fighting round Neuve Chapelle which was taken by the British in mid October, 1914, lost again on October 27th, retaken next day by the Indian Corps, but only to be driven out again almost at once by the Germans, had obliged our line to run well west of the village from then till now.

This quiet country village before the war with its walled gardens and orchards and neat dwellings, had been considerably knocked about during the earlier fighting, and the Germans had later during January and February somewhat altered it further in adaptation for defensive purposes generally. Buildings had been put into a state of defence and machine guns had been mounted in houses and cottages, while strong points were arranged for flanking village approaches. Between our lines and Neuve Chapelle were fields intersected by deep, waterlogged ditches, and hedges, and heavy rain had turned the land into a morass of tenacious mud, in which the going was most difficult. Beyond to the east, the slightly rising ground of the Aubers Ridge could be seen commanding the approaches to Lille from the west and north-west; to the south-east ran the dark line of the Bois du Biez, in front of which stood a few houses and between which and the village ran the Des Layes stream, small but still presenting an obstacle, being some 10 feet wide and 4½ feet deep. Such in brief was the terrain over which this coming struggle was to surge (*Sketch VI*).

Neuve Chapelle and Locality.

The attack was to be carried out in two stages—the first objective being the hostile front and support trenches west of the village; the second to be the trenches to the east of it and the extensive wood called the Bois du Biez. The 8th British Division (4th Corps) attacking the village, was to link up with the left of the Indian Corps at the south-east corner.

Objectives of Operations, 10/3/15.

Most detailed orders were issued for the operations so as to leave nothing to ill chance as far as humanly possible. Two lines of breastworks had been constructed, behind which the assaulting columns were to form up—step ladders were provided—drains and watercourses were bridged—and all manner of material such as barbed wire, sandbags, hurdles, pickets, planks, ammunition, etc., were stacked at various accessible advanced "dumps." All wire along our front was cut during the night of March 9th-10th, and the moves of troops went on all night until by daybreak all were in their appointed places.

The Battalion's operation orders ran :—

"The 4th and the Indian Corps are to attack Neuve Chapelle on March 10th. Further objectives will be the east edge of the Bois du Biez and the high ground between Aubers and Ligny le Grand.

"The Garhwal Brigade is to assault the trenches extending from the front of 'Port Arthur' to opposite the left of the line now held by the Meerut Division at 8.5 a.m.

Divisional Arrangements for attack, 10/3/15.

"The Dehra Doon Brigade is to be in support, and the Bareilly Brigade will continue to hold the present line of trenches.

E

"The 1st Corps is undertaking an offensive north-east of Givenchy. The Dehra Doon Brigade will be prepared to attack the Bois du Biez as soon as that of Garhwal has attained success.

"The order of march from La Couture to the front will be as below*:—

"Greatcoats will be worn and each man will carry 200 rounds of ammunition, his emergency ration, and to-morrow's cooked ration in the haversack."

Further detailed orders concerned transport, medical, tools, water, bombs, etc.

The 2nd Goorkhas duly reached their appointed locality, and were soon in position to support the Garhwal Brigade (*Sketch VI*). At 7 a.m. a hostile aeroplane flew low over "Port Arthur" retiring rapidly, having undoubtedly seen our trenches unusually crowded with men; for very shortly after its disappearance the enemy opened a heavy fire on the portion of the trenches occupied by the Leicesters and 1/39th Garhwalis, causing many casualties owing to their being so packed.

At 7.30 a.m. our guns opened on the signal from "Grannie," the big 15-inch howitzer, and for half an hour 480 guns and howitzers pounded a length of about 2 miles of hostile positions, the troops watching and waiting their turn seeing the terrific continuous explosions shattering the German trenches and hurling earth, bricks, and men into the air. The village of Neuve Chapelle was soon a mass of ruins, even the lines of streets vanishing, while "Grannie" got on to Aubers demolishing the church and "keep" round it. Then the guns lifted on to their next target and at once the assaulting columns swarmed over their parapets to the attack. No need to follow the Garhwal Brigade in their gallant and successful earlier advance which together with the 8th Division of the 4th Corps gained us the village, the carrying of the German front line trenches being accomplished it is stated in ten minutes, thanks to our overpowering bombardment; so we will turn to the Battalion's War Diary and follow its fortunes.

Opening Bombardment, 7.30 a.m., 10/3/15.

At 9.40 a.m. news was received that the Garhwal Brigade attack had been completely successful, and shortly afterwards the 2nd Goorkhas were ordered to move forward to replace the Seaforths, and on the way we passed 200 or more German prisoners taken by the Garhwal Brigade, reaching the point one hour later and being fired upon *en route* but happily without casualties.

---

* No. 4 Company; No. 3 Company; the Scouts; the Signallers; No. 1 Company; No. 2 Company; Machine Guns.

From this point we were ordered to the "Port Arthur" breastworks (*Sketch VI*), and from which our final advance on the Bois du Biez was to be

Battalion reaches "Port Arthur" for final advance, 10/3/15.

made. Here we got news that the 1/39th Garhwalis had gone too much to their right in the attack and were held up by the enemy in a strong "keep"—an impasse of affairs which lasted some time delaying our forward move and wasting precious time. Two companies of the Seaforths were sent forward to help clear the situation, but the "keep" proved too strongly held. Colonel Ritchie (Seaforths) and Major Boileau on being called to Brigade Headquarters to report what was occurring, received orders that the Seaforths should be detached to deal with the "keep," while the 2nd Goorkhas and 9th Goorkha Rifles were to commence the attack on the wood with the 4th Seaforths in support.

Owing to this delay the day was passing, and what with numerous barricades and obstacles to be crossed in our advance the afternoon was far

Battalion attacks the Bois du Biez, 10/3/15.

gone before the Battalions were in position to attack the wood, the front of which was equally divided between ourselves and the 9th Goorkha Rifles. In the front line we had No. 3 Company under Major Nicolay and Lieutenant Clifford, and No. 4 under Major Watt and Captain Dallas Smith, while behind them on the right came No. 1, with Major Sweet and Captain McCleverty, No. 2 under Captain Mullaly being in rear on the left, each company moving in column of platoons and then deploying for attack. As each line strung out in the open it came under fire from both flanks, a machine gun being particularly active, and casualties began to occur. The one obstacle, viz., the Des Layes stream, was luckily found to be in dead ground, and did not hamper the advance as much as was expected. Early in the attack Captain McCleverty became a casualty, shot through the upper arm, and Captain Dallas Smith's company with great dash reached the edge of the wood, followed closely by Major Watt with the rear platoons.

Our Companies reach the wood.

What happened to the leading line of No. 3 is not quite clear, but Major Nicolay (a little later reported missing) in trying probably to keep touch with the 9th Goorkha Rifles on our left, lost touch with No. 4 on his right. Lieutenant Clifford, bringing up the rear lines of No. 3, met a few men who said they had been told to retire, he, however, took them on until he was held up by machine-gun fire and forced to retire.

Meantime Nos. 1 and 2 Companies had come up successively in close touch with each other, and advanced up to the right of the wood, halting in rear of No. 4 which had now seized the outer line of the Bois du Biez, and had begun to dig in, sending scouts into the wood and the various houses along the road at its western edge, where some German snipers were busy, five being captured. During this attack Riflemen Manjit Gurung, Partiman Gurung, Ujiar Sing Gurung, and Hastabir Roka, distinguished themselves by attending to wounded and bringing them back under fire, while the last mentioned Rifleman brought up machine-gun ammunition across fire-swept ground although badly wounded. All were rewarded with the Indian Order of Merit, 2nd Class.

Incidents of Gallantry, 10/3/15.

Firing now had more or less subsided, there seemed few of the enemy in the part of the wood immediately in our front, and it was getting dark; so Nos. 1 and 2 were ordered by the Commanding Officer to dig themselves in where they lay, and they were here joined by a company of the 9th Goorkha Rifles, which had become detached, and which now extended the left of No. 2, throwing back its exposed flank (*Sketch VI*). Touch with the 9th Goorkha Rifles had been maintained till we reached a ditch beyond the Des Layes stream, but it was lost after this as that Battalion did not reach the edge of the wood with us. It was now that Major Nicolay could not be found, the last seen of him being when with an orderly and a section commander he was going across to try and link with No. 4 Company. Reported as missing, it was not till nearly a year and a half later that the society in Geneva for tracing out missing men, got into communication with the Commanding Officer of a German unit which had fought in this part of the field, from whom it was learnt they had come across the dead body of Major Nicolay with the Goorkha orderly lying near him badly wounded, who became a prisoner.

Major Nicolay killed, 10/3/15.

Major Watt went back to Brigade Headquarters to report the situation, as apparently resistance in our immediate front had been overcome Captain Mullaly in a letter alluding to himself and another officer "roaming in the wood at will," while scouts sent into it for some distance reported no trenches. From German prisoners taken in the houses, information was extracted under threats, that they were not in strength about here, but that some distance on our left front were some 1,200 Germans entrenched in the wood well protected with barbed wire. No. 3 was then withdrawn as a reserve, and more detached men of the 9th Goorkha Rifles having come up, still further extended our line to the left of No. 2.

Hostile Resistance ceases at the wood.

On the position having been referred to the General Officer Commanding,

GROUP OF GOORKHA OFFICERS, 2/2nd K.E.O. GOORKHAS.
FRANCE, JULY, 1915.

Major Boileau was ordered to consolidate the line where he was, and a wing of the Seaforths was ordered up in reserve; but before much could be done further orders reached us to withdraw behind the Des Layes stream (*Sketch VI*). This was carried out, the company nearest the wood retiring through the supports and reserves, each of which then similarly retired alternately. The men were employed digging in behind the stream most of the night, which passed uneventfully save for a few Germans being fired on who were scouting towards the stream. More bridges were sent up during the night and placed in position across the Des Layes.

Battalion withdrawn behind the Des Layes Stream, 10/3/15.

Very early on March 11th we received orders to renew the attack on the Bois du Biez at 7 a.m., provided the right Brigade of the 8th Division which had taken and passed beyond Neuve Chapelle the previous day, came up level with the 9th Goorkha Rifles. The morning opened with a thick fog, but all preparations were made and supporting companies advanced to the positions best suited for carrying out the attack. During this movement heavy machine-gun fire was opened on us from new hostile trenches on the left, causing some casualties, amongst these being Major Watt, badly wounded in the leg, but who continued with the attack until too exhausted. He later received the Distinguished Service Order for the conspicuous ability and bravery with which he led his company in the attack on the wood, while Captain Dallas Smith and Lieutenant Corse Scott received the Military Cross for their services in this action.

Attack on the wood resumed, 11/3/15.

Major Watts wounded.

The two leading companies in the fire trench along the Des Layes bank crossed and lay down in attack formation in the open so as to occupy a good jumping off position; but the attack being delayed and many casualties occurring, they withdrew again behind the trench. This delay was due to the fact that the two right Brigades of the 8th Division were badly checked, one by a strongly held bridgehead, the other by machine guns towards Piètre.

8th Division checked.

At 2 p.m. news came to hand that a fresh attack of the 8th Division was to start a quarter of an hour later away to our left; the Battalion was warned to be in readiness, and from this time on till dark the enemy kept up a heavy fire of guns and rifles, appearing to have been strongly reinforced. Their machine guns also enfiladed our position in which the slightest movement

Further Advance on this Section of Front checked, 11/3/15.

caused more casualties, so every effort was made to deepen the trenches. About dark on the 11th the Commanding Officer was informed that the 8th Division was again checked, no advance could be made, and we were to stand fast in our present position. Here the Battalion remained till 1.30 a.m. on the 12th, when the Sirhind Brigade, coming up to relieve us, the Battalion with the rest of the Dehra Doon Brigade was withdrawn, suffering some casualties in the process. The brigade marched to Vieille Chapelle for rest and refitting, which was reached at 4 a.m.

Sirhind relieves Dehra Brigade, 12/3/15.

Our casualty list in these two days' fighting showed :—

	Killed.	Wounded.	Missing.
British officers ...	0	2	1
Goorkha officers ...	2	1	0
Other ranks	17	41	27

Casualties, 10–12/3/15.

a total of 91, the Goorkha officers in the list being Subadar Jagbir Thapa and Jemadar Sanman Sing Gurung killed, Jemadar Jit Sing Bohra being wounded.

The fight for the Bois du Biez was to be continued on the 12th by the 4th and the Indian Corps, and as we were again sent to the front to take part in its later stages, although not being drawn actively into it owing to change of views on the general situation, the narrative of this series of actions may be continued.

The Germans forestalled the British advance early on March 12th by opening a heavy bombardment on "Port Arthur," and its neighbouring work the "Crescent," following this up by an attack in mass of a nature showing the recently arrived presence of considerable reinforcements. The attack of such a moving multitude from the direction of Piètre as well as from the wood, in which at least two officers were seen mounted, seemed almost impossible to check. But the fire of our lines—withheld till the enemy were barely 200 yards off, now broke out in a furious tornado of shells, machine-guns and rifle fire, to such an extent that in a short time their solid formations broke up, which forced to retreat under the hail of bullets, left our front littered with dead and dying men, only about 100 or so getting to within 30 yards of the "Crescent" work. The slaughter was great, over 2,000 bodies being counted in front of the Meerut Division alone.

Germans attack, 12/3/15.

These massed attacks of the Germans, to which in the early days of the war they pinned much faith, were colossal imposing efforts which could

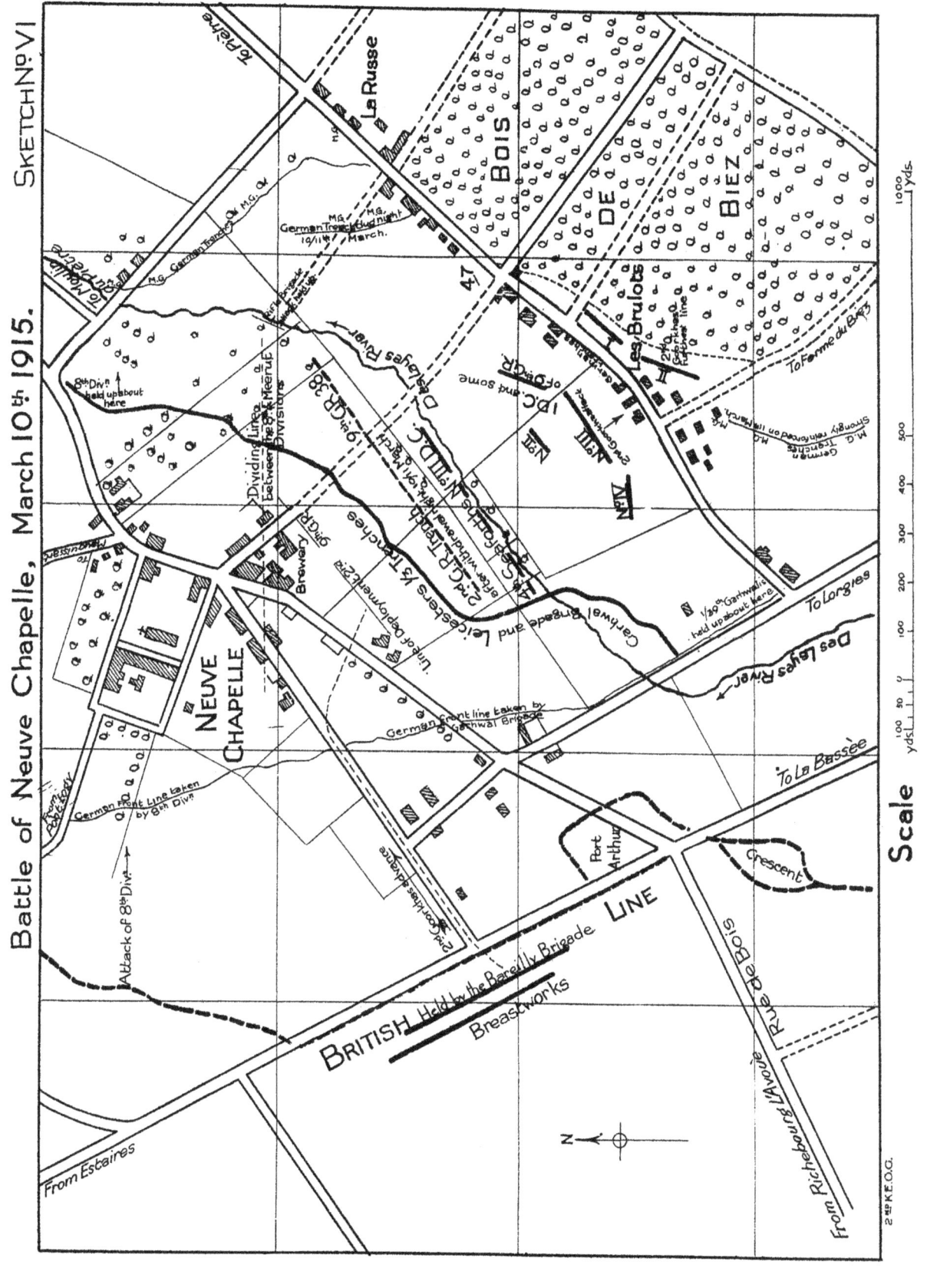

hardly have been believed possible of attempt in these days and in the face of modern weapons. Although here and there evidences appeared as to their men having been given drink to stimulate them for the supreme but hopeless task, many have testified to the gallantry with which the German troops came on. An officer of a British regiment in telling the writer of his first experience of such an attack said that when they saw this avalanche of humanity moving forward he could hardly get his men to fire—they were new to the war and the trenches having just relieved another regiment, and they simply looked on over the parapet in astonishment at the spectacle. The German troops came on in a long line of units in quarter column formations without firing, and all singing " Deutschland über Alles." They advanced as if on parade, even when our guns got on to them, ploughing great holes in the moving masses, holes which were filled up at once by those in rear until the limit of human endurance was reached and the masses, pounded by artillery and rifles, broke up in disorder and were forced to retreat, leaving the field an indescribable litter of dead and wounded in thousands.

<small>German Massed Attacks.</small>

To return to our line. Our guns now turned on the Bois du Biez, a fresh assault on which was timed for 1 p.m. on the 12th. It started but again got no farther than the edge of the wood, suffering heavy losses from frontal and enfilade fire, the Germans having brought up more reinforcements. The Dehra Doon Brigade, which had hardly settled in billets after being relieved by that of Sirhind, found itself once more *en route* to the front to join in the last attack on the wood ; but owing to darkness then (it being 10 p.m.) further attempt was vetoed by Sir James Willcocks. The troops were ordered to dig themselves in where they stood, and early next morning an order came from General Sir Douglas Haig, G.O.C. First Army, to suspend all further active operations and to consolidate our present position.

<small>End of Battle of Neuve Chapelle, 10 p.m., 12/3/15.</small>

This closed the great battle of Neuve Chapelle, in which our gains were not only the entire village but a successful advance had been made on a front of 2 miles to a depth of 1,000 yards (*Sketch IX*), but at the expense of exceedingly heavy losses—the Indian Corps having over 4,000 casualties, while an estimate of the German losses in this three days' fighting puts them at not far off 18,000. It was also the first time during the war that the German line was broken.

<small>Results of Battle.</small>

It has been stated that our first attack on the 10th was a complete surprise to the Germans, and it may well have been so, there being evidence showing that the German 8th Corps in this area was then in process of reorganization. As before mentioned, a hostile aeroplane flew over our line very early that morning and must have seen us lining up for attack, but its report could not have been in time to be usefully acted on. A captured German officer said they had become aware of the British concentration in the small hours that day, and they had immediately asked for strong artillery support, but were told such could not be given without direct orders from Corps Headquarters, to obtain which there was no time.

It was said at the time we first attacked that Neuve Chapelle was only weakly held by three battalions, but this was not so. The 11th Jägers certainly only held the village, but both flanks were also **Strength of Germans** held by the 12th and 16th Regiments of three battalions **at Battle of Neuve** each and reinforcements soon came up of the 13th and **Chapelle, 10–12/3/15.** 56th Regiments of similar strengths. Later on more arriving gave some 18 or 19 complete regiments in the first day's fighting, while on the 12th at least 9,000 more reinforced the Bois du Biez according to the statements of prisoner officers.

In this operation we took a leaf out of the French book in method of artillery preparation, and interest is attached to these actions as witnessing the first introduction by us of intensive bombardments, followed at once by the infantry assault. Many lessons were learnt at Neuve Chapelle, but that transcending all others was the protection afforded to infantry by the terrible effects of the concentrated fire of a large number of guns. Later on it seemed as if this had run us short of ammunition, for the supply of shells being found insufficient for a time our guns were terribly restricted in rounds to be fired, to the extent that field guns were allowed only three per day, larger ordnance being often entirely silent

CHAPTER IX.

MARCH 13TH TO MAY 10TH, 1915. (*Sketches IX, VII.*)

ON March 13th the Lahore Division relieved that of Meerut at the front, and the 2nd Goorkhas were more or less quiet in billets for some days at Vieille Chapelle, where on the 15th they were inspected by the General Officer Commanding Meerut Division, and congratulated on the work done in the recent operations. A draft of 50 men from the Burma and the Assam Military Police Battalions was also received. Here we lost the services of Captain Dallas Smith for a time, he being evacuated on account of ill-health, but on the 18th we were joined by Captain G. D. Mathew, one of our own officers who had been on duty with the Assam Military Police Force and at the depot, while a day or two later Major Rooke, 10th Goorkha Rifles, who was with us before and was wounded on December 20th, and Captain E. R. L. Browning, 34th Pioneers, joined us for duty. On the 21st we received another draft of 2 Jemadars and 93 men from Assam, these drafts bringing our strength almost up to its proper complement again. The Military Police drafts were all Goorkhas of good physique and a most useful addition to the Battalion, but they necessarily required a lot of training when in billets to put them on a level with Regulars.

Billets at Vieille Chapelle.

Military Police Draft, 15/3/15.

After moving to another billet at Paradis our Brigade had orders to relieve the 25th Brigade on the night of March 24th-25th, and it was stated the Indian Corps would take over the front of the 4th Corps, north north-east of Neuve Chapelle, our Battalion and the 1st Seaforths to be the two units in the front line.

On the 23rd the Commanding Officer, Adjutant, and Company Commanders went off to see the trenches we were to occupy, till now held by the 3rd Kensington Regiment. They found the line to be held was some 500 yards in front of that held by us on November 2nd, 1914, prior to the German attack that day and consequently full of unhappy memories. Though the Kensingtons had buried between 600 and 700 bodies there were still many lying about waiting burial. This actual trench line had only been occupied a few days and was in consequence not a strong one as yet, the fire trench not being bullet proof, the only existing support trench was not yet connected up with the front, and communicating ones had not been begun. Heavy rain was falling, trenches and ground generally being in a bad state.

Battalion moves to front trenches, 24/3/15.

The following day the Battalion marched to Bout Deville (*Sketch IX*), and up to the front by 6 p.m., the 1st Seaforths being on our right with a unit of the Bareilly Brigade on our left. The relief worked smoothly as the Germans were not busy with this part of the front just then, and our Nos. 2 and 4 Companies were soon in their front trenches, commanded by Captain Cruickshank, a length of 250 yards with another 250 yards to be taken over later, and Nos. 3 and 1 Companies in support on the Rue Tilleloy. The old Battalion Headquarters house, now in ruins, was passed on the way up, and it was sad work continually coming across dead bodies of our men killed on November 2nd and burying them, as well as a number of Germans, the enemy not seeming to have taken the trouble to bury any while in occupation of this area. The body of Captain Barton was found, removed to the rear, together with Subadar Jitbahadur Gurung, who was shot through the head on March 28th, and buried close to Major Macpherson's grave near the old Battalion Headquarters. A few days later the 21st Sappers and Miners came across Major Becher's body which was buried where he fell, the 129th Baluchis fashioning and erecting a cross.

Finding of Officers' bodies, killed, 2/11/14.

During this tour of trench duty we were visited by the Divisional Commander (General Anderson) and General Jacob our Brigadier, both of whom expressed themselves satisfied with the work in hand. Much spadework had been put in improving and strengthening the line, but the depth of water in the trenches rendered the work slow and difficult. Fortunately the Germans appeared to be similarly busy, firing very little and causing only two casualties. Later a certain amount of sniping started and the hostile guns became a little more active, but doing us no damage.

On the night of March 28th-29th we were relieved by the 9th Goorkha Rifles, and proceeded to billets in Croix Barbée for a welcome rest after five days' exceedingly hard trench digging. By the 31st the relief of the Meerut Division by that of Lahore was completed, and our Brigade was moved to other billets at Bout Deville, the 2nd Goorkhas being sent on to l'Epinette, where they remained some ten days. Our chief occupation here lay in giving our Military Police drafts, now over 200 strong, a thorough training, which they undoubtedly lacked, good men though they were. We

Lahore relieves Meerut Division, 31/3/15.

also had to send fatigue parties to the front, in which we had 3 casualties. On April 2nd the General Officer Commanding Division inspected our drafts and men reported unfit (14) passing all the latter for discharge, and we were joined by Lieutenants H. V. Brandon, 18th Infantry, and Burne, I.A.R.O., also by Captain Park, 10th Goorkha Rifles, recovered from his wound, but Lieutenant Clifford in ill-health had to be evacuated.

Battalion in Billets, Rue l'Epinette.

April 10th saw the Dehra Doon Brigade inspected by the Commander-in-Chief (Sir John French) who addressed the units, thanking them for their share in recent operations, alluding in particular to the gallant behaviour of the 9th Goorkha Rifles and 2nd Goorkhas at the Bois du Biez and Neuve Chapelle. His address to the men will be found in Appendix *D*. Two days later we were moved up to the front again to take over the line of trenches just south of Neuve Chapelle, held by the 5th Royal Sussex Regiment. These trenches more or less in the same locality we were getting to know so well were in the line originally dug by the Battalion after the Battle of Neuve Chapelle, and considering a month had elapsed since then, it was remarkable how little appeared to have been done by other units to improve them. Four battalions of the Dehra Doon Brigade were now to hold the front line, each unit having two companies in the firing line with two in support. The Germans appeared to have a very good observation position in the Bois du Biez, while the ruined houses in its front which faced us on March 10th seemed full of busy and accurate snipers, for one of our officers records in a letter how " you could not put up a periscope without its being smashed." A 13-pounder field gun also got the range of our front trench and was very active, though so far only gave us three casualties. Continuous digging went on and fresh machine-gun emplacements were built in the front line and also behind it to guard against eventualities, and by April 18th our position was a strong one, the 6th Jāts helping with fatigue parties.

Inspection by Sir John French, 10/4/15.

Battalion in front trenches again, 13/4/15.

The 2/2nd Goorkhas held this portion of the front for a fortnight, each company doing a week in the advanced trenches, and during this time our casualties were 1 killed, 10 wounded, a howitzer shell which struck and splintered a tree in the centre of the line being responsible for most of them. A certain amount of shelling by the Germans was experienced during the 17th and 18th, but without doing much damage, and a pleasant change in the weather set in drying up the ground quickly.

On the 21st news came that our Brigade was to be relieved by that of Ferozepore on the night of April 25th-26th, but as the Lahore Division was shortly detailed to assist the Second Army in its operations round Ypres this relief was postponed.

We now received a list of prisoners of war which showed that 51 of our men were in Germany out of 101 missing, and we lost the services of Lieutenant Burne, who was transferred to the 59th Rifles, but were joined by Captain Colenso, 7th Goorkha Rifles.

Our Prisoners with the Enemy.

About this time we learnt of the first use by the Germans of asphyxiating gases at Ypres which necessitated rough precautions being taken by us, in the event of such being used against this portion of the front. To this end tins of water containing bicarbonate of soda were placed in the trenches, every man being directed to wear a piece of cloth tied round his neck which could be dipped in the solution; this had to do until proper masks, now being made in England, could be supplied. All hose pipes noticed in the German lines had to be reported, as although they possibly were only for pumping water from trenches they might have some connection with the use of gas, especially as a small weathercock was spotted near one such pipe. Intermittent shelling and a good deal of sniping occurred during the 28th, and for a short time the Germans opened a heavy bombardment on Neuve Chapelle, otherwise this period to April 29th was without special incident. That evening our Battalion was relieved by the 2/8th Goorkha Rifles, and moved back into billets at Vieille Chapelle. During this spell in the trenches our casualty list showed 1 killed, 18 wounded, and 25 men evacuated for ill-health.

First use of Gas, April, 1915.

Battalion in Billets, 29/4/15.

The weather had now changed, fine summer days succeeding the interminable cold and wet experienced almost continually till now. The day after reaching billets came a list of awards by the Commander-in-Chief for the operations at Neuve Chapelle, showing Major D. Watt to have gained the Distinguished Service Order, while Subadar Dan Sing Lama with five Riflemen were awarded the Order of Merit. Here we had to part with Subadar Arjun Rana, whose health having broken down, rendered him unfit for duty in the field. He was returned to India, the loss of his excellent services being much felt. The only incident recorded while at Vieille Chapelle this time was the burning of certain billets in which the 4th Seaforths were, when three of our companies doubling down

Honours.

got to work at once with their useful kookeries cutting down and smashing in the roofs so as to cut off the fire, for which assistance their Commanding Officer was most grateful.

Our rest was short this time, for with a heavy bombardment by the Germans on Pont Logy, "Port Arthur," and the Rue du Bois, which it was believed heralded an attack, we were ordered to move up to the front line on May 3rd. No attack, however, following the bombard-

Battalion in front trenches South of "Port Arthur," 3/5/15. ment, we relieved the 9th Goorkha Rifles in the southern section of the Indian Corps, slightly south of " Port Arthur " (*Sketch IX*). The Battalion took over the new line by 10.30 p.m. that day, Nos. 1 and 2 companies being in the front line about the "Orchard Keep," almost on the Rue du Bois, the remaining ones being located at "Lansdowne Post," in reserve, with the 6th Jāts on our right (*Sketch IV*). This post, 1,000 yards north of the Rue du Bois, and some 1,600 yards south-west of Neuve Chapelle, was a perfect maze of trenches and dug-outs, holding 400 men, and intended as a local defensive work. An improvement in rationing facilities, removal of wounded, etc., was found in new railway lines, which had been laid from the nearest railhead to three points close up to the front, but good communicating trenches about here being again found almost non-existent required making, and our officers and men invariably worked up to that unwritten law of trench life, viz., "to always leave a place better than you find it." Captain Cruickshank, our machine gun officer, who had been in this line before we arrived, reported the Germans to have their machine guns (of which they had numbers) in action every 50 yards, while we were severely handicapped by having only two guns per battalion still, although in January we had been told four more were being sent to each unit. So far only British troops

We relieve 6th Jāts 7/5/15. had received this much-needed increase. Another move took place during the night of May 6th-7th, when our Battalion took the place of the 6th Jāts in the front line a little farther south.

We now approach the next great offensive effort to be made against the German line; an effort arranged for late April but postponed till the return of the Lahore Division from their part in the Second Battle of Ypres. Orders

Preparations for fresh offensive, May, 1915. were received to send back to the train all blankets, waterproof sheets, and such like impedimenta which always heralded coming activity, to say nothing of the country which as one letter says was "alive with parties burying telephone wires." We were informed our Brigade would attack on a front of three battalions and capture the Ferme du Biez, Quinque Rue, and the Distillery in front; the Bareilly Brigade moving towards Ligny le Petit, and Ligny le Grand (*Sketch IX*). Our Battalion would be on the right of the attacking line with the 1st Seaforths on our left, beyond them the 4th Seaforths, the 9th Goorkha Rifles supporting the left, the 6th Jāts the right.

Definite orders for operations by the First Army, viz., the 1st, the Indian, and the 4th Corps reached us to move into position of assembly by 11 p.m. on May 9th, preparatory to an attack at dawn provided that a French attack which was to take place a little earlier came off; so we can now review briefly the Allied situation stating the why and wherefore of these operations and their objectives.

During April and early May Russian successes on the Eastern Front had been checked by the Germans to the extent of turning such offensive success into a desperate defensive, and the French were **Situation of Allies** engaged fairly successfully in hard fighting in the Woevre **and Intentions,** district between Verdun and Metz with a view to breaking **May, 1915.** the German line on the extreme south end of the Western Front. It appeared that the present was the time to effect a diversion of the enemy's attention in these two directions by a vigorous offensive from our portion of the line against the area containing the important railway centres at Valenciennes and Douai, from which ran lines supplying three of the hostile armies. Such action if successful would also render Lille and Roubaix untenable, while materially assisting the French Tenth Army in their projected attack on Lens in the Arras area, a little south of La Bassée.

To this end the Commander-in-Chief, Sir John French, ordered a general attack to take place on May 10th by the 1st and the Indian Corps, between Neuve Chapelle and Givenchy, and the 4th Corps north of the former village.

The operations were to be of a well sustained nature by the **Orders for General** whole of the three Corps in close co-operation with the **Offensive, May 9th–** French, and are known under the name of the Battle of **10th, 1915.** Festubert. The 1st Corps was to attack on a broad front the line Rue du Marais—Illiers, with its right still on Givenchy—the Indian Corps to cover the left of the 1st Corps by attacking the strongly held Ferme du Biez, continuing the advance towards Ligny le Grand and La Cliqueterie Farm, the 4th Corps farther north to operate so as to break the hostile line near Rouge Bancs and turn the famous Aubers Ridge from the north-east (*Sketch IX*).

Most detailed instructions were issued to ensure proper communication between corps and units and to obviate the delays in pushing up supports and reserves, which had unfortunately marked previous actions militating against their complete success. The Meerut Division was to assault the hostile first line trenches on a front of 600 yards, and capture the village of La Tourelle and the Ferme du Biez (*Sketch VII*), its leading Brigade that of Dehra Doon, working on a three-battalion front, with the Bareilly and Garhwal Brigades in support and general reserve respectively.

We can now turn to the doings of the 2nd Goorkhas in this, following its War Diary.

The three assaulting battalions of the Dehra Doon Brigade were the 2nd Goorkhas, the 4th Seaforths, the 1st Seaforths, the two last named being on our left, while on our right were a company of the 6th Jāts, and then the Welsh Regiment. Nos. 2 and 4 Companies were detailed to carry out the first assault advancing in column of platoons at 25 yards distance, No. 3 in support, No. 1 in reserve, with which were the machine guns.

Brigade Orders for attack, 10/5/15.

The British officers present with the Battalion were as noted below*:—

The three phases of the bombardment were:—

       1st phase   ...   40 minutes on German front trenches.
       2nd phase   ...   35 minutes on La Tourelle and Quinque Rue.
       3rd phase   ...   30 minutes on The Distillery.

and the assaulting columns were to deploy before the first bombardment ceased.

During the night May 9th-10th the scouts under Havildar Sarabjit Gurung had been out placing bridges across a ditch in front and cutting our wire, ladders had also been placed in the trenches, and by 2 a.m. most of the men had settled down for a little rest, and all was quiet.

The dawn broke fine and clear, at 4 a.m. all moved quietly into their respective places for assault and waited. An hour later our guns opened in a terrific bombardment which however did not seem effective in keeping down the enemy's fire, for their machine guns were very busy while some of our own shells burst near our men wounding several, including Captain Mullaly in the hand. At 5.36 a.m. our assaulting companies went " over the

Bombardment opens, 10/5/15.

---

* Colonel Boileau, Major Sweet, Major Rooke, Captain Cruickshank, Captain Park, Captain Mullaly, Captain Mathew, Captain Colenso, Lieutenant Corse-Scott, Lieutenant Collins, Lieutenant Browning, Lieutenant Brandon.

top," No. 2, led by Captain Mullaly with Captain Colenso, No. 4 by Captain Mathew with Lieutenant Collins, the company of the 6th Jāts under Captain Dudley and Lieutenant Hebbert going into action along with us. The moment our men appeared in the open a most appalling fire from rifles and machine guns met them, men fell in heaps and all the British officers who were the first to cross the parapet became casualties, viz., Captains Mullaly and Dudley (6th Jāts), and Lieutenant Collins, killed ; Captain Mathew mortally, and Lieutenant Hebbert badly wounded. The survivors of this line and others coming on behind made a dash for a ditch in front, forming the only bit of cover, where they lay for some time with the storm of bullets passing close over them. On our left both battalions of the Seaforths suffered heavily, and the attack was held up. Captain Park with No. 3 Company now rushed forward to support No. 4, but got no farther than the ditch where he too fell mortally wounded. The advance thus checked was then definitely ordered to halt, and await a further bombardment to take place at 8.30 a.m.

Our Attack starts, 10/5/15.

Heavy Losses. Attack held up, 10/5/15.

Meanwhile our men in front were getting it hot and were trying to dig more cover with such entrenching tools as they had with them, but the slightest movement brought down a hail of bullets. The second bombardment also was not good, the " heavies " being inaccurate, dropped several shells amongst our line causing more casualties. At 8.40 a.m. the first platoon of No. 1 Company in reserve led by Major Rooke, mounted the parapet and rushing forward crossed the ditch, being joined by more of our men lying there. This party doubled on across the open under heavy fire, when Major Rooke was killed, and Jemadar Bhagatman Gurung with a few men reached a point about 25 yards from the German trench, where the Jemadar fell dead. Two of our men—Riflemen Gorea Gurung and Alam Sing Chettrie—though their fate will never be known, did reach the German trench, their action being distinctly seen by the Royal Artillery observing officer near by who recorded the fact in his notes, further stating the bombardment to have been ineffective owing to the high wind, and that thus the Germans (as he could see) were able " to stand up looking over their parapets and shooting down our attackers while lyddite shells were bursting yards behind them." The few men left at this farthest point got into a shallow ditch and remained there for hours eventually crawling back to the ditch where the rest of our advanced line lay. The

Fresh Bombardment and Attack, 10/5/15.

Attack again held up, 10/5/15.

Black Watch now attacked close to our right losing heavily, the few who crossed the ditch being all killed except one man badly wounded, whom Naik Bambahadur Gurung with Rifleman Anarupe Rana pulled back across the open into cover where he died. The enemy's machine guns, which played such havoc, appeared to be excellently sited, either low in the trench or at the bottom of the parapet, and our guns failed to dislodge them (*Sketch VII*).

Hardly had Major Rooke's platoon gone forward than orders came for the line to halt, as no further attack was to be made just then, both the 1st Corps to the south, and the 4th to the north of the Indian Corps having been similarly held up. Shortly after this, there being evidences of some disorganization among the enemy, Major Boileau went along the trench to the Commanding Officer of the Welsh Regiment to inquire if he would take advantage of this condition opposite and attack with him. But orders had already been sent to relieve the Welsh, who had had heavy casualties, so nothing further could be attempted. The Germans could now be seen retiring to their left, and a hot fire was directed on them from our men lining the parapet and from the machine guns under Captain Cruickshank. The 9th Goorkha Rifles were now ordered forward to reinforce the 2nd Goorkhas, but our trenches, packed with dead and wounded, had been so battered by high explosive shells causing parapets to fall in and scattering direction boards, that only some 200 of them were able to reach the front.

Whole Attack checked, 10/5/15.

9th Goorkha Rifles reinforce us, 10/5/15.

Later orders for another assault were received only to be cancelled almost at once, and we were directed to consolidate our line. During the actual course of the operations the German guns had not been so very active, but they now commenced to play on our parapets in earnest, also shelling the Rue du Bois and our support trenches. The enemy were apparently strongly reinforced and more casualties occurred, Jemadar Patiram Pun, our scout Naik, and several others being killed.

Captain Mathew, who had been badly hit in the stomach during the first rush was brought in by pulling down the parapet to get at him. As he was being carried back he remarked he was afraid he was done for, his one thought was of his duty, and he apologized, poor man, to the Commanding Officer for not having been able to do more. He died next morning at Vieille Chapelle and was buried in that cemetery.

Officers killed, 10/5/15.

Men tried to bring in Captain Park but he begged not to be moved then; later he was brought in but died of his wounds next day. Major Rooke was buried just behind the fire trench, but the bodies of Captain Mullaly and Lieutenant Collins were never found, they must have been entirely destroyed by shells.

About midday May 10th the Battalion was relieved by the Black Watch and withdrawn to billets at Riez Bailleul (*Sketch IX*), where it constituted the Corps Reserve.

Battalion relieved by Black Watch, 10/5/15.

Casualties, 10/5/15.

Our total casualties in this battle were 101, viz. :—

	Killed.	Wounded.	Missing.
British officers ...	4	0	0
Goorkha officers ...	2	2	0
Other ranks ...	25	62	6

Failure of Offensive, 10-11/5/15.

Fresh efforts all along the line during that afternoon and on the 11th met with no better results, such ground as had here and there been gained having to be vacated under the ceaseless enfilade fire of the enemy. The 2nd Goorkhas not being concerned in these later stages of the operations, it will suffice to say that fresh efforts on May 15th and again on the 22nd meeting with only slight successes at heavy cost, all further operations were cancelled, leaving the three corps with a stretch of only some 600 yards in a length of 4 miles to their credit. Actual objectives had nowhere been gained owing to the strength of the enemy and his defences.

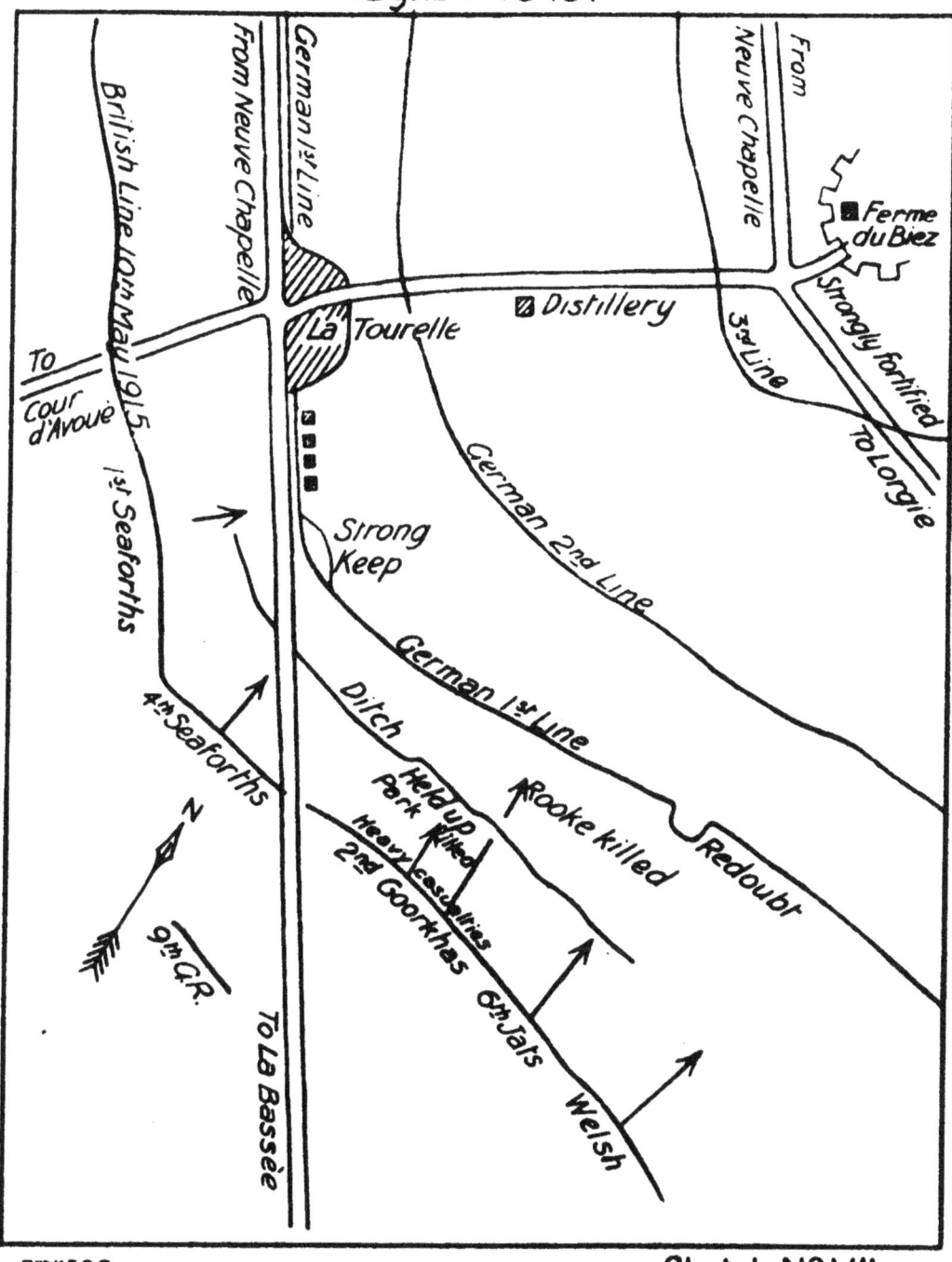

To illustrate attack of the Dehra Dun Brigade May. 10th 1915.

Sketch No VII

CHAPTER X.

May 10th to September 24th, 1915. (*Sketches IX, IV, V, VIII.*)

A PERIOD of comparative inactivity for the Meerut Division now set in, that is to say there was an absence of stirring incident or interesting operations during the next two months and more.

Billets at Riez Bailleul, May 10th–18th, 1915.

The 2nd Goorkhas were at Riez Bailleul till May 18th, and while there were joined by Captain H. K. Bruce, of ours, who had been for some time on duty with the Egyptian Army. With casualties and sick men the ranks of the 2nd Goorkhas were by now sadly depleted, being down to about 400 effectives only; and reinforcements badly needed, did not reach us for a long time. In British officers too we were short, as this month Captain Colenso was evacuated in ill-health, while Captain Molloy and Lieutenant Hay Webb, whose return from hospital was expected, were sent to other regiments when fit. Major Boileau also had to be sent back sick, but only for a fortnight, during which time Major Sweet officiated in command. Twenty recovered sick and wounded men rejoined us from various hospitals, but we lost Jemadar Nake Thapa, who died of his wounds, and Subadar Lal Sing Thapa had to be sent away suffering from acute rheumatism, his absence being much felt.

Need of Drafts, May, 1915.

On May 18th orders came for the Dehra Doon Brigade to move into the second line trenches there to be in a constant state of readiness, and it was well into the night before the Battalion reached its allotted position near the cross roads at Rouge Croix, 1½ miles north-west of Neuve Chapelle, where some of our units occupied two redoubts in the vicinity, the others having to bivouac as best they could in pouring rain. Next day better shelter was found for them in a few small houses near by; however, this did not last long for the 21st saw us moved to Vieille Chapelle till the 23rd, when we were sent to the front again to assist in relieving the Sirhind Brigade after their unsuccessful attack on the Ferme du Biez the previous night. The move was quietly effected that evening, and we occupied the redoubts on the Albert Road with the Highland Division, new to trench life, on the right of our Brigade. Their newness showed itself early when Major Sweet and the Adjutant with two orderlies who were reconnoitring that flank were made prisoners by an over zealous subaltern of the 5th Seaforths and

Battalion in front trenches on Albert Road, 23/5/15.

detained some while till the Commanding Officer could be communicated with, and an absurd and inconvenient situation was cleared by a Major of the Seaforths with apologies. It appeared our little party had just left a house a few minutes before it was set on fire by a German shell and the subaltern attributed the act to them, under the belief they were spies in English uniforms.

The evening of May 26th saw the 2nd Goorkhas relieving the 9th Goorkha Rifles in the front line nearly opposite the Ferme du Bois, due east of "Chocolate Menier Corner" (*Sketches IX, V*), and the night being quiet our men were employed burying bodies lying around and in improving the position which fronts the German line about and including the Ferme du Bois, north of the Ferme Cour d'Avoué. For a few days both sides were too busy over their own affairs, and only a little firing took place causing us 6 casualties, while Major Sweet had a narrow escape—a shell burst knocking down the parapet behind and partially burying him. One of our shells had made a gap in the hostile trench in front of us, and Lance Naik Jitman Gurung of the Machine Gun Section, did a good bit of work in shooting down ten Germans in succession who were trying to repair the gap, a Seaforth Sergeant spotting for him.

Battalion relieves 9th Goorkha Rifles near Ferme du Bois, 26/5/15.

The night of May 30th the 6th Jāts relieved us in the front trenches, and we returned to the redoubt on the Albert Road, leaving one machine gun at the front, and having had casualties to the extent of 2 killed and 8 wounded. Next day the Battalion was sent to La Couture where orders came concerning a readjustment of the sections of the Indian Corps' frontage, by which the Dehra Doon Brigade would hold the north section of the Meerut Division's line with the Bareilly Brigade on its right, the Ferozepore on the left, while the Highland Division with the Indian Corps was transferred to the 4th Corps, its place being filled by the 8th Division of the 4th Corps, and the 49th Division New Army.

Battalion moves to Albert Road Redoubts, 30/5/15.

Captain Bailey rejoined us here from duty at Marseilles, and after a very short spell of billets, sufficient to get up the baggage wagons, issue fresh clothing, and let all have a bout of washing, the Battalion was back in the trenches, relieving the 9th Goorkha Rifles. A part of this line facing the Ferme Cour d'Avoué (*Sketch V*) we were now in was that held recently by the Highland Division, and was here some distance from the German trenches. A stir was going on amongst our front troops owing to an attack being in progress not very far away to our right about Festubert.

Battalion relieves 9th Goorkha Rifles, Ferme Cour d'Avoué, 4/6/15.

Our duties were, as usual, working on trenches, connecting up our flanks, building a redoubt, patrolling, and reconnoitring the Ferme Cour d'Avoué to our front in the vicinity of which the Germans were very busy, and our only casualty was Bugle-Major Budh Sing Gurung, badly hit by a sniper. When we took over this part of the trenches an immense number of sandbags were collected, some 7,600, which apparently the Highland Division, new to this work, had evidently used to floor the " dug-outs " with.

The Garhwal Brigade succeeded ours on the night of June 7th-8th, the 2/3rd Goorkhas relieving our Battalion, which went into billets on the Locon Road at Les Lobes, a new area west of Vieille Chapelle, whence after ten days it was shifted to La Couture, where we became the Reserve Battalion to the Brigade in the advanced trenches. During this period of rest a letter was received from the Committee of the " Bureau de Secours aux Prisonniers de Guerre," at Berne, informing the Commanding Officer that all but a few men of the Regiment officially reported as prisoners of war had been located at Zossen in North Germany, so arrangements were now made to send parcels of food and money to them through the Secretary of the Committee. Ordinary drills, route marching, instruction in the use of stink and inflammable bombs, and in the setting up of wire entanglements filled our time here, where we were joined by a party of 11 men with Subadar Manbir Thapa from the Field Ambulance. A welcome draft of 73 men from Dehra under Jemadar Narbir Thapa also rolled up, and an excellent cinema show, hired for a few days, was greatly enjoyed by all.

Battalion relieved by 2/3rd Goorkhas, 8/6/15.

Battalion in Billets, Les Lobes, June, 1915.

Draft arrives.

During June 18th an aviator reporting the Germans to be concentrating opposite the Rue du Bois, arrangements were made for the 4th Corps (now on the right of our Brigade, south of Neuve Chapelle) to make an attack at 3 a.m. after a short bombardment, the 2nd Goorkhas being ordered to be ready to repulse a counter-attack. Nothing occurred, however, and the night passed quietly. While here Captain A. S. B. Roberts, of the Burma Commission, was sent to us for duty, and on the 21st La Couture was treated to a shelling in which we were lucky in having only Major Sweet's horse wounded, but the gunners bivouacking in a field next to us had 4 men and 23 horses killed, and 7 men wounded.

Our Billets shelled, 21/6/15.

June 23rd found the Battalion back in the firing line taking over a new line east of " Chocolate Menier Corner " (*Sketch V*) on the left of the

Seaforths, as the Meerut Division was taking up a longer frontage and extending northwards. The Commanding Officer and Officers went up to reconnoitre our new ground then occupied by the 39th Garhwalis and 3rd Londons, and on return to La Couture while at tea the party had a narrow escape, a large shell exploding within a few yards of the room wounding 2 orderlies, while a second shell killed and wounded 3 more men. Our casualties in this tour of trench duty were 1 killed and 10 wounded of whom 2 died, and 2 were knocked out with deafness and shock. By 1.30 a.m. on the 24th the relief was complete, No. 4 Company with Captain Bruce and No. 3 with Captain Browning being in the firing line which faced the Ferme du Bois and Ferme Cour d'Avoué (*Sketch V*), about 300 yards from the Germans, whose line ran immediately beyond both farms. "Farm Corner" was a prominent point about the centre of our defences, and the following days it was subjected to a considerable shelling which damaged parapet and works badly, also destroying the machine gun emplacements, the gun itself was saved but a certain amount of equipment was lost. The Germans, having the exact range of "Farm Corner," the salient there was blunted by making a retrenchment behind it, while the front of the destroyed area was strongly wired. Work was thus heavy what with digging, clearing the front of underwood, improving communications, etc., and the men being constantly shelled by day and having to work all night had no rest ; but it resulted in a very strong position being made, and our last day's casualties occurred during patrolling causing us 2 killed and 1 wounded.

Battalion relieves 3rd Londons, 24/6/15.

An extract from the Corps Intelligence Diary at this time was pleasant reading ; it ran :—

Extract from Corps Intelligence Diary, June, 1915.

"Thanks to (1) the capture of certain prisoners near Neuve Chapelle ; (2) excellent reconnaissance work ; (3) the killing of a number of Germans near Ferme du Bois and recovery of their bodies, all by the 2nd Goorkhas ; a general idea of the disposition of the German forces on this part of our front and its vicinity can now be formed."

Further pleasing news also reached us in the promotion of Major Boileau to a Brevet Lieutenant-Colonelcy and of Captain Dallas Smith with Lieutenant Corse Scott who were awarded the Military Cross for services in the field.

The 6th Jāts relieved our battalion during the night of June 29th-30th, and we learnt that in future as far as possible arrangements would be made for regiments to have four days in the trenches and four days in billets. This relief did not go so smoothly and took much longer than usual, due to the bad condition of communicating trenches which with recent heavy rain were 2 feet deep in mud, clay, and water. The enemy's shrapnel during the move also caused us a few casualties.

Battalion relieved by 6th Jāts, 30/6/15.

Our billets on King George's Road, some 600 yards east of La Couture were very crowded, and as we were ordered to be in constant readiness boots and putties could not be taken off; fatigue parties were also in frequent demand to convey materials up to the front.

During the night of July 3rd-4th the Battalion moved to the front in relief of the 4th Seaforths in the "Kinkroo" section near La Quinque Rue almost facing the Ferme Cour d'Avoué (*Sketch V*) and not far from the scene of our losses on December 20th, 1914. These trenches were quite good and strong, but contained an awkward salient held by us, beyond which came the Highland Brigade (9th Division). Here "No-Man's-Land" was of considerable width, the hostile trenches being mostly 300 yards and more away. Between our two sections of defence ran an old German trench, 50 yards up which we placed a listening post. This post, in which 1 man was killed, was much knocked about together with the "Kinkroo" communicating trench in the shelling we were treated to on July 4th, this being brought on by the 9th Division, whose men moved about far too much in the daytime. Trench improvements, patrolling, and the reconnoitring of the Ferme Cour d'Avoué went on nightly amid intermittent shelling, and a "minenwerfer" which bothered the listening post and that neighbourhood was fortunately located and silenced by our supporting battery.

Battalion relieves Seaforths near La Quinque Rue, 4/7/15.

Our next relief was by the 4th Seaforths when we retired to billets in King's Road just behind Rue l'Epinette (*Sketch IX*), and here we heard a rumour to the effect that the whole of the Indian Corps was shortly to be sent back for rest, it having been almost continually employed on or near the front lines since March, and this was followed by orders reorganizing the corps by grouping all its British units into the Lahore Division, while that of Meerut was to contain only the Indian ones. By the middle of July this reorganization was complete and the bulk of the Meerut Division was withdrawn into rest billets, the 2nd Goorkhas being sent to Calonne where it was

Battalion in Billets, Rue de l'Epinette, 10/7/15.

expected three weeks would be spent. In splendid weather with good fields for parading, football, etc., the men now thoroughly enjoyed life. Leave to England was given, of which Major Sweet, Captain Bruce, Captain Cullen (our doctor), and Lieutenant Brandon, availed themselves at once. A beer canteen was also arranged for and was soon in great demand. Under these conditions and with daily drills the bearing of the men soon improved, and they threw off the round shoulders and somewhat slovenly ways induced by life and work cooped up in trenches. Lieutenant C. G. Barker joined us from the 2/8th Goorkha Rifles for duty on the 14th, and Lieutenant Scoones with 2 non-commissioned officers returned from a machine-gun course at Mollinghem, while on the 22nd the welcome addition arrived from Dehra of a draft of 83 men under Lieutenant N. G. Hind and Subadar Champa Sing Gurung; some of these were this year's recruits and all were fit and thoroughly well equipped. These now brought the Battalion strength up to 692 of all ranks, but we lost the services of Major D. Watt, who went to the 25th Divisional Staff.

Meerut Division withdrawn to Billets and leave home opened, 15/7/15.

A Draft from Dehra, 22/7/15.

A "gymkhana," held for units of the Dehra Doon Brigade proved a great success, attracting a large number of people including the Army Corps Commander and the General Officer Commanding Meerut Division. This was followed by sports given by the 8th Brigade Royal Field Artillery, in which some of our men competed and carried off prizes. On July 30th Lieutenant Clifford with 14 men rejoined us from the convalescent hospital at Boulogne, our officers had returned from leave, and we received orders, closing down this the pleasantest rest period the Battalion had enjoyed, in that the Dehra Doon Brigade was to march next day to La Gorgue near Estaires north-west of Neuve Chapelle, there to be in Divisional Reserve (*Sketch IX*). Apparently the recent reorganization of the Indian Corps did not work well, for on reaching La Gorgue after a hot, trying march, we found our former Brigade and Divisional component units were to be reverted to.

Amusements in Billets at Calonne, July, 1915.

Battalion at La Gorgue, 31/7/15.

Near Estaires the Battalion remained till August 8th, the period not being marked by anything particular except for the starting of a Brigade Grenadier Company with its special training, the issue of a "sniperscope," a means of firing a rifle from a position below, telescope and night sights, all new and requiring practice; also about this time platoons of units of the New Army were being attached to old regiments to learn work, to which of necessity they were new. For amusement there was a fine open ground north of the canal in Estaires, where football and scratch games of polo were played and a first-rate concert was given one night in La Gorgue by the Red Cross which was heartily supported and enjoyed by the garrison.

This came to an end with the night of August 8th-9th, when the Dehra Brigade succeeded that of Garhwal in Brigade Reserve, and we were located in a deserted hamlet on Rugby Road, north north-east of Neuve Chapelle (*Sketch VIII*), the sole inhabitant being an old peasant woman who had remained through all the shelling the place had undergone, and who laboured over washing our clothes most efficiently. Two days later we relieved the Seaforths in the front trenches, and were now on comparatively new ground in front of that first held by us in early November, 1914, our aid post being placed not far from the old farmhouse in which our battalion headquarters was first housed and where Major Macpherson was buried. Hitherto most of our activities and interests had centred in areas south of Neuve Chapelle.

Dehra relieves Garhwal Brigade north of Neuve Chapelle, 9/8/15.

The front we now held with No. 4 Company under Captain Bruce with Lieutenant Clifford on the right, and No. 3 under Captain Bailey with Lieutenant Brandon on the left, occupied 250 yards and was a strong one excepting for one salient called the " Duck's Bill " (*Sketch VIII*) near the centre, the machine guns being so placed as to cover the ground in front of this weak spot which invited attack. In two days this salient was improved by the neck being made into a defensive work on each side, the whole parapet was thickened and its entrance barricaded. This corner having been much fought over was in a pestilent state, so many bodies lightly buried covering the area.

Battalion relieves Seaforths, 11/8/15.

Patrolling went on continually but all was quiet and uneventful in both lines, the Germans in their trenches barely 130 yards off being frequently heard singing merrily or shouting abuse at us, which was heartily responded to.

The " Duck's Bill " Salient, mid Aug., 1915.

A curious accident happened one night in the " Duck's Bill " to one of our men with Captain Roberts who was going round these trenches. He heard a loud explosion just behind, and naturally jumped round the nearest traverse. The explosion was followed by loud screams and, turning back, he found a man all in flames struggling on the ground. Earth was thrown over him and after some seconds they extinguished the fire, but being pitch dark and the man incoherent it could not be found out what had happened. When he could speak it was found he had a "Very" pistol with cartridge inserted and cocked in case it might be wanted; in some way the trigger caught in his clothes discharging the light into his thigh, where it continued to burn and set his clothes on fire. The wound was extremely bad and necessitated amputation of the leg.

The fine, summer weather had now changed, heavy rain soon waterlogging the trenches, and making the going above ground very heavy.

In Billets on Rugby Road, 16/8/15.

Draft from 7th Goorkha Rifles.

We returned to billets on Rugby Road (*Sketch VIII*) on August 16th, leaving one platoon in Tilleloy Post, and found a draft of the 7th Goorkha Rifles, under Captain J. G. Faris and Lieutenant M. R. Jerram waiting, and who were to be attached to us—a good looking lot, all Limbus and Raies. Captain Bailey having a bad foot, had to be evacuated from here, and Lieutenant G. Sanderson, 15th Sikhs, was sent to us for duty.

First moves of Indian Units from France, Aug., 1915.

Battalion sends Detachment to Gallipoli with 4th Goorkha Rifles, 18/8/15.

Not long before this three regiments of the Indian Corps had been sent from France to Egypt, which led to various rumours as to the future of the Corps; and now it was the turn of the 2nd Goorkhas to supply men for another theatre of war; for on August 18th we were called on to send 100 picked men to the 4th Goorkha Rifles, who were being despatched to Gallipoli. These left us on the 20th under Lieutenant Brandon with Subadar Guman Sing Gurung and Jemadar Santbir Gurung, and the same night the Battalion relieved the 9th Goorkha Rifles in the front trenches for the next four days, during which we had 10 officers of the New Army (19th Division) attached for instructional purposes. Numbers of these officers were distributed among the various sections of defence held by old regiments to learn something of trench life and warfare. These days at the front were singularly quiet and unproductive of interest, very little spasmodic shelling and bombing only occurred with but equally little result. Aircraft activity on both sides increased, and one day an Allied biplane was shot down by German anti-aircraft guns in front of our position with fatal results to both occupants. Both sides were busily employed perfecting their own defences and often in the evenings the enemy (Saxons) whose trenches were a bit nearer to those of the Seaforths and Highland Light Infantry on our right and left, used to shout across a regular flood of badinage. On one occasion these Saxon troops put up a notice in one part of the line saying: "Don't waste ammunition now; to-morrow about 10 a.m.

GROUP OF OFFICERS, 2/2nd K.E.O. GOORKHAS.
FRANCE, AUGUST, 1915.

Captain Cruickshank. Captain Roberts, I.A.R.O. Captain Cullen, I.M.S. Captain Brandon.
Captain Bailey. Colonel Boileau. Captain Corse Scott. Major Sweet.
Lieutenant Scoones. M. Gantes (*Interpreter*). Lieutenant Hind

GOORKHAS (THE SIRMOOR RIFLE REGIMENT)

our General, a Prussian, comes inspecting, then fire away," and on another, a placard they pushed up said: "Stop wasting ammunition on us, to-morrow evening we are being relieved by a Prussian Corps, then fire like hell." Evidently the Saxons had no love for the Prussians.

The Bareilly Brigade took over this front section on the night of August 24th-25th from our brigade, the 2nd Goorkhas marching back to their former billets near Estaires. As usual, the first day here was spent in washing and indenting for clothes, and Colonel Boileau with Captain Roberts went on leave, while Captain Bailey rejoined us; we also lost the excellent services of our interpreter, M. Gantès, who was promoted and went to General Headquarters. He had been with us from our arrival in France, and was greatly missed. His place was taken by M. Le Gras, from the 6th Jāts.

Battalion in Billets near Estaires, 25/8/15.

The Indian Corps were now directed to lengthen their frontage which necessitated three Divisions in the line and the 19th Division (New Army) therefore was added to the corps. Consequent on this addition the 2nd Goorkhas had to move on August 27th to other billets at Lestrem where, being now 5 miles from the front, a long "trek" was imposed on the large numbers of fatigue parties we had to send forward. Occasionally carts were available to help the men over the distance to and fro. From Lestrem a move took place to Riez Bailleul, whence on September 4th the Battalion formed part of the Brigade Reserve near the "Moated Grange" a little north of Neuve Chapelle, with No. 4 Company garrisoning the "Colvin" and "Lafone" posts (*Sketch VIII*). The usual eternal digging work went on, and we had a visit from Colonel Norie and Major Wigram of ours (now on the Army Staff), both going over ground a little to the south of our present position, the scene of the first heavy fighting the 2nd Goorkhas were engaged in on November 2nd, 1914.

Battalion at Moated Grange, 28/8/15.

Changes now occurred in the higher commands, in that General Sir James Willcocks, General Officer Commanding Indian Corps, to the great regret of all, left us, being succeeded by General Sir Charles Anderson, while our Brigadier (General Jacob) was promoted to command the Meerut Division, the latter taking Lieutenant Scoones as his aide-de-camp, and Colonel Harvey of the Black Watch succeeded to the command of the Dehra Doon Brigade.

Changes in High Commands, early Sept., 1915.

The evening of September 8th the Battalion took over its former front section from the 4th Seaforths, viz., from "Sunken Road" to "Colvin" Trench, including the "Duck's Bill" Salient. Sounds of great activity could clearly be heard behind the German lines—that of much traffic, cutting timber, and dropping iron sheeting, while from visual observation it seemed as if the enemy were mining opposite the "Duck's Bill," and patrols constantly went out to see if this could be verified, when three places were noticed where a lot of slate-coloured sandbags were lying, suggesting such work. Our anti-aircraft guns brought down a German aeroplane one day, which fell in flames behind their lines to the sound of tremendous cheering all along our front.

Battalion in Front Trenches, "Duck's Bill" area, 8/9/15.

September 12th to 18th were spent near Estaires, 7 miles back, where a draft of 31 men joined us from India and we lost Captain Roberts, invalided with rheumatic fever, also Lieutenant Clifford transferred to another unit, the latter date seeing the Battalion back in its old front line trenches near the Moated Grange. Here additional shelter and dug-outs had to be prepared, the Dehra Doon Brigade having been warned to concentrate on this section of the front. This pointed to probable offensive operations and generally more stir was noticeable, a heavy bombardment could be heard going on to the south, our guns and aircraft became more active, and two flocks of 15 or more aeroplanes in each passed over us *en route* for a big raid.

Billets near Estaires, 12/9/15.

Battalion back at Moated Grange, 18/9/15.

We were now to use gas for the first time although doubts existed as to its utility, but it was thought desirable in this way to cope with the German new and barbaric method in warfare. Smoke screens were also to be tried with which to cover the advance of assaulting columns. Cylinders of gas began to reach the front and were distributed to the various points decided on for their use. The Meerut Division having to extend its front to the north, the Bareilly and Garhwal Brigades now took over the whole section (*Sketch VIII*) from the "Sunken Road" to "Winchester Street," a distance of some 900 yards or more, the Jullunder Brigade continuing south to and including Neuve Chapelle, while a Brigade of the 3rd Corps carried the line on beyond "Winchester Street." The Dehra Doon Brigade was in Divisional Reserve on the Tilleloy Road near the "Moated Grange" and on the night September 23rd-24th all were in their respective locations ready for coming events.

First Trial of Gas and Smoke Screens, Sept., 1915.

CHAPTER XI.

SEPTEMBER 24TH TO NOVEMBER 9TH, 1915. (*Sketches IX, VIII.*)

WITH this chapter we enter the last of the big operations on the Western Front with which the 2nd Goorkhas were directly concerned ; indeed, the last in which the Indian Corps generally took a prominent part during its stay in France.

The First Army, under Sir Douglas Haig (1st Corps, Indian Corps, 3rd Corps), in September, 1915, stood on a line stretching from a point slightly north-west of Lens where it linked its right to the French Tenth Army, through Givenchy to Neuve Chapelle, joining with the right of the Second Army at a point a little south-west of Armentières (*Sketch IX*). The decision now to force the main effort into the Champagne district east of Laon and Rheims in order to cut the enemy's supply communications from the Rhine, brought about several big subsidiary actions intended to prevent German reinforcements reaching Champagne. The most important of these subsidiary actions was that affecting the First Army on the line mentioned, in which the rôle of the Indian Corps was to carry out an attack so as to hold the enemy on his main positions, viz., Aubers, Pommereau, Illiers, La Bassée (*Sketch IX*), thereby inducing a doubt as to the actual locality of the Allies' main attack, and to cause his reinforcements to be wrongly diverted.

General position in this area of front, late Sept., 1915.

Plans for fresh action, Sept., 1915.

Three objectives were assigned to the Indian Corps, viz., to attack his line fronting ours north of Neuve Chapelle, then to advance against the Haut Pommereau—La Cliqueterie positions, and finally if all went well, to incline to the south and turn the La Bassée defences from the north. The 20th Division 3rd Corps on the left, and Lahore on the right, were to cover with their fire the advance of the Meerut Division in the centre, which was to commence the attack. Of this latter Division the Bareilly Brigade was intended for the left, that of Garhwal for the right attack, the Dehra Doon Brigade being held in reserve for action as might become desirable (*Sketch VIII*).

Objectives for the Indian Corps.

The most elaborate artillery preparation and detailed instructions in general seemed to leave nothing but every hope of complete success to follow, the weather only appeared the doubtful factor as heavy rain and mist were followed by high winds, the trenches again became waterlogged, and there were many opinions against the possibility of using the gas. Four days of bombardment by guns and mortars were to precede the assault, a large mine was to be exploded under the salient hostile parapet opposite the left of the Bareilly Brigade just before the gas and smoke barrage started, behind which the assaulting lines were to advance at 6 a.m. on September 25th.

Battle of Loos, Arrangements for attack, 25/9/15.

Just before 5 a.m. mischance brought a German shell into the "Duck's Bill" salient, its explosion blowing off the heads of the gas cylinders there, the escaping gas causing many casualties before they could be covered with earth, thus averting a serious contretemps. In fact the wind changing nullified our efforts to use gas at all, as it got blown back into our own trenches.

Use of Gas a failure, 25/9/15.

At 5.48 a.m. our big mine on the left was sprung, resulting in the total disappearance of the German salient in a dense cloud of earth and debris, and at 6 a.m. following the smoke screen the infantry crossed the parapets and swept forward to the assault, to be soon lost sight of and mixed up in the battle, which for hours surged back and forth. At 7.30 a.m. the Dehra Doon Brigade went forward into the "Home Counties" and other trenches ready for the further advance, which was to take them through the captured German trenches and on to assault the enemy's next positions at La Haute Pommereau, and La Cliqueterie (*Sketch IX*). At 11 a.m. the brigade again moved forward to the front trenches preparatory to attack, as Bareilly required support and the direction of our next move was to be towards Piètre, necessitating a change of front. Nos. 2 and 4 Companies, 2nd Goorkhas, leading our attack, were first in position, there being no block in this part of the trenches as there was elsewhere, to hinder movement.

Dehra Brigade advances, 25/9/15.

But it was not till 2.15 p.m. that orders were received for the Brigade to advance, which commenced at once—the 1st Seaforths and 2nd Goorkhas in centre, 9th Goorkha Rifles and 4th Seaforths on the flanks. Hardly had they all got under way than the order for advance was cancelled and a return was made to the trenches. The early attacks, at first successful in capturing trenches

Further advance stopped, 25/9/15.

GOORKHAS (THE SIRMOOR RIFLE REGIMENT)

at Mauquissart and near Piètre, had now been driven back by superior numbers of the enemy who had reoccupied their old trenches. Certain British troops, it was believed, were still remaining in parts of the hostile lines and a company of 1st Seaforths with No. 2 of the 2nd Goorkhas, under Subadars Mansur Rai and Bhagatbir Limbu, were sent forward to establish touch with these troops. They crossed the parapet making towards a German flag (red, white, and black) floating over the line in front of them, and at once came under a storm of bullets chiefly from machine guns, which checked the rush, forcing all to take such cover as was possible. A fresh bombardment now became necessary and both companies were withdrawn, our casualties being 3 killed, 18 wounded, and 2 missing.

No. 2 Company sent forward, 25/9/15.

Towards the end of the day and after heavy fighting, with here and there success to both forward Brigades but only to be driven back again suffering severe losses, orders were sent stopping further offensive efforts—the Battle of Loos as it is officially called and in which the above was a subsidiary operation, ending in failure in this area, in spite of the utmost gallantry on the part of all concerned. The defences and numerical superiority of the enemy proved too strong.

Failure of offensive, 25/9/15.

At 11.30 p.m. that night the 9th Goorkha Rifles took over this section of the front, and the 2nd Goorkhas withdrew to billets on Rugby Road (*Sketch VIII*) till 10.30 a.m. next day, when we were sent forward to repair parapets, clear trenches of equipment, etc., and bury bodies, during which work 2 men were wounded by shell fragments. The Shropshires relieving us on the night of 28th-29th, the Battalion was sent to La Couture, where two new officers joined us (Lieutenants Swayne and Helm, both I.A.R.), and to the regret of all, Major Sweet left us on transfer to the officiating command of the 2/8th Goorkha Rifles. While here we came in for a little shelling, which killed 1 man and wounded 2 others. Intimation now reached us that the Dehra Doon Brigade would very shortly be sent south to take over the front section just beyond Festubert, and on October 1st the Battalion moved to Croix Marmuse, the following day marching to Gorre, and thence to our new locality which was found to be slightly north of Givenchy extending to opposite Festubert, and here we succeeded

Battalion in Billets, 26/9/15.

Shropshires relieve Battalion, 29/9/15.

Major Sweet transferred to 2/8th Goorkha Rifles, 30/9/15.

the 8th Gloucesters (*Sketch IX*). The trenches now held by the Battalion were in bad repair, much knocked about, and with few dug-outs, all of which had to be taken in hand. Fortunately, quiet reigned here at this time. On our right the 1st Seaforths held Givenchy Ridge, the 9th Goorkha Rifles were on our left, and our company distribution was with Captains Bruce and Faris in the fire trenches, No. 1 in support, No. 2 in reserve. The usual digging and repairing work went on daily in bad weather, both sides being busy, and we had only 1 man wounded by a sniper. This quiet continued save for a sudden stir on October 4th from the direction of the La Bassée Canal, which turned out to be only a bombing affray. Lieutenants F. M. Daly and E. De Brath, both I.A.R., joined us here for duty and Jemadar Adjutant Chandan Sing Gurung had to be evacuated owing to ill-health, so also had Captain Macintyre. The winter work was now directed to be undertaken, viz., the building of trenches above ground level, in the commencement of which we had 1 man killed and 1 wounded, and the 93rd Infantry relieved the Battalion during the night October 6th-7th, which withdrew to trenches round Festubert village and became the brigade reserve. This locality came in for considerable hostile attention, the Germans shelling both Festubert and Le Plantin near by fairly frequently, and the 10th saw us back at the front till the 20th, during which period we made a demonstration, the men of the Brigade Grenadier Company using smoke balls to divert attention from a gas attack to the south near Givenchy. The Germans replied with shrapnel, and we lost Lieutenant Sanderson, a most keen and promising young officer, who was hit in the head while looking through a periscope, and was buried in the Gorre Cemetery. Two men were also badly wounded. Naik Amer Sing Pun did a useful bit of scouting here in misty weather getting close to the German trenches, where he located a troublesome machine-gun, and made a good report on their wire.

Battalion sent to new front near Givenchy, 1/10/15.

Disposition of Battalion and work, Oct., 1915.

Battalion relieved by 93rd Infantry, 7/10/15.

Battalion back in trenches, and last casualties in France, 10/10/15.

Our "unfits" were now being turned to some use in being sent to Nieppe Forest for wood cutting, together with those of other units.

The North Staffords relieved us on the evening of the 20th, the Battalion marching to Vieille Chapelle, and the following day to

Rough Plan shewing the Meerut Division in the battle of Sept. 25th 1915.

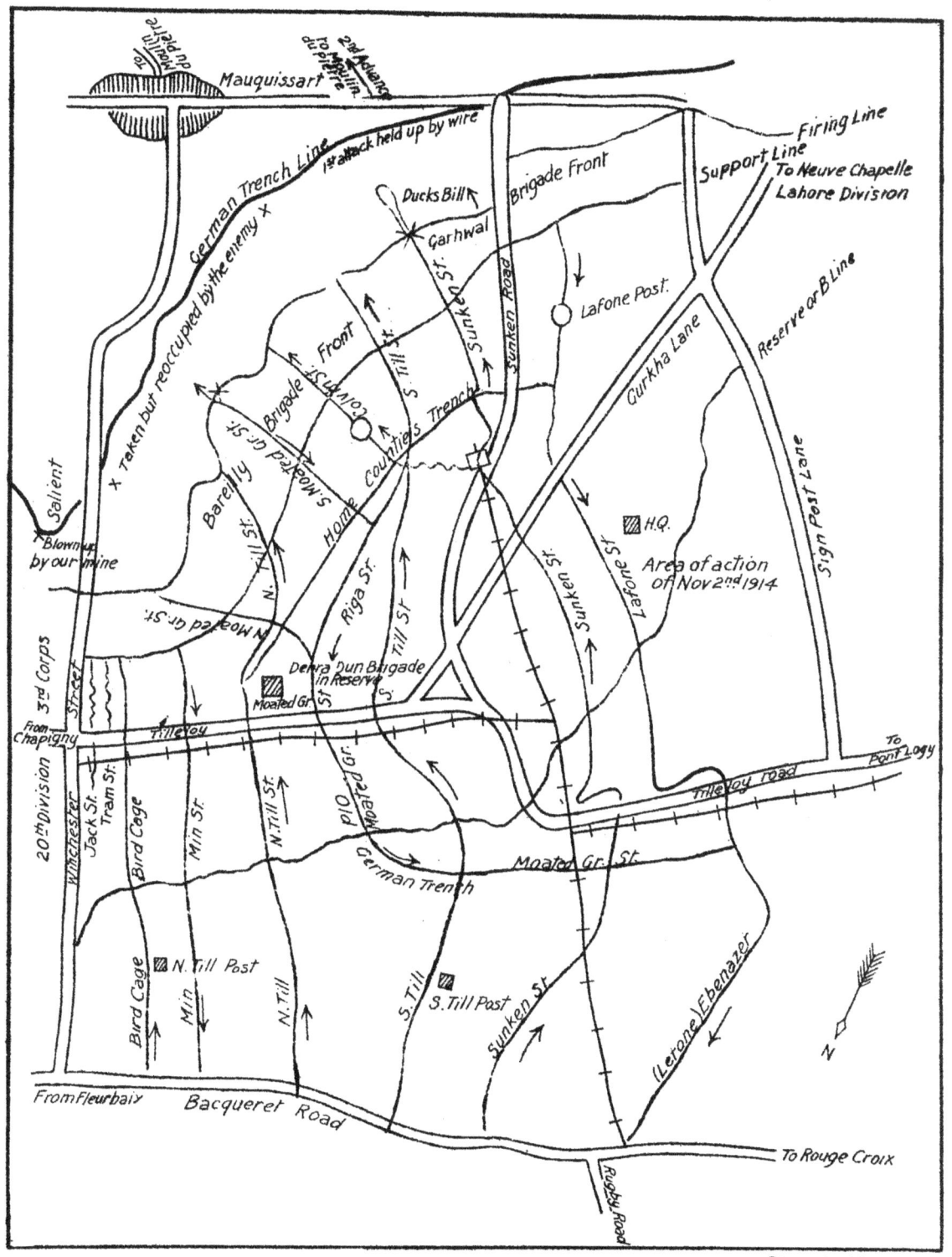

2ND K.E.O.G. Sketch No VIII.

GOORKHAS (THE SIRMOOR RIFLE REGIMENT)

Battalion relieved by North Staffords, 20/10/15.

Battalion near "Port Arthur," 21/10/15.

"Lansdowne Post," west of "Port Arthur," which it had been in prior to the assault on May 9th; "Windy Corner Post" being held by No. 1 Company; and the Brigade generally occupying the old front from the "Cinder Track" to the "Crescent" work near "Port Arthur" (*Sketch IV*). Our four days here were uneventful, 1 man only was wounded, and on the Black Watch taking over from us the Battalion marched to billets at Quentin (8 miles back), near Calonne, in company with the rest of the brigade, Bareilly having succeeded our brigade at the front.

On October 28th the 2nd Goorkhas marched to La Pannerie (2 miles), where the Dehra Doon Brigade assembled for inspection by His Majesty The King who was visiting the front. After waiting in pouring rain and cold till noon, it was learnt that His Majesty had had a fall from his horse that morning, and though not seriously injured was unable to come. A very disappointing day for all units, who returned to their billets.

Visit of H.M. the King, 28/10/15.

Colonel Boileau here left us for England on leave, his duties being carried on by Captain Bruce, Captain Bailey and Lieutenant Hind getting a week's leave also. October 30th was observed as a holiday to celebrate the "Dassera" and "Dewali" festivals, a dance and "show" being given by the men, and the only goat procurable slaughtered to mark the occasion.

Former rumours relative to the future of the Indian Corps now became more certain as definite orders came to hand showing that arrangements were being made for the whole corps to leave France about the middle of November, but where for was still unknown. The reason for this impending change had been foreseen for some time, and it lay chiefly in the fact that the Indian Reserve Organization had been a complete failure. Heavy casualties at the front, sickness, unfit men sent with drafts from India, had all reduced units dangerously in strength. Reinforcements at first good, began not only to deteriorate but to be sent at long intervals. The heavy losses in British officers made such most difficult to replace with those who knew India and its soldier classes. It was after the actions of September 25th that these conditions constrained serious notice to be taken by the higher authorities, with the result that it was deemed the best course to transfer the entire Corps to theatres of war where their presence was much

Withdrawal of Indian Contingent from France late Oct., 1915.

Reasons for withdrawal.

needed, and where they would not be so far removed from India and their sources of reinforcements. The cavalry only of the Indian Corps was to be retained in France for some while longer.

The 2nd Goorkhas moved to the front on November 2nd for the last time into the breastworks behind the Rue du Bois near Edward Road (*Sketch IV*), in relief of the 2/3rd Goorkhas, and two days later orders came to withdraw entirely to Croix Marmuse. This marked the end of the Battalion's services on the Western Front, as this move was followed at once by instructions to embus at Lestrem for Hazebrouck, there to entrain for Marseilles. The last march from La Couture and Croix Marmuse was one full of memories, passing as we did many billets occupied by us during our sojourn in France, and of sadder thoughts of the gallant men in all ranks left behind for all time to mark how troops from the far off mountains of Nepal had given their best in the service of the King and Empire.

Battalion's Last bit of trench duty, 2/11/15.

Orders to entrain for Marseilles.

The following statement shows the total casualties sustained by the 2nd Goorkhas in France during their share in the campaign :—

Casualty.	British Officers.	Goorkha Officers.	Other Ranks.
Killed	13	9	135
Wounded	3	7	303
Missing	1	2	106
Sick	9	21	380
Died of Wounds	3	1	16
Died in Hospital	—	—	10
	29	40	950

Total casualties in France.

a total of 1,019. Of the wounded and sick :—

Wounded and returned to duty	1	1	52
Sick and returned to duty	2	5	177
Wounded and sick returned to India	—	11	131
	3	17	360

The Prince of Wales in November was sent over to France to convey His Majesty The King's farewell message to a large gathering of representatives

PART OF THE INDIAN CONTINGENT CEMETERY AT GORRE, NEAR FESTUBERT, IN WHICH MANY OF THE 2/2nd K.E.O. GOORKHAS ARE BURIED.

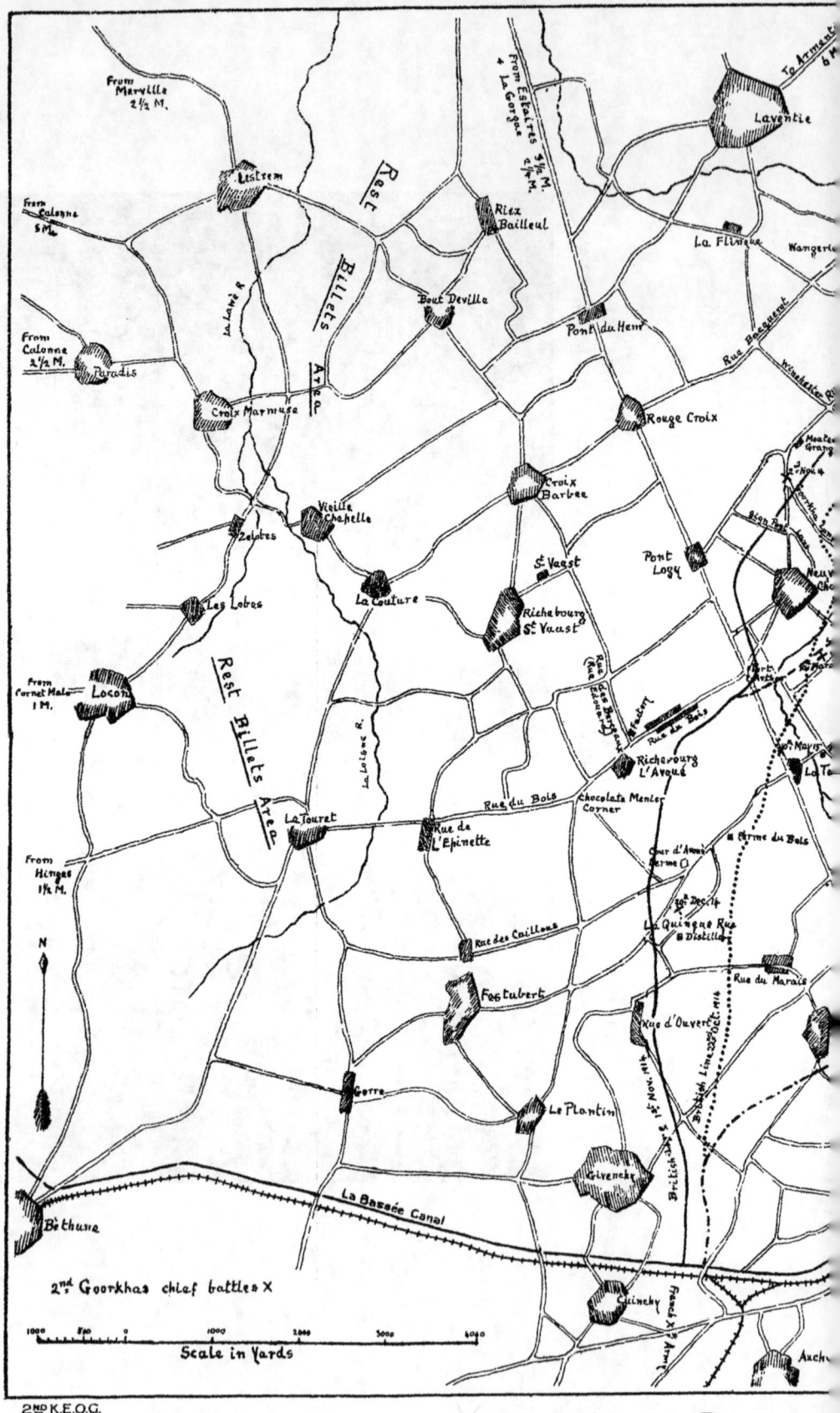

Plan of area in France where the Meerut Division o[perated]

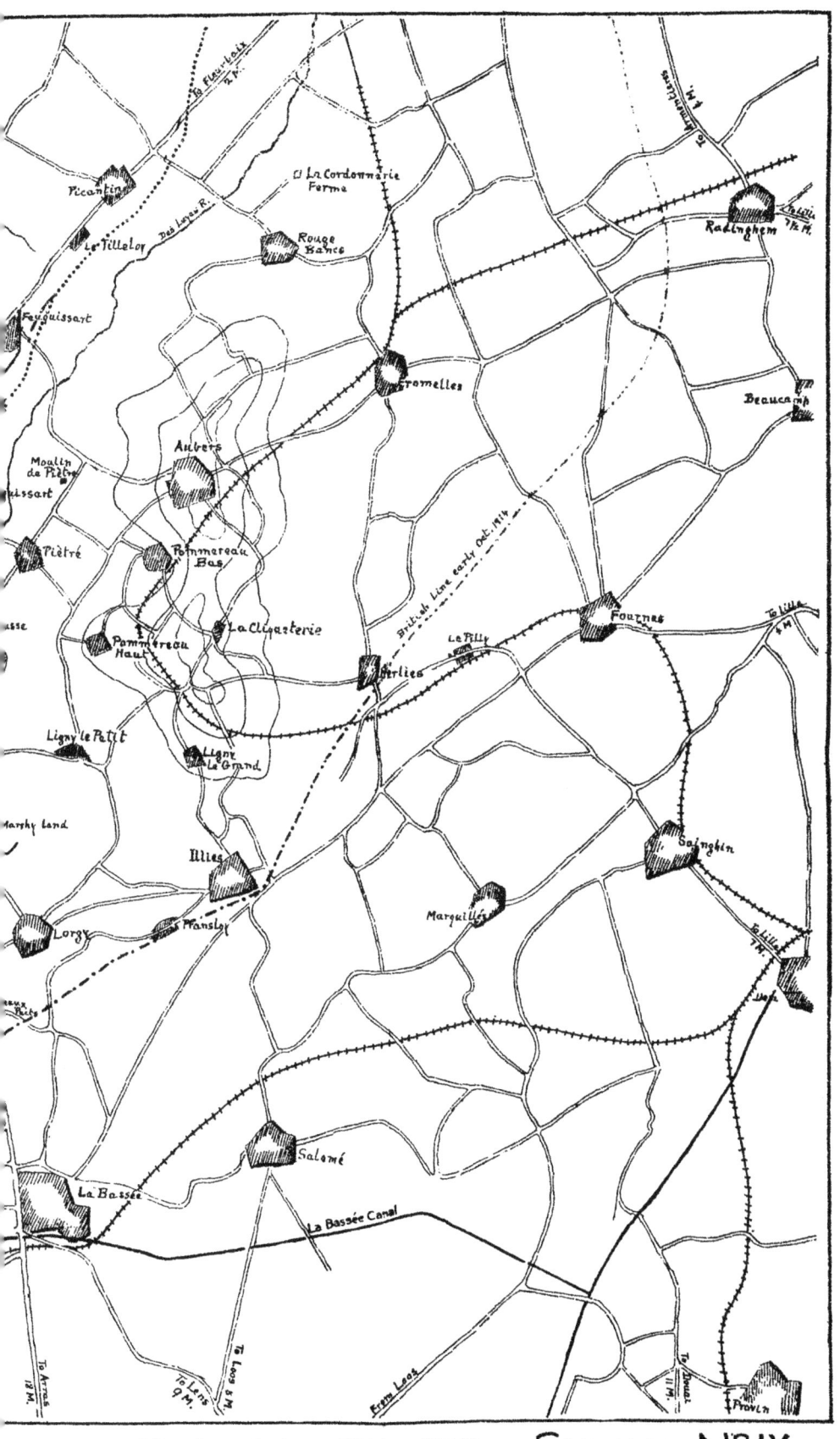

ced from 29th Oct.1914 to 6th Nov.1915   SKETCH Nº IX

Prince of Wales's visit to Indian Contingent, Nov., 1915. of the Indian Corps at the Château Mazinghem, and the Commander-in-Chief, General Sir John French, issued a special " Order of the Day " thanking all for duties carried out and heavy losses sustained in a manner worthy of the best traditions of the Indian Army. The Royal message will be found in Appendix D.

The Garhwal Brigade was the first Indian Brigade to leave the front and France, to this unit the 2nd Goorkhas were attached, and we entrained at **Battalion entrains at Berguette, 7/11/15.** Berguette on November 7th, Colonel Boileau, Captains Bruce, Bailey, and Lieutenant Hind rejoining from leave in time for the last move. At the station were General Blackader (General Officer Commanding Garhwal Brigade) and Staff to speed us on our way at 2.40 p.m. The next two days were spent in the train, at various places *en route* the men receiving tea, food, and pleasant kindly ovations. Marseilles was **Marseilles and embarkation, 9/11/15.** reached during the night of the 9th, the Battalion embarking straight away on board the *Coconada* together with a wing of the 39th Garhwalis, and steamed out of harbour eastward bound by 9 a.m. next day.

CHAPTER XII.

NOVEMBER 9TH, 1915, TO MARCH 3RD, 1916. (*Sketch X.*)

THE voyage to Alexandria in delightful weather after the first day out which was rough, was uneventful, and port was reached at 10.30 a.m. on November 16th, but only to stay a few hours as the *Coconada* steamed at 4 p.m. for Port Said, where anchor was dropped next morning. Here the Battalion was directed to disembark and entrain for Kantāra on the Canal, there to form a unit of the Army in Egypt and to relieve the 51st Sikhs.

Arrival Port Said, 17/11/15.

The situation in this war area was briefly :—

During January and February, 1915, the Turks with their Arab allies, had made a rapid move with a force of some 14,000 men from Palestine against Egypt. They had been defeated in their attack on our Canal defences in the vicinity of Serapeum, where they had managed to launch pontoons and had got two across with troops, but had retired again to El Arish there to consolidate their forces, push forward a railway, and generally to make more elaborate preparations for a further effort. During the summer desultory skirmishes had taken place, and reconnaissances been made by them towards various points on the Canal, in one of which they managed to float a mine which blew up one of our steamers. Our Canal defences had during these months been greatly improved, but more troops were needed, and these released from the Western Front began arriving in November, 1915.

Situation on the Suez Canal during 1915.

Kantāra Camp was reached on the 18th, where we were greeted by Captain A. J. H. Chope, of ours, who had been on duty in Egypt with the Bikanir Camel Corps since the early months of the war. The camp (about 1,000 yards east of the Canal) proved comfortable, and the men were naturally delighted with the space and freedom of the place after the cooped up life in trenches and the general restrictions necessary in France. Kantāra was then occupied by three Battalions, a Regiment of Cavalry (Mysore State Lancers), and a 4-gun Battery of the Honourable Artillery Company, the whole of this No. 3 Section of the Canal Defence extending from Port Said to Kantāra being under the command of General Sir Herbert Cox.

Battalion located at Kantāra, 18/11/15.

HISTORY OF THE 2ND KING EDWARD'S OWN GOORKHAS

Captain McCleverty, badly wounded in France, rejoined us here on the 19th, but later had to go to Helouan for further massage treatment.

Drills now were steadily attended to and much needed, also the amalgamation of the Battalion units, conditions at present being ideal for this. For amusements the men had football though not of the best owing to the heavy sand, and unlimited fishing in the Canal. Cavalry reconnaissances were frequent, with them going Colonel Boileau, Captain Corse Scott, and other officers as available in order to get acquainted with the ground. In No. 3 Section the 2/3rd Goorkhas and 2/8th Goorkha Rifles supplied men for the desert posts north of Kantāra, as well as for the armoured train and night picquets 1,500 yards beyond the perimeter; the 2nd Goorkhas were in reserve and formed the Movable Column.

Work, etc., at Kantāra.

The first outing the Battalion was engaged in was with a force of Cavalry and Camelry, which marched for Hod el Aras (13 miles north) on the night of November 22nd-23rd to block the route from Mahādat to Bir el Jaffeir, a force of Turks and Arabs having been reported as near Mahādat. Wireless linked the force with Kantāra, while an aeroplane was in attendance on the column. The Cavalry only came in for a short engagement, but after working round the enemy's flanks these retreated pursued by the Cavalry for 7 miles, who captured 12 prisoners and some camels with rifles and ammunition, an Arab leader being killed. Meanwhile the Infantry, considerably fatigued toiling through the sand, reached Hod el Aras as dawn was breaking. Picquets were placed on surrounding sand hills, and helio communication opened to Hill 70 (7 miles from Kantāra). Towards midday news was to hand of the Cavalry's action, and at 2 p.m. orders were flashed out for the return of the Infantry, camp being reached at midnight. Considering our men had only their thick khaki to wear and were not as yet accustomed to marching in sand, they did very well, only four men falling out.

Battalion on reconnaissance in desert, 23/11/15.

On the 25th Sir Herbert Cox inspected the Battalion, and as none of the kits containing the men's thin khaki had arrived from the Indian depot at Marseilles, nor had any news of their despatch been received, new khaki was now indented for though there was small hope of such being forthcoming for long, but General Cox promised to push the matter for us.

Battalion inspected by Sir Herbert Cox, 25/11/15.

We also received here a kindly letter from General Jacob (lately commanding the Meerut Division in France) congratulating the Battalion on work done in the field, and wishing it all success in the future (*vide* Appendix *D*).

December 2nd saw the Movable Column composed of 300 of the 2nd Goorkhas with machine-gun detachments and a squadron of Cavalry and some Bikanir Camelry proceed on a week's tour to the north, as intelligence agents reported small hostile bodies to be in the El Katia valley and its neighbourhood. No Infantry had been so far as El Katia before, and the tour though without contact with the enemy proved interesting as an experience. The first camp at Bir el Dueidar was reached at 3 p.m. where good water was found and helio communication established with Kantāra, and the Cavalry patrolled towards Hod el Aras. The next march, starting at 8 a.m., brought the column to Abu Ramel by 7.30 p.m., our aeroplane during the march reporting camels and the collection of stores at Bir el Abd, which the Cavalry were sent on to destroy. An intelligence agent also arrived reporting he had seen some 200 of the enemy moving towards El Katia. Later a mounted unit pushed on to try and gain contact with them, and a halt on the fifth day was made by the column to scour the neighbourhood, when it was found the hostile party had made off to the south-east without touching the place. Romāni was reached at 11.30 a.m. on the 6th without any signs of the enemy, Hod Negeiret Ali next day at 2 p.m., and by 7.30 p.m. on the 8th the column was back in Kantāra. These desert marches were all heavy going, but the men were very fit and none fell out.

Battalion with Movable Column advances to El Katia, 2/12/15.

Rush cutting and brick making were now added to our varied works in camp, the detachment of the 1/7th Goorkha Rifles attached to us in France, was now ordered to join their regiment which had arrived in Egypt, and arrangements were made for our detachment sent from France to Gallipoli with the 4th Goorkha Rifles to rejoin us.

This latter detachment's experiences were as follows :—

Leaving France on August 25th, 1915, the 4th Goorkha Rifles, with our detachment, disembarked at Lemnos on September 1st and were sent across to Gallipoli on the 13th, disembarking in Anzac Bay. They formed for a few days part of the Divisional reserve, thereafter taking turns in the front trenches with the 2/10th Goorkha Rifles, 1/6th Goorkha Rifles, and 1/5th Goorkha Rifles. During their four months here their life was practically entirely in the trenches, often under heavy shell fire, mining and counter-mining, and warding off Turkish attacks, these, however, not being so formidable as in the earlier months of the expedition. Work, of course, was continuous, heavy, and the climate very severe. Casualties in action, however, were not numerous apparently, but dysentery and

Our Detachment with 4th Goorkha Rifles rejoins, Dec., 1915.

SUEZ.
1. Defensive Post, 2nd/2nd Goorkhas near Ayun Mūsa.
2. 2nd/2nd Goorkhas Camp on the Suez Canal.

other diseases, due to exposure, took a heavy toll. On December 13th confidential orders were received relative to the evacuation of our positions which took place throughout the night of the 19th via Suvla Bay without hostile interference, the movement having been a complete surprise to the enemy. On December 24th, 1915, the 4th Goorkha Rifles sailed from Mudros for Alexandria and Suez, our men rejoining the Battalion in early January, 1916.

The Battalion now had to garrison Hill 70 (7 miles north of Kantāra) with two companies, the other companies holding the picquet line, Battalion Headquarters with the machine-gun detachments only remaining in the main camp, which had recently become a great centre of activity, roads being laid out and metalled, pipe lines laid to different points, and preparations made for the reception of a large number of troops.

Christmas at Hill 70 in desert. Christmas Day, 1915, was spent here where sports were held, all who could be spared gathering at this desert post, and the following officers dined together:—Colonel Boileau, Colonel Pridham, Royal Engineers, Captains Bruce, Bailey, Chope, Faris, Taylor, I.M.S., and Lieutenants Jerram and Hind; when, in spite of culinary difficulties, a very pleasant evening was spent.

Battalion moves to Ayun Mūsa, 30/12/15. On the 27th the Battalion was withdrawn to Kantāra as it was under orders to proceed to the southern end of the Canal on December 30th; a move which duly took place, Suez being reached by rail that afternoon, where a draft of 50 men (mostly recruits) awaited us. The following day orders came to proceed on January 1st, 1916, to Ayun Mūsa, south-east of Suez and across the Canal, lighters transporting the Battalion as far as El Shatt, whence a 7-mile march. While passing Port Tewfik at the entrance to the canal we were met by Brigadier-General H. D. Watson—a former officer of the Regiment for many years, who latterly had commanded a battalion of the 9th Goorkha Rifles, and now was in command of the Suez section of Canal defences. That night we bivouacked at El Shatt, and reached Ayun Mūsa at 10.30 a.m. next day, the baggage coming on in the lighter. (*Sketch X.*)

Stay and work at Ayun Mūsa. The Battalion's stay here of one and a half months, was entirely devoid of any stirring interest; it was employed along with other troops mostly in preparing the defences of the place, much of which being over rocky ground entailed heavy labour, in garrisoning certain posts on the desert side, one of which was $2\frac{1}{2}$ miles in front, in forming at times part of the Movable Column, in the usual drills and training, and we were over 100 short of strength. Small parties of recovered sick and wounded from various hospitals rejoined us from time to time, also Captain McCleverty, who had benefited much by the massage treatment to his arm at Helouan. The Corps Commander (General Byng) and Staff came out on January 19th and carefully inspected the new defences.

Intelligence summaries showed that the Turkish desert garrisons away to the north-east of the Canal had been increased and that the main forces in South-West Palestine were gradually pressing on from Rāfā and Auja, intent on attacking Egypt; but so far no hostile effort on the part of their troops in Sinai enlivened our sojourn at Ayun Mūsa (The Wells of Moses) (*Sketch X*).

Recently received despatches by Field-Marshal Sir John French showed that Major Sweet, Captain McCleverty, Captain Cruickshank and Lieutenant Scoones had been " mentioned," and in a later notification the last mentioned officer was awarded the Military Cross, while No. 1759 Havildar Bambahadur Gurung with No. 2693 Rifleman Anarupe Thapa were to receive the Indian Order of Merit 2nd Class. Both these men had been recommended for the Victoria Cross by General Jacob for gallantry in having during the action of May 9th, 1915, gone to the assistance of a wounded man of the Black Watch and under heavy fire had brought him under cover. Unfortunately no eye-witness except men of their own unit saw their act, hence disqualification for the coveted Cross.

Military Police sent to 1/2nd Goorkhas in Mesopotamia, 9/2/16.

It was on February 2nd that the first intimation of the Battalion returning to India was received, followed on the 9th by orders directing all men of the Military Police Battalions to be sent to Suez, there to be despatched to join the 1/2nd Goorkhas at Basra—the first we had heard that our other Battalion left so long at Dehra chafing at inaction, had at last gone to the front in Mesopotamia.

Battalion relieved by 58th Sikhs, and leaves Ayan Mūsa, 11/2/16.

Embarkation for India, 17/2/16.

The 10th saw our Battalion relieved by the 58th Rifles, and the following day it marched to El Shatt, where it camped till the 17th, when the s.s. *Baroda* arrived and embarkation was completed by 2 p.m., the vessel sailing for Bombay shortly after. While at El Shatt an interchange of visits took place between our officers and those of H.M.S. *Jupiter*, guarding this part of the Red Sea, some of their officers dining with ours one night, and a football match was played between the sailors and Goorkhas. The voyage passed comfortably, one man was lost from enteric fever, and on the 22nd a wireless message changed our destination to

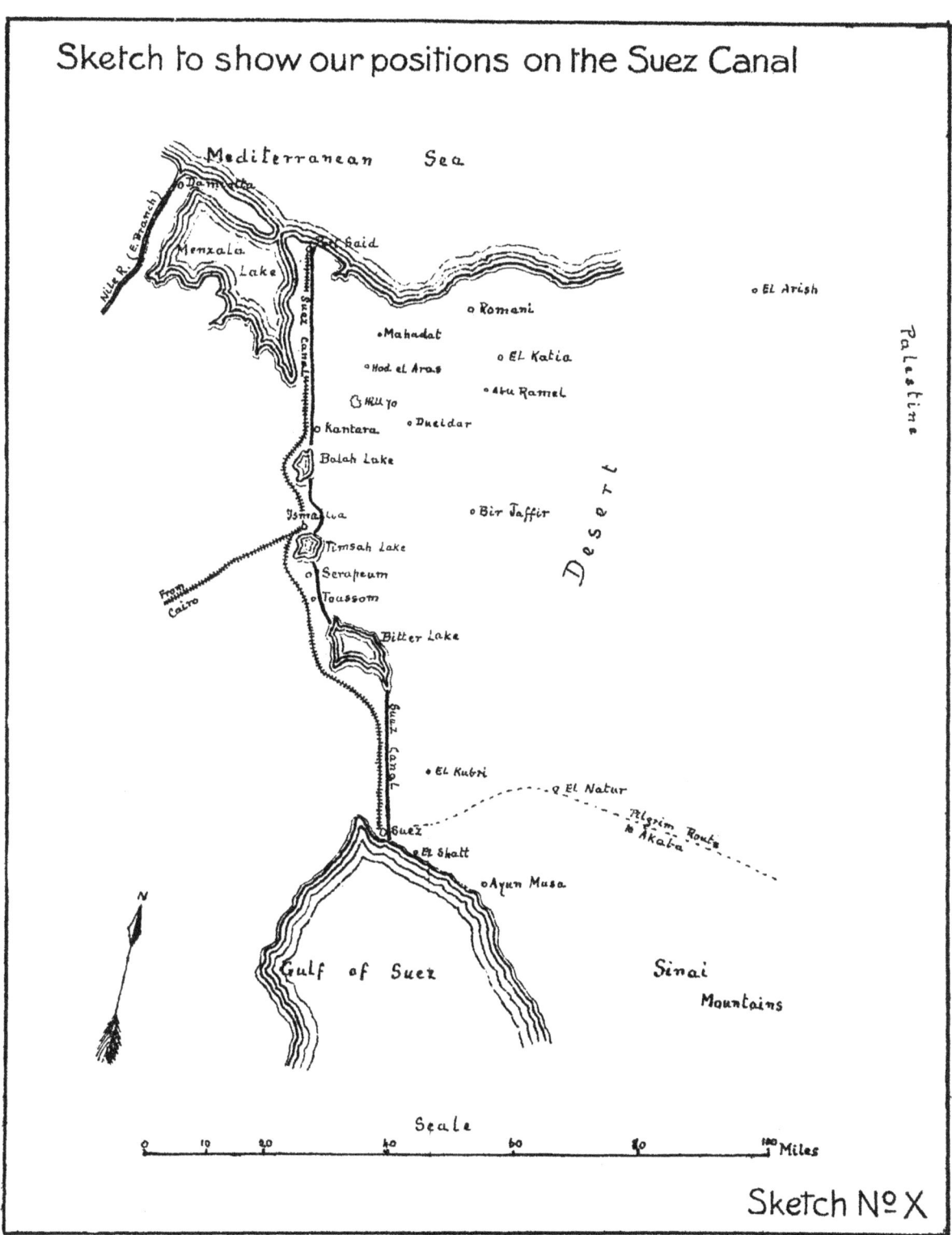

Disembarkation at Karachi, 28/2/16. Karachi, which port was reached at 3 p.m. on February 28th. No time was lost in disembarking and entraining, and before the Battalion left the station a telegram from the Commander-in-Chief India welcoming the 2nd Goorkhas back, was received.

It ran :—

"My heartiest welcome to you all and all ranks under your command on your return to India from field service where all have so gallantly and devotedly maintained the high traditions of Indian Army."

A letter also from the Adjutant-General notified that our men would be allowed the requisite period at Dehra for " Pani Pattiya," viz., the ceremony necessary to be gone through by Goorkhas who had crossed the sea, in order to regain their caste.

A four-hour halt was made at Lahore where the Commanding Officer received a telegram of welcome from the Mahant Lachman Das of Dehra— " Congratulate you all on your bravery and good service for our Government and General Maharaja blessings on the Regiment."

The 2/2nd Goorkhas reached Dehra at 10.30 a.m. on March 3rd, 1916, once more home after a period of strenuous life and war in a far off foreign country, such as had never fallen to its lot before, covering **Battalion arrives at Dehra, 3/3/16.** as it did 18 months of excessive toil and ceaseless danger, and the delight of all at its ending can better be imagined than described. At the station a large gathering of all civil and military officials greeted the Battalion, the band striking up the Regimental quick-step as the train drew up. Leading Mahomedan and other Indian gentlemen distributed gifts of cigarettes and light refreshments to the men, and the march to cantonments was through decorated streets and applauding throngs. Passing the " Jhanda " temple, **Battalion's home-coming.** wreaths were flung over the men as they went under one arch with the words on it : " Welcome ye Guardians of the Doon," and under another with : " You have deserved well of your country." The Battalion in its march was headed by the Truncheon, accompanied by many old pensioned Goorkha officers and Honorary Captain (pensioned) Subadar Major Santbir Gurung rode beside the Commanding Officer. From the Bindal Bridge to the Memorial Arch the roadway was lined by the recruits of both Battalions, the Lines were a mass of coloured festoons, and after ranks were dismissed all was joy and feasting for a grand repast had been prepared for the returning warriors, who soon settled down to a happy period of well-deserved peace amongst their pals and families.

CHAPTER XIII.

March 3rd, 1916, to end of 1920. (*Sketch XI.*)

THE lines in Dehra were empty now with our 1st Battalion away in Mesopotamia and only their Depot left here, while the Mess called up sad memories of the old cheery friends fallen in France whose vacant places could hardly be filled again; but life in the old cantonment was soon taken up as formerly and went happily on for nearly a year. Much training of recruits and the preparation and despatch of drafts and officers for the 1st Battalion on service occupied the time till early November, when the 2nd Battalion marched for Tuglokabad near Delhi, to attend a Camp of Exercise lasting till the end of December, and where we were brigaded with the 1/4th Wiltshire Regiment, the Somerset Light Infantry (both Territorial units) and the " Mahendra Dal" Regiment of the Nepalese Army, under the command of Brigadier-General the Earl of Radnor.

Delhi Manœuvres, Nov., 1916.

The last named unit was one of several lent by the Nepal Durbar which, throwing in its lot with the British Rāj, offered assistance with troops. This was accepted by Government for internal defence and for service on the Indian Frontier, but not for overseas. Early in 1915 two of these regiments arrived in Dehra, each 1,000 strong, of excellent material, and were located in the Gangora Lines vacated by the Mountain Batteries usually in occupation but now at the war, and were under the command of General Tej Shumsher Jang. A fine body of troops, to train which on modern lines Captain Nicholl with Lieutenants Marsh and Woodyatt were detached from the 1st Battalion, and under their care very great improvement in efficiency was soon visible. Eventually patient hard work was rewarded by some of these regiments seeing active service on the North-West Frontier. It was pleasant to find that the necessities of war had brought back an old officer of ours once more to the Regiment in Major W. H. K. Gough, who some years earlier had left us for a political career. He rejoined at Dehra during 1915, and was in command of the Depot for a year, after which, the Political Department claiming his services again, he was sent to Persia.

The Nepalese Contingent.

A 1st Reserve Goorkha Battalion was now started, to which we had to

BRITISH RESIDENCY, MANIPUR.

add our quota of one company, which went off under Captain Bailey and became subsequently the 4/3rd Goorkhas; while a few months later 2 British officers with 1 Goorkha officer and 50 Riflemen were sent to form part of the new 3rd Reserve Goorkha Battalion at Rawal Pindi, which later became the 3/6th Goorkha Rifles.

Formation of new Goorkha Battalions during 1916.

This pleasant stay at Dehra came to an end in January, 1917, when the 2nd Battalion was ordered to Burhān near Rawal Pindi, to join the new Indian 16th Division, which was being formed there. Colonel Boileau, having recently been appointed Commandant of the Cadet College at Quetta, had left us, so the Battalion proceeded to Burhān under the command of Major J. G. Faris, until on March 6th Lieutenant-Colonel A. B. Tillard, D.S.O., was sent from the 3rd Goorkhas to command temporarily.

Battalion joins 16th Division at Burhān, Jan., 1917.

During February and March, 1917, we moved with other units to Hassan Abdul for purposes of brigade and divisional training, after which the Battalion was sent for the hot weather to Rewat in the Murree Hills—a pleasant change to the heat and dust of the plains about Burhān.

Battalion at Rewat, April, 1917.

Throughout these two years a constant stream of officers and recruits passed through our hands—young officers from Sandhurst or the Cadet Colleges at Quetta and Wellington—Indian Army Reserve officers recruited from commercial, legal, engineers, police, forests, and other branches of civil life also officers recruited from British regiments in India or England. These kept arriving, being trained, and passed on to the 1st Battalion on service, or elsewhere. In all some 2,500 men were trained during this period, involving no small amount of effort and responsibility on the part of the few instructors and trained officers we had.

During this summer orders having been received regarding the raising of a 3rd Battalion to the 2nd Goorkhas in June, the 2nd Battalion sent 2 British officers, 2 Goorkha officers, 32 Non-Commissioned Officers, 150 Riflemen, and 150 recruits to make the nucleus of the new unit forming at Dehra. As practically all the Goorkha regiments were to raise third battalions, it was naturally a wonder as to whether such was possible; could a small State like Nepal stand the strain of so much extra recruitment of its man-power? But it did, thanks to the good offices of the Prime Minister of Nepal; recruits came in freely, and it is estimated that during the period of the war and up to about 1920 some 210,000 men left that country to serve the British Rāj in various capacities connected with that period of stress.

With the autumn came a return to Burhān Camp, and prolonged brigade training that winter at Kālā Serai, some distance nearer to Rawal Pindi, our Brigade consisting of the 1st West Riding Regiment, 2/2nd Goorkhas, 3/6th Goorkha Rifles, the " Pasupati Prasād " Nepalese Regiment, under Brigadier-General Paterson.

Burhān Camp was left in early January, 1918, for Tank on the North-West Frontier, to relieve the 2/113th Infantry; a desolate spot noted for its bare surroundings, great heat, prevalence of appalling dust storms, and scanty water supply. Hardly had the Battalion reached this delectable land than it was ordered to despatch 200 rifles to the extreme north-east of India, where a serious rebellion had broken out among the Kukie tribes on that border of Assam and Burma. This detachment left the Battalion on January 18th, under Major J. E. Cruickshank, with whom were Lieutenants Duff and Buss, and railing five days across India marched the 134 miles from the railway at Dimapur through the Naga and Manipur Hills, dropping Lieutenant Duff with 100 rifles at Kohima, while the remainder marched on to Imphal the capital of the Manipur State, the hill country surrounding which was the area of disturbance. It was a country of forest clad hills and dense vegetation, very different to that frontier they had left; but as the detachment was only for garrison duty and to support the Assam Rifles if need arose, who, with the Burma Military Police in the Chindwyn Valley, were dealing with the trouble, Major Cruickshank and his men were not called on to take active part in suppressing the rebellion; and after a pleasant sojourn of four months there they were ordered to rejoin the 2nd Battalion, which was reached in the end of May.

Battalion moves to Tank, Jan., 1918.

Detachment sent to Manipur, 18/1/18.

Meanwhile disturbances had arisen on the other side of India in Baluchistan in the hills between Sibi and Quetta, where the Marri tribe had risen in revolt, necessitating the operations of a Field Force under Brigadier-General T. H. Hardy to quell it. To join this force the 2nd Battalion was ordered to move on March 7th, 1918, and joined by a detachment of 1 Goorkha officer, with 25 rifles, from the 3/5th Goorkha Rifles they reached the base of operations at Harnai on the 12th. The following day it marched to Duki by the 16th, where the western column of the Marri Field Force was concentrating; this force consisting of the 1st South Lancs Regiment, 2/2nd Goorkhas, 107th Pioneers, 1 squadron 3rd Skinner's Horse, No. 3 Mountain Battery, and 1 Machine Gun Company. The force moved forward on March

Battalion joins the Marri Expedition, 7/3/18.

TYPICAL HILL COUNTRY IN THE MANIPUR STATE.

GOORKHAS HALTING AT A RIVER IN MANIPUR.

18th, reached Gūmbaz on the northern boundary of the Marri country, and on the 22nd the seizure of the Watwangi Pass, the main entrance to the country, was effected without loss to the column and with little opposition. The locality operated in now was one typical of that along the north-west border, very difficult to work over consisting as it does of steep, bare, rugged hills and broken valleys in which only a scanty vegetation is found owing to the very small rainfall (*Sketch XI*).

At Zrind on the summit of the Pass, the Battalion was split up, the Headquarters with two companies remaining here to picquet and protect the road up, the other two companies under Captain E. J. Corse Scott continuing on with the main column. It was on April 4th that the Marris were met in any force, in number some 1,500 or more, and who **Action of 4/4/18.** were holding a position on a high and almost inaccessible hill where they made their only stand. The attack was led by one company of 2/2nd Goorkhas and one platoon of the South Lancs, who succeeded in laboriously scaling the hill and attacking the enemy, of whom over 100 were killed, while many wounded were **Casualties.** carried off by their retreating comrades. Our casualties were slight, only 5 wounded; but this action broke the back of the revolt for further resistance soon ceased. Kāhan, their chief village, was occupied on April 18th, when the tribe **Chief village occu-** made full submission, and in early May the Field **pied during the** Force broke up. The following were mentioned in **Expedition, 18/4/18.** the subsequent despatch for good work done, viz., Subadar Gamer Sing Gurung, and 2403 Lance Naik Dhanraj Gurung.

While in the Marri Hills the much regretted news **Brig.-Gen. Fulton** was received that Brigadier-General H. T. Fulton, of ours, **killed, 29/3/18.** had been killed in France while in command of the 3rd New Zealand Infantry Brigade.

The Battalion returned to Tank by May 23rd, where it spent the hot weather in wretched huts in great heat and discomfort, which caused a high rate of sickness. A little later we were much split up, **Return to Tank,** having to furnish detachments at Pezu, Sheikh Budin, **23/5/18.** and Dera Ismael Khan, while a little later again the outposts of Jandola, Khirgi, Girni. and Jatta were added to our charge—all of them being places no one would ever desire to see again!

On December 3rd, 1918, the Battalion welcomed the return of Lieutenant-Colonel D. M. Watt who had been commanding the 145th Infantry Brigade in Italy, and who now took over temporary command for some months, Colonel Tillard rejoining his regiment.

Gen. Sir Arthur Barrett's Inspection, 14/1/19. While at Tank General Sir Arthur Barrett, G.C.B., K.C.S.I., commanding the Northern Army, inspected the Battalion on January 14th, 1919, and after presenting medals, made an address which will be found in Appendix D.

From January to March, 1919, brigade training was carried out in the neighbourhood of Pezu, and in the latter month the Regimental Band which had come up to Tank in early January, 1919, was sent back to Dehra. *En route* there the party was met at Kundiān railway station by a civil official who requisitioned their assistance, as a mob of rioters was threatening the railway station and public buildings of that town. The sudden appearance of our party of Bandsmen though armed solely with kookeries, was sufficient, and the mob dispersed. Rumours now began to get about relative to possible trouble with Afghanistan, but it was thought most unlikely that such would

Opening of 3rd Afghan War, 2/5/19. happen. This, however, did come about, for on May 2nd, 1919, an Afghan force crossed our border near Landi Kotal and descended on the Khyber Pass. In consequence of this and its probable effect all along the border land, the 2nd Battalion was ordered to mobilize at Dera Ismael Khan on May 6th for operations in the Derajāt district. It was the intention of General N. Woodyatt, General Officer Commanding

Battalion mobilizes at Dera Ismael Khan, 6/5/19. Derajāt Brigade, to despatch a column at once to Wāna, which was held by the Waziristhan Militia, whose attitude was very doubtful. This proposal was, however, vetoed by Simla with the result that later, lacking the support of Regulars, this militia unit mentioned, threw in its lot with the Afghans, killed their five British officers, and made off with a considerable amount of arms and loot.

Instead of to Wāna then the Battalion was sent with a squadron of the 27th Light Cavalry to Murtāza to assist in the withdrawal of the civil officials from the Gomal, Sarwakai, and other posts to the south,

Battalion in Waziristhan, May to Oct., 1919. and which in spite of intense heat was successfully carried out. The Battalion then marched to Khirgi to form part of the column assembling there under Brigadier-General Miles, and later was employed in picqueting the Zam River during the Relief of Jandola, also in establishing permanent picquet posts on both sides of the high road for some days, thus initiating the permanent picquet system which was adopted in all subsequent operations.

One of our companies under Captain A. L. Donaldson, took part in the action at Girni on June 4th, in which they had 2 men wounded, and ten days later Major J. E. Cruickshank took over temporary command of the Battalion from Colonel Watt, who left us for the Abbottabad Brigade. While here we learnt with much regret of the death of Captain D. Macintyre while in Switzerland for his health. He had been with us in France, had got very ill and had to be invalided.

Affair at Girni, 4/6/19.

The end of this month saw us moved into the hutted camp at Manzai, where our headquarters remained till the Battalion finally left Waziristhan, and during July two companies under Captain Donaldson were employed with a small column sent to protect the post at Murtāza, which was threatened by the enemy and with whom a brief encounter at long range ensued. The Mahsūd Waziris made several attacks on convoys and posts during August, necessitating various columns being sent out in which our Battalion took part, notably against raiders on the Murtāza—Khirgi road on the 7th, the second relief of Jandola on the 14th, Kaur Bridge action on the 22nd, and repelling an attack on the Girni Post on August 28th. None were of great importance or productive of the interest going with a good fight, but all entailed much hard marching in very great heat. In the last-named action a detachment of the 2/2nd Goorkhas attacked and drove a band of Mahsūds off the hills commanding the post, inflicting a number of casualties on them with a loss to us of 1 man killed and 2 wounded, 1 stretcher bearer was also killed (*Sketch XI*).

Various small attacks on Convoys and Posts, Aug., 1919.

Girni Post attacked, 28/8/19.

The next two months were spent at Manzai more or less quietly, small parties only occasionally being sent out after raiding gangs, in escorts, or reconnaissances; and in late October a mixed column of which we formed part, was attacked while returning from Girni. Some confusion occurred here owing to the Mahsūds penetrating the front of the rearmost unit, but a counter-attack by one of our companies restored the situation, the tribesmen being driven off with considerable loss, our casualties being only 1 wounded.

Our Column attacked on march, Oct., 1919.

Trouble of a political nature now showed itself in Scinde low down the Indus Valley, and the 2/2nd Goorkhas were ordered to Hyderabad and Karachi

Battalion ordered to Karachi and Hyderabad, 23/10/19. as a protective measure, leaving the dust and discomfort of Manzai and Waziristhan generally to the relief of all on October 23rd, 1919. Prior to quitting this most unpleasing part of the North-West Frontier where the Battalion had spent nearly two years, most of which was on active service, the General Officer Commanding Waziristhan Field Force (General Sir S. H. Climo) inspected us thanking all for the part they had played in the various operations, and expressing his regret at having to lose our further services. His order of the day will be found in Appendix *D*.

The casualties of the Battalion in this tour of service were slight, amounting to 2 men killed, 4 wounded, while 4 men died of disease. The undermentioned men became the recipients of the award of the Indian Distinguished Service Medal for services in Waziristhan, viz , No. 1935 Havildar Dhanraj Gurung, and No. 4176 Lance Naik Ude Bura ; while the following were " mentioned " in subsequent despatches :—

Honours and "Mentions."
Major J. E. Cruickshank.
Captain N. J. Hind.
Lieutenant H. Green (I.A.R.O.).
Lieutenant G. H. Woollcombe.

Subadar Bahadur Ghale.
No. 3677 Havildar Bhanu Gurung.
No. 1935 Havildar Dhanraj Gurung.
No. 2092 Havildar Gajbir Thapa.
No. 2346 Havildar Gamu Sing Gurung.
No. 1803 Quartermaster Havildar Lilambar Gurung.
No. 4166 Lance Naik Gagan Sing Thapa.
No. 4176 Lance Naik Ude Bura.
No. 2944 Rifleman Hira Sing Newar.

An extract from the despatch by His Excellency the Commander-in-Chief, India (General Sir Charles Monro) on the operations of the Third Afghan War (May to August, 1919), shows that General Climo brought the Battalion to his notice as being one of those specially deserving of mention.

The Battalion Headquarters with two companies were located at Hyderabad (Scinde), and the other two companies at Karachi till January, 1920, being chiefly employed in garrison duties until the political atmosphere in that district had calmed down, when the 2nd Battalion was **Battalion returns to Dehra end of Jan., 1920.** released from duties far afield and returned to Dehra Doon by the end of that month.

On April 2nd, as Colonel Boileau's tenure of command

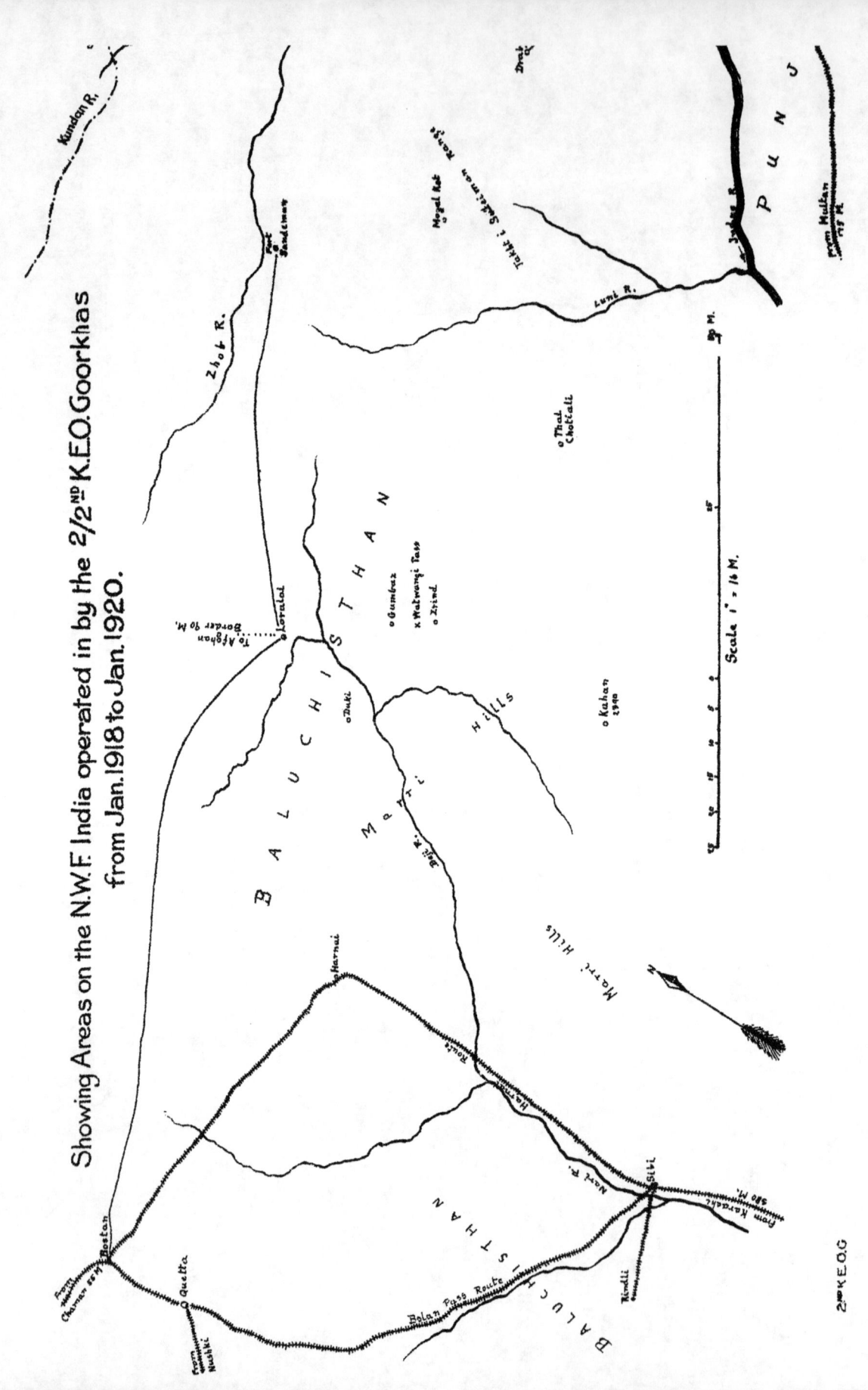

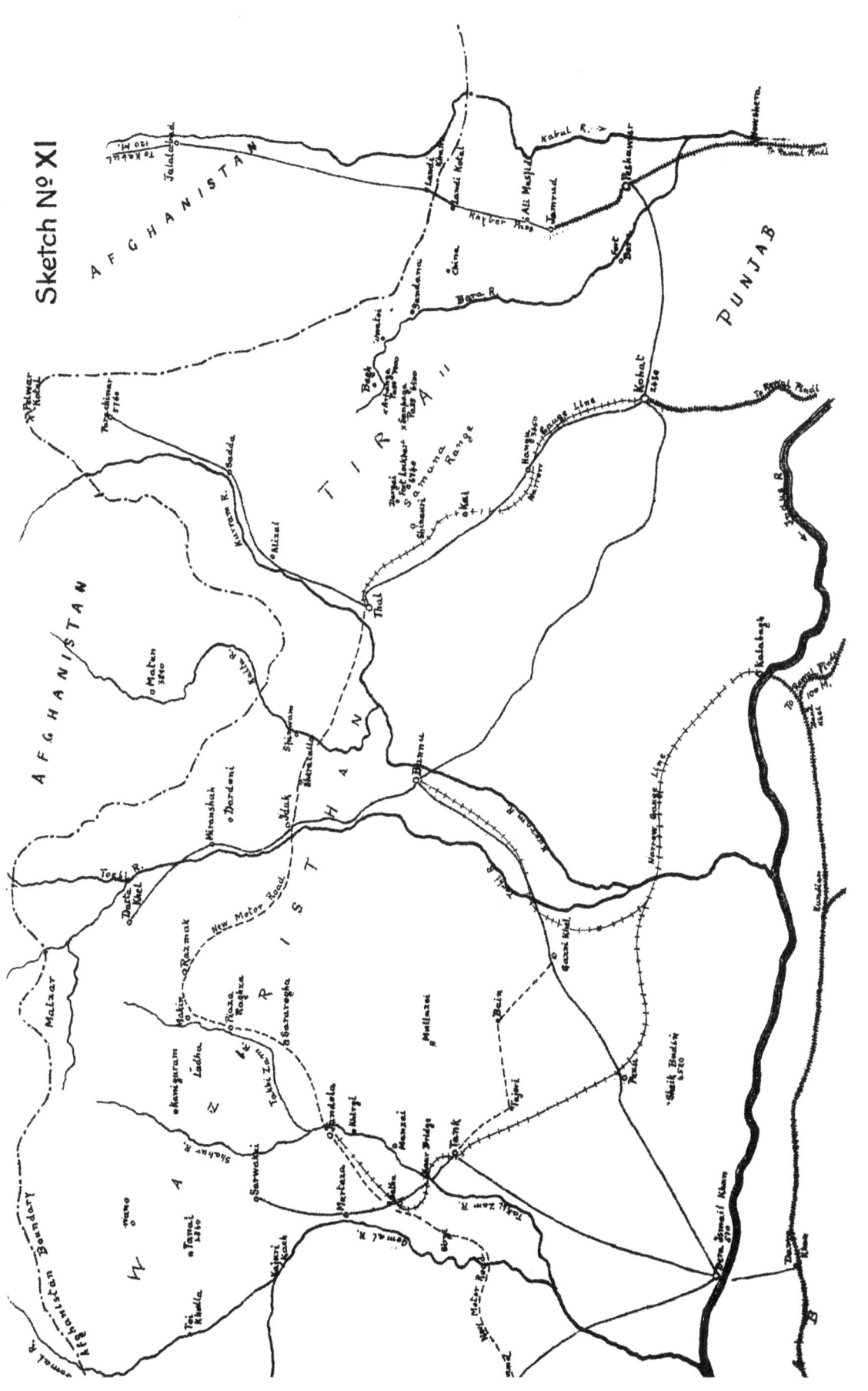

had expired, he was succeeded by Brevet Lieutenant-Colonel K. Wigram, of ours, who had been for some years holding important positions on the Staff of the Army at Simla and in France during the war.

The business of reorganizing the Battalion and demobilizing surplus men was taken in hand when all had settled down once more in cantonments, and this occupied most of the hot weather. The 3rd Battalion, which had returned to Dehra from Peshawur, had also to be disbanded, those men desiring to remain on in the service being absorbed in the old battalions together with a proportion of British and Goorkha officers.

3rd Battalion disbanded, 3/10/20.

PART II. MESOPOTAMIA AND NORTH PERSIA

SUBADAR-MAJOR SARABJIT GURUNG, M.C., SIRDAR BAHADUR, BEING PRESENTED WITH THE KING'S COMMISSION AS LIEUTENANT BY H.R.H. THE PRINCE OF WALES, AT DEHRA, ON MARCH 13th, 1922.

CHAPTER XIV.

OCTOBER, 1914, TO APRIL, 1916. (*Sketches XII, XIII, XV.*)

HAVING set forth the doings of our 2nd Battalion in Europe and India during the period covering the Great War, we can now turn and follow the fortunes of our sister unit in Mesopotamia and Persian fields ; but first we may briefly note occurrences affecting our cantonment in this period.

During 1914 the Forest Research Institute, which since 1906 had been located in cantonments a little to the south of the Mess House, was increased by new buildings which were occupied in 1915. Later on, viz., in 1920, a new site was chosen for this institute west of the Kaulaghir Tea Estate abutting on our cantonments, and building commenced the following year. The new extension was indicative of the enormous progress made by this go ahead department, for in 1915 the new buildings in cantonments were considered large enough for all contingencies, yet five years later the Institute was able to prove that the revenue resulting from research was so great as to justify much larger and better equipped buildings, the actual cost of which was 7% of the total revenue resulting from one year's work of the department.

Cantonment and Regimental matters.

A reference to the first volume of the Regimental History will show the start of the Imperial Cadet Corps in cantonments for Indian Princes, under the direction of Lord Curzon in 1900. From various natural causes the institution declined in numbers until from Princes, later not forthcoming, it had to take in young Indian gentlemen of lesser rank, and finally the whole expensive scheme was abandoned in 1914-15. The buildings thereafter were first utilized as a War Hospital, and later on (1918) as a Motor Transport School. In 1922 it developed into the Royal Indian Military College for the training of young Indian gentlemen desirous of obtaining commissions in the Indian Army, and was opened on March 13th, 1922, by His Royal Highness The Prince of Wales, who also during his visit to Dehra held a parade at which he presented Subadar-Major Sarabjit Gurung with the King's Commission as Lieutenant.

During 1914 important alterations in the lighting of cantonments came into being as the Dehra Municipal Electric Supply were able to extend their power. The Mess now sold their engine, and private houses gradually had electric light installed.

The Regiment, which had already bought up certain of the privately-owned houses in our cantonment extended its purchasing powers in 1920, taking over the bungalows owned by Colonel Boileau, Major Macpherson, and Captain Nicholl, also one known as " Orange Lodge," whereby it became possessed of most of the house property in the old cantonment.

A reference to our little hill camp at Sarona was, I find, omitted in the first volume, so may be entered here. A desire had long been felt to own a bit of land as the Regiment's own property somewhere up in the hills within easy reach to which recruits, sickly men, and families could be sent during the hot weather; also companies in turn for hill training. To this end about 1907 search was made for suitable ground in the outer range by Subadar-Major Santbir Gurung and Subadar Man Sing Bohra, who in due time reported a good site available near the village of Sarona on one of the southern spurs of Jālki (Tōp Tiba) at an elevation of about 4,400 feet, and some 12 miles from cantonments. This site was then visited by Captains Wigram and Nicholl and myself, who all finally decided on buying the piece of land ourselves and making it over to the Regiment. The two Goorkha officers mentioned arranged the purchase, the site becoming ours the following year. It is some 4 acres in extent, capable of holding tents for a company, the recruits, and 3 or 4 officers, on the top of a spur facing east and the Donalti Range. Water was good from a spring in a ravine below and to north of the camp. A pucca building with an upper storey was then built at its eastern end for the use of families, and a short rifle range arranged for. During the first three or four years the approach from Sahansadāra was difficult, our fatigue parties made a roughly graded path up a steep spur from Majhāra hamlet to Sarona village; but it was not till 1912 that a decent road was made by the Raja of Tehri, who, to get a shorter outlet for his country's produce to the Dehra markets without having to go through Mussoorie with its octroi posts, put his Imperial Service Troops (Sappers and Miners) on to construct a proper bridle path from the high road near Jālki village to Sarona thence slanting gradually down into the valley at Sahansadāra and so to Nāgal and Dehra. The site was regularly used every hot weather season and was generally approved by all.

Questions having lately been asked me *re* the origin of the dice border on the 2nd Goorkhas' head-dress and the red piping round the collars in khaki and black serge—points which I had forgotten in the early volume of the History—I may state here that the dice border was introduced by Colonel

Macpherson (later General Sir H. Macpherson) when he commanded the Regiment from 1862 to 1876, and the authority for this information was Colonel W. Hill, formerly Commandant of our 1st Battalion, who had served under Colonel Macpherson and who told us this when the 2nd Battalion was raised in early 1886. Whether Colonel Macpherson introduced it in memory of any Scotch regiment with which either he or the Regiment had been associated in early days is not known. It may well have been either, or even his own clan tartan pattern, for in days prior to the abolition of John Company a certain licence in dress distinctions seems to have been allowed to units. In the Mutiny time we wore black Kilmarnock caps, and the earliest pictorial record of the dice border which the writer remembers seeing was in an old *Illustrated London News* depicting the various Indian officers of the Contingent at Malta in 1877, and in which it is distinctly shown on the caps of our Goorkha officers.

The red piping on the collar we were told was instituted in the early "sixties" by the same Commandant, probably when we became a Regular Rifle Regiment, discarded our colours, and adopted the uniform of the 60th Rifles, who most probably wore it in the white drill uniform of those days. When the 2nd Battalion was raised in 1886 the old battalion wore a darkish grey drill cloth in the hot weather, and all ranks wore trousers (slacks), the wearing of putties and fast dyed khaki came in about 1888 or 1889. Previous to the introduction of fast dyed khaki our hot weather uniforms had to be steeped frequently in liquid abomination which when fresh smelt to high Heaven, and for which purpose there was a "rangrez" (dyer) with each company.

The latter part of 1914 and the whole of the next year was passed by the 1st Battalion in Dehra, chafing at not being able to take part in the world struggle, but amazingly busy in training recruits, preparing and despatching drafts to France, training Indian Army Reserve Officers, furnishing detachments for Allahabad and Cawnpore, and as we have seen, some of its British officers attending to the efficiency needs of the Nepalese battalions sent to Dehra. It had also been called on to despatch a draft of 100 men under Lieutenants Thomson and Trotter with Subadar Lachman Khattrie and Jemadar Narain Sing Gurung, which left Dehra on December 10th, 1915, for

Draft for 5th Goorkha Rifles in Gallipoli, 10/12/15.
Gallipoli as a reinforcement for the 1/5th Goorkha Rifles. By the time they reached Suez the operations there had been brought to a close, so here they were detained to await the arrival of that battalion. The 2/2nd Goorkhas arriving at Suez from France, the draft hoped to be attached to them, but owing to the 1/5th Goorkha Rifles being sadly

reduced in strength this was not allowed. This unit on arrival was sent out to El Kubri, a post in the Canal defences 10 miles north of Suez, and 5 miles out in the desert, with only occasional interchange of shots with mounted Turkish patrols to enliven the time.

As soon as the Canal was free of danger troops began to be moved back to India or to Mesopotamia, and in April, 1916, the draft (still attached to the 1/5th Goorkha Rifles) returned to India, where they spent two months at Peshawur and returned with that battalion to Abbottabad till September, 1916, when the draft was sent back to our depot at Dehra Doon. Of the 2 British officers Lieutenant Thomson had a little before this been sent to East Africa, while Lieutenant Trotter went to join our battalion in Mesopotamia.

Colonel W. Beynon, D.S.O., having been appointed to command the Nowshera Brigade, the officiating command of the 1/2nd Goorkhas had at this time devolved upon Major B. Nicholl.

Mobilization orders received early Feb., 1916.

Embarkation at Karachi, 13/2/16.

At last in early February, 1916, rumours as to probable active service became a joyful fact, for instructions to mobilize for Mesopotamia were soon followed by orders to move, and the 1st Battalion left Dehra in two troop trains on February 10th, reaching Karachi at 9.30 a.m. on the 13th; and embarking on the s.s. *Thongwa*, sailed at 7 p.m. that night for Basra.

The strength of the Battalion on leaving India was as noted below*, making a total of 824 of all ranks.

The British officers proceeding with the Battalion were:—

Major B. R. Nicholl, officiating in command.
Captain P. A. R. Pritchard, 4th D.C.C.
Captain H. F. Marsh, 1st D.C.C.
Lieutenant N. G. R. Woodyatt, 2nd D.C.C.
Lieutenant F. I. S. Tuker, 3rd D.C.C.
Captain A. H. R. Saunders, Adjutant.
2/Lieutenant H. R. Traill, Quartermaster.
2/Lieutenant W. G. H. Gough, No. 1 D.C.O.

Battalion strength for active service, Feb., 1916.

2/Lieutenant I. A. S. H. Monro, No. 2 D.C.O.
2/Lieutenant F. S. Harrison, No. 3 D.C.O.
2/Lieutenant W. H. M. C. Brodie, Signalling Officer.

* British officers, 14; Goorkha officers, 17; S.A.S., 1; non-commissioned officers, 80; riflemen, 654; ward orderly, 1. First reinforcement:—Goorkha officers, 2; non-commissioned officers, 8; riflemen, 47.

ASHAR CREEK, BASRA.

A STERNWHEELER ON THE TIGRIS.

2/Lieutenant L. E. Morgan, Machine Gun Officer.
2/Lieutenant G. H. Bruce Kerr, Transport Officer.
Lieutenant A. M. Ramsay, I.M.S., Medical Officer.

Major Harcourt being reported on as unfit for active service owing to a weak heart, took over the Depot on rejoining from leave. Captain R. D. Hill rejoined the Battalion on April 1st from duty with the Chitral Scouts. Major E. Ridgeway on recruiting duty at Darjiling was asked for, but could not be released at the time and was not able to join on service till some months later, and Lieutenant Newall was with the Air Force.

Basra was reached after an uneventful voyage on the morning of February 18th, 1916, and early next morning the transport moved up to Māgil, 3 miles above the town, where disembarkation at once began, and by evening we had pitched camp and all impedimenta had been brought up; though this had to be carried up by the men 1½ miles owing to lack of transport carts. Here it was learnt that we were to belong to the 37th Brigade, newly forming under Brigadier-General F. G. Fowler, D.S.O., of which ours was the first unit to arrive, the next to come up the following day being the 1/4th Somerset Light Infantry (a Territorial battalion), but the Brigade was not completed till some while later.

Basra reached, 18/2/16.

This country being absolutely new to us, a few remarks on it and the reasons for this particular expedition having been undertaken as a large side issue of the Great War, may be of interest to our future officers. The general aspect of the country is dead level, a desert of sun-baked alluvial soil through which flow the Euphrates and Tigris Rivers, both uniting at Kurnah to form the Shatt el Arab, which then flows on roughly 110 miles to the Persian Gulf. The only greenery to be seen anywhere is along the banks of the rivers which are bordered by large and valuable date palm groves varying in breadth from 200 yards to 2 miles in the vicinity of Basra; beyond this belt on either side stretches the desert. A country as we found it of sand, mud, mirage, and blazing heat according to the season (*Sketch XV*).

Description of country and Basra.

The city and port of Basra was famous in the East for ages, but centuries of Turkish misrule had brought about its decay; though in modern times its prosperity has somewhat revived, chiefly through the date and liquorice root trade, for which it is the central mart. It has been styled the "Venice of the East" by some writers, a title far too flattering as such little beauty it possesses is due solely to its setting of palm trees, some gardens, and its numerous and evil smelling intersecting canals on which ply "bellums"—long narrow boats with some slight resemblance to gondolas, and which canals are a constant source of fever. The main portion of the city lies 2 miles inland, a quarter as we found it in November, 1914, with narrow unpaved insanitary streets, and two to three storied houses of half burnt bricks. The population, some 70,000, is composed largely of Arabs, Armenians, and Jews—a low class crowd, the whole place rather recalling Port Said in the early " eighties " before we instituted law, order, and sanitation. Ashar town on the Shatt el Arab constitutes the so-called port and here dwell the various Consuls, commercial people, and so forth.

A little above Basra is Māgil, which the Germans intended to be the terminus of their Berlin–Baghdad–Persian Gulf Railway, where we found certain of their buildings and miles and miles of railway lines and sleepers carefully stacked. Below it some 20 miles from the sea is Abadān with its oil refineries, etc., the end of the oil pipe line which comes down from the Shustar Valley just in Persian territory and 120 miles off.

The Turks entered the war against us in late October, 1914, and in the beginning of November the 6th Poona Division, under General Sir Arthur Barrett, formerly commanding the 5th Goorkha Rifles and subsequently raised to the rank of a Field-Marshal, was despatched to Mesopotamia. The intention of the Government of India at the time was to occupy Basra and

Brief account of early part of Campaign, Nov., 1914, to Feb., 1916.
to hold only that " vilayat " viz., up to Amāra on the Tigris, and to Nasiriyeh on the Euphrates, this being all that was required to round off our complete control of the Persian Gulf to protect the Shustar oilfield, pipe line and important works at Abadān, and to block the projected German Baghdad–Basra railway scheme. Other incidents and views plus ambition landed the British in difficulties farther afield, the original expedition developing into the long and serious campaign into which our 1st Battalion now was to make its debut (*Sketch XV*).

Basra was occupied unopposed on November 23rd, 1914, after some fighting on the way up, and what was spoken of as a port which presupposed jetties, wharfs, cranes, etc., was found by the 6th Division to be entirely destitute of any such needs and appliances, the Germans only having built a small, decent jetty with two movable cranes at Māgil. Steamers lay in midstream, here some 800 yards wide, and discharged cargoes into small boats, which landed their loads on the mud bank anyhow. By the time the 1/2nd Goorkhas landed a certain number of good jetties and wharfs had been built by the Sappers and Labour Corps with endless toil and expense, every bit of timber having to come from India, and stone from the neighbourhood of

Koweit on the Gulf, the country being entirely lacking in either article. Kurnah, 48 miles upstream of Basra, was attacked and taken in February, 1915, and serious fighting took place during March and April at and around Shaiba, 12 miles west of Basra, ending in the Battle of Burjesiah and rout of Suleiman Askāri Bey's force. The second Battle of Kurnah on May 31st, 1915, followed by the pursuit and destruction of the Turkish gun-boats next day, led to the capture of Amāra a few days later. In August the 12th Division under General Gorringe, after completing a most arduous task in clearing the Turks and Arabs from the neighbourhood of Ahwaz and Hawaisa, where they threatened (and at one time did break) the oil pipe line, proceeded up the Euphrates and took Nasiriyeh after hard and continuous fighting. In September, 1915, the British move beyond Amāra (not originally intended by the Government of India) resulted in the successful battle of Ctesiphon, a prelude to advancing on Baghdad which now was deemed politically desirable, that city being the focus of all Turkish lines of advance down the two great rivers or into Persia. Its seizure if possible—and the Turks had been well beaten—would be the outward and visible sign to our credit against the serious conditions in Gallipoli, while failure to take advantage of the apparently favourable conditions would be looked on as weakness. Optimism on the spot had prevailed in spite of our scattered forces and long line of communications. But large and unexpected forces of Turkish Regulars arriving, compelled the retirement of the 6th Division under General Townshend to Kūt-el-Amāra, where the force was cut off and surrounded. To effect his relief was the object of the large force under General Aylmer, V.C., which had incurred heavy fighting at Sheikh Saad, Orah, and other places during the winter of 1915-16 before our 1st Battalion arrived to join in the struggle ; and this force was now engaged on both banks of the Tigris—the 3rd Lahore Division opposite the Es Sinn and Dujailah positions on the right bank, the 7th Meerut and 13th British Divisions opposite the Falāhiya and Sannayat positions on left bank. Every effort was being made to break the Turkish opposition, and get through to relieve Kūt (*Sketch XV*).

Russian Allies. A Russian force was also operating in Asia Minor against the Turks, the nearest unit to General Aylmer's force being a Division under General Barātov advancing from Hamadan to Khānakin in the Persian hill country some 250 miles from the British right flank.

During their stay at Māgil the Battalion was chiefly employed on road making and building embankments to keep out the flood water which covers this part of the country in the spring, and is due to heavy rains followed by the melting of the snow in the mountains of Asia Minor.

The third unit of the 37th Brigade, viz., the 36th Sikhs, arrived on February 26th, and three days later the Battalion received orders to move, proceeding up-river in detachments as boats were available; *P7*, a paddle-boat, and the *Mejidieh* river steamer taking three Double-Companies, both towing barges on which the men were accommodated. The fourth Double-Company left Māgil a day later on barges carrying loads of high explosive shells for the front, towed by the little tug *Shurur*.

37th Brigade forming at Māgil, Feb., 1916.

The voyage was monotonous to a degree above Kurnah for the flood water covered the country as far as the eye could see, and Amāra was reached on March 3rd, where a day's halt was made. Above Ali Gharbi the next stage the war zone was entered, necessitating precautions for defence by placing the machine guns at stern and bow, allotting alarm posts, etc., as hostile cavalry with guns were reported moving on the right bank.

Battalion reaches the front, 5/3/16.

On March 5th Orah, on the right bank, was reached at 9 a.m., and landing commenced at once, followed by orders to move up to the front next day. The 1/4th Somersets and 1/2nd Goorkhas at this time represented the 37th Brigade—the 36th Sikhs being still at Māgil and the 64th Pioneers not yet in the country.

Composition of 37th Brigade.

That day was spent in loading up the two country boats (mahelas) allotted us to take the 10 days' rations, kits, etc., by river, while we marched; the scale for the latter now being, British officers 20 pounds, others 1 blanket each only. Our fourth Double-Company having arrived, the two Regiments moved off at 7 p.m., marching 4 miles to Senna Camp which was not reached without much delay and confusion, the routes of several other units crossing with ours.

Orders and arrangements for attack, 7/3/16.

On March 7th came orders for operations against the Dujailah Redoubt, the southern end of the Turkish Es Sinn entrenched position. The operations were under the direction of General Sir F. J. Aylmer, V.C., and were intended to relieve the situation on the left bank where the Meerut and 13th Divisions had assaulted the enemy, strongly dug in at Um el Hanna, in mid January several times, being repulsed with heavy losses. It was the failure of our assaults on Um el Hanna that started trench warfare in Mesopotamia. Before this position was captured on April 5th nearly 16 miles of trenches, deeper than those in France, had been dug by our troops.

COUNTRY BOAT AND SMALL "MASHOOF" NEAR AMARA.

Sketch by L.W.S.

The Brigades of the Lahore Division to be employed were as noted below,* and were divided into three columns—" A," " B," and " C," which were to rendezvous at the Pool of Siloam 3 miles south-west of Senna Camp, and move from there south-west by west to the position for deployment where the columns would separate. " A " to proceed to the south of the objective—" B " to take position still farther south-west, both being under General Kemball—" C," with which was the 37th Brigade and our Battalion, also the 7th and 8th Brigades under General Keary (General Officer Commanding 3rd Lahore Division) to take position 1,200 yards east of the redoubt. At dawn on March 8th " A " and " B " columns were to open the attack, and while this was in progress " C " column was to advance to within 500 yards of the redoubt and attack, but was not to press the attack home or to enter the position on this side owing to reports as to it having been mined; their entry was to be from the south side after the first assaults had got home. (*Sketch XII.*)

The 37th Brigade marched at 6.15 p.m. reaching the rendezvous an hour later and halted till 11.20 p.m., the three columns then moving forward over the open plain in line of double companies at deploying interval. At 5.30 a.m. on March 8th " C " Column arrived at the deploying position, advancing again as soon as its front was cleared by the movements of " A " and " B."

Night march, March 7th-8th, 1916.

This night march of some 20 miles presented unusual difficulties in the assembly and guidance of so large a force in the dark, over a country previously untrodden by the British, and featureless save for a few nullahs and low scattered sand-hills, but it was successfully accomplished, and the columns struck their objective points accurately. We were in position some 1,400 yards east of the redoubt with the Somersets on our left by 6.35 a.m., the only enemy to be seen thus far having been an Arab mounted patrol which the Battalion scouts dispersed, and this was followed by a short burst of rifle fire from the enemy. Our guns now opened on a group of tents to south-east of the position creating considerable confusion among Arab troops camped there, it was getting light and the high mound marking the Turkish main position standing up well on the plain could be clearly seen. There was however, little or no movement on the enemy's part, and it appeared as if the position was inadequately held, but no sound came as yet from " A "

Action at the Dujailah Redoubt, 8/3/16.

---

* *C* : 7th, 8th, and 37th Infantry Brigades ; *A* : 9th and 28th Infantry Brigades ; *B* : 36th Infantry Brigade. *Reserve* : 35th Infantry Brigade, 6th Cavalry Brigade, 90 guns.

and "B" columns, and advantage was taken to dig ourselves in on the line we had reached and to bring up the machine guns under Lieutenant Morgan. About 10 a.m. the enemy began a desultory shelling of our line and that of the Somersets in which Rifleman Gagan Sing Thapa had the uncomfortable honour of being our first casualty, hit in the leg. A little later a stream of Turkish reinforcements were seen entering the redoubt by what appeared to be a hole in the top of the mound, their rifle fire increased, and the roar of battle was heard from the other columns. Our machine guns were now in action but owing to instability of their mountings were of little effect. Meanwhile unfortunate delays occurring to "A" and "B" columns their attack did not start till too late to effect the intended surprise. To "C" column it was evident, and also from an aviator's report, that the portion of the redoubt facing it was weakly held, and had this force been allowed to attack then, the results of the day would have been very different. But as one account states, the shelling of the camp by the Corps Artillery in rear of "C" column apprised the enemy of what we were up to, and they poured reinforcements into the place from Magasis and from across the river, as fast as they could. The strict orders *re* time of attacks of each column and other details were not to be departed from, and so the 37th and 7th Brigades waited through the morning under heavy shelling knowing the golden opportunity to be gone. General Kemball's force—36th, 9th, and 28th Brigades—advanced on the south end of the redoubt in face of heavy opposition from concealed positions to left and trenches in front of the main position, and were held up again and again, incurring great loss. It later transpired that the reinforcements poured into the Dujailah Redoubt early that morning were picked troops recently arrived from their success in Gallipoli ; add to this that the position sloped up a long glacis to the redoubt some 20 feet or more above the plain over which the British were attacking, and it will readily be understood how costly such an attack would prove. By 4.30 p.m. no material progress had been made, and it was then that General Keary's column ("C") was let loose.

Returning to our Battalion. After a long wait a message was received from General Kemball that he would attack at 2.30 p.m. and asking that the 1/2nd Goorkhas might advance their left flank to assist the assault. This was done under heavy fire from snipers in concealed trenches, when Captain Marsh, later rewarded with the Military Cross, was wounded in the leg, and many other casualties occurred. Nos. 1 and 4 then remained in this position till they joined in the final assault. At 4 p.m. on receipt of information that the 7th Brigade would assault on our right, Captain Saunders went forward to see the ground and was hit in the

TURKISH PRISONERS MARCHING INTO AMARA.

arm, but completed his reconnaissance and returned to the support trench from which he later again advanced with No. 2 Company leading the assault. They were covered by Nos. 1 and 4 who then followed on, the troops penetrating and occupying two of the enemy's trench lines, where severe hand-to-hand fighting went on. But the assaults all failed in face of the superior numbers the Turks had had time to bring up, and our supply of bombs giving out we were driven out again, the enemy leaving their trenches and from the flanks bombing our men back. At about 5.30 p.m. the final retirement of the 37th Brigade was ordered and a more or less quiet night was spent some miles back.

Assault on Dujailah Redoubt, 8/3/16.

In this our first action, our casualty list was a heavy one, for it showed we had lost Major Nicholl, known to have been wounded, but missing and believed killed, and Captain Saunders with Lieutenant Woodyatt also missing and later found to have been killed—officers, indeed, whom we could but ill afford to lose, they being of the very best. Our total casualties came to 204, viz., 96 killed, 108 wounded. Rifleman Padam Sing Gurung was awarded the Indian Order of Merit, and several others received recognition for acts of gallantry. Captain Saunders was recommended for the Distinguished Service Order, but this was refused on the grounds that posthumous Distinguished Service Orders were not granted.

Our Casualties, 8/3/16.

On March 9th at 3 p.m. orders were received to retire on Wadi Camp, the 1/2nd Goorkhas forming the right flank guard, during which movement a number of casualties were caused by Turkish shrapnel, the enemy following and occupying the Twin Canal position from which eventually they were pushed out by the 7th Brigade (*Sketch XII*).

Retirement from Dujailah Redoubt, 9/3/16.

That evening a position was taken up for the night, and our guns for a time were active; there was no water, as the so-called Pools of Siloam were too brackish for drinking, and our men suffered severely from thirst and lack of food till camp on the Tigris opposite Wadi was reached on the afternoon of March 10th, and most of that night was spent in digging defences. The next two days were passed at Wadi in bad weather, heavy rains turning the plain into a morass. In the action at the Dujailah Redoubt our Brigadier had been wounded, and it was a pleasure to find his successor for a time was to be General S. H. Edwardes, D.S.O., an old friend of the Regiment's in former years at Dehra.

Wadi Camp reached, 10/3/16.

The next move of the Battalion was back to Senna camp on the evening of the 13th and in better weather, where we relieved the 93rd Infantry, who were holding a front of 700 yards with the 92nd Punjabis on the right and the Somersets on the left. Later, as the 92nd were sent to Arab Village, their vacated line was added to ours, increasing the Battalion's frontage to 1,200 yards. While here the following message from General Aylmer was communicated to the Brigade :—" I wish to tell the 37th Brigade how much I appreciate what they did at the Sinn battle (Dujailah) on the 8th inst."

<small>Battalion relieves 93rd Infantry, 13/3/16.</small>

Here we remained till the end of the month, with the exception of two double companies which were sent forward to hold a position on the Twin Canals (*Sketch XII*), the days being mostly spent in building a strong embankment to keep off flood water, as the Tigris, $1\frac{1}{2}$ miles to our right, was rising rapidly, and already the water was entering some of the flank trenches. When this was drained off large numbers of fish up to 6 pounds in weight were left behind, forming a welcome addition to the men's rations. We also were able to learn much of trench life and routine from our old Dehra friends, the 1/9th Goorkha Rifles, who occupied part of the line not far from us, and who had been much longer on service than we had. On March 24th 2/Lieutenant Gough, with Havildar Ran Sing Thapa and Naik Jitia Sing Gurung, were sent to the Divisional Headquarters for a course of instruction in the use of the new " ball bomb " (Mills), of which the Battalion had just received a supply. A few days later we relieved the 1/9th Goorkha Rifles and also formed a Depot under Lieutenant Traill at Orah a little below Wadi on the right bank. Work in this new position was the building of a redoubt and assisting the R.A. in digging gun positions, and until the arrival of Colonel Sweet the temporary command of the Battalion had fallen to Captain Pritchard.

<small>A Wing at Twin Canals.</small>

On April 1st we were joined by Captain R. D. Hill, who had been on duty in Chitral, the return of an old officer being very welcome now, in view of the casualties which had taken toll of our seniors. Road works were now taken on in addition to ordinary fatigues until the 5th, when fresh operations were to be started, co-operating with renewed efforts against the Turkish entrenchments on the left bank at Um el Hanna, Falāhiya, and about Sannayat, and the 37th Brigade moved north to the Abu Romān position which the enemy had vacated without much opposition, and dug itself in. The 36th Sikhs and Somersets held the front line,

<small>37th Brigade moves to Abu Romān to co-operate in left bank offensive, 5/4/16.</small>

with the 1/2nd Goorkhas in reserve, while the 8th Brigade moved up on the right, the 7th on the left. Here we came under shell fire from the direction of Beit Aiessa, which our aeroplanes reported as being held in force. The position we now occupied was almost in line with that of the troops at Falāhiya (left bank); the enemy's lines at Um el Hanna and Falāhiya had just been successfully taken on the 5th after a heavy bombardment and casualties to our force of 2,700 men; and the 13th British Division was about to attack Sannayat, the Turk's next position.

The hostile position at Beit Aiessa lay about $2\frac{1}{2}$ miles in front of us to our right, and covered the river flank of the Sannayat entrenchments. However, operations had to be delayed owing to flood water conditions, the river having burst one of the "bunds," covering the country to our rear and left flank. Turkish activity showed itself in addition to shelling, by building up observation mounds—the only way of getting any extended view over the vast dead-level plains, some 2,000 odd yards in front of our lines, and which the "Tommies" somewhat appropriately named "The Pimple" and the "Boil." Lieutenant Morgan, with his machine guns, frequently disturbed their working parties, who finally gave up the effort of completing them.

Floods delay operations.

The country all round was not only a dead-level, but was covered at this season with low-growing scrub jungle, which made it easy for snipers to get concealment and very difficult and hazardous for our patrols to get information. We had a number of casualties during reconnaissances, and the only effective way of dealing with the trouble was to sweep the ground with machine-gun fire before any advance was made.

The country on Tigris Front.

Continued heavy rain during April 10th and 11th made any advance impossible; the first attack on Sannayat had failed, and our only move was to support the 36th Sikhs south of Abu Romān (*Sketch XII*), where the 37th and 8th Brigades were directed to establish a strong line of picquets and to concentrate near the Somerset Headquarters. The following day two Double Companies were sent to strengthen the picquet line, which was much harried by snipers, through whose successful attentions that day the Battalion had 1 man killed and 19 wounded, Lieutenant Tuker being among the latter. April 14th saw Lieutenant-Colonel Sweet, who had been in France with our 2nd Battalion, then in temporary command of the 2/8th Goorkha Rifles in France and Egypt, and Major Bruce, who had also been with the 2nd Battalion in France, join us, the former taking command.

Casualties near Abu Romān, 12/4/16.

Next day orders came to push forward the strong picquet line to a new position some 150 yards west of "The Pimple" mound, where our left would link with the right of the 7th Brigade, the Somersets carrying on the line to our right.

New front line formed. Casualties, 13/4/16. This was carried out by evening and the new front consolidated, not without loss to us, for the move was exposed to heavy machine-gun fire, which accounted for 2 riflemen killed, 2/Lieutenant Monro, Jemadar Champa Sing, and 21 riflemen wounded. During April 16th the 27th Punjabis relieved us, and the Battalion bivouacked about 500 yards in rear of the trenches, having 6 men wounded in the move.

Battalion in Divisional Reserve during action, Beit Aiessa, April 16th-17th, 1916. Next day the 37th Brigade found itself in reserve to the 3rd Lahore Division, which was attacking the Beit Aiessa (*Sketch XII*) position, and we advanced some distance north of "The Pimple" under shell fire, the 1/2nd Goorkhas and Somersets in the front line, followed by the 36th Sikhs in support. Hardly was this done than fresh orders sent us back 4 miles south to occupy a line previously held by the Turks, and from which direction it was expected an attack might be made. A bombing party was sent ahead to see if these trenches were held, when they were fired on by three picquets, who retired, and it was found the Turks were in no strength about here. At 10 p.m. that night another change of position was ordered, which was hardly effected when at 1 a.m. we were told to hand over this new position to the Somersets and to move north to relieve the Manchester Regiment. While all these vexatious moves were being carried out the action at Beit Aiessa could be heard going on, which then died down, to break out again with renewed intensity indicating serious counter-attacks.

Capture of Beit Aiessa position, 17/4/16.

We learnt later that the 3rd Division had been successful in capturing Beit Aiessa after heavy fighting, that it was occupied and held against several very stiff counter-attacks by the Turks during the night, who were said to have lost near 4,000 men in the action, and the Manchesters had been sent up to assist in defence of the ground won. The casualties on the British side were severe, our friends the 1/9th Goorkha Rifles being badly cut up. Towards dawn firing almost ceased, and with the first streaks of daylight we could see in the distance the enemy retiring towards Chahela, line through line in most perfect order, although our guns were playing on them. Casualties in the Battalion during the last two days had been 17 men wounded and 3 missing (later found killed), among the former being Subadar-Major Motilal Lama and Jemadar Pertab Sahi.

Our casualties, April 16th-17th, 1916.

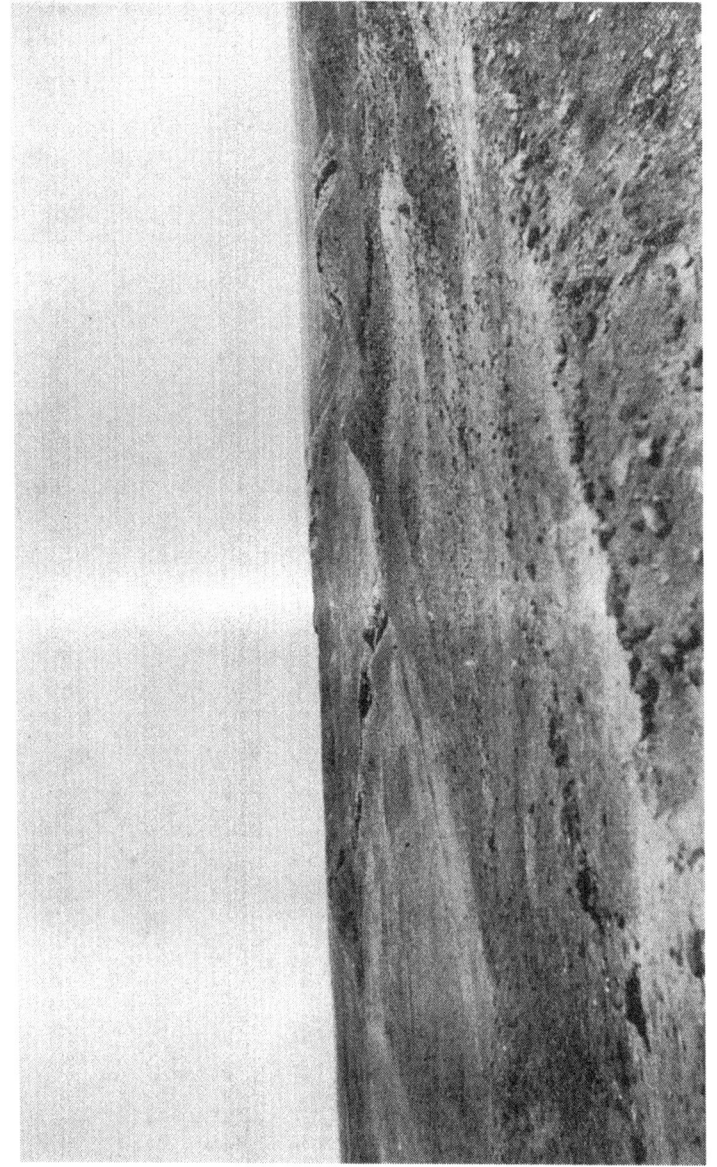

COUNTRY AND TRENCHES NEAR BEIT AIESSA.

THE TIGRIS BELOW KURNA.

GOORKHAS (THE SIRMOOR RIFLE REGIMENT)   115

April 18th saw two more changes in the Battalion's position, till in the evening we were sent northwards to form night outposts covering our Brigade.

We return to Twin Canal position, 20/4/16.
At 5 a.m. on the 20th the outposts were withdrawn, the 37th Brigade returning to the Twin Canal Redoubt (*Sketch XII*); and there we remained till the end of the month, only detaching 100 rifles under 2/Lieutenant Harrison, to hold an entrenched post at the west end of the causeway running through a marsh in front of the Redoubt.

Bombing practice accident.
It was during our stay here that a most unfortunate accident occurred at bombing practice, whereby 1 man was killed and 5 badly wounded, while 2/Lieutenant Gough lost an eye. On April 30th information was received relative to the relief of the 37th by the 35th Brigade, and that we should probably be sent back to Sheikh Saad for rest and refitting about May 3rd.

Last efforts to relieve Kūt, April, 1916.
Of events generally in other portions of the British force during the latter part of April, when all efforts to relieve the besieged garrison in Kūt seemed doomed to failure it may be said that on April 22nd another strenuous effort by the 7th Meerut and the 13th British Divisions against Sannayat was delivered, and two lines of trenches were taken; but a desperate Turkish counter-attack drove the troops back, and ended what was practically the last effort to get through to General Townshend's beleaguered Division, who were now at the last point of resistance and almost starving. On the 25th we heard of the failure of the desperate effort made to run the blockade by the river steamer *Julna*, laden with food supplies for Kūt. The *Julna*, under her captain, Cowley, with some Royal Naval officers, reached a point 4 miles below Kūt, when she ran on to a cable placed diagonally across the river which drove her on to a sandbank, where she stuck under heavy fire almost in sight of General Townshend's force, who now fully saw the end was near. It was on April 29th,

Kūt falls, 29/4/16.
that we heard what all expected with deep regrets, that Kūt with its gallant garrison, had been forced to surrender after a siege of 143 days. Much has been written about this siege, and what might have been done to obviate it in earlier days. No doubt mistakes were made at Kūt and by the force sent to relieve the place, but nothing can dim the glory of the old 6th " Poona " Division, first to reach Mesopotamia, and which had borne the stress of every action (save that at Nasiriyeh) from November, 1914, to this last lamented day, which sent the Division (or all that remained of it) into captivity until the end of the Great War. The numbers of the Kūt garrison were 2,500 British and 6,000 Indians

all told, and the losses incurred by the relieving force from all causes totalled nearly 20,000 from early January to late April, 1916. Large numbers died of wounds and sickness through the hopelessly inadequate medical arrangements, which with the transport deficiencies formed the subject of a very great scandal.

CHAPTER XV.

MAY 1ST, 1916, TO FEBRUARY 21ST, 1917. (*Sketches XII, XIII.*)

EARLY on May 2nd our Brigade was duly relieved by the 35th, we marched for Sheikh Saad at 10.45 a.m., and when 2 miles from this post the Brigade was ordered to halt and bivouac till the 5th, when it would take over the place, our Battalion relieving the 3rd Brahmins. Here, after settling in, we found ourselves chiefly employed in furnishing daily fatigues for loading and unloading steamers—Sheikh Saad at present being the Advance Base, and for endless other work connected with shifting ordnance stores, road-making, etc., while guard duties were by no means light. The strength of the Battalion had by now dwindled through casualties in the field and sickness to 383 men, and of these 315 were daily required for the duties mentioned. The need of a draft was badly felt; we knew long ago that Dehra had sent two such, and no one could understand why these never arrived at the front, but only later did the reason for their non-arrival transpire; when it was found the drafts had been detained at Basra for nearly two and a half months doing all sorts of fatigue works without any reference being made to the Battalion badly in want of them. If ever men went into distant hospitals or were sent far off on special duties, we often found that when convalescent or the particular duty was completed, we lost sight of them for long periods, as they were taken by some one for other works—a most annoying state of affairs.

Battalion at Sheikh Saad, 2/5/16.

Delay in sending up Drafts.

Sheikh Saad on the river bank, was at this time a pestilent place, though it was improved later. Fully half the area of the post was still occupied by an Arab village; it was appallingly dirty and by no means easy to organize a system of sanitation. A few cases of cholera had also occurred, and every effort had to be made to ward off an epidemic. A few of our men later on being taken with the disease, the Battalion was sent into camp 2½ miles south of Sheikh Saad on the 20th, which proved a blessing, for it was fresher and healthier out there, the men had a real rest, and there was leisure for overhauling kits and refitting. While at Sheikh Saad we were joined by Captain Ross, 2/8th Goorkha Rifles.

Cholera starts.

Captain McCleverty, of ours, and Lieutenant Dunlop, I.A.R.O.; and on the 25th at last a welcome draft reached us of 67 men under Subadars Mansur Rai, Jitman Thapa, and Jemadar Gutman Rai. They were all from the Assam and Burma Military Police Battalions, and had served with our 2nd Battalion in France. These were followed a few days later by a large draft of 192 men, under Lieutenant Snow, I.A.R.O., which brought the Battalion nearly up to field service strength again.

One night we were treated to the attention of expert Arab thieves, who succeeded in getting off with five rifles. This was the first occasion that thieves had ever taken a weapon from the 2nd Goorkhas, **Arab thieves.** and many parties lay out at night trying to ambuscade them, but only succeeded in capturing one Arab, which scared them from our immediate neighbourhood. They continued their thieving operations, however, with other units, including on one occasion actually the General Officer Commanding and Brigade Staff as victims, who woke up one morning to find they had no breeches or even drawers to wear; the thieves having made a clean sweep of all clothes they could rapidly lay hold of. This nuisance to all troops had become so great that a reward of Rs100 was offered for each Arab thief shot or captured. The country about here simply swarmed with sand grouse, but few were those with shot-guns. Captain Ross one morning brought back 63 birds in a comparatively short outing. Supply difficulties frequently presented themselves, and just at this time we had been left for days without firewood or vegetables, the men being put to extra trouble in collecting grass and scrub where possible, which was all they could cook with.

The news we got of the Russian force under General Barātov showed them to be making good headway against the Turks north-east of Khānākin, and on May 24th we heard of the arrival in camp at Ali Gharbi **Arrival of Cossacks** between Sheikh Saad and Amāra of 3 officers with 120 **at Ali Gharbi,** Cossacks from Barātov's force then operating near Kerind. **24/5/16.** This party had undergone a long and most trying march to link with the British, and the success of their effort seemed to presage well for the near future. Other news stated the Turks had, on May 20th, vacated the Es Sinn lines of which the Dujailah Redoubt was such a strong feature; due to their left flank having been turned **Turks abandon the** by the 3rd Division, which later proved incorrect, though **Es Sinn position,** the Turks had given up those defences. This action on **20/5/16.** their part was found due to their having had to send a large force to oppose the Russians near Kerind, and finding the

GOORKHAS (THE SIRMOOR RIFLE REGIMENT)

positions below Kūt too extended to hold with the forces left, they had to abandon the Es Sinn positions, taking with them guns, ammunition, and all. A Turkish aviator one day flew over us and dropped a letter, the contents of which ran that " if by chance the Turks had to vacate the Sannayat defences, would General Gorringe (commanding the force at this time in place of General Aylmer) mind stating in his report that, owing to the Turks having evacuated Sannayat, he had now occupied it "—a polite if sarcastic remonstrance on the British occupation of the whole Es Sinn lines, which had been quietly entered without a shot being fired, our only casualties being those from heat stroke— yet the published report stated the position had been taken by assault ! Certain changes in our Brigade took place here, the Somersets being replaced by the 1/4th Devons and the 64th Pioneers by the 45th Sikhs.

The enemy so far always got the better of us in the air, for our aeroplanes were few, old, and slow; they had several expert airmen, Germans and Turks, with rapid Fokker machines. It was here, while our men **Turkish air** were working near the river bank where three ammunition **superiority.** barges lay, that one of their airmen located these and dropped some smoke bombs for their guns to fire on. Their third shot sunk one barge, and with the tenth hit another which blew up, exploding at the same time the third barge. Parts of the wreckage were hurled over 400 yards away, and we were lucky in having only one man killed by the explosion.

On June 2nd the 37th Brigade was inspected by General Sir R. Egerton, General Officer Commanding 14th Division, newly formed in early May, of which we were now a unit, and that afternoon two Double **Formation of new** Companies were detached to guard the transport camp on **14th Division, May,** the bank of the Tigris called " Gomorrah " till the 13th, **1916.** when the whole Brigade was sent back to the Twin Canals. The scale of baggage was 10 pounds kit and 10 pounds tentage per man; for officers, 80 pounds kit and tentage each; the remainder of the Battalion stores and baggage were to be left in a dump at Sheikh Saad. The men's health was now anything but good, **Scurvy trouble.** and scurvy from scarcity of meat and vegetables had started; 103 men had to be left behind under Captain Pritchard, as being unfit to march (*Sketch XII*).

The Battalion (535 rifles) reached the Twin Canals **Battalion back at** after a march of 12 miles, and found their work to be **Twin Canals, June,** corn-cutting fatigues and picqueting the cornfields. Con-**1916.** voy escorts were frequently fired on by marauding Arabs, but otherwise nothing of interest occurred. Water presented a difficulty, having to be brought in " puckals " a distance of some 3 miles, and the heat being now great working hours were from 4.30 a.m. to 9 a.m., and from 6 p.m. to 9 p.m.

Move forward to Es Sinn Area. 20/6/16.

Our next move on June 20th was 8 miles to the Es Sinn area (*Sketch XII*), where we were camped not very far from the scene of our action and heavy losses at the Dujailah Redoubt ; and the line to be held by the 37th Brigade ran from the Tigris near Magasis to near Dujailah, our left being watched by cavalry patrols. The heat was now excessive and most trying, the temperature in large E.P. tents rising to over 120°, and it was consequently worse in 40-pound tents and sepoy " pāls." From a point near Magasis, Kūt el Amāra with its minarets and trees was visible in the distance —a pleasant-looking spot compared with where we were, for not a sign of a tree or vegetation enlivened the vast plains surrounding us and nothing to break the horizon, though in very clear weather the outline of the Persian mountains could be seen far away to the north. Not long after the Battalion got here it received a large consignment of war comforts, including 2,500 cigarettes and 1,300 shirts, which it is needless to say were very greatly appreciated. Our labours now were the digging of new support trenches, the old ones being full of graves, and in work on the new " Pentagon Post," while the nights were continually disturbed by the visitations of parties of marauding Arabs.

War Comforts.

Pentagon Post established early July, 1916.

The " Pentagon," about 2 miles south-west of Magasis and 4½ miles west of the Dujailah Redoubt (*Sketch XII*), was to consist of five redoubts all linked by trenches, and to have 60-pounder guns (our heaviest) mounted in them, with which to hammer the enemy's bridge-head defences over the Hai River near its junction with the Tigris, as also their strongly entrenched positions at Mahomed Abdul Hassan on the right bank of the Tigris, and Fort Khadairi on the left. The building of these redoubts was a big task, and occupied us and other units a considerable time.

With July active operations in general came to a standstill owing to excessive heat, sickness, etc., the temperature now showing 124° daily in tents, while scurvy and dysentery were taking a large toll of most units. Roughly, some 500 men a week were being invalided from our Division (the 14th), and there was no news of reinforcements coming up. Transport and supply arrangements always presenting an endless difficulty, with

Active operations cease for hot weather, July, 1916.

river steamers as few as they were, had to be improved from Basra up, to which end a light railway was in progress of building towards Amāra. The intention was to run it on from Sheikh Saad to the front at Es Sinn, the river between Amāra and Sheikh Saad being wide and presenting no difficulties to river steamers such as existed above Kurnah. A broad gauge line was also under construction from Basra to Nasiriyeh at the junction of the Hai with the Euphrates—the Hai River really being a branch of the Tigris. The "Pentagon" works having been completed and occupied in the later part of July, orders were received relative to the taking up of Battalion training, though how this could be effectively carried out it was not easy to see in view of heavy guard and convoy duties, and sickness. And on the top of this came an addition to our programme of works in the shape of the preparation of two "strong points," each to hold 100 rifles in our area of defence. Towards the end of the month we sustained a bad loss in the stampeding of five officers' chargers—from what cause was unknown. They bolted off towards the Hai and were caught by the Turks. All were saddled and equipped, which intensified the loss, as both saddlery and remounts were almost impossible to get at this time.

Much sickness and Supply difficulties.

Battalion training to start.

Fortunately for the troops exposed to this trying climate the enemy appeared to be similarly feeling it and to need rest, for he showed few signs of activity beyond an occasional and desultory shelling and in his aircraft, in which, as stated before, he had the advantage of us.

Most units about this period were loud in complaints *re* the looting of their stores on the way up from Basra, scarcely any officers' mess escaping this worry. It was usually attributed to the native boatmen, but signs were not wanting that this was by no means always the case and that subordinate officials were not above helping themselves, though this was not easy to prove. The wrath of officers looking forward to consignments of, say, whisky can be imagined, when cases were found on arrival to have had the bottles abstracted and mud put in instead, which frequently occurred!

Looting of stores.

With this cessation of operations leave in India for one month was opened, Colonel Sweet and Lieutenant Dunlop availing themselves of it, together with Subadar Mansur Rai and a number of men who qualified for leave, such qualification being that they had left India during the first nine months of the war and had not been invalided or had leave from the country in

Leave to India opened, July, 1916.

which they were serving. All who now went on leave were riflemen from Military Police Battalions who had served in France. At the end of July a draft reached us under Jemadar Dhanbir Sunwar somewhat depleted by sickness on the way up, as only 34 out of the 45 arrived at the front.

Several changes in the higher commands took place about now, General Gorringe, commanding at the front, and who had been wounded earlier, for one, leaving for France, rumour having it because of inability to get anything he had requisitioned India for, although absolutely essential. This time it appeared as if rumour spoke the truth, for it was amazing to all how little attention India gave to the urgent needs of the force. This, however, was soon to be altered under a new régime. News also came up from Basra as to signs of much greater activity down there which it was hoped indicated resumption of operations at no very distant date. As a set-off against these hopes was the knowledge that, roughly, some 10,000 men per month were being evacuated to India from sickness and wounds, but it was cheering to learn that reinforcements in fairly large numbers were beginning to arrive at Basra, and that it was confidently expected at least 100 steamers more would be plying on the river in the coming winter. Why this much needed form of transport had not been collected a year earlier was beyond anyone's comprehension, for such had been urgently required long ago. Another small draft of 38 men reached us before the month was up, and news from the Russians was good, as they had taken Ersingjān in Asia Minor.

Changes in High Commands.

Draft arrives.

Several interchanges of wounded prisoners recently took place between us and the Turks, but so carelessly that the latter were able to note much of what was going on and where; for instance, on one occasion two barges full of ammunition lying near the front were used as a gangway to the steamer taking the prisoners to Kūt. This was naturally reported on to their headquarters, and the following day Turkish guns opened on and blew them up.

Interchange of wounded prisoners.

With August came two really good aeroplanes to the front, and it was a pleasure to note how at last we could get the better of "Fasul" or "Fritz," as the Tommies used to call their airmen. They had not been long here before they were able to bring down one of their Fokkers in full view of our loudly cheering men; it fell, however, on their side of the river, but was smashed up by our guns. Our aviators also made a night raid on the hostile aerodrome

Better aeroplanes at last.

TRENCHES IN ES SINN AREA, AND LIGHT RAILWAY TO THE FRONT.

near Shumrān above Kūt, dropping bombs and effecting considerable damage.

But the greatest change and improvement for the force in Mesopotamia took place at the end of this month, when the entire operations taken over by the War Office from the Government of India some **Improved conditions** months earlier made itself felt under General Sir Stanley **of Tigris Force.** Maude, who succeeded General Sir Percy Lake in command of the whole Expedition, the latter retiring from the service. With him came Colonel Grey to take over the running of the Inland Water Transport, and as both apparently were given a free hand and an open purse in a few weeks things were humming, although activity at the front could not yet be resumed owing to need of complete reorganization **Composition of** during the hot weather. The force at General Maude's **Force and plans,** command now consisted of 1 Cavalry Division, 5 Infantry **Sept., 1916.** Divisions (viz., the 3rd, 7th, 13th, 14th and 15th Divisions), mixed Brigade, Lines of Communication troops, and proportionate numbers of guns. The whole in two Army Corps (1st and 3rd) of 2 divisions each, with the 15th Division at Nasiriyeh on the Euphrates guarding the left flank of the Tigris force. His plans were to hold the enemy to the left bank of the Tigris by constant activity and threats of attack while advancing step by step on the right bank, clearing the Turkish bridgehead defences on the Hai River opposite Kūt, attacking if possible, the weakest point in the hostile line, and cutting his lines of communication at Shumrān.

At present only a little gun fire on the Sannayat side of the river occasionally broke out, otherwise things were quiet. Captain Hill was sent to attend a Lewis gun course at 14th Divisional Headquarters, and four of these useful weapons were made over to the Battalion. Lieutenants Jerram and Baker joined us here in the Es Sinn area, followed a few days later by Lieutenants Sheridan and Rowbotham, all I.A.R.Os., and a good deal of Battalion training, field firing, and some tactical staff tours were put in during the month, which was also marked by many very severe dust and sand storms.

September saw the cases of scurvy increasing in most units, at one time the 1/2nd Goorkhas had 170 men in hospital from this malady alone, and we lost our Brigadier-General Fowler invalided to India **Scurvy increases,** with bad fever, Colonel Carey, 27th Punjabis, succeeding **Sept., 1916.** him. The excessive heat, however, was passing, for the temperature dropped to 100° about the middle of the month, a blanket at night was found comfortable, and it became desirable to get up the warm kit from the Sheikh Saad dump. The railway had now actually reached Es Sinn, so the transport and supply difficulties were at an end, as also the endless convoy escort duties from Sheikh Saad to the front. The enemy appeared to wake up a little, as he now indulged in some shelling of the camps in this area, Magasis Fort coming in for some attention, though but little damage was done.

Railway reaches front, mid Sept., 1916.

On September 15th we received a large draft of 189 men under Lieutenant Goodall, I.A.R.O.; Captain McCleverty, who had been ill at Amāra, also was able to rejoin us, and the Battalion was moved to a new camp 1½ miles west, all the " Strong Points " and trenches we had been labouring over for a month or more being given up. The very next day the Turks dropped a number of shells on to our old camp and that of the 36th Sikhs close by, causing them a number of casualties. During August a number of regimental Bands had been sent from India to enliven the slack period, that of the 105th Mahrattas coming to our Brigade, whose efforts towards our entertainment were much appreciated. Many of the New Army units also had a number of music hall artists in their ranks, who combined and gave really first-class shows.

Bands arrive, also concert parties, Sept., 1916.

Nasiriyeh, 120 miles roughly away on our left flank, blocking the Euphrates approaches to the enemy by the presence of the 15th Division, sent news of a battle at Es Sahilan on September 11th a few miles north of that town, when a large force of Arabs came down the Hai to attack the place, but were beaten off. Severe fighting took place here, notably when a body of Arabs charged the 5th Goorkha Rifles in true Ghāzi style. Turkish aeroplanes from Kūt twice got as far as this Division, and managed to do some damage amongst the transport (*Sketch XV*).

The 15th Division on Gen. Maude's left flank.

At the end of this month Colonel Sweet rejoined from leave, and with him came one of our most valued officers, Major Ridgeway, who had at last been relieved of his recruiting duties; this brought us up to eleven British officers, and four more were *en route* to join. Climatic conditions having very greatly improved, the men became healthier; at one time during the end of September the Battalion had actually 322 in hospital, but these were now rapidly recovering.

Col. Sweet and Major Ridgeway arrive, end Sept., 1916.

About this time the Intelligence Branch computed the Turkish strength opposed to General Maude's force at 18,000 men of the 51st, 52nd, and 45th

GOORKHAS (THE SIRMOOR RIFLE REGIMENT)

Divisions, while their guns were put at 60, and not 110, as previous reports had stated. But their entire strength in this theatre of war—viz., on the Tigris, Euphrates, Khānākin (Persian border), and Baghdad—came to 41,100 rifles, 3,200 sabres, and 125 guns.

The beginning of October found the Battalion still camped in the Es Sinn area doing as much training and attack practices as possible considering the heavy guard and other duties, and three more " Strong Points " were ordered to be prepared and finished in a week's time. We also formed part of the Movable Column. Our machine guns were now taken away to help in forming the new Machine Gun Company, the personnel of which **New Machine Gun** was to be half British and half Indian. A Stokes mortar **Companies and** battery—a weapon new to us—had arrived at the front, **Stokes Mortars,** and an exhibition of its uses was given one afternoon at **mid Oct., 1916.** Divisional Headquarters. In the middle of the month there was a cessation of hostilities to effect an exchange of prisoners, and at the same time the 37th Brigade was ordered to move back into the central brigade area on relief by the 26th Punjabis. Here lectures were given in the use of gas masks and in defensive measures to be taken in the case of gas attacks, but this form of warfare was not resorted **Battalion inspected** to by the Turk in this theatre of war. Three parades daily **by Gen. Maude.** went on, and we were inspected by General Sir Stanley Maude, while sports and football enlivened the men's leisure, and the 37th Brigade held a successful and well-attended " pagal " gymkhana. On another occasion the Y.M.C.A. treated us to a first-rate cinematograph show, and so the period of inaction drew near its close.

On November 12th the 1/2nd Goorkhas were ordered to relieve the 82nd Punjabis in the right area near the river bank which it **Battalion moves to** includes for some distance above Magasis Fort (*Sketch XII*), **Magasis Fort,** and while the move was in progress it came under shell fire **12/11/16.** from their position at Mahomed Abdul Hassan, but fortunately with no bad effects, most of the shells being " duds." A draft of 58 men, under 2/Lieutenant Toogood and Subadar Sarabjit Gurung, joined us here—quite the best lot we had received for some time—but these had been sent straight up instead of being detained in Basra. **Draft arrives.** Some useful scouting work was done from this section by Lieutenants Jerram and Baker, notably when one evening with fifteen scouts they reached a point some 400 yards from where the enemy's trench was supposed to be. Jerram then went on with three scouts,

Scouting work under Lieuts. Jerram and Baker, Nov., 1916. the rest remaining to support him. They entered the hostile trench, and were proceeding along it when a sentry challenged them 30 paces off and fired, and two picquets at once opened fire on our little party, who by great luck got away unharmed, though nearly all had narrow escapes, with bullets through clothes and head-dresses. Lieutenant Jerram's information brought back *re* the enemy's new trenches and their position proved most useful. On November 14th the whole of this area and its defences were closely inspected by General Marshall, commanding the new 3rd Corps, to which the 14th Division now belonged. The distance between our right at Magasis and the Mahomed Abdul Hassan position was about $3\frac{1}{2}$ miles or less, and our patrols frequently were almost in touch with those of the enemy in the vicinity of Abbas village. Fatigue parties had to be sent to Imām Mansur, nearly 4 miles to the south, to assist in trench-digging there, but quiet reigned until the 28th, when the Turks indulged in a short but heavy bombardment. The position of the two opposing forces was out of the ordinary, for the enemy,

Unusual position of opposing forces, Nov., 1916. having made a seemingly impregnable series of entrenched defences at Sannayat on the left bank, were holding off every effort of ours against them, while the river on one side and the wide Suwaikieh marshes on the other secured their flanks.

On the right bank, since the successful Beit Aiessa assault in April no further heavy fighting had taken place, but our lines had been able to advance owing to the enemy abandoning the Es Sinn positions till we fronted the Turks at their Hai bridgehead and at Mahomed Abdul Hassan at 4 and $2\frac{1}{2}$ miles respectively, and we were now some 10 miles in rear of the Sannayat position. A plan for crossing the Tigris at Guwam a little above Magasis was under discussion, but was given up. The ground north of the river favoured the enemy, particularly where the dry Dahra Canal ran, up which for a long distance they could reinforce Sannayat under cover. The 7th Meerut Division had been holding the enemy there, while the 13th British Division, now at full strength, was in rest at Amāra for two months after a most strenuous spring and early summer. This latter Division, on return to the front, was sent to the right bank front.

The 1/2nd Goorkhas in early December, relieving the 2/4th Goorkha Rifles in the central area (Es Sinn) for some days were busy road-making, and as the weather was now exceedingly cold and wet, warm clothing was issued to all troops.

On December 13th the first moves heralding coming operations took place when the 37th Brigade was ordered to advance and cover the right flank of

First moves of winter operations, 13/12/16. the 13th Division (3rd Corps), which was to effect a crossing of the Hai River at Atāb, the objectives now being the Turkish entrenchments covering the Liquorice Factory just opposite Kūt and their bridge defences over the Hai, all held in strength with elaborate trench systems; the 1st Corps having to deal with the Turkish positions from Mahomed Abdul Hassan (the Khadairi Bend) to Sannayat. The 35th Brigade the while held the Tigris River line about Magasis and Abbas village, the 36th that stretching from Dujailah to Atāb (*Sketch XII*). This duty over, the **Battalion part of Corps Reserve, mid Dec., 1916.** 1/4th Devons and our Battalion were sent to Imām Mansur as Corps Reserve, a little later being moved forward again into Divisional Reserve until December 17th, when our Brigade took up the line north and south of " Dead Calf Pond," linking the 35th and 36th Brigades. The 3rd Lahore Division was still at Es Sinn.

The 13th Division, effecting the Hai crossing with little opposition, moved up the west bank with the Cavalry Division away on its left flank towards Shumrān, where they were held up by machine-gun fire. The Division reached the neighbourhood of Ummas Saad, where they reported on the 15th the Turkish defences to the south of the Liquorice Factory to be very strongly held, the enemy having been reinforced by a force released from Asia Minor. Our aeroplanes got busy, and, finding the *Firefly* (one of our captured monitors) attempting to tow the Shumrān boat bridge up river, dropped bombs, forcing the proceeding to stop and sending both *Firefly* and bridge on to a sandbank. Meanwhile the 7th Meerut Division demonstrated against Sannayat to draw off attention from our moves about the Hai, which succeeded to the extent of making the Turks despatch large reinforcements down river.

37th Brigade crosses the Hai at Ummas Saad, 19/12/16. On December 19th the 37th Brigade, led by Lieutenant Jerram and the Battalion scouts, who had previously reconnoitred the ford at Ummas Saad, crossed the Hai, and, proceeding on to Lake Khor Abbas, bivouacked there. For several days there was marching and counter-marching, with fresh digging at each halt, doubtless with objects not apparent to us; but it was weary work and in bitter cold, with only overcoats for the men. On the 20th we were holding a line of outposts facing west, and linking the 40th Brigade on the right with the 36th on the left, and the 13th **Capture of Kāla Haji Fahān position by 13th Division, 20/12/16.** Division had taken the hostile position at Kāla Haji Fahān. All companies were up in the front line some 3,500 yards long, with no supports or reserves. From this next day the 37th Brigade was moved forward some 4 miles in reserve to the 40th and 38th Brigades, who were to attempt to cross the Tigris near the brick-kilns about 6 miles above Shumrān, cavalry and guns accompanying them. We bivouacked for the night near Nahr el Massag (*Sketch XII*). The attempt, however, failed, and had not been a serious effort, but rather a demonstration in the vain hope of drawing the enemy out of Sannayat. The troops returned to the neighbourhood of the Khor Abbas, and on the 23rd we moved a little farther north in line with the Ummas Saad ford and 1½ miles from it, and here the Battalion spent quite a cheery Christmas Day, regaled by presents of champagne from Lord Curzon and plum puddings from the kindly ladies of Poona and Bombay.

Demonstration towards Shumrān, 21/12/16.

Christmas, 1916.

On December 30th, in the vilest weather imaginable, the 1/2nd Goorkhas marched south to a point a little above Basrugiyeh Fort on the Hai west bank, where we relieved the 82nd Punjabis in the picquet line there, and where we had tents to shelter us from the violent storm raging. This picquet line was 8 miles in extent, so the Battalion was much split up and officers lived in company messes. There was a good deal of sniping going on from the west, and on January 1st, 1917, our line was advanced about a mile to more favourable ground, where we dug in, as reports pointed to a possible Turkish attack on this flank, which if successful, would have brought them well in rear of the 13th and 14th Divisions, now at Kāla Haji Fahān, where heavy rifle and gun fire proclaimed them busy. Here we were employed in arranging several "Strong Points," and it seemed we were in for a long stay. Meanwhile another demonstration was made by two Brigades towards Shumrān, the cavalry getting as far as Baghailah, where they destroyed a Turkish supply depot. This drew attention from the attack of the 3rd Division (1st Corps) on January 9th against the Mahomed Abdul Hassan position (sometimes called the Khadairi Bend position), where the Division captured the first line of trenches; but five Turkish battalions crossing from Khadairi Fort counterattacked and drove us out with considerable loss, chiefly to the Highland Light Infantry, Manchesters, and 59th Rifles, and success was only achieved by this Division after hard fighting on January 17th, which cost General Cobbe's force some 2,100 casualties. Large Arab forces being reported in Hai town 12 miles south of Atāb, two Brigades of Cavalry were

Battalion relieves 82nd Punjabis near Basrugiyeh Fort, 30/12/16.

Cavalry success at Baghailah.

Mahomed Abdul Hassan positions attacked unsuccessfully, 9/1/17.

despatched there on the 13th and nearly had a reverse, due to Arab treachery, necessitating the 82nd and 62nd Punjabis being sent to extricate them. For us and our immediate part of the line, which now ran facing west from the Bessouia ford on the Hai in a semi-circle to Kāla Haji Fahān (*Sketch XII*), nothing stirring occurred, beyond small scraps with parties of hostile Arabs, and constant patrolling went on until January 23rd, when the 2/1st Goorkhas relieved our Battalion, which moved up to near Kāla Haji Fahān and the 13th Division, which two days later made a vigorous assault, the 39th Brigade capturing certain trenches, but being driven out again. On the 26th the 13th Division was on both sides of the Hai, its 39th Brigade having successfully captured trenches at P10, and the Division's main attack had now reached the Andrew trench line and were consolidating their gains (*Sketch XIII*). The Battalion was now warned to be ready to support the 36th Brigade, and so the threshold of our second battle was crossed. On the 28th the 37th Brigade moved up into the trenches just north of Kāla Haji Fahān, less the 1/2nd Goorkhas, who moved into the Lunette line and "Emperor's" trench at 7 a.m. next morning. At this time the 36th and 45th Sikhs were holding the line P12g—P15b, and had established a few bombing parties in a channel now converted into a trench P16—P13a; but the enemy held the remainder of this line westward, and between this line and the Liquorice Factory the ground was covered with an elaborate and well-dug series of trenches on both banks of the Hai, the 3rd Division and part of the 13th Division operating on the east bank, the 14th and remainder of 13th Division on the west bank.

Cavalry reverse at Hai town owing to treachery, 13/1/17.

We move up to Kāla Haji Fahān, 23/1/17.

Battalion enters the offensive against Liquorice Factory position, 28/1/17.

About 6 p.m. on January 28th our bombers were ordered forward to join those in the Sikh front line, and after a short bombardment, that both 36th and 45th Sikhs should occupy the whole of the trench P13a—P17. After this was accomplished, 200 of the Devons and the same number of our men were ordered to go up and dig a fresh communicating trench in place of that at P12c—P12g, which was so blocked with corpses as to be impassable. The bombardment started, and was followed by a roar of rifles from the Turks, but the Sikhs gained their objective, and the fatigue parties under Major Ridgeway and Lieutenant Jerram, with two Sapper officers, carried out the digging, in which we had 10 casualties and Lieutenant

Our Bombers join the front trenches, 28/1/17.

Jerram shot through the arm. On the 31st the Battalion, less No. 4 Company, moved forward to "King's" and "Queen's" trenches (*Sketch XIII*), No. 4 being sent to a position in rear of the 45th Sikhs, and all were employed in either digging or carrying up stores and munitions to the front line, in which work Jemadar Gopi Lama was mortally wounded.

<small>Battalion fatigue parties at front, and casualties, 30/1/17.</small>

Our next orders were for the 1/4th Devons and 1/2nd Goorkhas to support the 36th and 45th Sikhs on February 1st who were to assault at noon. As they went over the parapet Major Bruce, who had rejoined from sick leave on December 30th, and Captain Hill, with their companies, occupied the vacated trench, the right of which was on the Hai River. A terrific bombardment was in progress, but did not seem to keep down the enemy's machine-gun and rifle fire which greeted the Sikhs. The 45th got into the Turkish second line, but the 36th were unable to reach the position under the hail of bullets, and shortly after both regiments were driven back, the former with about 600 casualties, the latter with about 500. This attack was premature; our guns had not registered on the right of the Turkish trenches which the 36th Sikhs assaulted; thus as they appeared in the open they were mown down by machine guns and rifles, few reaching the enemy. The repulse of the 36th exposed the left flank of the 45th, who were unable to hold the two trenches they gained; while in support of this assault we had 1 Goorkha officer and 41 men hit, and Major Bruce was killed. The command of our front companies then devolved on Captain Hill, who at 1.15 p.m. was ordered to push forward two companies to help the 36th Sikhs, but before this could be carried out it was changed to one for attack at 4.45 p.m. after a further bombardment, and this again was postponed till the following day.

<small>Battalion and Devons support Sikh attack, 1/2/17.</small>

<small>Sikh Attack premature, and fails—heavy losses, 1/2/17.</small>

<small>Our Casualties, 1/2/17.</small>

Towards evening the Battalion sent out stretcher-bearers and parties to help collect and bring in the wounded, which was done under continual sniping, while Arabs looting wounded and stripping the dead had to be driven off and shot down. Towards 8 p.m. things quieted down and patrols were sent out on both flanks. One of these patrols, under Lance/Naik Randhoj Limbu, did a good piece of work in advancing up a nullah (*Sketch XIII*), at the far end of which he came on some Turks, whom his patrol bombed out,

<small>Patrolling and collection of wounded, 1/2/17.</small>

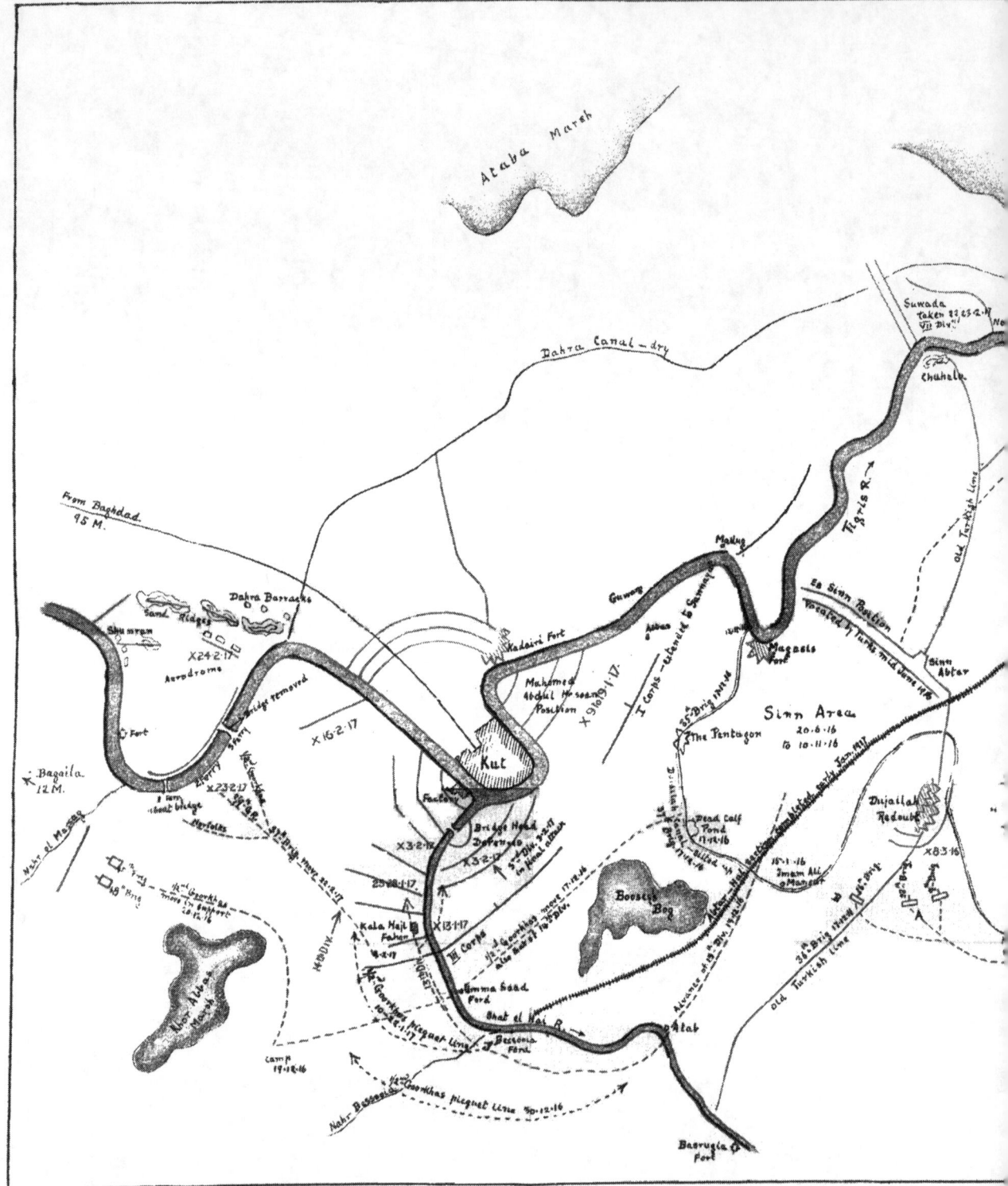

Sketch showing area operated [on]
between March 5th 1916 and F[...]

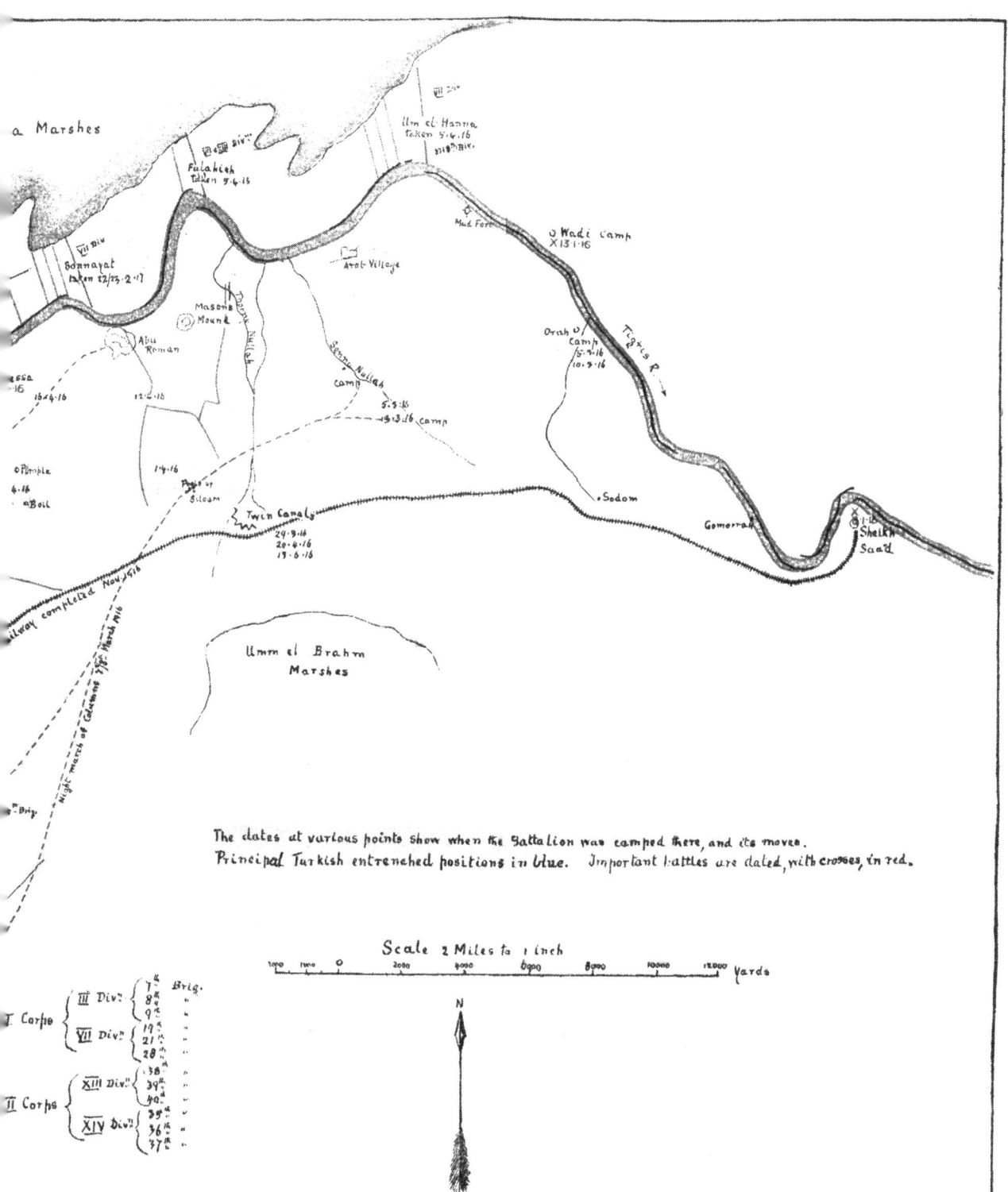

following them actually into their front trench. Here they threw bombs, which created confusion among the enemy, noted his strength and position of the trench, and by good luck got safely back. Lieutenant Trotter, who with some stretcher bearers after nightfall was trying to get Sikh wounded away, was joined by Captain Marsh and some men, and while **Capt. Marsh killed, 1/2/17.** getting the wounded out of a small nullah Captain Marsh was hit badly in the knee, and, in spite of first-aid dressing being applied at once, died of hæmorrhage before he could be got to the Field Ambulance. Marsh, who was a most popular and first-rate officer, had been awarded the Military Cross for gallantry during March 8th at Dujailah, and was Adjutant of the Battalion, Captain McCleverty now succeeding to that billet. During the night the Battalion dug the trench known as "Warwick" 60 yards farther forward, which brought this part of our line within 200 yards of the enemy (*Sketch XIII*).

The next attack was ordered for 9 a.m. on February 2nd, preceded by a fifteen-minute bombardment, and the 1/2nd Goorkhas and 1/4th Devons were in position to mount the parapet when the attack was **Attack by Devons and 1/2nd Goorkhas ordered, but postponed, 2/2/17.** twice ordered to be delayed for an hour each time, and it was then once more postponed till next day. Naturally all this waiting about and continually getting attack orders changed was not only vexatious, but entailed a great strain on the troops having to make the attack. Both the 1/2nd Goorkhas and the Devons had been 6 days in the trenches exposed to constant fire, with endless fatigues to carry out, with but little rest, and they were now to attack a position, in the first attempt to take which two battalions 50 per cent. stronger in numbers had been nearly exterminated, and the ground over which this second attack had to pass was littered thick with the bodies of those who had gone before. The Devons was a Territorial Battalion which had not been in action before, and most of the 1/2nd Goorkhas were young soldiers new to the work, though, fortunately, they had a fair sprinkling of men who had seen service in France. Still, in spite of these disadvantages, the results of this coming attack surpassed the highest expectations.

At 9.30 a.m. on February 3rd the bombardment opened, and our front companies in eight waves on a front of 150 yards, led by Captains Hill and Pritchard and Lieutenant Baker, began going over the **Our attack, 3/2/17.** parapet, the Devons being on our left, the leading lines rushing forward to some 30 yards from the Turks' trenches, where they lay down until our barrage lifted. Here the first platoons took the pins out of their bombs, and as they charged the trench threw them in. As it was full of Turks, considerable execution was done before bayonet and kookerie got to work. The 8th Brigade across the Hai assisted with enfilade fire.

With great dash our first platoons, under Subadar Sarabjit Gurung and Jemadar Dhanraj Gurung (who was killed), and those following closely took the first two lines of trenches, two more platoons going on into the third line under Subadar Karakbir Thapa, who fell badly wounded, as also were Lieutenants Trotter (whose thigh was badly smashed) and Dunlop and Baker, both hit. This did not, however, stop the former—viz., Dunlop—who, taking two parties of bombers and a platoon under Jemadar Dhanbir Sunwar, went up the Hai bank and entered that flank of the enemy's third line trench, losing nearly half their number by machine-gun fire from the Turkish position on the opposite bank, which the 3rd Division were also attacking. In this trench they succeeded in making a block, which, unfortunately, twice was unintentionally destroyed by our guns, but was gallantly rebuilt a third time under direction of Jemadar Dhanbir Sunwar, Lieutenant Dunlop having been killed while fearlessly directing the bombers. This forward block in the enemy's third trench our party managed to hold for some hours in spite of counter-attacks by Turkish bombers and bayonet men. On our left Captain Hill had also penetrated well forward with No. 3 Company, and formed a block which they held all day, in spite of many efforts to dislodge them by parties with bombs, of which the Turk had plenty. Nearly all our bombers and Lewis gunners were knocked out.

Trenches captured, 3/2/17.

Dunlop's action, 3/2/17.

Consolidation of our gains went on all the afternoon of February 3rd under heavy shell fire, causing numerous casualties to our Battalion and the 62nd Punjabis, who had come up earlier. By about 4 p.m. the whole of the 37th Brigade was up, and the captured trenches were now strongly held (*Sketch XIII*). Our troops in this area of attack had in the last twenty-four hours pushed forward some 1,400 yards towards the Liquorice Factory, the biggest advance at one swoop that had yet been done here; and during the night of the 3rd the enemy withdrawing from our immediate front enabled our men to advance again another 600 yards. The lines were reorganized, the 1/2nd Goorkhas holding the right flank in all three captured trenches; and the Hants were also now up in support. Both Devons and 1/2nd Goorkhas signified their readiness to remain on in the front if desired.

Consolidation of ground gained, 3/2/17.

The Battalion had serious losses in these actions, into which they went

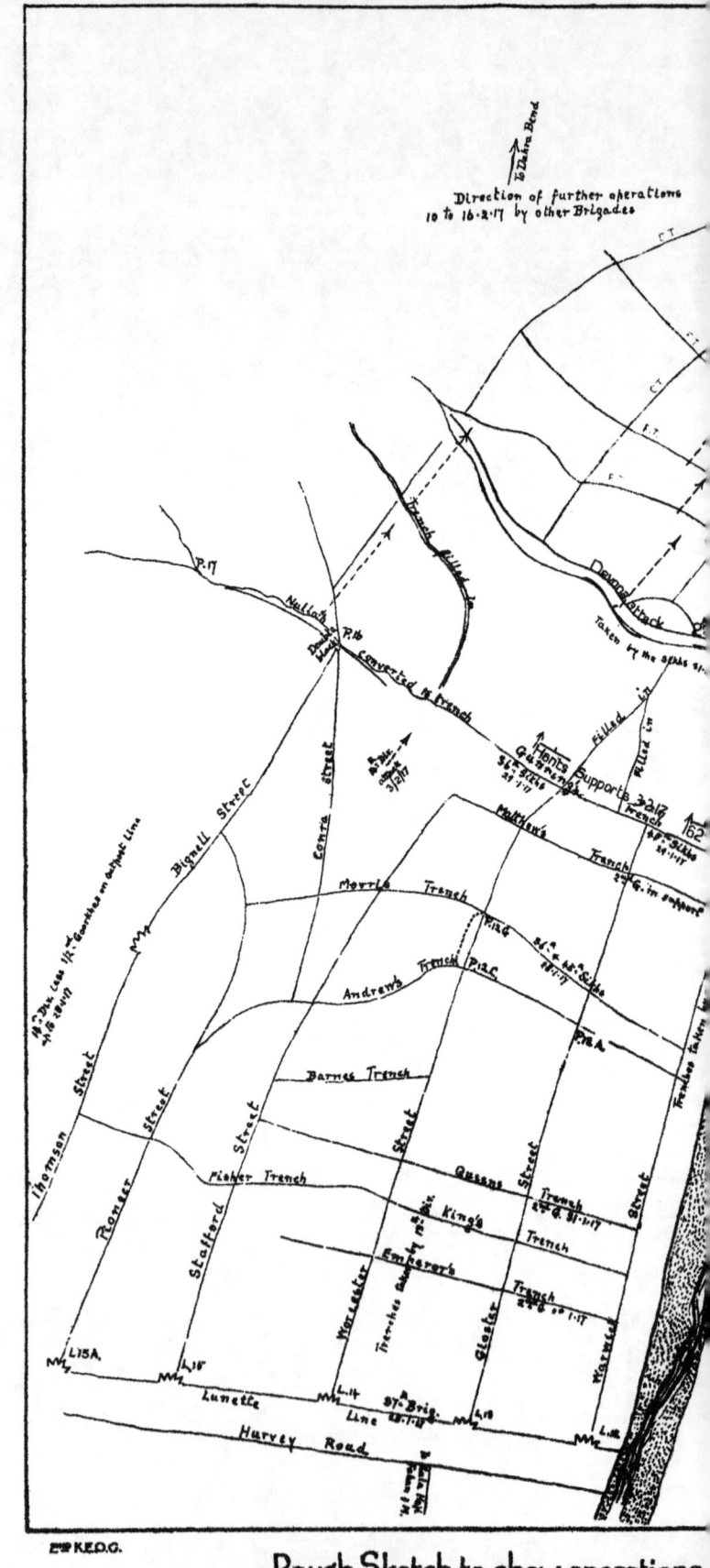

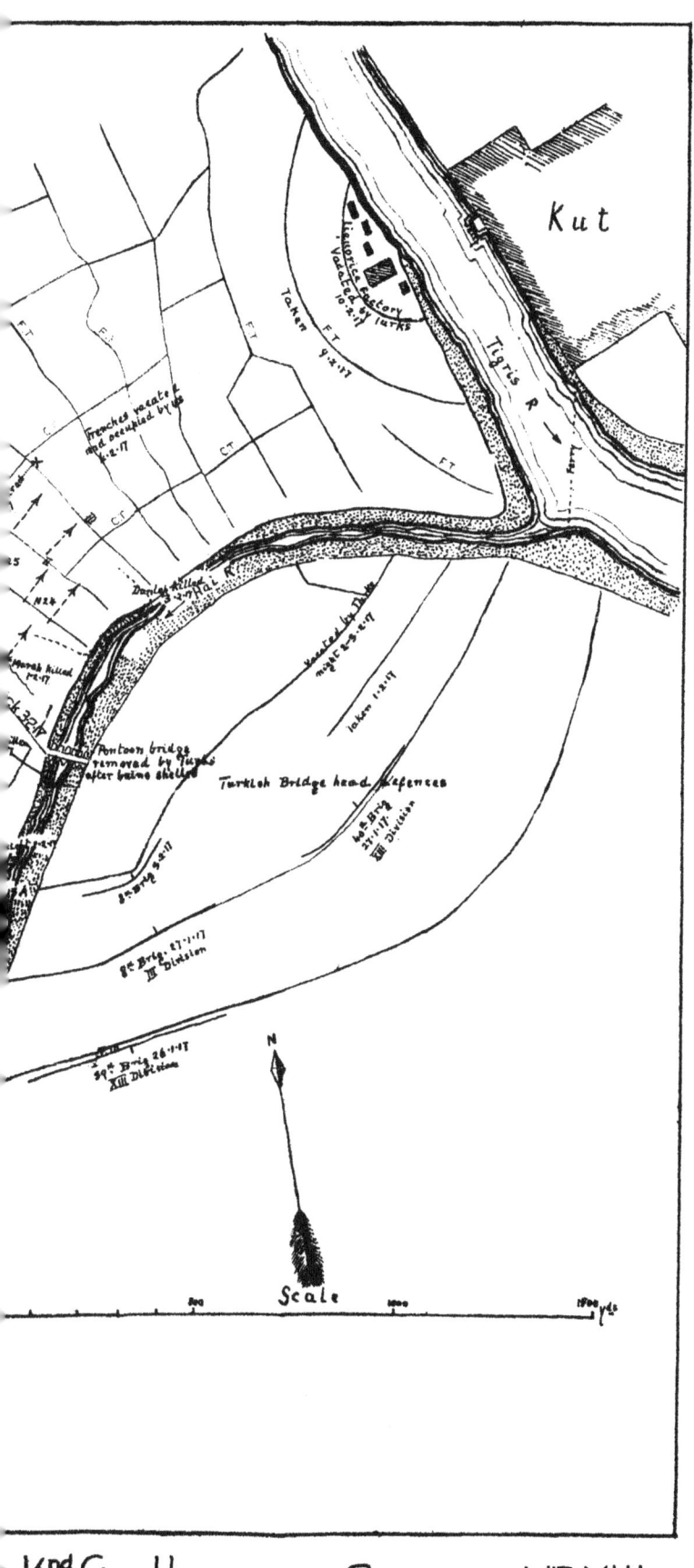

SKETCH Nº XIII

GOORKHAS (THE SIRMOOR RIFLE REGIMENT)

545 strong, the casualties being 3 British officers, 2 Goorkha officers, and 82 men killed, while 2 British officers, 5 Goorkha officers, and 197 men were wounded—a total of 292 of all ranks. Of these, 90 were in Captain Hill's company, which went into action 170 strong. Our British officers—viz., Major Bruce, Captain Marsh, and Lieutenant Dunlop—were all buried in a wired in cemetery on the Hai west bank. The losses of the Devons on our left were several officers and 214 men. The major portion of these casualties occurred after the trenches had been reached.

Our casualties, 3/2/17.

Major Ridgeway during this day had been left behind with Subadar Major Tulsiram Gharti and Subadars Lachman Sing Khattrie and Narain Sing Thapa with one platoon, where they organized working parties for sending up bombs, sand-bags, ammunition, etc., to the front in a most efficient way. Through their labours they were able to supply not only our Battalion, but others in the fighting line until it was dark, after which ample supplies could be got forward by other parties detailed from the Brigade.

Working parties in rear, 3/2/17.

During the night all the wounded were brought away and trenches improved, and when daylight came it was seen the 8th Brigade on the east bank of the Hai were advancing, the enemy having vacated their positions on that side. Resistance had ceased in our immediate neighbourhood, for the Turks had withdrawn into the Liquorice Factory defences, which were bombarded and attacked by another brigade on the 9th, whereupon the enemy retired across the Tigris (*Sketch XIII*). The 1/2nd Goorkhas remained in this vicinity some days, employed in salvage and burying, reorganizing units, road-making, in practising trench attack and blocking of trenches, most of which was done in bad weather, which flooded the camps and obliged us eventually to move back to our former camp near Kāla Haji Fahān till February 22nd.

Turks abandon Liquorice Factory defences, 9/2/17.

Salvage work, Feb., 1917.

Shortly after the action of the 3rd the Turks being found still holding certain new entrenchments upstream of the Factory and at right angles to their previous line, these were attacked by the 35th and 38th Brigades, who cleared them out, and the entire right bank of the Tigris was in General Maude's hands. The fierce fighting in the early days of this month had cost the enemy 89 officers and 1,916 men taken prisoners, besides much war material and 344 dead were buried.

Turkish losses, early Feb., 1917.

Concerning the past three days' fighting, an extract from a letter of the General Officer Commanding 37th Brigade to 14th Divisional Headquarters is of interest. He writes:—

"I consider the following units particularly distinguished themselves in the recent operations—viz., the 36th Sikhs, 45th Sikhs, 1/4th Devons, 1/2nd Goorkhas, 62nd Punjabis.

Extract from Brigadier's letter on the fighting, 1–3/2/17.
"The 36th and 45th Sikhs made a most determined and gallant assault against the Turkish positions on the west bank of the Hai on February 1st. The two regiments advanced under a heavy enfilade fire from guns and machine guns on both flanks, and although many men fell as soon as they left our trenches each succeeding wave pressed on until they finally reached the enemy's position. They were, however, unfortunately unable to maintain themselves there and had to fall back, but the spirit of the survivors was in no way impaired and reflects the greatest credit on these two regiments.

"The 1/4th Devons, the 1/2nd Goorkhas, and the 62nd Punjabis attacked the same Turkish positions on February 3rd. These three regiments, in spite of the fact that the Devons and Goorkhas had seen their trenches full of wounded Sikhs two days before, attacked with the greatest gallantry and determination. They captured three lines of Turkish trenches, and maintained themselves there all day against several counter-attacks. When withdrawn next day they were still ready to continue the offensive.

"The severity of the fighting during these two attacks may be judged by the casualties suffered, the losses being over 50 per cent. of the total strengths of the regiments engaged."

37th Brigade reconstituted.
Our Brigade (37th), having suffered very heavily, was now rearranged, the Norfolks succeeding the Devons, who had lost 5 officers and over 200 men out of the 350 who went into action on February 3rd, the 62nd Punjabis also suffering considerable losses. The 2/9th Goorkha Rifles and the 67th Punjabis replaced the remains of the 36th and 45th Sikhs.

While near Kāla Haji Fahān we were ordered to arrange to practise the men in river crossing by means of pontoons during the next four days. Pontoons were allotted to units and company after company was instructed in entering and settling in, rowing across and landing, and at once taking up picquet or laying out trench lines, all of which pointed to a coming move and further operations above Kūt.

BIVOUAC ON THE TIGRIS BANK—EARLY BREAKFAST.

CHAPTER XVI.

FEBRUARY 22ND TO MARCH 26TH, 1917. (*Sketches XV, XIII, XIV.*)

WE now come to the final stage of the long period of fighting around Kūt, one in which the most strenuous resistance was expected to be met with; the enemy now driven entirely from the Tigris right banks, occupying strongly entrenched positions at the impregnable Sannayat, at Kūt, and at the Dahra and Shumrān bends of the river some 6 miles above Kūt. The intention was to cross the river above that town, and, if success attended the operation, it might bring about the capture of Khalil Bey's entire force. The "if" in this case seemed a very large one, for the Turk was well aware of our probable new move. The seriousness and doubtfulness of success

The Tigris crossing and arrangements, late Feb., 1916. would seem to have been shown in the orders, which stated " the crossing would be *attempted*," in contrast to all former orders, which had been worded such and such an operation "*will be carried out.*" Every effort was made to conceal our move and the points at which the crossing would be made, such as demonstrations before Sannayat, raids and noises as of preparations at several places down stream during the night of the 22nd-23rd; and at dawn, when the actual crossing was to commence, the 7th Division was to fling itself on the Sannayat entrenchments.

On February 22nd, 1917, came orders showing the 37th Brigade had been given the honour of leading what was considered almost in the light of a forlorn hope, and that it was to move into position on the right

Our Brigade to effect the crossing, 22/2/17. bank of the Tigris almost opposite Dahra preparatory to crossing that river. Late that afternoon the Brigade advanced in company with the Sappers and Miners with their pontoon train, under Captain Fardell and Lieutenant Eustace, R.E. The vicinity of the crossing was reached by 6 p.m., and we halted in a nullah, when detailed orders for the operation were issued, and the 1/2nd, 2/9th, and Norfolks were to lead with the 67th Punjabis supporting, the 35th Brigade being in reserve.

The points for crossing were three, with a ferry master at each, all under the direction of Major Pemberton, R.E., and the Tigris, swollen by the recent heavy rains, was now a stretch of fully 400 yards of water, presenting a serious obstacle to be overcome in face of an active and vigilant enemy. No. 1 Ferry, to be used by the Norfolks, was opposite the extreme right of the enemy's defences; No. 2, for the 2/9th Goorkha Rifles, lower down; and No. 3, for our Battalion, farther down again, the intervals being about 300 yards or more. After the crossing had been effected the Sappers were to throw a boat-bridge across just above No. 1 Ferry.

The points for crossing Tigris.

The carts with the pontoons (thirteen to each ferry) were brought into the nullah in the dark, taken forward by hand, and placed behind a specially thrown-up bank some 12 yards from the water's edge, under the direction of Lieutenant Eustace; each unit was soon at its place, and spent the night in getting such rest as was possible in the open and in bitter cold. Certain sections of the 13th Divisional Machine Guns were directed to proceed to a point on the right bank higher up and dig in on a position whence they could assist the crossing when daylight came (*vide Sketch XIV*). These later not only greatly aided the crossing, but were able to give assistance to the subsequent advance. All guns of both 13th and 14th Divisions were also to take up positions whence a barrage could be formed on the southern end of the Shumrān peninsula, and no firing of any description was to take place until the enemy opened on our troops crossing.

Battalion reaches No. 3 Ferry, 22/2/17.

According to orders, at 5.40 a.m. on February 23rd the first boat pushed off with Lieutenant Toogood, Jemadar Guman Sing Gurung, L./Naik Chandra Sing Gurung, and ten men, and the rest of the flotilla of thirteen boats (first trip) followed with Lieutenant Baker, Subadar Sarabjit Gurung, and No. 1 Company, including two Lewis guns. With these were two boatloads of No. 2 Company, each boat holding ten men and five rowers. It was hoped the current would carry the boats to a point a bit down stream where the mouth of a nullah pointed to a likely landing-place. However, the excellent rowing of the Hampshire men (130 of that regiment and some of the 13th Company Sappers and Miners having been sent to the crossings as rowers) brought the boats to a point higher up where a high "bund" afforded some cover for landing, the curve of the river somewhat protecting the right flank. But the Turks soon became aware of what was in progress, and opened heavy fire on ours and the boats of No. 2 Ferry 300 yards above us. Lieutenant Toogood, with eleven out of thirteen boats, landed on the mud bank, and

Crossing commences, 23/2/17.

Landing effected under heavy fire, 23/2/17.

fighting with bomb and bayonet began at once. He was able to place a bull's-eye lantern on the rallying-point to guide the other boats soon to cross, but the hail of bullets was such that only two boats of the first trip were able to return to the right bank, almost all the other rowers had been killed or wounded before their boats could be got under way.

At 7 a.m. these two boats and two others which we retrieved as they floated down from No. 2 Ferry, went across with Major Ridgeway, Subadar Karbir Thapa, and thirty-eight men of No. 2 Company.

Major Ridgeway crosses and is killed, 23/2/17. They pulled out into the tornado of bullets, and only eight men of one boatload which began to sink at once were able to return to the Battalion, almost all the rest, including Major Ridgeway, being shot down before they could land on the far bank, and the Battalion could now see with dismay all its boats stranded on the opposite shore filled with dead and wounded, and Toogood's and Baker's men defending themselves desperately on the top of the bank. Major Ridgeway during the crossing was seen to have been hit, but he pluckily seized the oar of a rower killed and was pulling hard when he fell riddled by machine-gun bullets. One man only from his boat, a Naik of Sappers and Miners, was able to land. Major Ridgeway's loss was deeply deplored by all who knew him; he had been Adjutant of our 2nd Battalion, and was a sound, capable officer, popular with all ranks. The last boat to make the crossing with Jemadar Manbahadur Gurung (later Jemadar Adjutant) had all its rowers killed or wounded before they got halfway across, and, drifting back, returned to the Battalion.

Meanwhile Lieutenants Toogood and Baker, with the remains of the two companies across the river (fifty-six all told), had managed to maintain their position at one end of the "bund," with a signaller keeping **Lieutenants Toogood** up communication with the Battalion. Through him useful **and Baker on far** information as to the enemy's position was passed to the **bank, 23/2/17.** guns, which were then better able to break up attacks on our gallant little party. Of many gallant deeds performed by men of this party that of Rifleman Jagia Rana may well be recorded, who was hit in the jaw and again in the neck, but continued to fight and use his bombs till compelled to stop through loss of blood and weakness.

Six of our riflemen, of whom five were wounded, had crossed in No. 12 pontoon and were taken prisoners. The rowers and the rest in the boat were badly hit, and it drifted down on to a part of the bank held by the Turks, who captured them. They were taken to a Turkish trench, where their wounds were dressed with their own field dressings, and then sent to a hospital.

Next morning (February 24th) they were put on a river steamer, the *Basra*, and taken up stream. When in sight of CTesiphon Arch they were overtaken by one of our "Fly" boats, and after the interchange of a few shots the *Basra* surrendered. They were then sent to hospital at Sheikh Saad, where they recovered and rejoined the Battalion later. They stated the Turks had plenty of medical attendance and appliances, but the Turkish doctor made no attempt to redress their wounds; they were merely given dry coarse bread and had to lie on the deck.

The following list gives the boats and their commanders:—

Boats and their Commanders, 23/2/17.

Company.	No. of Boat.	Commander.	
1	1	Havildar Santbir Thapa	⎫ Rowers from
1	2	Havildar Narain Mal	⎬ Sappers
1	3	Naik Ragbir Rana	⎭ and Miners.
1	4	Lieutenant Toogood and Jemadar Guman Sing	⎫
1	5	Lieutenant Baker and Subadar Sarabjit Gurung, M.C.	
1	6	Havildar Kehar Sing Thapa	
1	7	Jemadar Narbahadur Thapa	
2	8	Naik Kangsu Gurung	⎬ Rowers from 1/4th Hants.
1	9	Naik Khatai Gurung	
1	10	Havildar Manbahadur Ghale (missing)	
1	11	Naik Puran Sing Gurung (missing)	
1	12	(Acting Jemadar) Havildar Hari Sing Thapa (missing)	
1	13	Havildar Gamai Sing Gurung	⎭

2nd Trip.

2	1	Havildar Dhan Sing Thapa (missing)	⎫
2	2	L./Naik Kulman Thapa (missing)	⎬ Rowers from Sappers and Miners.
2	3	Major Ridgeway and Subadar Karbir Thapa	
2	4	Jemadar Manbahadur Gurung	⎭

The failure of the second effort to cross showed that this ferry, the most exposed of the three, was no longer of any use, and a message **No. 3 Ferry useless.** to this effect was sent to Major Pemberton, who tried to get pontoons and rowers across from No. 2 Ferry to retrieve some of our stranded ones, but he was unable to effect anything under the heavy fire.

At 9.30 a.m. orders came from the Brigade to abandon further attempts to cross at this point, and, directing the rest of the Battalion **Battalion crosses** to move up to No. 1 Ferry as soon as possible, and having **by No. 1 Ferry,** crossed there to reinforce Toogood and Baker. At 10.15 a.m. **23/2/17.** Lieutenant Rowbotham and No. 3 Company crossed at this ferry, and not only succeeded in reinforcing Toogood (who had been slightly wounded), but managed to push forward gallantly and turned the Turks out of a nullah in front of Toogood and Baker, when both parties combining had a fine little action on their own, **Rowbotham's** killing and wounding a number and capturing close on 100 **company reinforces** Turks. No. 4 Company, under Captain Pritchard and **Toogood, 23/2/17.** Colonel Sweet, with Battalion Headquarters, were across by 11.30, only a small party being left at No. 3 Ferry to keep up communication with Toogood and Rowbotham, and by 5 p.m., with more troops across by the boat-bridge built by the Sappers directly the crossing was effected, the position was secure for our force stretching now practically all round the south bend in which lay the Turkish hangar pits to the north, with the Dahra barracks and ridge of sandhills beyond and the **Crossing succeeds.** buildings at Shumrān to the west, while we had linked up **23/2/17.** with the 2/9th Goorkha Rifles on our left, whose casualties in effecting the crossing had been considerable. As General Maude's despatch puts it : " By nightfall, as a result of this day's operations, our troops had by unconquerable valour and determination forced a passage across a river 340 yards wide in face of heavy opposition, and had secured a position 1000 yards in depth covering our bridgehead." Here we remained till 9 p.m.; fire had died down, the Turks having retired to hold the Dahra ridge and barracks (*Sketch XIV*), and we then bivouacked about 2 a.m. near the river bank on being relieved by the 1/4th Hants. Our **Our casualties,** casualties this day came to 80 killed and 43 wounded. **23/2/17.** amongst the former being Major Ridgeway and Subadar Karbir Thapa. Acting Jemadar Hari Sing Thapa was wounded and taken prisoner by the Turks, but was subsequently recovered on an ambulance boat captured by the R.N.

The 37th and 36th Brigades were ordered to attack the enemy at the Dahra barracks and ridge beyond, some 4000 yards north of us, at 6 a.m. next day (February 24th), our Brigade to be on the left, the 36th on the right, with the 35th and 38th Brigades in support and reserve respectively. The advance was made by the Norfolks and 67th Punjabis in the front line, with the 2/9th Goorkha Rifles and 1/2nd Goorkhas in support, and the Battalion moved out with Nos. 3 and 4 Companies in four waves of platoons, followed by Nos. 1 and 2 in similar formation, our left being on the river bank (*Sketch XIV*). It was not long before our leading platoons came under machine-gun and rifle fire, and we reached a point east of the Shumrān buildings with few casualties, though Captain Pritchard, while leading his company, got severely wounded—a serious loss to us. Now began the most strenuous opposition of this action, for the west end of the barracks in front of the ridge was strongly defended, and here the 67th Punjabis were checked, necessitating our Battalion pushing into their line to carry it farther. This was done, and after a short advance, in which Subadar Shamsher Khawas was killed and Jemadar Lal Sing Rana wounded, we again took up a line in rear of the 67th, prolonging it to the right to fill the gap between ourselves and the 2/9th Goorkha Rifles.

Attack of position at Dahra Barracks and sand ridges, 24/2/17.

Meanwhile the Norfolks, finding somewhat less vigorous opposition in their front, had succeeded in taking at 7.30 a.m. one bit of the ridge, but the resistance in our front not being overcome the 35th Brigade was sent up, the 1/5th Buffs and 2/4th Goorkha Rifles joining us and the 67th, carrying our lines a short distance forward with them, and the buildings were taken, the 1/2nd Goorkha bombers being first into them. Further advance was finally hung up before another hostile position north-east of the Shumrān buildings. Here our lines and units reorganized themselves, our Battalion lining a sunken road in rear of the 67th Punjabis. We remained thus awaiting further orders to continue operations, and wondering how things would end and what had happened at Sannayat, until the evening, when orders were issued withdrawing the 37th Brigade to bivouac near Shumrān Fort, leaving the 35th and 36th Brigades to hold the front line, along which only spasmodic firing occurred, and the night was fairly quiet.

35th Brigade reinforces 37th, and position taken, 24/2/17.

37th Brigade withdrawn; relieved by 35th, 24/2/17.

Our casualties in these two days' fighting were 1 British officer, 3 Goorkha officers, 69 men killed; 2 British officers, 1 Goorkha officer, 72 men wounded—total, 148 of all ranks.

Our casualties.

Sketch No XIV

Rough sketch showing position of the ferries for the crossing on 23·2·17 & Turkish position at Dahra taken on 24·2·17 (By one of our officers)

2ⁿᵈ K.E.O.G.

Turkish trenches in blue.
British positions in red.

GOORKHAS (THE SIRMOOR RIFLE REGIMENT)

Next day (February 25th) it transpired that while the crossing was being carried out the 7th Division had pushed home successfully its assault at Sannayat, routing the enemy there, who retreated on to Kūt, fighting various units of the 1st Corps which had crossed about Guwam during the 24th, where news greeted them of the successful river crossing and the succeeding action at Dahra. Realizing further resistance was useless, the enemy withdrew rapidly in the night from its last positions above Kūt, and the whole of Khalil Bey's army was in full retreat on Baghdad, covered by a strong rearguard. The Cavalry Division was sent across the river during the afternoon of the 24th with intent to cut off the Turks, but unfortunate delays or some misconception of orders caused them to return, giving the enemy the opportunity of escape before the cavalry advanced again at dawn on the 25th.

Sannayat assaulted, Turks in retreat, 23–24/2/17.

There was no delay in starting the pursuit of the retreating enemy, and the duties that fell to the 1/2nd Goorkhas for some days were those of rearguard and then escort to the second line transport of the 14th Division, this latter being onerous and fatiguing work, as bodies of Arabs were frequently hovering on the right flank watching for opportunities of attacking a convoy 5 miles long. The Battalion was on the march practically from 3.30 a.m. on the 25th to 2 a.m. on the 27th January, when the men were so fagged out they could go no farther, and were allowed to halt till 6 a.m., when the march was resumed and the 37th Brigade rejoined at Sāma.

Pursuit of Turks, 25–27/2/17.

On the way many signs of the retreat were seen in deserted Turkish camps, hastily dug trenches, and in one spot seven Krupp guns of 1876 manufacture; in fact, from Kūt to Azizia (*Sketch XV*) the country was strewn with material left by the enemy in his hurry, which became less beyond the latter place. Between February 25th and arrival at Azizia, during the fighting that occurred in the pursuit, and which chiefly concerned the 13th, 3rd, and Cavalry Divisions, the Turks lost 188 officers and 4,300 men taken prisoner, while 38 guns, 11 machine guns, ships and barges with munitions, also fell into our hands.

Turkish retreat and losses.

The Battalion was warned to be ready to march at the head of the main body at 8 a.m. on the 28th, but the move was postponed and finally was cancelled for that day, so the men had a good rest, No. 3 Company furnishing the picquet posts that night. The 14th Division led on March 1st, and the

Halt at Azizia, 2/3/17.

Battalion moved with its Brigade to Rawiyat (17 miles) the following day, a short march bringing the troops to Azizia, where the non-arrival of ration supplies obliged a two days' halt, which most unfortunately allowed the enemy to get well away. The cavalry only got up with them at Lajj, near CTesiphon, and had an action in which they were severely handled by machine guns. A certain amount of flour badly sifted, found on a captured barge, was issued; but this did not go far in satisfying large and urgent needs. The fact was the Commissariat at Sheikh Saad, not expecting so successful a crossing and rapid advance, were not prepared to follow it up with supplies in time.

While at Azizia General Sir Stanley Maude held a parade of the Battalion, at which he presented Subadar Sarabjit Gurung with the ribbon of the Military Cross; Havildar Bahadur Gurung and L./Naik Randhoj Limbu with that of the Indian Distinguished Service Medal. Lieutenant Jerram, who had recovered from his wound, rejoined us here from hospital at Amāra and took command of No. 4 Company.

General Maude presents ribbons, 3/3/17.

The advance was resumed on March 5th to Zeur, the 13th Division leading, the 1/2nd Goorkhas being left behind to guard the supplies which had at last arrived. Early on the 6th the 7th Division coming up released the Battalion, which made camp 16 miles on in a most violent dust-storm blowing for several hours. The following day, moving off at 6.30 a.m., Bostan (15 miles) was reached by noon, where the 14th Division was just moving out; so after a halt for food till 4 p.m. we did the remaining 5 miles to Bāwi, rejoining our Brigade, and a halt was made on the 8th. From Bostan on we found ourselves on pasture land for the first time in this country, making marching pleasanter, in place of the interminable desert of sand and sun-baked alluvial soil. Before reaching camp we passed close to the stupendous arch of CTesiphon, the interesting remains of a palace of the Sassanian rulers in a far-off past, this ancient city attaining its prime in the early part of the fifth century. Across the Tigris, nearly opposite CTesiphon, are the remains of another venerable city, Seleucia, once famous in history, but now covered deep in driftsand, as are all the many ruined cities in Mesopotamia.

Hard marching, 6/3/17.

At Bāwi the force was within 16 miles of Baghdad, and we heard the Turkish rearguard was strongly entrenched at and about Diāla village where the river of that name joins the Tigris about 15 miles by water below Baghdad, or 8 to 9 miles across country. The 35th Brigade and Cavalry Division were crossing the Tigris to

Force at Bāwi crosses Tigris and forces passage of Diāla River, 7–11/3/17.

CAMP AT BAWI.

BAGHDAD.
1. A typical Kelek on the Tigris. 2. A general view from the barracks.

the right bank in order to make a dash for the railway, the 7th Division was to follow them, and the 38th Brigade was under orders to attack Diāla and force the passage of that river about 6 miles to our front. The Intelligence reports about it were found misleading, fords being mentioned and crossing it being treated as easy of accomplishment, whereas the river was found to be in flood, swift, 20 feet deep, and 60 feet wide, with steep mud banks; in fact, not many days elapsed before our steamers were plying up it to Baquba.

On the night of March 8th-9th the 38th Brigade, with the 36th guarding the right flank, endeavoured to force the passage of the Diāla, but failed with considerable loss, all the men in the pontoons being killed by machine gun fire. Eventually an officer with some sixty men did manage to cross, and effected a landing, where they maintained themselves against repeated attacks until next morning, when two battalions got across.

First failure at crossing Diāla, 8–9/3/17.

That night explosions were heard and fires seen in Baghdad city. At 8.15 a.m. on March 9th the 37th Brigade received orders to move at once from Bāwi and relieve the 36th Brigade about 5 miles above Diāla village and 2 miles from the river, and that evening a party of 25 men of ours and of the 2/9th Goorkha Rifles were despatched under Lieutenants Jerram and Gladstone (2/9th Goorkha Rifles) to reconnoitre the river down to Diāla, as reports stated parties of the enemy to be on our side between the two Brigades. During their reconnaissance very heavy firing was going on about Diāla village (the 38th Brigade were then effecting the crossing), but no enemy was seen on our side of the stream (*Sketch XV*).

37th Brigade relieves 36th above Diāla village, 9/3/17.

Very early next morning, the 10th, we were directed to cover with our fire the advance of the two battalions 38th Brigade which were across, but checked. The distance being too great, the Battalion moved up to the bank, dispersing some hostile patrols who had come from farther up river, but we had no means of crossing. Searching a few deserted houses for materials such as could be found for constructing a raft, one of our search parties luckily discovered a buried "gūfa," or coracle—a large circular sort of wicker basket covered with bitumen, and used by the Arabs for crossing rivers. This was got into the water with Havildar Manbahadur Rai, L./Naik Jaicharan Rai, and two or three men, a couple of paddles were hastily improvised, and with doubled telephone cords attached they got over, the coracle being pulled back for others to cross in. All this took a long time over three hours to get one platoon over; so as news was received that the pontoon bridge at Diāla was ready and the

Battalion on Diāla river, 10/3/17.

Brigade was to cross by it, the 1/2nd Goorkhas and 2/9th Goorkha Rifles who were picqueting the right flank were ordered to move as rapidly as possible during the evening of the 10th to that point and cross there. During the move, which was harried somewhat by Arabs, we could hear the 13th Division in action in the distance across the plain in their final attack on the last position (Tel Mahomed mounds) of the enemy's rearguard before Baghdad, who eventually were able to get away during a violent dust-storm. We did not share in this last action south of the city, as before we could cross fresh orders came for the Battalion to remain at Diāla to form bridge defences and a covering force to the 14th Division, the 36th, and remainder of the 37th Brigade, who crossed over. Baghdad was occupied without opposition during the morning of March 11th, the 35th Brigade on the right bank being the first to enter, all Turkish troops having rapidly cleared off up river.

Battalion halted at Diāla village, 11/3/17.

Diāla village was more or less in ruins after the severe shelling on the 9th and 10th, and groves near the river had the appearance of having been subjected to a blizzard stripping all leaves and branches; but a few houses fairly intact were found which were occupied as mess house and quarters, forming the first roof shelter we had had in Mesopotamia, and since early December, 1916, the first shelter of any sort we had been under. The place was surrounded with fields of onions, beans, and beetroot, some of course, trodden into pulp, while others escaped injury; and some gardens of orange, fig, and peach trees had also survived the storm of battle, their contents proving useful additions to our very low rations, just now reduced to biscuits and bully beef. Our duties during our stay here were those of salvage and the burying of dead, with which both banks and the plain as far as the Tel Mahomed mounds were littered—a most unpleasant task, as the corpses had been lying for several days, making numbers of the men very sick, and the free tot of rum issued was well earned. On March 13th the Battalion received the pleasing notice of the following rewards for gallantry at the Tigris crossing on February 23rd—viz., Lieutenant C. G. Toogood, the Distinguished Service Order; 2/Lieutenant Baker, the Military Cross; No. 3699 Havildar Kesar Sing Rana, the Indian Distinguished Service Medal; No. 2896 Rifleman Jagia Rana, the Indian Order of Merit, 2nd Class.

Diāla village and duties.

Rewards for Tigris crossing.

During the Battalion's stay at Diāla, March 11th to 21st, a number of our men who could be spared and wanted to see Baghdad (*Sketch XV*), of which all had heard so much, were marched to the city 10 miles off, and returned in a thick dust storm tired and disappointed. Many of these had seen Cairo, and naturally, after the exaggerated accounts all had heard of the place, they expected something here similar to the Egyptian capital. The river front only of Baghdad is of pleasing aspect; a couple of hundred yards inland one is lost in a maze of narrow insanitary streets and squalor—Basra on a larger scale. The celebrated covered bazaars had been looted and knocked about by Arabs even in the short space of time between the Turks evacuating and the British entering. Later, when these bazaars were reopened and filled with motley crowds of Arabs, Khurds, Persians, Chaldeans, in their distinctive dresses, certainly interest was aroused, and the scenes became animated and picturesque. A few mosque domes and their minarets, both bright with coloured encaustic tiles (an art said to have died out), give pleasing bits of colour standing up amongst the sea of drab dun-coloured houses. There are also here and there picturesque street corners, as the Baghdadis love to build their upper windows standing well out from the wall above the street, the timber supports of which are often carved. The better class houses show a small amount of greenery in palms and vines in little enclosed gardens, but, taking it all round, the Goorkhas' disappointment was justified, seeming, as they declared, " a place not worth fighting for."

Brief description of Baghdad, March, 1917.

The city of some 170,000 inhabitants which occupies both sides of the Tigris, here about 280 yards wide—the old original circular city of Haroun el Rashid being the portion on the right bank, is really in a large oasis; for beyond its old ruined walls, $1\frac{1}{4}$ miles from the left and $\frac{3}{4}$ of a mile from the right bank, the only remaining old fortified entrances in which are the Bab el Wastāni gate to the north and that of Bab el Sherqi to the east, stretches at once the open desert as far as the eye can reach. These walls are of great breadth, and motors can be driven along the top in spite of their ruinous state, attesting the strength, as do the mosques the earlier opulence, of this city, once the greatest seat of learning and trade in the East. A narrow belt of fruit gardens and date palm groves stretches along the river banks above and below Baghdad to the suburbs of Kazimain 3 miles up, and Karrāda 2 miles down, stream, where many units of the force were now billeted or camped.

On March 20th Captain McCleverty, with 100 rifles was sent to the Mismai ruins 6 miles east, as a support to the cavalry reconnoitring towards Medūr, and that flank being found clear all returned by nightfall. The following day half the 37th Brigade marched north for Baquba, 43 miles up the Diāla River,

Reconnaissance, 20/3/17.

Battalion sent to Hanaidi camp; Brigade moves to Baquba. while the 1/2nd Goorkhas and 2/9th Goorkha Rifles were sent to Hanaidi, 3 miles south of the city, where camp was formed in a pleasant date palm grove close to the river. The few days here were passed in washing clothes, bathing, company drills, certain escort duties, and Lieutenant Harrop was sent back to Azizia to bring up our dump. Captain Hill rejoined us here from hospital at Amāra, and took over temporary command of the Battalion, Colonel Sweet being ill in hospital.

The long series of operations during late 1916 and early 1917 having ended with the taking of Baghdad, it will be of interest to record some extracts from General Maude's " Summary " in his despatch of April 10th, 1917, covering the period from August, 1916, to end of March, 1917. He says:—

" During the past winter months the fighting has been strenuous and continuous, and the strain imposed on all ranks, both at the front and on lines of communication, severe. But they have responded whole-heartedly to every call, and their reward is the measure of their success. **Extract from Gen. Maude's " Summary " of Operations."** The nature of the operations has been as varied as it has been complex, and the training of the troops has been tested, first in the fierce hand-to-hand fighting in trench warfare round Kūt and Sannayat, and later in the more open battles which characterized the operations in the Dahra Bend, the crossing of the Tigris, the advance on Baghdad. From this ordeal they have emerged with a proud record, and have dealt the enemy a series of hard blows the full significance of which will not easily be effaced. British and Indian troops working side by side have vied with each other in their efforts to close with the enemy, and all ranks have been imbued throughout with that offensive spirit which is the soldier's finest jewel. As regards Regimental Commanders and those under them, it is not easy to do full justice to their sterling performances. Leadership has never faltered, whilst all ranks, by their heroism, endurance, and devotion to duty, have almost daily affirmed their superiority over their opponents in the bitterest struggles. The fierce encounters west of the Hai, the passages of the Tigris and Diāla, and the final storming of Sannayat, may perhaps be mentioned as typical of all that is best in the British and Indian soldier. For the success achieved the fighting spirit of the troops has been mainly responsible, but the dash and gallantry of individuals and units have been welded into a powerful weapon by that absolute sympathy which has existed between all services and all branches."

The tide of war having now rolled well beyond the historic city, we may look briefly into the reasons for going so far, and further still, it having been

CAMP ON TIGRIS AT HANAIDI, NEAR BAGHDAD.

Sketch by L.W.S.

Military situation and reasons for continued operations, March, 1917.

held by many that Baghdad should mark our farthest point. The questions propounded by the occupation of March 11th were—should we stop here and adopt a defensive rôle, or should we go on ? The city, which, as stated before, had been the focus of all Turkish lines of advance down the two great rivers or into South-West Persia, and also of German propaganda and assistance generally to the enemy, was in our hands, but was endangered by approach on three lines—viz., those of the Tigris, Euphrates, and Diāla rivers. The Turks still had a considerable force below Mosul, another operating against the Russians on the upper Diāla in South-West Persia, and a force about Hit on the Euphrates which could be reinforced from Aleppo (*Sketch XV*). The enemy on the Tigris having been beaten and more or less demoralized, co-operation with our Russian allies being desirable, and it being necessary to secure the approaches to Baghdad, were the determining factors in settling the matter. Hence the forward moves by the British forces even beyond Sāmarra when that was taken, and up the Euphrates and Diāla ; Mosul and Hit eventually marking the limit of our progress on the Tigris and Euphrates respectively, while political considerations and the frustration of German schemes in North Persia obliged us later to go still farther afield, even to the Caspian. It should, however, be remembered that General Allenby, operating in Palestine successfully, was drawing off Turkish troops who might otherwise have been reinforcing their Euphrates or Tigris fronts, and so materially assisted the British forces in Mesopotamia

CHAPTER XVII.

March 27th to April 30th, 1917. (*Sketch XV.*)

WE were wondering in what direction the Battalion would next be called upon to operate when, on March 27th, orders came to march to Baquba, which had been occupied by General Keary's column a few days earlier, escorting a battery and field ambulance, and a start was made at 7 p.m. Cassel's Post, 15 miles, was reached by 2 a.m., and a halt made till 6.30 a.m., when the march to Conningham's Post, 12 miles on, was resumed, and completed by 10.30 a.m. Here a few men of the last draft, unable to continue marching, were sent up on a river steamer. At 2.30 p.m. on the 28th the column continued the route, entering Baquba, 13 miles on, by 10.30 p.m. The latter part of this march saw much delay from carts falling into water channels, but the whole performance for heavily-laden infantry (no transport being available for Lewis guns and magazines) of 40 miles in 27½ hours over the desert was, under the circumstances, a remarkably good one. That night we took over a number of picquets from the 67th Punjabis.

Battalion marches to Baquba, 27/3/17.

Baquba (*Sketch XV*) was found to be a fair-sized town situated on both banks of the Diāla, with large orange-groves interspersed among the houses, a quaint feature of the place lying in the large numbers of storks nesting on almost every roof. We soon settled down in bivouac in a large palm-grove on the right bank for a welcome rest, which, however, did not last long, for about 10 p.m. on March 29th we received orders to get under way again to escort a Howitzer battery and a machine gun section to a place beyond Deltāwa, 16 miles off, where part of the 13th Division were after their action on the Marl Plain, and where the Turks were attacking them again. Transport was collected, rations drawn, and the column moved off at 2 a.m. on March 30th. It was a pitch-dark night, the Sapper guide lost the way, and after much wandering till daylight Deltāwa was reached at 10.30 a.m., the last half of the march being through a very fertile, well-watered country, in pleasant contrast to the drab, dusty lands below Baquba. Deltāwa was found to be a very extensive village with large gardens full of fruit-trees and date-palms, intersected by numerous canals

Baquba.

Escort duty to Deltāwa, 29/3/17.

THE LEANING MINARET IN BAGHDAD.

Photo by   *Exclusive News Agency*

1. The "Mejidieh" river steamer lying off Baghdad.
2. The Bridge of Boats at Baghdad.

and water channels, which later did not make for healthiness as they produced a good deal of fever. Three miles beyond this, and the 13th Divisional Headquarters at Khan Nahrwan was reached by 11.30 a.m., but the action was found to be over, so a halt was made till 7 p.m., when the return tramp started. After bivouacking for some hours till 6.30 a.m., the Battalion got back to Baquba by 9.30 a.m. on the 31st, where Colonel Sweet, rejoined from hospital at Baghdad, greeted us.

General Keary's column at this time was pressing the Turks beyond Sharobān to the Jebel Hamrin range on the Khānākin road (*Sketch XV*), but had failed before greater force in men and guns (the Turkish 2nd and 6th Divisions retiring before the Russians), and had been obliged to withdraw.

We were in camp here for a week busy over endless fatigues, occupying 270 men daily in unloading barges and stacking commissariat stores, also in sending out parties to search for arms in neighbouring villages, the rest of the Battalion being on guards and furnishing part of the Movable Column. The evening of April 7th the Battalion was ordered, together with a section of the 187th Machine Gun Company, to start at 4.30 a.m. next morning for a point 17 miles south-west of Deli Abbas (*Sketch XV*), there to report to the General Officer Commanding Cavalry Division, he being in need of reinforcements, as a Turkish force from Persia *en route* to join their retiring Tigris army was menacing him. Deltāwa was reached by 9.30 a.m. on the 8th, where a halt was made for two hours; and Abu Tamar, 18 miles farther, by 7.30 p.m., where Lieutenant-Colonel H. Champain's camp was met, with whom we bivouacked that night, tired out with the long tramp. Fortunately the day had not been hot, but a strong gale raising clouds of dust made for considerable discomfort.

Battalion sent to reinforce Cavalry, 8/4/17.

Resuming the march next morning at 5 a.m., the 16 miles to Dishdāri were covered by noon, the sound of distant gun fire being audible from 11 o'clock on. Here information was received as to what was happening—viz., that the enemy, estimated at 6,000 infantry with 28 guns and 700 cavalry with 9 guns belonging to the Turkish 2nd Division from Persia, were in front and threatening our left. It appeared their intention was to attack the line of communications of our two Divisions (3rd and 7th) advancing up the Tigris, and to delay that advance by obliging reinforcements to be sent from the Tigris to this right flank of General Maude's army, while the Turkish 18th Corps was advancing down the Shatt el Adhaim.

Joins Cavalry at Dishdāri, 9/4/17.

The 1/2nd Goorkhas were first ordered to take up a position astride the Deli Abbas road facing north-east, but at 5 p.m. the whole force was directed to retire 6½ miles, where we dug in on the right of the Cavalry near the mosque of Mahomed Ibn Hassan, and where, fortunately, our transport mules got water—their first drink after twenty-six hours. At 5 a.m. on April 11th all stood to arms, and the Cavalry with the Royal Horse Artillery guns moving out, came in contact with the Turks, who were advancing and trying to work round the right of our line. Our guns were soon active checking the hostile move for a time, till two Brigades from the 13th Division near Dogāmeh, on the Tigris, coming up during the afternoon, surprised the enemy, who drew off, and our position was rendered more secure. The Battalion, temporarily attached to the 35th Brigade, was further strengthened by the arrival out here of a draft of 190 men under 2/Lieutenant A. E. Warhurst and Jemadar Aiman Rana.

Turks attack, but retire on our reinforcements arriving, 11/4/17.

At 3 p.m. on the 12th the 35th Brigade advanced, with the 37th Dogras and 2/9th Goorkha Rifles in the front line, the 1/5th Buffs and 1/2nd Goorkhas in support, and the 102nd Grenadiers in reserve; and on reaching the junction of the Nahr Tawila and Nahr Khalis Canals the Battalion was directed to fill the gap between the 2/9th Goorkha Rifles on our left and the right of the 40th Brigade (13th Division), which had been sent from Sindiah on the Tigris, to this flank. A certain amount of shelling went on, causing the Battalion 3 casualties, and the following day the force advanced, being vigorously opposed, in which our casualties were 35, including Lieutenant Tanburne killed and Jemadar Adjutant Tilbir Thapa badly wounded. One of our batteries close by suffered heavy losses. That night, the enemy being only some 800 yards in front, an attack was ordered, but later cancelled, the enemy having retired. The 35th Brigade followed up towards Deli Abbas, but touch with him was not gained, though the Battalion had 3 more casualties from his shells. On the night of the 15th the Brigade bivouacked 6 miles from Deli Abbas, when it was found the enemy had withdrawn into the hills, where it was not considered desirable to follow them. The force therefore returned to Abu Tamar, where we were on picquet duty for a short while, and thence proceeded to Deltāwa, where a draft of 30 men and Lieutenant Baker, rejoined from hospital, met us.

Force advances, 12/4/17.

Action of 13/4/17 and our casualties.

Turks retreat into hills, 15/4/17.

Arrival of a Draft.

On April 21st the Battalion, together with the 2/9th Goorkha Rifles, received orders to march to Dogāmeh on the Tigris, to join General Marshall's force on the lower Shatt el Adhaim, who was about to attack the Turks (part of their 18th Corps) on that river; while General Keary's Column and the Cavalry Division held the rest of the enemy on the Deli Abbas—Sharobān line. On the way we passed over the Nahrwān Canal, a very ancient work for irrigating the country between the Tigris and the hills; and a marvellous work it was, almost as wide as the Suez Canal, with banks in places rising 40 feet above the plain, and with remains of bridges and dams. It took off from the Tigris at Daur, a little above Sāmarra, and ancient history states the canal head was adorned with a golden statue of Nebuchadnezzar, who conceived the idea of this stupendous work and carried it through. We also crossed the Turkish light railway connecting the Kifri coal mines with Sindiah on the Tigris, and which as far as Chāliyeh had fallen to General Cayley's force, together with rolling stock, on April 10th.

Battalion to join Gen. Marshall's force, 21/4/17.

The Nahrwān Canal.

At Dogāmeh, where Captains Hill and McCleverty, with Lieutenants Snow and Baker, left us on leave, we joined the 35th Brigade (13th Division), to which we were attached for these operations. The Shatt el Adhaim River, coming down from the Khurdistan hills, runs through a fairly broad valley with high cliffs on each side, and joins the Tigris a little above Sindiah (*Sketch XV*). The Turks, having been worsted by the 3rd and 7th Divisions at Mushaidie and Beled on the Tigris right bank, had now retired to positions about Istabulat, their main defensive line being at Sāmarra with their left flank on the Shatt el Adhaim in the neighbourhood of Band i Adhaim village, where they were strongly entrenched and expecting the support of their 2nd Division coming from the Kirkuk side, after their 14th Division had been driven up the river with heavy loss in the action of April 14th.

The Shatt el Adhaim and situation, late April, 1917.

Three days were occupied in reconnaissances, the guns on both sides were busy, and the 38th and 40th Brigades advanced to attack Band i Adhaim village on the left bank at dawn on April 30th, that position being now held by the Turkish 2nd and the remains of the 14th Divisions. The 35th Brigade advanced at the same time up the right bank, and the assault following immediately after the Artillery bombardment was successful; but the 35th Brigade, with 102nd Grenadiers and 2/9th Goorkha Rifles in front line,

Attack on Band i Adhaim, 30/4/17.

followed by the Buffs and 1/2nd Goorkhas in support, were checked by the Turks, with machine guns well dug in on a ridge jutting out into the valley, and from its shape named the " Boot." Our initial success on the left bank, however, obliged the enemy to give up the " Boot " so as to help on the other bank, on which our Battalion was ordered to cross the river to support the 40th Brigade, who were being heavily counter-attacked. A severe sand-storm sprang up during the battle blotting out everything, and in the murky atmosphere the two Brigades on the left bank got separated; a Turkish counter-attack happened during the storm to strike this gap, which for a time cut off a portion of the 40th Brigade, and they recaptured seven of their guns previously taken by us. The Brigade extricated itself after heavy hand-to-hand fighting just as the air cleared and the storm passed, and reserves coming up the situation was restored in our favour. The Turks drew off with heavy casualties, several guns and 750 prisoners being captured, but of the latter, some 400, taking advantage of the sandstorm, escaped. That night our Battalion relieved the 8th Cheshires in Brigade support, the only incident being that of an attack on one of our batteries by a party of mounted Arabs, to repel which we sent out one company; and early next morning our aeroplanes reported this portion of the Turkish force to have retreated to a position in the hills some 8 miles away. Our own casualties in this action were very slight, but some units of the 38th and 40th Brigades lost 50 per cent.

Battalion sent to support 40th Brigade, 30/4/17.

Sketch by L.W.S.

CORNER IN BAGHDAD CITY, AUGUST, 1917.

CHAPTER XVIII.

May 1st to December 31st, 1917. (*Sketch XV.*)

During the last week in April, 1917, the stubborn battles round Istabulat had been fought by the Tigris main force. The Turk's last stand at Sāmarra had been broken down with serious losses to them, several guns, and 27 officers and nearly 700 prisoners being taken. Their total casualties in this four days' fighting were 3,700 men. General Maude now brought operations to a close, the hot weather being upon us. Sāmarra became the advanced summer headquarters, and those of General Marshall's force of the 14th Division on the Shatt el Adhaim, returned to the Diāla side. Our Battalion, together with the 2/9th Goorkha Rifles and a Brigade Royal Field Artillery, returned to Baquba by May 9th, where Lieutenant Ennis with a draft of 85 men (52 of whom were wounded recovered) met us.

Operations close for hot weather, May, 1917.

The Battalion was soon to be split up, for on the 11th it was sent back to the Tigris where we garrisoned the river posts of Kasirin, Khan Jadidah, Daudieh, and El Mimar, relieving the 2/5th Goorkha Rifles (*Sketch XV*). Here till early August, we were employed in laying out and arranging the posts, in work on a road connecting Khan Jadidah and Daudieh with Baquba, escorts to convoys, etc., ordinary drills filling in spare time. Parties were also sent to Baquba for transport and Lewis gun courses. Our strength now was 11 British officers, including the Medical Officer, 8 Goorkha officers, 651 other ranks, and 38 followers.

Battalion in posts on Tigris, May to Aug., 1917.

During June we were ordered to send 40 non-commissioned officers to help raise our 3rd Battalion, and were still further split up by having to send a company to hold Cassel's and Conningham's Posts on the Diāla below Baquba. This month the following Serbian decorations were awarded for gallant and distinguished services :—

Foreign Decorations. 3030 Havildar Atibal Gurung, the Cross of Karageorge, 2nd Class ; 4487 Rifleman Khumba Sing Gurung, Gold Medal ; 4216 Rifleman Raskar Gurung, Silver Medal.

In spite of great heat the health of the Battalion was remarkably good, rationing matters went well, and all ranks received an issue of ice daily, which was duly appreciated.

In early July Colonel Sweet proceeded on leave to India, the command in his absence being held by Captain Ross, 2/8th Goorkha Rifles, as Captain McCleverty on return from leave was sent to Baghdad as Staff Captain. The posts at Kasirin and Daudieh were now closed, our units there being sent across the Diāla to occupy a post on the Mahrūt Canal 14 miles east of Baquba, where they relieved the 2/9th Goorkha Rifles detachment. We now learnt our next move would be to Beled Rūz 25 miles east of Baquba, so as Lieutenants Jerram and Snow were returning from leave with a large draft of 254 men, these were ordered to proceed to Beled Rūz direct and await the Battalion there. This move took place on August 10th, when Khan Jadidah was vacated and the 13th Divisional Transport Company escorted to Baquba. Here Captain Ross was sent to the 2/4th Goorkha Rifles, being succeeded in temporary command by Captain Blandy, 2/9th Goorkha Rifles, and Captain Auret from the 127th Baluchis also joined us. We also were directed to send Jemadar Banbir Sing Thapa and 50 rifles to join Colonel Hesketh's Column co-operating with other troops near Sharobān.

Large Draft arrives early Aug., 1917.

Battalion moves to Beled Rūz, 10/8/17.

Mahrūt Post was reached on August 15th, and Beled Rūz next day, when we learnt of coming operations against the Turks in the Jebel Hamrin positions, north of Sharobān on the way to Kizil Robāt, where our troops had been unsuccessful in April, and it was expected the Russians from near Kasr i Shirin would co-operate. Reconnaissances were pushed to the north, in which we took part, otherwise the usual drills and duties went on, varied on August 25th by our being rearmed with the new H.V. rifles, and on Captain Blandy falling ill he was succeeded by Major Brett, 1/7th Goorkha Rifles. Railhead now at Baquba from Baghdad, was pushed on to Sharobān, greatly easing supply affairs for the 14th Division watching this flank towards Persia.

Reconnaissances and coming operations, Aug., 1917.

Railway pushed on beyond Baquba.

Turkish aeroplanes frequently reconnoitred in this direction from Kifri, on one occasion in July two came over, and one getting its water tube damaged had to come down some distance off. The other then descended and tried to rise again with the whole party—2 pilots, 2 observers, kits, 3 machine guns, and carbines, etc., with the result they could not rise more than 400 feet, but they got away before we could capture them. They eventually smashed up in the desert, two of the men only succeeding in reaching our lines at Sāmarra. The Turkish force in the Diāla—Kifri area were estimated

CAMPS AND TRENCHES NEAR BAQUBA.

GOORKHAS (THE SIRMOOR RIFLE REGIMENT) 155

Estimate of Turks' force in the Diāla —Kifri area. at between 6,000 and 7,000 rifles forming part of their 13th Army Corps with 650 sabres, 20 guns, 4 howitzers, 4 mountain guns, and 24 machine guns. This force was divided up in positions on the Jebel Hamrin range right bank Diāla, at foot of the same hills on the Kizil Robāt road, at Mansuriyeh north of Sharobān, and Kāra Tepe (*Sketch XV*). The great heat obliged active operations to be delayed till October, meanwhile the Battalion remained at Beled Rūz, escorting survey parties in the district, and digging the usual defences, with amusements in the way of polo and football for the men. Those who had shot-guns were

Shikar. able to enjoy small game shooting, for this locality swarmed with sand grouse (the pin tailed variety) and black partridge, while gazelle were also to be found. Colonel Sweet rejoined us from leave and despatches showed he was awarded the Distinguished Service Order, while Captain McCleverty and Lieutenant Jerram gained the

Honours and Rewards, 15/9/17. Military Cross, and on September 15th at a Battalion parade Brigadier-General Maclachlan, 37th Brigade, presented the Indian Distinguished Service Medal to Jemadar Guman Sing Gurung, 3551 Havildar Narain Mal, and 4383 Naik Parsabahadur Thapa, and 132 Rifleman Padam Sing Thapa, the Indian Order of Merit to 3893 Havildar Gorea Gurung; also notifying that Subadar-Major Tulsiram Gharti was to be awarded the Order of British India.

Regimental Band arrives, Sept., 1917. Our Regimental Band from Dehra arrived during the month and enlivened the evenings several times a week.

Lieutenant Loftus Tottenham joined us from the 51st Sikhs, and the strength of the Battalion at the end of September stood at 11 British officers, 12 Goorkha officers, and 959 other ranks.

Activity started at the end of the month when on the 29th our Cavalry Brigade with slight opposition captured Mendali, 30 miles east of Beled Rūz, on which the Battalion was ordered to send out a company

Mendali occupied, 29/9/17. under Lieutenants Jerram and Tottenham to improve the ford and approaches at Baghdadia on the Abu i Naft river, the whole Battalion moving to Mendali on October 7th. Before leaving the cheering news had come in of General Brooking's (15th Division) great success at Rāmādie on the Euphrates, where after a severe battle the Turkish force had been completely routed, 14 guns and 3,200 prisoners being taken.

At Mendali (*Sketch XV*) defence works were begun at once, but on October 13th the Battalion was ordered back to Beled Rūz on relief by a detachment of the Norfolks, there to join Brigadier-General Maclachlan's Column for operations in the Jebel Hamrin range, and we were directed to reduce to old war strength, leaving surplus men there under Lieutenant Duncan. We also received 8 new Lewis guns. On October 17th the column consisting of the 37th Brigade Headquarters, 67th Punjabis, 2nd Norfolks, 1/2nd Goorkhas, 2/9th Goorkha Rifles, Wing 128th Pioneers, a Battery Royal Field Artillery, and another of howitzers, 2 Mountain Batteries—marched for Tel Qubbah, 16 miles, and next day to Chahriz, where we joined up with Norton's Column from Mendali.

Battalion joins Gen. Maclachlan's Column, 13/10/17.

Column's composition.

The objective of operations was Kizil Robāt and the Turkish positions on right bank Diāla from the Jebel Hamrin passes northwards. The 13th Division was to take Deli Abbas, and force the passes north and east of Suhāniah, the 35th Brigade to attack Mansuriyeh, the 37th Brigade and Cavalry Brigade to cross the range, and move on Kizil Robāt. The 1/2nd Goorkhas were detailed to assist the 35th Brigade by a flank attack along the range towards the Diāla (*Sketch XV*).

Objectives of operations.

On October 18th the 13th Division were successful at Deli Abbas, the 35th Brigade also at Mansuriyeh, both then moving on the Jebel Hamrin hills. Our Battalion found the Turkish trenches on the range unoccupied, and reached the Sharobān—Kizil Robāt road without incident, but the rest of the 37th Brigade after crossing the hills were soon in action beyond the Kardarra River, running along the northern foot of the range. By evening the town was taken, the Turks blowing up the bridge just before our troops entered. The success was damped by General Maude's order to vacate the place, which was done next day, the Battalion with the 2/9th Goorkha Rifles being sent to Sheikh Sālih, whence they joined the Brigade at the Kardarra crossing. Naturally the Turks returned to Kizil Robāt, but made their main positions on the right bank opposite the town. Thus we remained with desultory artillery duels for six weeks, awaiting the nearer approach of the Russian force under Generals Barātov and Bicherakov, who in the country west of Kermanshah devastated by long periods of fighting, were having the greatest difficulties with supplies and transport.

Kizil Robāt taken, 18/10/17.

Approach of Russians awaited.

It was on November 18th that the regrettable news reached us of the death of General Sir Stanley Maude in Baghdad, it was said of cholera; later rumour had it he was poisoned. A most capable and energetic commander his place was by no means easy to fill. A few days later we learnt of the changes in higher commands necessitated by the sad occurrence—viz., that General Marshall commanding the forces on this flank was to succeed in command of the Army; General Egerton commanding our 14th Division to command the 3rd Corps; while Brigadier-General Thompson, 35th Brigade, became the 14th Divisional Commander.

Gen. Maude's Death, 18/10/17.

Changes in high commands.

Arrangements were now made for a push across the Diāla River near Kizil Robāt, towards Kāra Tepe, with the Russians to co-operate from Kasr i Shirin. These were for the 13th Division to attack the Abu Zenabi and Sakal Tutan passes in the Jebel Hamrin, west of the Diāla, the 35th Brigade to force a crossing between Tawila and Kizil Robāt; the 37th Brigade to move north of the latter town, and attack the positions of Tel Burdan and Tel Ahmādiat, the bulk of the cavalry moving by a detour to the north-west of Kāra Tepe. On December 2nd our Brigade (37th) left the Kardarra crossing, advancing up the Kirchand nullah, the 2/9th Goorkha Rifles and 67th Punjabis to force the crossing 3 miles and 1 mile respectively above the town, the Norfolks to cross opposite it; our Battalion forming the rearguard. The crossings were somewhat heavily opposed, the 2/9th Goorkha Rifles suffering many losses, the 67th Punjabis unable to cross at their point moved upstream and followed the Goorkhas, and the Norfolks were unable to cross at the town until our guns put up a heavy bombardment of Tel Burdan; when the 67th Punjabis and 2/9th Goorkha Rifles having gained a long ridge on the enemy's left the enemy rapidly retreated. The troops on the left had great difficulty in forcing the Turks out of the strongly-defended passes, where 2 guns and 180 prisoners were taken; this delay giving the Turk his opportunity of getting back to Kāra Tepe pursued by the 35th Brigade, and out of which he was again driven to Kifri by our cavalry and some Russian troops. This was our people's first acquaintance with the Russians, whom they described as a fine lot of men, especially the Cossacks and Mountain Artillerymen as yet untainted by the revolution in their

Resumption of operations, Kizil Robāt and Kifri, early Dec., 1917.

Plans and arrangements.

37th Brigade advances, 2/12/17.

Crossing effected above Kizil Robāt, 2/12/17.

35th Brigade pursue Turks; Russians co-operate.

own country and with discipline still good, but which excellent state of affairs did not last much longer. A number of their wounded, including a cavalry colonel, were tended in our Ambulance and were under the care of a Russian lady (Princess Lievin), who had been with their Red Cross for two hard years. Two of our young officers hearing she spoke English and desiring to pay their respects, went to call on her at the Ambulance, taking a goose they had shot for her But to their disappointment the doctors did not play up or introduce the young fellows, who in their shyness left the bird, which the doctors enjoyed.

Impressions of Russians.

On December 7th the 35th Brigade returned from Kāra Tepe, further pursuit being unnecessary as our airmen reported all Turkish troops being now in retreat to Mosul from Kifri (*Sketch XV*), where they had fired the coal mines. The Battalion returned to the Kardarra crossing where it remained till the end of the month, chiefly being employed in road making across the Jebel Hamrin and in bridging, with leisure spent in shikar for which this locality was a paradise. Captain McCleverty had rejoined us from Staff duty in Baghdad, on December 9th and became Adjutant again. The weather was now bitterly cold, and a good deal of snow and rain interfered with work and comfort. Kits were brought up from the dump at Sharobān, and Christmas Day was pleasantly spent with sports for the Brigade. On December 31st a further move towards the hill country was made, the Battalion being sent to Mirjāna, 10 miles north of Kizil Robāt (*Sketch XV*).

Turk's fire Kifri coal mines and retreat.

Battalion at Kardarra Crossing, and Christmas, 1917.

Battalion moves to Mirjāna, 31/12/17.

At this time the British officers present with the Battalion were as noted below*, and the strength of the Goorkha ranks stood at :—Goorkha officers, 17 ; rank and file, 1,140 ; followers, 88.

The War Diary records that so far during its active service in Mesopotamia the casualties in action came to 164 killed, 480 wounded, 105 missing believed killed.

---

* Lieut.-Colonel E. H. Sweet, D.S.O. ; Major A. S. Auret, from 127th Baluchis ; Captain A. Dallas Smith, M.C. ; Captain G. McCleverty, M.C. (Adjutant) ; Lieutenant C. G. Toogood, D.S.O. ; Lieutenant K. M. Coxe ; Lieutenant J. S. Lloyd ; Lieutenant M. R. Jerram, M.C. ; Lieutenant C. A. Snow ; Lieutenant W. S. Baker, M.C. ; Lieutenant A. E. Warhurst, from 2/6th Goorkha Rifles ; Lieutenant F. T. Loftus Tottenham ; Lieutenant R. D. Bucknall ; Lieutenant D. L. Duncan ; Lieutenant B. S. Mould ; Lieutenant P. Meyrick Jones ; Captain D. H. Murray, R.A.M.C.

Sketch of area of Mesopotamia Campaign 1914-18

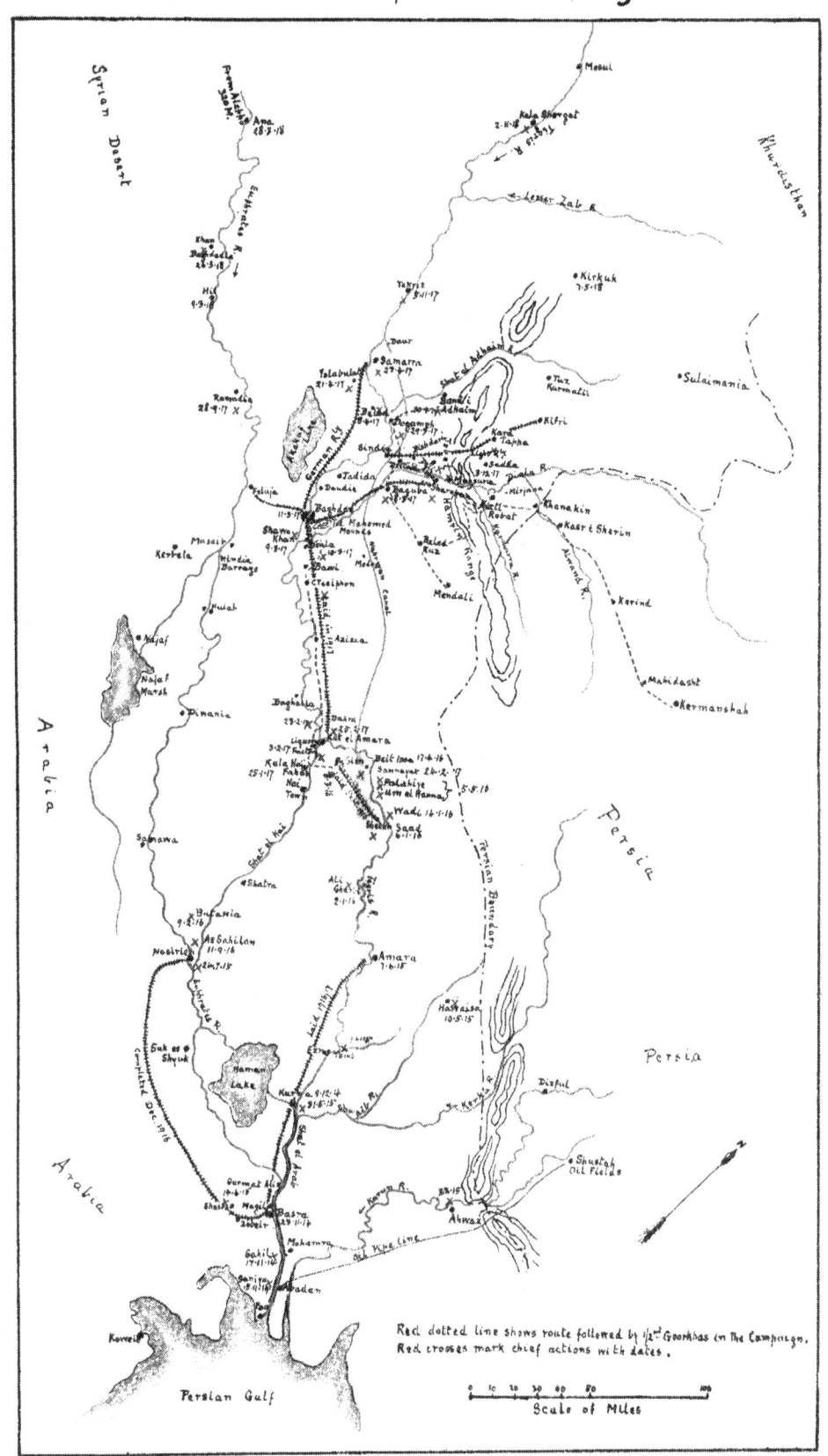

Sketch N° XV

CHAPTER XIX.

January 1st, 1918, to Christmas, 1918. (*Sketches XVII, XV.*)

The stay of the Battalion at Mirjāna (*Sketch XV*) was uneventful, the chief activity lying with our aeroplanes which bombed various villages beyond Kasr i Shirin occupied by Turks, also reconnoitring over Kifri and Tūz Karmatli, and reporting the return of the enemy to that region in strength, which spies and the Intelligence Branch put at near 8,000 rifles, 52 guns, and 78 machine guns. In the middle of the month the Hants Regiment passed through on its way to a point beyond Kasir i Shirin (*Sketch XVI*) to bring away the Australian Wireless Section lent to the Russians and which they had left behind stranded when they recently retired to Kermanshah. It now became known that as a result of the Revolution in their country these far distant forces had practically broken up as formed bodies of troops, except a small force of Cossacks, which still preserved its discipline under General Bicherakov. The disorganized Russian troops proclaimed their country had made peace with Germany and that it was only the English who were intent on carrying on the war. A little later a column under Colonel Bridges with the 14th Hussars passed through on its way north, and it was said the Hussars were destined for the Caspian Sea; but what actually was afoot was not yet known. Turkish airmen were now busy and our camps were bombed several times, but without much damage, Sharobān and Baquba also coming in for their visitations. The weather was bitter cold, snowstorms alternated with heavy rain, and water in basins was almost always frozen in the morning. Still much work on roads and defences was put in.

Russians withdraw under effects of Revolution.

First news of move into Northern Persia.

On January 27th the 37th Brigade was ordered to concentrate at the old Kardarra crossing, there to prepare a line of defence in case the Turks knowing the Russians had withdrawn, should attack this flank again. General Headquarters Baghdad, had ordered this particular line to be taken up, which for many reasons known to those on the spot was not good, and was reported as such, but without effect. We found all our former trenches and defence works had melted away with the heavy rains, so an entirely fresh series had to be dug in very bad weather. A particularly violent storm on February 5th blew our camp flat.

With the passing of General Dunsterville and a small party *en route* to Persia about the middle of January, it transpired a new and distant scheme of operations was in the air, and rumours as to the 1/2nd Goorkhas probably following him became prevalent; such a possible move being viewed with pleasure as taking us up into high ranges far from the hot, drab plains of Mesopotamia. It was not till later that we learnt of the scheme afoot or that our move into Persia was to become a fact, but the reasons for this venture so far from the base at Baghdad may here be explained.

First Advance of "Dunster" Force, mid-Jan., 1918.

Owing to Germany's pre-war schemes having now broken down for absorbing Asia Minor, penetrating into farther Asia and obtaining domination there, for which their Berlin—Baghdad railway was primarily intended, they had shifted their plans to a more northern area. These new plans being to work their Asian penetration along the line Berlin—Bāku—Bokhara, whence they could exercise a most disturbing influence on Afghanistan and India. The object of General Dunsterville's move was to prevent this by occupying towns in the neighbourhood of the Caspian Sea, by exerting our influence in Northern Persia, by reorganizing the broken units of Russian, Georgian, and Armenian soldiery, and with them to stem the advance of Turko-German forces from the Black Sea eastward.

Reasons for bringing "Dunster" Force into existence.

It was found impossible to spare sufficient troops to meet a situation so far off, for Bāku on the Caspian is about 800 miles from Baghdad, the 3rd, 7th and 13th Divisions were fully occupied in the further advance up the Tigris to Mosul, and the 14th Division in dealing with the Turks round Kifri and Kirkūk, and as something had to be done a mission headed by Brigadier-General Dunsterville composed of 200 British officers with 400 non-commissioned officers, was formed for the purpose. All were specially selected, a large number being from Colonial regiments, and they were to take the place of leaders and instructors of the reorganized units. Some time was taken to collect and despatch this mission, which from the secret nature of the venture became known familiarly as the "Hush Hush" Brigade, officially as the "Dunster" Force, the first detachment of which with the Brigadier set out from Baghdad in mid-January 1918, the rest following at later intervals, and all travelling in Ford vans or in lorries.

The Mission formed —its composition and duties.

Returning to our Battalion, it remained at Kardarra crossing till April 22nd, the weather during February and March being particularly trying with terrific gales and heavy rain; it then marched again to Mirjāna, a portion going on to Saddah (*Sketch XV*), on the way it was thought to join in operations at Kifri and the advance on Kirkūk. But this was not to be, for after establishing a marching post at Saddah we returned to the Diāla near Kizil Robāt, and it seemed evident the Battalion was being kept for other work. The bridging of the Diāla on which we were employed proved a difficult job, and was on completion by us swept away in a severe storm before it could be used, and we had to laboriously ferry ourselves across in a few small boats. Jason Camp was reached on May 5th, where we started work on the railway now nearing Kizil Robāt, and to be pushed on to Quraitu close to Khānākin. The heat in these low valleys was now great, but nights fortunately still cool, and the health of all was good. The strength of the Battalion now was 12 British officers, 19 Goorkha officers, 1,098 men, but in the end of April this was reduced as we were called on to send 2 British officers, 4 Goorkha officers, 250 men to assist in forming the new 2/11th Goorkha Rifles, and with them went Lieutenants Jerram and Duncan. Not long before this the *Gazette of India*, January, 1918, showed the following men had been awarded the Indian Distinguished Service Medal for gallantry in the field, viz., 4466 Lance Naik Bhudibal Thapa, 547 Rifleman Gagan Sing Gharti, 1695 Lance Naik Makardhoj Rai, 2923 Rifleman Narbir Bura; while 248 Lance Naik Haridatta Jaici, 4042 Lance Naik Jaibahadur Thapa, and 4366 Havildar Jiwan Sing Lohar received the Meritorious Service Medal.

On May 30th we at last learnt our future, for orders came for 600 men of ours to proceed towards Hamadān in Persia, to occupy three posts from Peitak to Kerind (*Sketch XVII*), and to guard that section of the route from the troublesome Sinjābi tribe, who were being stirred up against us by a German agent Von Dreuffel, and who was also arming them. Accidentally being drowned, his activities, which might have caused much trouble, ceased.

Captain McCleverty who had been acting Brigade-Major recently, with Lieutenants Coxe and Mould went with the first detachment which started on June 6th in 68 Ford vans, the second detachment followed four days later—an imposing procession of 200 Ford cars, vans, and light lorries of the Mechanical Transport Corps, making a total sent forward of 3 British officers, 8 Goorkha officers, 592 men, and 8 Lewis guns, 23 followers. Battalion Headquarters and the remainder stayed on at Tel Suleiman, to which spot we had recently moved.

The reason we were told to send two strong companies of 300 each was because it was not desired to acquaint the British public that more than a very small force as yet was right up in Persia. The military authorities wanted the equivalent of a strong battalion which these two strong companies and two of the 1/4th Hants would make, totalling 1,000 men. Lieutenant-Colonel Sweet would have got command of this force being senior, but Lieutenant-Colonel Mathews, 1/4th Hants, had already done good work in Persia, and was on the spot there, so the command fell to him.

On June 17th came news that Captain McCleverty with one company had been sent on to Kermanshah and Hamadān, but was hung up at the former place for lack of petrol. A few days later all reached Hamadān, and Lieutenant Coxe's detachment was hurried forward to Kāsvin. So the 1/2nd Goorkhas were now well into Persia in new and pleasanter fields for operations, although all sorts of difficulties connected with politics and with the famine which was heavy on the country, often made life anything but easy. A strong draft of 2 Goorkha officers and 157 men under Lieutenants Thomson and Murray, reached Tel Suleiman on the 23rd, when the former Officer took over the Adjutancy, and two days later owing to our Brigadier going on leave Lieutenant-Colonel Sweet took over temporary command of the 36th Brigade, to which we were now attached. On the 26th information was received that Jemadar Manbahadur Gurung and 1915 Lance Naik Dalbahadur Gurung had been awarded the Indian Distinguished Service Medal for good service in the field. From June on the Battalion was formed into four Companies instead of Double Companies.

Capt. McCleverty at Hamadān, mid-June, 1918.

Strong Draft arrives, 23/6/18.

At last on June 27th came orders for the rest of the Battalion to march for Kermanshah, and after forming a dump of spare kits, stores, etc., at Kizil Robāt, they proceeded to Khānakin, 22 miles, reaching Kermanshah via Peitak and Chasma Safed in twelve days under command now of Major Collingridge, 2/9th Goorkha Rifles. Except for the trouble and difficulty in getting the transport over some of the high passes, three of which were over 5,000 feet, the march was uneventful.

Rest of Battalion, marches into Persia, 28/6/18.

This part of Persia (the west and north-west) stands high, the general level being between 3,000 and 7,000 feet consisting of successions of barren mountain ranges interspersed with fertile valleys; fertile only in the vicinity of rivers

Shows road difficulties in the ranges between Khānākin and Kermanshah.

Photo by
Exclusive News Agency

1. Resht—Where serious fighting occurred in late June, 1918.
2. Māhidasht near Kermanshah, where the 1st/2nd Goorkhas held a post in 1918.
3. The British Consulate at Resht, saved by Capt. McCleverty and his detachment in late June, 1918.
4. Kangawār between Kermanshah and Hamadān where the 1st/2nd Goorkhas held a post in 1918.

GOORKHAS (THE SIRMOOR RIFLE REGIMENT) 163

or where irrigation channels had been dug. Except near villages or towns there is scarcely a tree to be seen between the Peitak Pass and the Elburz Mountains, a distance of nearly 450 miles. Only on the northern slopes of the great Elburz range near the Caspian Sea do forests occur, and these are very dense, while the Province of Gilān and country round Enzeli on the coast for which we were eventually bound, is most fertile, rice, and fruit growing luxuriantly. The route from Baghdad (the Base) which we were soon to know so well may be briefly described as in four sections (*Sketch XVII*):—

Description of country and route through it.

1. Baghdad to Khānakin, 94 miles, over the ordinary hard clay soil of the desert till the low Jebel Hamrin Range is reached, and which by the summer of 1918 was crossed by a railway to Kizil Robāt.

2. Khānakin to Hamadān through Kermanshah, 240 miles, through mountains, the road improved and made just passable for motors by the Russians during their operations in 1915-1916 was difficult in good, but almost impassable in bad, weather.

3. Hamadān to Kāsvin, 147 miles, a good road made to the Caspian by the Russian Road Company many years ago, and now in much need of repair.

4. Kāsvin to Enzeli, through Menzil, 120 miles, was the same, but with the last 40 miles on the level. Snowstorms in winter frequently blocked the passes for days. Enzeli lies on the flat coast of the Caspian Sea among low sand dunes with wharves and shipping, and is the nearest port to Bāku.

A word may be said as to politics which bulked largely during our stay in this country. Persia nominally neutral, had much sympathy with Germany, treating the British as uninvited and undesirable guests, and often refusing supplies or boycotting us, probably because they were anti-Russian—our Allies. In parts there was actual hostility, while in the north between Kāsvin and Enzeli the Gilān Chief Kuchik Khan was in open rebellion working with the Bolshevik Committee. He was said to have 5,000 or more reliable and well-armed men under him, they having bought large stocks of rifles and ammunition from the disbanded Russian soldiers. Kuchik's force was under German and Austrian officers, the whole being led by a German Colonel, Von Paschen, and while allowing the Russian troops to pass, they defied the British to do so. The British officers with General Dunsterville as they arrived were dispersed to various centres to try to collect and train men for gendarmerie or for fighting units, others again formed the " Dunster " Staff. The first Regulars to reach him were the 14th Hussars, who were pushed on to Kāsvin; then the Hants Regi-

Politics.

ment followed by the 1/2nd Goorkhas and a Battery Royal Field Artillery; later a certain number of aeroplanes came up and more troops.

One of the chief troubles in view of the unfriendliness of the Persians to us lay in the feeding of these troops, scattered as they soon were about the country. This part of Persia also was in the throes of famine, having been fought over by various Russian and Turkish forces in the past two years to the destruction of crops and granaries, while a drought followed on, and German propaganda imputing the cause of famine to the English intensified the trouble. The British as soon as possible started relief works and as far as could humanly be done to feed the starving people, crowds of whom had to be sent down to refugee camps in Mesopotamia; in fact, a great feature of General Dunsterville's work lay in famine relief. Usually it took a convoy of 700 Ford vans to bring up supplies for one battalion at Hamadān, so the magnitude of this work alone can be imagined as more troops were sent up, viz., the North Staffords, Warwicks, and Worcesters. These were passed straight on to Enzeli (*Sketch XVII*) after the action at Menzil, where Kuchik Khan had been defeated in mid-June by a force of Bicherakov's Cossacks and some of the 14th Hussars, who attacked Kuchik's force in position at the bridge in the Menzil Gorge, and in a short fight routed them and their German leader in spite of the commanding positions his "Jangalis," as they were called, occupied. This opened the road to Enzeli and the companies under Captain McCleverty were then sent to Resht, a city of some 40,000 inhabitants, where they formed part of a Movable Column during late June and July under Lieutenant-Colonel Mathews, meeting the "Jangalis" on several occasions with a fair amount of fighting before Kuchik Khan finally gave in, notably at Imam Zādeh Hachem (*Sketch XVII*), where our men under Lieutenant Coxe, getting well home into the enemy, gave them a wholesome dread of the Goorkha kookerie, the fame of which weapon spread through the countryside. One of this Chief's last big efforts was an attack on Resht in July, when a large number of his men managed to enter the town, the garrison of which was not strong enough to defend all round. Severe fighting took place. The British Consulate, with a small garrison of the Hants and the 1/2nd Goorkhas, was surrounded and other prominent buildings captured by the "Jangalis." The first-named place was saved by the

Famine difficulties in Persia.

First action at Menzil, June, 1918.

Capt. McCleverty's detachments at Resht, late July, 1918.

Casualties at Resht, late July, 1918.

timely action of Captain McCleverty, who led detachments of the 1/4th Hants (35), 1/2nd Goorkhas (45), with one Light Armoured Motor Battery car, through the city under considerable opposition. The Consulate was reached just in time, for the " Jangalis " had set fire to the main and another gate, and the little garrison was in a tight corner. A hand-to-hand fight took place in which McCleverty's casualties were 1 British officer and 7 men killed, 28 wounded, of which the 1/2nd Goorkhas detachment had 4 killed and 13 wounded. The enemy lost heavily, and the garrison with the flag were brought away. Three days later McCleverty's force drove the enemy from the Hotel Metropole and Cinema House, and a further action relieved the detachments holding the Telegraph Office and Bank, where an American, Mr. Lacy, was rescued. Kuchik Khan's force then withdrew from this neighbourhood, having lost heavily. The following month Kuchik Khan gave up the contest and came to terms for a time. Detachments from McCleverty's two companies were now sent to Menzil—Enzeli—Zinjān.

At the end of July General Lewin passed through Kermanshah where our Battalion Headquarters were, *en route* to Hamadān to command the troops in Persia, as General Dunsterville was now occupied at Bāku with his own force. Kermanshah, a large town of some 50,000 inhabitants, proved a fairly pleasant place with very hospitable English and Russian officials and their wives. The Battalion, now in the 36th Brigade, was much split up—Captain Dallas Smith, Lieutenants Snow, Smith, Warhurst, and Bucknall being out with detachments at Mahidasht, Sahneh, Kangavar, and Asādabad (*Sketch XVII*), while Captain McCleverty was still in Resht with his separate command of our 600 men (officially still called two companies), and which now furnished detachments at Zinjān, Kāsvin, Imam Zādeh Hachem, and Resht. At this time with him were Lieutenants Mould, Meyrick Jones, and Toogood, the latter unfortunately being in hospital with typhus. Lieutenant Coxe had left for India on leave, his place being filled by a new officer, Lieutenant J. L. Smith, I.A.R.O. At the end of this month an unfortunate incident occurred here; Lieutenant Loftus Tottenham with a party had gone out at night to try to ambush rifle thieves who were causing much trouble. On their return towards dawn a sentry of the Hants fired on them by mistake, wounding Tottenham in the arm, and his orderly in the leg.

Battalion at Kermanshah and posts, July, 1918.

Unfortunate incident, late July, 1918.

In this locality, viz., near Kermanshah are the ancient and famous rock cut inscriptions and sculptures at Bisitūn and Taq i Bostān, representing hunting scenes, etc. These were visited by Lieutenant-Colonel Sweet when touring to his posts, who describes the carving and lettering as being marvellously clear still in spite of their hoary antiquity.

On August 13th the Battalion which had been more or less occupied on the Line of Communications, became a part of the "Dunster" Force, and more troops continued to arrive from Mesopotamia, viz., the Glosters, three aeroplanes also, but unfortunately one crashed badly on landing. Our next move on relief by the 26th Punjabis who were on the road up, was to Hamadān on August 26th, marching via Kangavar, the pass up which being very steep and rough, ambulance cars had to be pushed and dragged with ropes. Here we picked up our detachment and found the place crowded with Nestorian (Assyrians) refugees, escaped from their country round Lake Urmia near Tabriz, which was being overrun by the Turks. They were not Asiatic in appearance being a remarkably fair people, and it was a curious sight seeing a whole tribe of some 40,000 in flight with horses, bullocks, carts, and all their belongings. Another bad pass of 7,600 feet was crossed and Hamadān (*Sketch XVII*) reached on the 31st, where we camped 2 miles out with a detachment of the Glosters recently arrived. Colonel Sweet now returned to us, Brigadier-General Champain having arrived to command the 36th Brigade.

Battalion moves to Hamadān, 26/8/17.

Refugees.

We were all struck by the wonderful cleanness of this town, so very different to most we had seen, large gardens well irrigated, surrounded the place, fruit and vegetables being plentiful. There were many Russian and English officials, commercial and otherwise, who were most helpful and hospitable. We learnt that Brigadier-General H. Champain was now to command the troops in Northern Persia as distinct from the 39th Brigade, and "Dunster" Force, who were the troops for Bāku, and also that the Turks in the region of Lake Urmia were stirring up the Khurds against us, and that much of the trouble with this tribe had originally been caused by the refugees who had pillaged many Khurdish villages on their way down to British protection.

Hamadān.

On September 4th we marched out for Kāsvin and had gone some way when fresh orders recalled us, the reason being it was thought, in consequence of the serious situation at Bāku, where 30,000 Turks were attacking the town, and General Dunsterville's small force there had had heavy losses.

Situation at Bāku, early Sept., 1918.

On September 6th Battalion Headquarters and two companies were sent to Asādabad and Yangi Khan, two marches off, to relieve detachments

GOORKHAS (THE SIRMOOR RIFLE REGIMENT)

We relieve detachments of Glosters, 6/9/18.

of the Glosters, who were to move further north to Bijar on the road to Lake Urmia. There were also fears as to having to retire from Resht on Hamadān, which caused many reconnaissances to select suitable positions for defence of the latter, and work was added to at all posts by having to collect refugees and escort them to points on the high road to Mesopotamia, these sometimes being fired on by marauding tribesmen.

Our Resht detachments move to Zinjān, late Aug., 1918.

Captain McCleverty and the Resht detachment had been sent up to Zinjān, and on to Miāne in the end of August, as the Turks about Lake Urmia were showing much activity, and it appeared they might push south to cut our Line of Communications about Kangavar. A small column consisting of a weak squadron of 14th Hussars, a platoon of the Hants, a platoon of 1/2nd Goorkhas under Subadar Champa Sing Gurung, and 120 Persian levies had also gone towards Tabriz for reconnoitring purposes under command of Captain Osborne (*Sketch XVII*).

Reconnaissance to Tabriz.

Battalion leaves Hamadān for Zinjān, 15/9/18.

Owing to these hostile probabilities the Battalion with Headquarters was ordered to march from Hamadān to Zinjān, 92 miles, and started on September 15th together with 8 machine guns of No. 186 Company and No. 9 Anzac Wireless Company. Zinjān was reached on September 24th after some intensely hard marching through high and difficult hill country. Large parties of Russian and Persian refugees were met on the road with all their goods and chattels in wagons often drawn by four horses abreast, all covered with bells and gay flags with inscriptions in Persian.

Zinjān, 24/9/18.

Camp was formed in a pleasant orchard, 1½ miles from the town, which we found solidly built and with a very fine covered bazaar vying with the best in Baghdad. Shops full of china, carpets, and various wares, fruit and vegetables in plenty, and a fair number of inhabitants still about who seemed friendly. Altogether a flourishing little township and one which together with its neighbour, Sultanieh, had risen in far off times to considerable importance under the rule of the Caliphs.

The Tabriz reconnaissance forced back.

The news on arrival here concerned Captain Osborne's column in early September, and events following. His column had reached a point a few miles from Tabriz, when it was attacked by a force of 2,000 Turks, of whom 400 odd were mounted, and was driven back on Tegmidash, 55 miles or so north of

Miāne. Major Wagstaffe, then commanding the troops on the Zinjān—Tabriz line, at once ordered Captain McCleverty forward with 100 rifles to support Osborne, who was met at Turkimanchai beyond Miāne, opposed by the enemy in greatly superior numbers (*Sketch XVII*). Captain McCleverty as senior now took command, and as the Persian levies were useless, bolting as soon as firing began, he decided to continue the retirement, sending word back to Zinjān to this effect. Orders were then sent out for the column to retire through Miāne to a position on the Kuflon Kūh Range, 29 miles back. This was done by midnight on September 7th, the column fighting a fairly strenuous rearguard action for 11½ miles, when the enemy stopped advancing. The little column, weary with having covered 57 miles in 55 hours which included the rearguard action mentioned, remained in the position on the Pass, where they found Jemadar Nandbir's two weak platoons withdrawn from Miāne, three very weak platoons of the 1/4th Hants under Lieutenant-Colonel Mathews, who had succeeded Major Wagstaffe in command of the troops in this area, and one platoon of the Worcesters, holding the road over the range. Next day this force was strengthened by the arrival of 1 section of howitzers, 1 section 18-pounders, and 1 section mountain guns. Here on September 11th they were attacked by the Turks who concentrated their pressure against our centre, the Persian levies on the right bolting as usual. The 1/2nd Goorkhas on the left did not have much fighting, but Captain Bucknall was severely wounded in two places.

As the Hants and Worcester platoons in the centre were being pressed back by superior numbers in spite of splendid resistance, Lieutenant-Colonel Mathews ordered the whole force to retire on Zinjān. The Battalion's casualties were very slight, Subadar Champa Sing Gurung's platoon only having had 5 men killed on the way back from Tabriz.

Brigadier-General Champain arrived on September 28th and informed us that part of the 36th and of the 39th Brigades were now to protect the Zinjān—Bijar area, where the Turks were moving in the Kizil Uzun Valley, and it looked as if we should spend the winter up here. The weather had already turned autumnal and cold. The present effective strength of the troops here being very weak, reinforcements were to be sent up.

An epidemic of " 'flu " now struck us, and hospital arrangements none of the best had to be improved, there being only Captain Murray, I.M.S., with

PERSIA.
1. Kerind—The first place of importance in the Persian Hills beyond Khánākin.
2. Kermanshah—A general view.
3. An ancient stone bridge about ten miles north of Kangavār. British troops passed this way, on their route from Mesopotamia to Enzeli, on the Caspian Sea.

Photo by   *Exclusive News Agency*

1. Shows the "Jebel Hamrin" range and country in the neighbourhood of Kizil Robat.
2. The Russian Road through the Elburz mountains between Imām Zādeh Hachem and Enzeli.

2 British ward orderlies and 2 Persian menials to attend to the needs of 140 sick, and the men here being generally worn out with constant trekking, succumbed the more readily to the malady. Typhus was also rife in Miāne which added anxiety lest it should spread down the road.

We were joined at the end of September by Lieutenant Mould, the Subadar Major and 45 men from Resht and two days later Captain Dallas Smith brought up another 115 from Kāsvin, so our hitherto scattered Battalion was getting together once more, and all were soon busy on defence works at Sarim Sāgli, north of Zinjān, to which place we had recently moved. News of successes in Palestine was most cheering, and it also seemed not unlikely the Turks would follow Bulgaria and ask for an armistice. But against this had come news of General Dunsterville's failure at Bāku after serious fighting, ending on September 14th, when he had to evacuate the place with his guns and his 1,200 survivors. The utter uselessness of the Armenian troops there and failure of the Caucasian Government to help him, had led to this state of affairs.

Remainder from Resht and Kāsvin rejoin end Sept., 1918.

Battalion at Sarim Sāgli, Sept., 1918.

On September 29th an Order of the Day announced that Captain G. McCleverty had been awarded the Distinguished Service Order for gallantry at Resht. To punish the villages of Nikpai and Akhnazar, 27 miles northwards, for ill-treatment of certain men of the 1/4th Hants missing after the Kuflon Kūh action, a small column was despatched on October 6th under Captain Dallas Smith, consisting of 1 squadron 14th Hussars, 1 armoured car section, 100 rifles 1/2nd Goorkhas, and 2 companies of the Glosters, he also had to form an advanced base at the latter village for a probable move on Miāne and Tabriz, but after a month the troops left there were withdrawn. Near Nikpai they picked up Lieutenant Williams, R.A.F., who had been missing for days; his engine had gone wrong when beyond Miāne, luckily he was able to land out of sight of the enemy and burning his aeroplane he escaped into the hills. A few days later Captain Dallas Smith hearing of a Turkish detachment having reached Jamālabad village on the south side of the Kuflon Kūh Range (*Sketch XVII*) made a rapid march with part of his column surprising and dispersing them. He barricaded the road there thoroughly and two or three days later when out in an armoured car to see if it was intact, an ambushed party of Turks nearly got him—a very narrow shave as they waited till he was 40 yards off before they fired.

Dallas Smith's Column to Akhnazar, 6/10/18.

With the beginning of November on return of the Battalion to Zinjān came the cheering news of the successful battle at Kāla Shergat (*Sketch XV*) on the Tigris below Mosul and the collapse of the Turkish Army in Mesopotamia after 4 years' campaigning, which cost the British in total casualties 4,335 officers, 93,244 other ranks, of whom 29,700 were killed in action. The Turks signed the Armistice next day (October 31st), and all looked forward to being sent home before long; but in our case this was not to be before another $2\frac{1}{2}$ years had passed. The Battalion now settled down to a rough sort of cantonment life in Zinjān and its neighbourhood; winter was on us and the cold in these hills was bitter. In the middle of this month we were joined by Lieutenant A. W. Holworthy, 1/3rd Goorkhas, with a draft of 60 men, a welcome addition, and the Battalion strength was now 12 British officers, 13 Goorkha officers, and 606 other ranks.

Battalion returns Zinjān early Nov., 1918.

Collapse of Turks in Mesopotamia.

A Draft arrives.

On the morning of November 12th a wire was received containing the joyful news of Germany's surrender, the Armistice having been signed and hostilities had ceased the previous day at 11 a.m. This was followed by orders from General Headquarters for a peace celebration to be arranged for in the shape of an entertainment to the Persian grandees of all people, who sympathized with Germany and were unfriendly to the British—not a word of any entertainment to the war-worn troops!

The news of the Armistice, 12/11/18.

At the end of the month the Battalion was directed to despatch two companies at once to Menzil and Resht who marched on November 28th under Captains Dallas Smith and Bucknall, with Lieutenants Campbell, Mould, and Holworthy; the rest of us remaining at Zinjān. We also learnt that the detachments in Persia under command earlier of Captain McCleverty had now been awarded honours as noted opposite the following names:—

Two Companies sent to Menzil and Resht, end Nov., 1918.

For actions at Imām Zādeh Hachem and at Resht:

Lieutenant Coxe	M.C.
Subadar-Major Tulsiram Gharti	M.C.
Subadar Aiman Rana	I.D.S.M.
Jemadar Nandbir Thapa ...	I.D.S.M.
3695 Havildar Kale Thapa ...	I.O.M. (2nd Class)
3966 Lance Naik Kuman Sing Gurung	I.O.M. (2nd Class)

Honours and Rewards.

3489 Havildar Tilakchand Gurung	...	I.D.S.M.
199 Lance Naik Kalu Gharti ...	...	I.D.S.M.
3222 Lance Naik Maniraj Gurung	...	I.D.S.M.
1833 Lance Naik Balbir Rai ...	...	I.D.S.M.
1234 Rifleman Singbir Thapa ...	...	I.D.S.M.
455 Rifleman Kahar Sing Rana	...	I.D.S.M.
4535 Rifleman Jagia Khattrie ...	...	I.D.S.M.

For action at Tegmidash—Retirement from Tabriz:
1032 Lance Naik Sherbahadur Ghale ... I.D.S.M.

For action at Turkimanchai—Retirement from Tabriz:
4848 Lance Naik Bahadurman Rai ... I.D.S.M.

Our Brigade (36th) consisting till now of the 1/6th Goorkha Rifles, 1/4th Hants, 1/2nd Goorkhas, 36th Sikhs, 186th Machine Gun Company, was much scattered, its distribution list for the end of 1918 showing that the 1/6th Goorkha Rifles garrisoned Enzeli, Resht, and Menzil; at Kāsvin were Brigade Headquarters, wing 1/4th Hants, 2 sections 186th Machine Gun Company, Brigade Transport Company, wing 1/2nd Goorkhas, *en route* from Zinjān; at Zinjān, wing 1/2nd Goorkhas, 2 sections 186th Machine Gun Company; at Shiah Dehan, Aveh, Hamadān, the 36th Sikhs; while the 1/4th Hants had 2 companies as far off as Merv and Krasnovodsk. Control of such widely dispersed units was one of considerable difficulty. At this time we had 13 British officers present, viz., Lieutenant-Colonel Sweet, Captains Dallas Smith, McCleverty, and Bucknall, Lieutenants Campbell, Mould, Smith, Thomson, Meyrick Jones, Snow, Warhurst, Holworthy, and Coxe, with over 800 Goorkha ranks. The Battalion's third Christmas was spent quietly here in intense cold, biting winds, and thick snow, which often closed the roads for days.

Distribution of our 36th Brigade end of 1918.

Battalion strength, Dec., 1918.

It is interesting to record from the War Diary that from March 8th, 1916, up to date the 1/2nd Goorkhas had been awarded the following number of orders and decorations :—

D.S.O., 3; M.C., 8; O.B.I. (2nd Class), 2; I.O.M., 6; I.D.S.M., 28; M.S.M., 4. Total, 51.
Serbian Decorations.—Cross of Karageorge (2nd Class) with swords, 1; Gold Medal, 1; Silver Medal, 2.
Italian Bronze Medal.—For Valour, 1.

Orders and Decorations received by Battalion since March, 1916.

The following, also from the War Diary, is the casualty list in action from May 16th, 1916, to end of 1918:—

	Killed.	Wounded.	Missing.	Total.
British officers ...	8	13	0	21
Goorkha officers ...	4	8	1	13
Goorkha ranks ...	174	393	41	608
	186	414	42	642

Casualties from May, 1916, to Dec., 1918.

The Goorkha casualties of March 8th, 1916, viz., 204, not being included in this list brings the grand total of casualties in action from our first arrival at the Tigris Front to 8 British officers killed, 13 wounded, and 846 of all Goorkha ranks killed and wounded. The number of reinforcements sent out in the same period was:—British officers, 42; Goorkha officers, 19; Goorkha ranks, 1993. The strength of the Battalion on arrival in Mesopotamia on February 18th, 1916, was British officers, 14; Goorkha officers, 17; Goorkha ranks, 793; and its strength at the end of 1918 was British officers, 13; Goorkha officers, 19; Goorkha ranks, 847.

Total Drafts sent.

CHAPTER XX.

CHRISTMAS, 1918, TO MAY 31ST, 1920. (*Sketches XVI, XVII.*)

JANUARY, 1919, opened with certain moves; a detachment under Subadar Aiman Gurung being sent off to Shiah Dehan, followed two days later by another detachment and a company of the 1/4th Hants; and we now heard

Detachments sent Shiah Dehan, early Jan., 1919.

there was a likelihood of our being supplied from Constantinople via Bāku, that route apparently being open, and that this would be the route to Europe in future, not via Baghdad. As, however, this part of the country, viz., about Bāku, was not really settled the new route did not promise success, and beyond some officers travelling by it was hardly made use of. Our mails at Zinjān were very irregular in arrival and at long intervals, which was much felt, sometimes being dropped from aeroplanes, sometimes

Irregularity of mails.

coming up by camel convoy according to the state of the road. These delays in postal arrangements were later, in the last half of 1920, due to the Arab revolt in Mesopotamia, and in early 1921 to prolonged blocking of the road by snow and landslips. On January 19th a *Gazette* showed that 3880 Havildar Keshar Sing Thapa had been awarded the Meritorious Service Medal.

A Vickers-Maxim Gun Course and ordinary drills, etc., went on when snow and weather permitted, also a little shooting for the officers; but the winter up here was monotonous, and it was a relief to know we should be moved before very long though it was not known where to.

Death of Capt. Chenoy, I.M.S., mid-Feb., 1919.

In mid-February we lost our Medical Officer, Captain Chenoy, of typhus to the regret of all. He was the best type of Parsi educated in England, had done well in France and on the North-West Frontier, and had served a year or more with us.

Lieutenant-Colonel Sweet now left us on a month's leave in England, the period being extended to October, as when at home he was placed on duty with the Indian Peace Contingent at Hampton Court

Col. Sweet and Capt. McCleverty on leave to England.

under the command of General E. Money, and given charge of a mixed company of Sikhs and Goorkhas. A party of the 2nd Goorkhas was also sent from Dehra to join this Contingent, and Captain McCleverty, also on leave in

England, and who had travelled via Bāku and Constantinople, assisted Lieutenant-Colonel Sweet in showing the men round the various sights. At the end of February Lieutenant Holworthy left us to rejoin the 1/3rd Goorkhas, and the following month Subadar-Major Tulsiram Gharti, M.C., left for India and pension after long years of good service.

The Peace Contingent.

During their absence in England the Battalion had left Zinjān in May, and was at Kāsvin and posts in the neighbourhood with detachments at Resht and Menzil, the latter place with its bridge being important to hold, as, owing to hills and forests in this region and few bridle paths, any fighting would be chiefly confined to this main route to the Caspian.

Battalion now at Kāsvin, 1919.

It was the trouble with the Bolsheviks and their intrigues with Persia which kept the British force up here; the former wanted the Enzeli—Kāzian port by which to regain North Persia; and General Denikin's Russian Volunteer Army, which the British were helping, was operating against the Bolsheviks on the west of the Caspian with a fleet on that sea as well. Efforts also were being made to stir up Kuchik Khan against us once more, hence our reoccupation of Resht and Enzeli. There was likewise fear that the unreliable Persian Cossacks at Teheran under Russian officers might cause trouble. Most of the former British units had been sent back, being replaced by the Berkshires at Hamadān, and Royal Irish Fusiliers at Kāsvin, the York and Lancaster coming up later. Certain fresh Indian regiments also came up, and the 42nd Deolis and 122nd Infantry had replaced the 1/6th Goorkhas, and 36th Sikhs in our Brigade. At Kāsvin General Sir G. F. MacMunn, K.C.B., now General Officer Commanding troops in Mesopotamia and Persia, inspected the Battalion.

Bolshevik troubles, 1919.

Changes in troops in North Persia, 1919.

In early December, 1919, we received a strong draft from Dehra of 256 men under Jemadar Lal Sing Rana, and Jemadar Nain Sing Thapa was despatched with a platoon to Tabriz escorting munitions. The distance was over 200 miles, across high ranges deep in snow, and fraught with various difficulties; 7 men suffered severely from frost-bite, and their work was highly commended by the Officer Commanding at Tabriz, and the General Officer Commanding 36th Brigade, when they rejoined us at Enzeli.

Strong Draft arrives.

Escort Duty to Tabriz, Dec., 1919.

On January 27th, 1920, Lieutenant-Colonel Sweet who had rejoined from England in time for Christmas at Kāsvin, was directed to move the Battalion, together with the 31st Mountain Battery, 2 sections 19th Sappers and Miners, and 1 troop of the Guides, to Enzeli, where the 42nd Deolis already had gone, with 2 mountain guns and the Machine Gun Company Royal Irish Fusiliers, but this was delayed for various reasons till March. The change proved a pleasant one to the cold of the interior, though even the Caspian coast was not free of snow, which in early February covered the country thickly, breaking down road and telegraph line between Enzeli and Resht for days. Woodcock and duck shooting proved extraordinarily good, and many excellent days were spent after both.

Battalion moves from Kāsvin to Enzeli, March, 1920.

Shikar.

Shortly after settling down in the new locality (*Sketches XVI, XVII*), a gun-boat and a troopship with 1,200 men of Denikin's force put into harbour but our orders were to allow none to land. A guard of the 42nd Deolis was put on board to see this carried out, and they left for Petrovsk after trading barley for meat. General Champain, commanding the North Persia troops, with Headquarters at Kāsvin having to go to Baghdad to discuss the situation, Lieutenant-Colonel Sweet took over the temporary Brigade command, and made a reconnaissance of the neighbouring coast east and west of Enzeli.

It was thought the Bolsheviks would make an effort to seize Enzeli as soon as the winter passed, and our policy was to keep them out of it. A message was received from the War Office *re* our attitude towards Denikin's fleet if they came to the port, which was that they should lower their flag, hand over the ships to the British, leaving only 16 men on each, and the remainder would be given safe conduct to Baghdad. The present situation had many involved points in it which could not be clear until the Home Government had given us its definite policy towards the Bolsheviks. Starosselsky, commanding the Persian Cossacks at Teheran, raised continual difficulties and objections to our desired action, and it seemed to all here that as the Anglo-Persian agreement was hopeless to carry out, it had better be torn up and the troops sent out of the country. The *Gretsia* lying in harbour and called a guard ship was now ordered by the Political Officer to leave port in 24 hours.

Orders from England re attitude towards Bolsheviks and Denikin's troops.

Measures for protection of the port and road to Resht were thoroughly taken up by Lieutenant-Colonel Sweet, General Champain on return also going into the matter, which was by no means easy, as a landing could be effected almost anywhere along the 25 to 30 miles of coast we had to watch, especially about Verst 13 east of Kāzian, or 9 miles away, on the narrow strip of land between the sea and the Murdāb Lake, where the highway to Resht turns inland and which if gained by the enemy would cut off our retirement. Our other two companies due to follow Battalion Headquarters had been detained at Kāsvin owing to a fresh situation having arisen at Teheran where uncertain conditions prevailed, and we were warned that Denikin's force, investing Petrovsk, meant to come to Enzeli later. They intended to make this their Base which, under our existing orders *re* his handing over his ships, would lead to complications. This was followed by the arrival of some of Denikin's officers from Petrovsk who had a long interview with General Champain on the subject of bringing their force here.

Protection measures.

The general situation in North Persia at this time was briefly as follows:— The Bolsheviks were gaining ground over Denikin's Forces in South Russia; Bāku was still Denikin's, but was not expected to hold out long; a Commission was sitting at Teheran evolving a scheme for co-ordinating existing Persian forces with a view to making them efficient to protect their own country; at Teheran Colonel Starosselsky commanding the Persian Cossack Division, and openly hostile to the Anglo-Persian Agreement, was doing his best to bring on a change in the Persian Government, British policy being to keep the present one in power; the Swedish officers of the Persian Gendarmerie were doubtful; Tabriz, where the British were supposed to keep order with a very small force, was on the verge of revolution; so it was no wonder all officials at Teheran were anxious for the near future.

Situation in Persia, 1920.

On March 30th the Enzeli garrison was increased by the arrival of a party of the Guides Cavalry and our two companies from Kāsvin, who with the 1/2nd Goorkhas were camped mostly along the road east of Kāzian at points where landings were probable, particularly at Verst 13, an important tactical point. Lieutenant-Colonel Sweet now commanded the forces at Enzeli, and Brevet Major Dallas Smith the Battalion. At this time came news that Petrovsk had fallen and that the whole of the Volunteer fleet and army were expected here. Lieutenant-Colonel Sweet on this despatched a wire stating his intention to forbid their entry into harbour, except under the conditions specified.

Disposition of force at Enzeli, 30/3/20.

The first ship to appear, viz., the *Asia*, with a coastal gun-boat, the *Vladimir*, were stopped, our machine and Royal Artillery gunners manned

GOORKHAS (THE SIRMOOR RIFLE REGIMENT)

their posts on the mole and harbour entrance, and Captain Crutchley, Political Officer, went out to inform them they could not enter the port except after disarmament. About 6 p.m. ten other ships arrived and Lieutenant-Colonel Sweet with the Political Officer went out to meet Admiral Sergiev and General Dratsenko on the *Kruger*, who were very indignant at finding the port closed to them, saying they would go on to Bāku and accept the offer of the Azerbaijān Government to take over the fleet. They left on April 1st and Captain Adamson, Royal Engineers, began making a boom to close the harbour mouth. The arrival on the 8th of the s.s. *Van* showed that she and another vessel containing officers and men had deserted Admiral Sergiev and gone over to the Bolsheviks; they were sent away. A day or two later more ships arrived and were visited, when it was found a Captain Buchen was now in command as the Admiral had left and gone to Poti on the Black Sea. Captain Buchen stated that as the fleet had not agreed to the terms of the Azerbaijān Government it was decided that, as the British had originally handed over the ships to them, it was right to hand them back to us on completion of their work. It also transpired that General Dratsenko had practically sold to the Azerbaijān Government a large number of his men by inducing them to go ashore then disarming them, and with them selling most of his munitions for a large sum of money, had decamped with it. And this after vowing to Denikin that he would never give in, but would fight the Bolsheviks to the last!

Captain Buchen agreed to the British terms, which were to strike their flag before entering harbour, to be disarmed, to come under British control, and to be interned pending arrangements for the men to be sent round to join Denikin's forces elsewhere. A camp then had to be arranged for them by Lieut. Lancaster, and wires were sent to General Champain and General Headquarters, Baghdad, on the situation, when to our dismay the latter replied ordering suspension of all landing. This, however, was altered next day, our arrangements receiving sanction, and Lieutenant-Commander Luke of Admiral de Robeck's staff, who arrived unexpectedly from Bāku, was most helpful in appreciating the situation, and was strongly in favour of the fleet being interned. This took days to carry out the weather being very bad, and the Russian Easter Day celebrations were on, during which period most of their men were drunk. General Champain came over from Kāsvin to inspect all

Side notes:
- Arrival of Denikin's fleet at Enzeli, 31/3/20.
- Fleet leaves for Bāku, 1/4/20.
- Fleet returns to Enzeli, 12/4/20.
- Fleet interned.

defensive and internment arrangements, returning after approving all that was being done. Of the fleet's personnel only some 140 did not wish to remain in Enzeli, the rest were quite content with internment and with our stated intention of giving them all possible assistance to ensure their safety in the event of the Bolsheviks attacking the port before they could be got away inland. Discipline among them was nil, their officers could do nothing with their men unless the latter were willing ; a most extraordinary condition for a fleet and troops to be in, and the wonder was that they carried on at all in any way.

By April 18th the bulk of the disarmament of ships and men had been completed, large quantities of ammunition and munitions were landed and carefully stacked, and a number of Lewis guns from the ships were distributed among the troops. Two days more and this work was finished though for a time the men were kept on the ships of which 16 different kinds were now in our hands. No Russian officers were allowed to go to Teheran which many wished to do, without a special pass from their chargé d'affaires through our Legation ; and as their men were without pay for months the officers wished to sell off all their cargoes to raise the necessary money. This was arranged for locally. These men of Denikin's, a cheerful crowd, were soon on a friendly footing with our men ; football matches were got up between teams from each side, concerts, etc., while an interchange of friendly entertainments between our officers and theirs took place. One night the officers on the *Kruger* held an official dinner inviting all our principal officers, when a most convivial time was spent with the drinking of many healths and speeches. Their custom of the honoured guest (in this case Lieutenant-Colonel Sweet) having to " drain a silver goblet on a gold tray to music," is described by one of our officers in his diary as being charming and picturesque, particularly as the voices were extraordinarily good. The night was a very late one, and a plaintive entry in another diary next day shows that vodka plus a variety of wines had had their due effect.

Disarming of Ships completed, 18/4/20.

Friendship between our Troops and Russians.

The climate was now delightful, wild flowers being everywhere and the inspection tours to Resht and elsewhere were a pleasure ; the spring green, the profusion of blue and white violets, yellow and mauve primulas, and cyclamen covered the countryside—a delight to the eye. At the end of April two sections of the 19th Battery Royal Garrison Artillery arrived, completing the little garrison composed of a detachment Royal Irish Fusiliers, 42nd

Strength of Enzeli garrison, April, 1920.

GOORKHAS (THE SIRMOOR RIFLE REGIMENT)

Deolis, 1/2nd Goorkhas with Vickers Maxim guns, detachment Guides Cavalry, 31st Mountain Battery, detachment 5th Battery Royal Garrison Artillery, two 4-inch guns taken off Denikin's ships, also one 5.2 gun mounted on a barge in harbour. The Berks and York and Lancaster Regiments were in reserve at Kāsvin. The bulk of the troops at Enzeli were distributed along the 9 miles of narrow strip of land from Kāzian east till the road turns inland, and where landings were likely to be attempted, though practically the coastline 14 miles west and 12 miles east of the port had to be defended. The Battalion's main camp was 2 miles east of Kāzian near the aerodrome (*Sketch XVI*), and the important point at Verst 13 was held by 1 company 1/2nd Goorkhas, a party Guides Cavalry, 1 section Machine Guns, Royal Irish Fusiliers, all under Lieutenant Lancaster of ours. Rumours

Rumours re Bolshevik Moves. were plentiful as to Bolshevik movements at Lenkorān on the Azerbaijān coast between here and Bāku, that they had landed there proclaiming they were enemies of the British only, that they wished to trade, etc. That province was stated to be unfriendly to the Bolsheviks threatening armed force to keep them out.

On May 9th Captain Jones, East India Squadron, arrived and took over all matters concerning the interned fleet and personnel. Further reports informed us Bāku was now occupied by 20,000 Bolshevik troops, their intention being to land at Lenkorān and to isolate Enzeli by marching inland to Resht. Nothing further occurred till May 18th; General Champain and Staff had come from Kāsvin to inspect the previous day, when suddenly at 4.30 a.m. all were

Bolshevik fleet bombards Enzeli, 18/5/20. aroused by the sound of a gun, then two or three more, a shell whistled over the Headquarters house in Enzeli, and the Bolshevik Fleet was found to be bombarding the port from a long distance off, being faintly seen on the horizon. Accounts, both private and from the War Diary vary, but from all sources the following is a fairly correct tale of what occurred here:—

All posts were at once manned, and the Political Officer, Captain Crutchley, went out in a motor boat with a white flag but was fired on and obliged to return. Later again going out he met the Bolsheviks who kept him with them, and sent a message to the port giving the Bolshevik Com-

Bolshevik Commander's intentions. mander's intentions which were, that he was ordered to take the Enzeli—Kāzian port which we must evacuate as he wanted the Volunteer fleet lying in harbour. He promised safe conduct to all British troops and to Denikin's men interned with us, many of whom had already been passed on to Baghdad, and he gave us a two-hour armistice. Our wireless of course at this critical juncture would not work properly causing delay which was increased by the fact that all instructions had to come from London via Baghdad and Teheran and all messages from the hostile fleet had to be translated from Russian into English. Meanwhile the armistice was not observed, some of the ships persistently continuing the bombardment causing some casualties. Other ships, mostly transports with two destroyers, were seen moving south and closing in to the coast to effect landings. Near Versts 13 and 6 boats (*Sketch XVI*) filled with men were seen approaching, which, about 10 a.m., Lancaster's detachments were able to stop for a time near their point, but other parties landed east and west of them, Subadar Narain Sing Thapa's platoon doing good work in opposing a landing, but without effect. By 11 a.m. considerable numbers of the enemy were on shore, and had cut the telephone line connecting the post at Verst 13 with Headquarters. Lieutenant Wingfield with a company 1/2nd Goorkhas was despatched to intercept the landing at Verst 6, but another landing had been effected at Verst 7, the Bolsheviks had occupied Shaluzar village and Wingfield's company was soon in action, their advance being covered by 2 Mountain Battery guns. The enemy was driven out of Shaluzar by noon with some loss, our casualties being 2 killed and 6 wounded. Orders then reached him to stop offensive action, remain where he was, and to try to parley. During the afternoon some 2,000 or more Bolsheviks had landed not without some fighting and casualties on both sides, and they had succeeded in blocking the road beyond Verst 13, where it turns inland from the coast (*Sketch XVI*). The armistice had been extended to 8 p.m., and the wireless working at last had brought down the Chief Political Officer from Resht who with General Champain interviewed Kājanov the Bolshevik Commander, who stated his orders were to take the port which they needed together with the Volunteer Fleet's ships (Denikin's), that he did not wish to fight us, nor were they invading Persia. Their strength in men and guns was far superior to ours, the fleet consisting of 26 ships of which 6 or 7 were transports with troops, the rest warships of various sorts. It also transpired a force had been landed at Astāra, and was advancing along the coast from the north on Enzeli.

The whole situation in this part of Persia was most unsatisfactory; it

GOORKHAS (THE SIRMOOR RIFLE REGIMENT)

had throughout been governed by political considerations rather than by military, and General Champain's clear orders from His Britannic Majesty's Minister at Teheran in the event of the Bolsheviks coming to Enzeli were:—To parley with their Commander, to avoid hostilities, and not to embroil Persia in trouble with them. Had we not been operating in a neutral country with political considerations uppermost we could have put up a good fight, though the end with the aid of their ships' guns would have been the capture of the port and possibly of the British force as well; some officers' diaries seem to show we could have cut our way out, their troops though more numerous being inferior to ours as fighters, but for the orders enjoining "no fighting and to avoid armed conflicts."

Situation difficult.

To save this ending to a trying and difficult situation it was decided to accept the Bolshevik Commander's terms, the firing ceased about 3 p.m., and our troops prepared to march out. Practically all our stores, kits, and record documents, etc., were lost to us having to be left behind owing to lack of transport, the Bolshevik Commander promising to send all after us later, which, however, was never carried out; and the Enzeli garrison marched for Resht about 9 p.m. as one officer's account states: "through lines of Bolshie troops with their machine guns in position at various points trained on to us as we passed." Our own casualties were slight and only in Lieutenant Wingfield's company as mentioned before.

Bolshevik terms accepted; Enzeli troops withdraw to Resht, 18/5/20.

A few days passed and reconnaissance reports showed the Bolsheviks to be occupying a position near Khoman on the road to Resht apparently with a view to advancing inland, and the 42nd Deolis with two Mountain Battery guns were sent back down the Enzeli Road. On May 22nd General Champain and Staff with the Political Officer and two Persian delegates went to Enzeli and had an interview with General Kājanov, who met the party in a flannel suit, suave and polite; and in evasive reply to the Persians' query as to why their port had been bombarded, stated he had orders to take the place and Russian property there, and having got it would do no more at present. He declined to give any written guarantee to this effect though pressed to do so, merely saying he would send an ultimatum to Teheran before any further operations.

Bolsheviks make a general landing. Fresh interview, 22/5/20.

Arrangements were then begun for handing over the old Volunteer fleet and finding out if any more of Denikin's men still with us desired to join the Bolsheviks, to which

Denikin's old fleet handed over to the Bolsheviks.

50 or so responded. Meanwhile more of Kājanov's force had crossed the Murdāb Lake and had occupied Pirri Bazaar (*Sketch XVI*).

The present position was hopeless from every point of view. Orders came from three different sources, viz., from Teheran, Baghdad, the Foreign Office, often conflicting, the country was full of armed men it being difficult to distinguish between Bolsheviks and armed Persians, so our men could not fire until shot at first. The Persian Gendarmerie and Police were useless. An incident on the Enzeli road when a Deoli sentry wounded a Bolshevik car driver who disobeyed orders inflamed the Russians, and hostilities at one time seemed imminent. It was also learnt that Kuchik Khan was again in the field and had accepted guns and money from Kājanov, so any assistance from his side was doubtful, although that chief continued to declare himself as being against the Russians.

Sketch map of the Enzeli-Kazian positions 18th May 1920
(Copied from one in the 36th Brig. War Diary.)

Sketch No XVI

Scale 1 inch = 1 mile

Enzeli-Kazian Garrison
½ 2nd Goorkhas (Less 1 C°)
42nd Deolis (" ")
½ 2nd C°G. & M.
M.G.s Royal Irish Fus.
31st Mountain Battery
½ Troop Guides Cavalry
Det. 5th R.G.A.
1 Sec. 48th Div'n Sig. Co.

1 C°. 42nd Deolis at Resht.

CHAPTER XXI

JUNE 1ST, 1920, TO JUNE 19TH, 1921. (*Sketch XVII.*)

ON June 1st orders were received to evacuate Resht prior to which action Lieutenant-Colonel Sweet was directed to again meet General Kājanov and get an explanation as to his apparent invasion of Persian territory, which further landing of troops and fighting towards Ardebil north of Enzeli implied, to inform him we were leaving Resht, and to enquire when he was leaving the port. Replies were still evasive, Kājanov stating he would probably stay until furs, skins, etc., Russian property looted by Denikin's force at Petrovsk and said to have been sold in Persia, had been restored. Meanwhile Enzeli and its neighbourhood was badly experiencing Bolshevik tyranny, looting, raiding, and rapine going on unchecked.

Resht evacuated, 1/6/20.

The orders for evacuation of Resht owing to the situation both military and political, placed Lieutenant-Colonel Sweet in command of a mobile column* to be located at Menzil and vicinity, where positions were to be prepared covering the Menzil bridge and road to Kāsvin against attacks along the Sefid Rud and Kizil Uzun Valleys. A second position to be arranged for further back at Loshān or Yusbashichai on which to retire if necessary, while mountain tracks which might be used to cut communications between Kāsvin and Hamadān were to be guarded and patrolled. The rest of the Enzeli and Resht force was to concentrate at Kāsvin.

Lieut.-Col. Sweet's Column formed at Menzil, early June, 1920.

The column with the 1/2nd Goorkhas doing rearguard, halted at Menzil to arrange defensive positions covering Kāsvin, it being apparent Russian intentions were to reoccupy all this part of Persia which they looked on as theirs, as it was practically before the war. Here our Battalion, now joined by Captain Tuker from Dehra who became Adjutant, and Captain Bucknall from hospital, remained till the end of June, taking part in many reconnaissances up the Kizil Uzun Valley towards Zinjān, and in other directions.

---

* 1/2nd Goorkhas; 1 company 42nd Deolis; 1 section Royal Irish Fusiliers Machine Guns; 1 troop Guides Cavalry; with 2 Hotchkiss guns, 1 section 31st Mountain Battery; 1 section 19th Sappers and Miners; 1 section 15th Light Armoured Mountain Battery; 1 section 48th Signal Company.

It then moved to Loshān on relief by the 122nd Infantry,
Battalion at Loshān, where with 1 section 31st Mountain Battery we formed a
30/6/20. support to the Menzil garrison consisting now of the 122nd Infantry, 42nd Deolis, and 2 guns of 31st Mountain Battery. The advanced posts were at Rudbar and Naglebar towards Resht and the road was regularly patrolled by the armoured cars, the whole being later under the command of Colonel Barclay. Captain McCleverty now left us for duty on the General Officer Commanding's Staff at Kāsvin, and Lieutenant Lancaster with a detachment of 1/2nd Goorkhas was sent up the Kizil Uzun Valley reconnoitring (*Sketch XVII*).

At the end of June we were notified that Kuchik Khan was proclaimed a rebel against the Persian Government, and that it was intended to send Colonel Starosselsky with his Cossack force to retake the Gilān province, which was threatened to be completely overrun by Kuchik and the Bolsheviks. The Shah appeared keen on the Anglo-Persian agreement and on British troops being here, but being weak he could not control affairs, and the whole of North Persia resented our presence. Conflicting advices came in from various sources in which the War Office favoured the idea of withdrawing the whole British North Persia force back to Hamadān, which would have meant handing over the north to the Bolsheviks and the futility of any British troops remaining in the country. However, no actual decision was arrived at, so affairs went on—drifting.

With the beginning of July the 42nd Deolis and some of the Guides being sent up to Zinjān, two of our companies under Lieutenants Warhurst and Campbell
were sent to strengthen Menzil from Loshān, and several
Two companies small "scraps" occurred between our patrol cars and
reinforce Menzil, Bolsheviks assisted by the "Jangalis" north of Menzil. A
2/7/20. force of these troublesome people were now reported at
Damash, 18 miles east of Menzil, necessitating a company under Captain Bucknall and Lieutenant Campbell being sent to Bivarzine to watch that flank, while another hostile gathering with 1 mountain
and 4 machine guns arriving at Obar up the Kizil Uzun
Reconnaissances. Valley obliged three platoons under Lieutenant Lancaster
to be sent to the Lohom Plateau, where they met a portion of the Obar force attempting to cross to Shiah Dehan, and drove them back after a short action (*Sketch XVII*). In late July a hostile gathering did make an attack at Loshān, but retired on our mountain guns opening on them, and stronger forces of the enemy occupying Rudbar and Aliabar attacked

Photo by
PERSIA.
Exclusive News Agency

1. On the road near Menjil.   2. The ancient fortress of Kâsvin, just outside the town.

Capt. Johnson's action, 28/7/20. Menzil seriously on the 28th of that month, obliging five of our platoons under Captain Johnson and Lieutenant Warhurst to make a sortie which drove the Bolsheviks out of certain entrenched picquets in which we had 2 killed and 8 wounded, including Captain Johnson hit in the hand. Fifteen of the enemy were bayonetted and many wounded.

Brigade distribution, July, 1920. The 36th Brigade was at this time distributed as follows:— 1/2nd Goorkhas, 1 section 31st Mountain Battery at Loshān; 122nd Infantry, 1½ troop Guides Cavalry, 31st Mountain Battery, at Menzil; Detachment 42nd Deolis, at Yuzbashichai; Royal Irish Fusiliers, Berks, wing of the York and Lancaster Regiments; 1 troop Guides, "A" Battery, Royal Horse Artillery, at Kāsvin; the rest of the 42nd Deolis and Guides *en route* to Zinjān.

Menzil evacuated, 3/8/20. General Champain came down from Kāsvin on July 30th, and was fired on before reaching Loshān. As it was evident the country was up all about Menzil and Loshān orders were issued to evacuate both places and concentrate at Kāsvin, which was effected on August 3rd in very great heat but without incident, a detachment of the 1/2nd Goorkhas being dropped at Kuhim as an advanced post, relieving that of the Berks Regiment. Here we heard that Kuchik Khan had again split with the Bolsheviks and was acting on his own against the Persian Government.

Kāsvin. Kāsvin, on a plateau at 4,500 feet, has been described as a very cosmopolitan town of about 40,000 inhabitants trying very hard to look like a city, with many hotels of high sounding names and shops with plate glass windows, out of place in an eastern town. It was full of German and Turkish agents trying to turn the Persian people actively against us. Shortly after settling down here Starosselsky's force of some 5,000 Cossacks from Teheran passed through Kāsvin and advanced on Resht, a column of 2 companies York and Lancaster Regiment and the 122nd Infantry being ordered to Menzil to remain there as a support and where a few days later they had an action capturing 75 men and 8 machine guns, knocking out the team of a 4.2 gun with our Battalion machine gun. This affair relieved the situation about Kāsvin where our Battalion was, for a time, and the Royal Irish Fusiliers were sent to Hamadān, leaving the Berks and the York and Lancaster as the British infantry units with the North Persia force.

On August 21st Starosselsky reached Resht out of which he drove the Bolsheviks, capturing large stores of munitions. We also now were informed of the intention to retain the troops in North Persia until the following spring to put down probable disorders; this was disappointing news as all had been looking forward to a return to India with the cold weather. At the end of this month came news of Starosselsky's defeat at Enzeli, where his force came under fire from the ships' guns causing heavy casualties. He then evacuated Resht in a demoralized condition, on which the General Officer Commanding began arrangements for sending all ladies back to Hamadān. The Cossacks, however, recovering themselves, were able to hold the road south of Resht at Imam Zādeh Hachem, and several strong reconnoitring parties of ours once more at Menzil scoured the different hill tracks, but found no sign of the enemy until early September, when a detachment from Kuhim fell in with a raiding party, dispersing them with the loss of two guns.

Persian Cossacks occupy Resht, 21/8/20.

Their Defeat at Enzeli, 30/8/20.

Reconnaissances, Sept., 1920.

A *Gazette* at this time showed that our Subadar-Major Sarabjit Gurung, M.C., had been granted an Honorary King's Commission as Lieutenant for his good services during the war. A fine type of Goorkha Officer with 27 years' service to his credit and medals for Tirah, Waziristhan, Aborland, the Great War, North Persia. He had received the Order of British India (2nd class), the Order of the British Empire (1st class), with the title of Sirdar Bahadur, and was given a sum of money in lieu of a grant of land in the Doon for valuable services in the field. On going on pension in October, 1922, he was further given a King's Commission as Honorary Captain.

Subadar Major Sarabjit Gurung.

With September the great heat was over and Delhi Day (September 14th) was celebrated by the 1/2nd Goorkhas and the Guides at Kāsvin, with sports for the men and a gymkhana for all. At the dinner that night it was learnt that General Champain who of late had not been in good health, was to be succeeded by General Ironside. The position at present was that a force of 3,500 Bolsheviks were holding a line between Resht (which had recently been reoccupied by Starosselsky) and Enzeli, covering the port, our advanced posts being at Jubin and Rustamabad, a little north of Menzil, at this time held by the 122nd Infantry. Changes among our officers had occurred from

Delhi Day, 14/9/20.

Our position and Bolsheviks', Sept., 1920.

time to time, those with us now being as noted below*. Captains McCleverty and Coxe with Lieutenant Bampfield were on the Staff of the 36th Brigade. The Battalion's strength now was 14 British officers, 12 Goorkha officers, and 793 men.

On October 3rd General Ironside arrived and took over command of the North Persia force, Brigadier-General Champain with his wife leaving for Baghdad and India, and late in the month Starosselsky was again turned out of Resht, which the Bolsheviks now occupied in force, terrorizing the countryside and committing excesses and outrages on the unfortunate inhabitants. Their presence at Resht had its effect at Kāsvin where trouble had been expected due to Bolshevik anti-British propaganda, and as stated before, nothing could be got out of the Persian heads who resented our being here at all, thought little of the services our troops had done for their country, and were only waiting to see who would come out top, Bolsheviks or British, so that each could then line his pockets at the expense of his country.

Gen. Ironside arrives to command, 3/10/20.

Persian Officials.

Winter was now on us and a large consignment of ill-cut thick serge uniforms was received, which took a long time to fit on the men, most of the clothing being far too large for our little Goorkhas. Major Dallas Smith, recently rewarded with a Brevet Majority, was appointed to command the Menzil Column on October 13th *vice* Major Van Straubenzee, and three days later the whole Battalion was sent forward in most villainous weather to be located first at Rudbar and neighbourhood, and in this locality north of Menzil we remained for the rest of our time in Persia (*Sketch XVII*).

Major Dallas Smith commands Menzil Column, 15/10/20.

Just before leaving Kāsvin orders came to reduce the Battalion's strength to 600 of all ranks by sending off surplus men on leave. This news was welcomed for a large number of us had had no leave for six years, so this leave party of some 200 odd was rapidly selected, and started for Baghdad a few days later. About the same time the York and Lancaster Regiment left for Hamadān and Line of Communications duty.

Battalion reduced, 18/10/20.

* Lieutenant-Colonel E. H. Sweet, C.M.G., D.S.O.; Brevet Major A. Dallas Smith, M.C.; Captain F. S. Tuker (Adjutant); Captain R. D. Bucknall, " C " Coy.; Captain A. S. Lancaster, " D " Coy.; Captain A. E. Warhurst, " A " Coy.; Captain C. H. Wingfield (Signalling Officer); Lieutenant C. M. A. Campbell; Lieutenant O. De T. Lovett, " B " Coy.; Lieutenant P. Meyrick Jones (Quartermaster); Captain P. R. Kapadia, I.M.S.; Captain Johnson (in hospital wounded).

In early November Colonel Francis, of the Berks Regiment, took command of the Menzil Column, to whom Major Dallas Smith now acted as Staff officer. Starosselsky's Cossacks retiring before Bolshevik pressure, passed through our lines, leaving the onus of holding off the enemy, whose positions were some 10 miles north of Rudbar, to the small British force. As this Cossack force showed signs of disaffection and of causing trouble, the 1/2nd Goorkhas were ordered to accompany them from Menzil to Kāsvin, returning a few days later, no trouble having occurred. We now lost Lieutenant-Colonel Sweet, who handed over command of the Battalion on November 14th to Major Dallas Smith and left for Dehra on leave pending retirement, and to settle up matters at the Depot. His field service throughout the war had been continuous, having first been in France with our 2nd Battalion, after which he was in temporary command of the 2/8th Goorkha Rifles in France and Egypt, then in command of our 1st Battalion during almost its whole service in Mesopotamia, and with exception of a leave period, almost all the time it was in Persia. He left with the hearty good wishes of all for his future. The Bolshevik troops now made a fresh advance, the 122nd Infantry moving out drove them back a few miles, and on the morning of November 18th the Menzil Column advancing with the 1/2nd Goorkhas on the left flank, cleared the enemy back with slight opposition beyond Imām Zādeh Hachem. This was our first offensive under General Ironside's orders, who records his appreciation of the good work and keenness of all concerned in it. The Battalion stayed here some days on one of which Captain Lancaster with a platoon of ours and a Newton mortar sub-section surprised a Bolshevik post at night inflicting casualties and driving the defenders out. He had 2 men killed and 2 wounded, and in this affair Rifleman Parbir Thapa gained the Indian Order of Merit for gallantry when, almost cut off from his platoon and severely wounded, he fought his Lewis gun and brought it out of action. On November 21st a large draft of 4 Goorkha officers and 204 men had arrived at Kāsvin under command of Subadar Lachman Sing Khattrie, who, later, on return to India of the Battalion, was made Subadar-Major of the Indian Army Educational School at Belgaum. The troops moved back on November 27th into positions about Rustamabad, Jubin, and Ganje where the winter and early spring of 1920–21 were passed.

Photo by   *Exclusive News Agency*

The "Goorkha Post," in the middle distance, near Imām Zādeh Hachem, beyond the Naglebar Ridge, and held by the 1st/2nd Goorkhas in 1920. Much fighting took place about here.

Photo by UNVEILING KING EDWARD'S MEMORIAL AT DELHI, 1922. *Central News, Ltd.*

The whole of this period the Battalion held the advanced picquet lines, supported by a troop Guides cavalry, a section of "A" Battery (Chestnut Troop) Royal Horse Artillery, and a mortar section, and which, known as the "Forward Area," was commanded by Major Dallas Smith. General Ironside inspected the 1/2nd Goorkhas and their posts here and expressed his complete satisfaction with all arrangements and his pleasure at the fitness, keenness, and turn-out of the Battalion.

Battalion holds advanced positions during winter, 1920-21.

The country about here was traversed by the Sefid Rud River, its valley near Rustamabad nearly a mile in breadth and bounded on either side by hills rising 2,000 feet, through gaps in which the higher ranges of the Elburz Mountains could be seen, attaining almost Himalayan heights and snow covered except in midsummer. Villages and cultivated patches dotted the valley and hillsides. The summer here was trying, shade temperature going up to 115°, while winter brought severe frosts, snow, or heavy rain, and gales; dangerous spates often came down the river then, and frequently our picquets on the hills would be waist deep in snow. Our billets in the valley were most uncomfortable as house roofs leaked like sieves with rain or melting snow. Menzil at 1060 feet, was perhaps the worst spot of all the Battalion was in, by reason of the everlasting hurricanes which blow down the gorge in which it is situated. Its name signifies "the home of a thousand winds."

Country round Menzil.

During December several minor actions occurred between small parties of both sides, notably when a patrol of the 1/2nd Goorkhas under Lieutenant Lovett on a bitter cold night in a heavy snowstorm successfully ambushed a party of Bolsheviks and in which he was wounded—our only casualty. On another occasion towards the end of the month, two of our platoons under Havildar Kharak Sing Thapa, attacked and drove a strong hostile picquet off the Naglebar Ridge (*Sketch XVII*), punishing them heavily being himself badly wounded in the knee and losing 1 man killed. Our fourth Christmas Day on service passed quietly though in considerable climatic discomfort, and on December 29th Captain Bucknall with three platoons finding the enemy had reoccupied the Naglebar Ridge attacked them though they were in superior strength, routing them with much loss and capturing a Russian officer and a few men. Bucknall, who distinguished himself here, was wounded in the arm early in the fight but continued to lead his men,

Lieut. Lovett's ambuscade, early Dec., 1920.

Action on Naglebar Ridge, 20/12/20.

Capt. Bucknall attacks Naglebar, 29/12/20.

and had one of them killed, while Havildar Mitralal (?) Thapa (later promoted to Jemadar) gallantly captured a machine gun single-handed, killing three of its team. This gun now stands an honoured trophy in front of the 1/2nd Goorkha Quarterguard at Dehra.

During the first half of January, 1921, two platoons under Subadar Tilbir Thapa had a small fight in the vicinity of Naglebar, on returning from which they ran into a large hostile gathering about to raid Jamshidabad.

Subadar Tilbir Thapa's Action near Naglebar, and our last one in Persia, 9/1/21. Our platoons attacked at once, aided by the troop of the Guides with their Hotchkiss gun, who got round the enemy's rear, while a Naik and four bombers of ours getting into their flank completed the Bolshevik's discomfort who lost 60 out of the 90 or so forming the party, including 27 prisoners, and a machine and a Lewis gun were also captured. This formed the last action worth recording in which the 1/2nd Goorkhas were engaged in North Persia, and for gallantry in which Subadar Tilbir Thapa was awarded the Indian Order of Merit (2nd class).

With April, 1921, the long sojourn of the 1/2nd Goorkhas in North Persia came to its end, and a little before this Major Dallas Smith left us for India to take up the appointment of Commandant 4th Assam **Major Dallas Smith** Rifles in Manipur, his place being taken by Captain Tuker. **leaves Battalion,** Under final orders from Baghdad the North Persia force **April, 1921.** was broken up, and on April 11th its various units began their return march to Mesopotamia and India, after handing over their posts to the Persian Cossack force now under British officers. The march began in greatest discomfort, heavy rain falling **North Persia Force** bringing down rivers in spate and breaking down the **broken up, 11/4/21.** road. A few days' rest at Kāsvin for collecting kits, etc., and for drill which all needed, and the Battalion when it started for Hamadān was quite its old smart self again. But now the influenza scourge got hold of us, affecting the **Battalion begins its** men seriously who fell victims to it the more readily that **return march,** the need for sustained interesting effort was over, and **13/4/21.** the long arduous winter had also used up their reserve strength. Major-General Cory, at this time commanding **Influenza.** in Persia, seeing the condition of the men, kindly obtained more transport for us and lightened the loads carried personally. At Hamadān Captain Tuker fell ill, the command devolving for a while on Captain Bucknall, and by the time Kasr i Shirin was

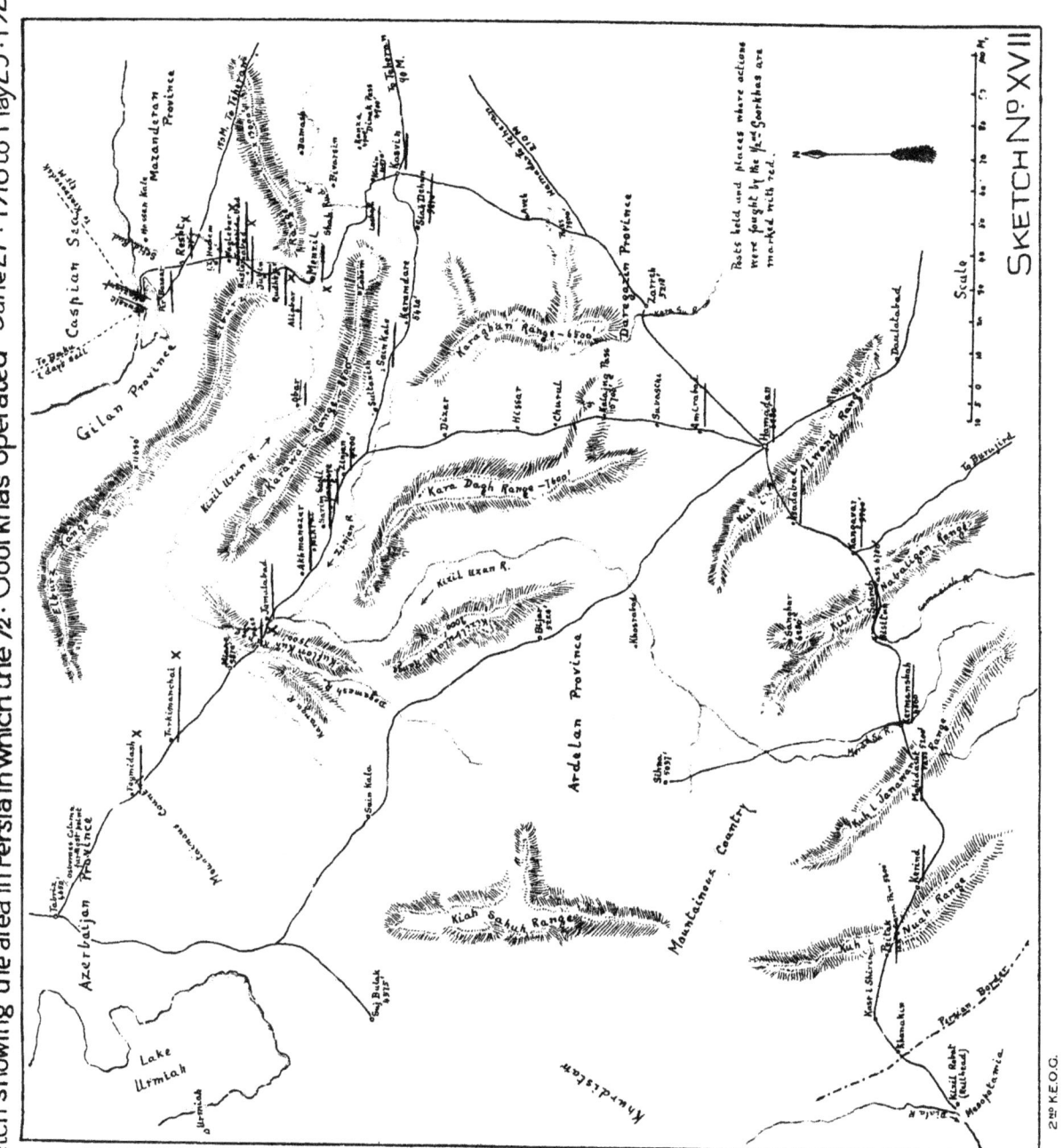

The last of Persia and Mesopotamia, May-June, 1921. reached the malady had worked itself out. It was in June, 1918, the Battalion had first entered Persia through this town, and on May 23rd, 1921, its last dust was shaken off our feet. Here Major McCleverty rejoined us, taking over command of the Battalion from Captain Bucknall on May 26th.

The long journey from Baghdad by rail, river, and steamer, ended at last when Dehra was reached early on June 19th, 1921, where the war-worn home comers received a welcome rivalling that accorded to our 2nd Battalion on its return from France, and the 1/2nd Goorkhas was once more in its old home.

Battalion arrives Dehra, 19/6/21.

Here this history will now leave them till a better pen than the writer's can record further services and glory which the future certainly holds for the old Sirmoor Rifle Regiment.

CHAPTER XXII.

THE 3/2ND GOORKHAS.

FROM JUNE 12TH, 1917, TO OCTOBER 31ST, 1920. (*Sketch XI.*)

TOWARDS the end of 1916 the Government of India decided that a certain number of new Goorkha Battalions should be raised for the duration of the war, and the 1st, 2nd, and 3rd Goorkha Reserve Battalions were raised, by transferring men from all the pre-war regiments including our two Battalions.

Raising of New Goorkha Battalions, late 1916. As, however, the necessity for more and still more men became apparent, it was soon seen that these three new units were not sufficient, and in June, 1917, the number was increased to nine, the old Reserve Battalions being renamed the 4/3rd, 3/5th, 3/6th Goorkha Rifles respectively. The 3/3rd Goorkhas had been previously formed in Egypt, and the remaining Goorkha Rifle Regiments were ordered to form a 3rd Battalion by the transfer of a nucleus from their 1st and 2nd Battalions, and it was thus that our 3rd Battalion came into existence.

This Battalion was raised at Dehra Doon on June 12th, 1917, by Major J. E. Cruickshank, and from the start it was in every way an "offspring" of the Regiment. Unlike those previously formed new Battalions, it was not formed from men of various units in the Goorkha Brigade, but solely from both Battalions of the Regiment. The original officers who joined the 3/2nd Goorkhas were our own, viz., Captain W. B. Shakespear, 1st Battalion, as Wing Commander; Lieutenant G. A. Bain, 2nd Battalion, and Second-Lieutenant G. H. Woollcombe, 2nd Battalion, as Adjutant and Quartermaster respectively.

3rd Battalion raised, 12/6/17.

The first few months in the life of a Battalion must always be a period full of difficulties and hard work, with few outward signs of progress. The 3rd Battalion was no exception to this rule, and it cannot be said that by December when it moved to Peshawur, it had the appearance of an old Battalion. During this period short as it was, many changes had taken place, and Major Cruickshank and Lieutenant Bain only remained of the original four. Lieutenant-Colonel A. Grant (late 4th Goorkha Rifles) had arrived to take over command, and the appointment of Left Wing Commander had been filled

Col. Grant to command.

HISTORY OF THE 2ND KING EDWARD'S OWN GOORKHAS 193

successively by Captain Shakespear, Captain Chope (1st Battalion), and Captain Brandon (1/4th Goorkha Rifles), while Lieutenant Woollcombe had reverted to our 2nd Battalion owing to ill-health. These many changes had naturally a disturbing effect, and although the number of officers with the new unit had been considerably increased by officers on probation for the Indian Army and others from the Indian Army Reserve, yet as these had had no previous experience with Indian troops and were ignorant of the language, their value to a newly raised Battalion was at first not great.

On December 11th, 1917, however, the 3/2nd Goorkhas arrived at Peshawur and joined the 1st Infantry Brigade under Major-General L. H. Dunsterville, and this move undoubtedly had a good effect on all ranks. The sense of competition with other regiments in the station soon began to develop its *esprit de corps*, and it was not long before the new Battalion pulled itself together to some purpose. Unfortunately Major Cruickshank, the only pre-war officer of the Regiment now serving with the Battalion, left to rejoin the 2nd Battalion in January, 1918. Two months later Lieutenant-Colonel Grant gave up command, to be succeeded by Major A. H. Arbuthnot (7th Goorkha Rifles), who held the appointment during the rest of the unit's existence, and Captain E. J. Corse Scott came from the 2nd Battalion as Second-in-Command.

Battalion moved to Peshawur, 11/12/17.

Major Arbuthnot succeeds Col. Grant, March, 1919.

Being now handled with more sympathy than had previously been shown, its progress and improvement was remarkable, a fact testified to in the reports on it by the Inspector-General of Infantry and others.

During the hot weather of 1918 at Peshawur an incident worthy of record occurred. A detachment of one company garrisoned Jamrūd Fort, and when drawing water one day from a deep well in the fort, Rifleman Prem Sing Bisht fell into it. Second-Lieutenant R. M. Newman in command of the detachment, hurried to the scene, and in spite of the fact that he was a big, heavy man, descended three times into the well by a thin rope at great danger to himself to try to rescue the man. This officer was granted a certificate by the Royal Humane Society, but unfortunately died from influenza four months later at Abbottabad.

Lieut. Newman's gallant action.

On the outbreak of the Third Afghan War in May, 1919, all ranks looked forward eagerly to their first active operations but to no effect, for although Major Corse Scott took the Peshawur Flying Column up to Landi Kotal and

o

3rd Afghan War. May, 1919. in spite of many applications made by the General Officer Commanding 1st Infantry Brigade to let the Battalion join his column, it was considered necessary for a Goorkha Battalion to be in Peshawur at this time on internal security duties. The general disappointment throughout the 3rd Battalion was very great, and it was further increased when in September at the end of the Afghan War mobilization orders were actually received for Waziristhan only to be cancelled, when for some reason all Goorkha Battalions were temporarily withdrawn from that front. The disappointment in this case was all the keener because there had been a good chance then that our new Battalion would see service alongside of our 2nd Battalion already in Waziristhan (*Sketch XI*).

In spite of the fact that it had no chance of taking part in these operations, there is no doubt that the rôle played by the 3/2nd Goorkhas in and around Peshawur was a very important one. In addition to very heavy station and escort duties the companies present in Peshawur were frequently called on to deal with gangs of raiders, while detachments were found at the following places :—Jamrūd Fort, 1 company ; Mobilization Godown, 1 company ; Cherāt, 1 company ; Peshawur City, 6 picquets of 1 platoon each ; Narai Khwar Fort, 1 platoon ; Badni Bridge, 2 platoons. It is of interest to record that it was the detachment at Jamrūd Fort which performed the duty of disarming the Khyber Rifles at the opening of the war. The 6 picquets were placed at the important gates and in prominent buildings in the city which then was seething with sedition, and the task of overawing seditionists and inhabitants was successfully performed. The only offensive action taken against our men was the throwing of a bomb at one picquet, which burst practically under a Havildar's bed but fortunately hurt no one. To the picquet at Narai Khwar under Jemadar Narbir Gharti, **Action at Narai Khwar.** belonged the distinction of being the only detachment actually to come into action with the enemy when it was attacked by a considerable body of tribesmen which was driven off with some loss.

After spending another cold weather in Peshawur the 3/2nd Goorkhas returned to Dehra Doon in February, 1920. Rumours were rife now as to the disbandment of all newly raised Goorkha Battalions, **3rd Battalion returns Dehra, Feb., 1920.** and eventually in July orders to this effect were received from Army Headquarters. Of the men many were transferred to our 1st and 2nd Battalions, others to pre-war Regiments in the Goorkha Brigade, while the remainder including a large

BRASS MEMORIAL TABLET IN DEHRA CHURCH.

number of recruits whose enlistment had at no time proved a difficulty, went on pension or took their discharge.

By October 3rd, 1920, our 3rd Battalion had ceased to exist, and its disbandment inevitable though it was, proved a real blow to those who had served with and seen it develop in so short a time into one of the keenest, smartest, and best units of the Indian Army, and a very worthy upholder of the great name of the 2nd Goorkhas.

Disbandment, 3/10/20.

APPENDICES

APPENDIX A.

LIST OF OFFICERS AND MEN OF THE 2ND KING EDWARD'S OWN GOORKHAS RECOMMENDED FOR REWARDS FOR SERVICES IN FRANCE, 1914-15, AND "MENTIONS" IN DESPATCHES.

Names.	Reasons.
Colonel C. de M. Norie, C.B., C.M.G. Major F. H. Norie (attd.), D.S.O. Captain G. M. McCleverty, M.C. Lieutenant E. J. Corse Scott, M.C.	} Mentioned for good work; Major Norie for gallantry November 2nd, 1914.
Major E. R. P. Boileau, C.B., C.I.E., C.B.E.	For good work done in action on December 20th, 1914. When Lieut.-Colonel Norie had been summoned to Brigade Headquarters the enemy suddenly attacked the Battalion's front line, breaking into the trenches in superior numbers. Major Boileau grasped the situation, and by rapid and excellent new dispositions checked any further hostile advance.
Major E. H. Sweet, C.M.G., D.S.O.	For capable handling of his Double Company during the action of May 9th-10th, 1915. His general good work and cheery behaviour throughout the attack gave confidence to both officers and men. His behaviour at Neuve Chapelle was similar, and his good work is worthy of mention. Again :— An officer whose sound judgment and excellent example to all ranks make him of great value in a Regiment. His quiet soldierly qualities make his services peculiarly valuable. He can best be described as being the whitest of white men under all conditions, and who deserves recognition.
Major D. M. Watt, D.S.O., C.I.E.	Commanded a Double Company at the attack on the Bois du Biez, March 10th-12th, 1915, with great ability and dash, securing the edge of the wood with few casualties. His dispositions on reaching it were admirable. On the morning of the 11th, when getting his command into preliminary position in support, although wounded in the leg, he brought his men into action, only giving up command when his wound prevented him getting any farther.
Captain A. Dallas Smith, M.C.	A very gallant officer. He led the attack on the Bois du Biez on the night of March 10th, 1915, and took command of the Double Company when Major Watt was wounded next day, and throughout the rest of the time displayed a splendid example of pluck. He is an exceptional officer.
Captain L. A. Bethell	On December 12th, 1914, when a small party collecting wood had drawn on themselves the enemy's machine-gun and rifle fire from trenches 400 yards off, losing 2 men killed and 1 wounded, Captain Bethell jumped out of his trench and ran across to where the wounded man had taken cover. He bound him up and brought him back to his own trench under a brisk fire from the enemy.
Captain J. E. Cruickshank	Did excellent work with his machine guns on May 9th, 1915. When the Battalion was held up he immediately mounted his machine guns, also taking command of those of the 107th Pioneers, whose officer was wounded. In spite of heavy shell fire he kept his guns in action, and was instrumental in keeping down the enemy's fire.

GOORKHAS (THE SIRMOOR RIFLE REGIMENT)

Names.	Reasons.
Captain W. B. Cullen (I.M.S.)	A particularly cool and efficient Medical Officer whose services since he joined us (January, 1915) are of the highest order. At the actions near Neuve Chapelle he was untiring in his efforts for the wounded. On May 9th and 10th, 1915, he displayed fine qualities in his duties by great energy in tending the wounded under very dangerous circumstances. On September 25th, 1915, he worked throughout the action and through the night. His strict sense of duty was remarkable.
Captain H. K. W. Bruce, M.C.	This officer possesses qualities of a high order. During the past four months he has commanded his company with ability and resource. On September 25th, 1915, when the Battalion was under heavy "minenwerfer" fire, he handled his company with conspicuous ability, and due to the prompt measures he took the Battalion escaped with slight casualties. He saved the machine-gun detachment and guns when their emplacements during the bombardment were shattered and levelled to the ground. His company is the best in the Battalion, due entirely to his energy and fine soldierly qualities.
Captain and Adjutant E. J. Corse Scott, M.C.	This officer throughout the day (December 20th, 1914) gave great assistance both as Adjutant and communications officer, and in the evening guided the Loyal North Lancs and Northamptons to the ground prior to their counter-attack on the enemy.
	Again :—
	This officer was invaluable throughout March 10th and 11th, 1915, in carrying messages to different parts of the Battalion, often at great risk. Due to the ability with which he carried out the duties of generally assisting the Commanding Officer during the attack and subsequent events, everything worked smoothly. He has twice before been recommended for good work.
	Again :—
	This officer was indefatigable during the preparation for and through the attack, May 9th, 1915. He was constantly up and down the line carrying messages and helping generally. This necessitated his moving under heavy shell fire and at great risk. His name has been brought forward three times for good work done, and he has twice been recommended for the Military Cross. He is an exceptionally capable and gallant officer.
	Again :—
	This officer's services have been repeatedly brought to notice for excellent work. He is very hard-working, capable, and possesses qualities of a high order. Though the Brigade as a whole was not called on to make an attack on September 25th, 1915, he was of the greatest assistance in bringing the Battalion to the front line under difficult and dangerous circumstances. His work throughout has been deserving of the highest praise. He has been three times mentioned in despatches, has received the Military Cross, and for services on May 10th, 1915, has been recommended for the D.S.O.
Lieutenant G. A. P. Scoones, D.S.O., M.C.	This officer is Quartermaster of the Battalion, and has done excellent work in various actions and on that of May 9th-10th, 1915. Whether the Battalion is in or out of action, there is no difficulty about rations, due to the energy and initiative shown by him in his work. He has repeatedly asked to be allowed to join the firing line, but his services are too valuable in his present capacity and he cannot be spared. His excellent work is worthy of mention.
Lieutenant A. P. Hay Webb	This officer is in charge of the Battalion scouts, and as such has continually done remarkably good work, often at great risk.

HISTORY OF THE 2ND KING EDWARD'S OWN

Names.	Reasons.
Major W. B. Bailey Captain G. H. D. Woollcombe Captain N. G. Hind, M.C. Lieutenant H. Green (I.A.R.O.)	Were "mentioned" for general good work done in France and with the Waziristhan Field Force.
Subadar Major Kara-Sing Rana, M.C., O.B.I. Subadar Sarabjit Gurung	Mentioned for gallantry and general good work in France.
Subadar Dhan Sing Lama, I.D.S.M., I.O.M.	Displayed great dash in command of a Company during the attack on the Bois du Biez, March 10th, 1915. Has done thorough good work throughout the period of the war.
Jemadar Patiram Pun, I.D.S.M.	During the withdrawal of the Battalion on the night of March 11th-12th, 1915, a shell burst on the road wounding several men. They were picked up, but Jemadar Patiram Pun was sent back to see if any had been left behind. He found only wounded men of another battalion, but remained helping them until a stretcher party arrived. He could get no volunteers to assist him, but stayed at his post although shells continued to burst on the road.
Subadar Mansur Rai, I.O.M. (*attached from 1st Assam Rifles*)	On September 25th, 1915, this Goorkha officer led his Company in the most gallant manner and was exposed to a very heavy fire of machine guns and rifles. Later in the day he succeeded in getting his men back when the attack was stopped, and again went out in front of the parapet, and was instrumental in bringing in several wounded men under most difficult circumstances. Ever since he joined the Battalion this officer has proved himself a capable and gallant leader of men. He is deserving of a good reward.
Subadar Bhagatbir Limbu, I.O.M. (*attached from 7th Goorkha Rifles*)	This Goorkha officer displayed a splendid example of dash and pluck when his Company attacked the German position on September 25th, 1915. His gallantry was most marked as he coolly collected his men for the advance, and due to his example all went forward splendidly. This attack was held up by a cross fire of machine guns which made further advance impossible, and the majority of his platoon were killed or wounded.
Subadar Arjun Rana, I.O.M. Jemadar Sarabjit Gurung, Order of St. George (Russian)	Both these Goorkha officers have done excellent service in France, their energy and hard work have been most remarkable, as well as their soldierly qualities in various actions.
Subadar Kharak Sing Rana, M.C. Jemadar Aiman Thapa, M.C. Jemadar Manbahadur Gurung, M.C. Subadar Fateh Sing Newar, O.B.I.	These Goorkha officers came under the Commanding Officer's special notice for bravery and good work during the action November 2nd, 1914.
	A detachment under command of this Goorkha officer was cut off during the action on November 2nd, 1914. He displayed great coolness and resource in keeping his men together, in withstanding the German attacks, and in eventually bringing his men back.
Subadar Arjun Rana, I.O.M.	On December 20th, 1914, when the enemy broke into the "Orchard" and after Major Rooke had been wounded, Subadar Arjun Rana took command of the Company and held his trenches for the rest of that day and all night, and kept the enemy from gaining foothold in them. On December 21st, when another British officer had been sent to take command, Subadar Arjun Rana continued to give him great assistance, supervising the fight in that part of the field until the Company was finally relieved.
Havildar Ranpati Gurung, I.D.S.M. Havildar Janglal Gurung, I.D.S.M. Havildar Nandlal Thapa Havildar Judbir Sarki Havildar Paspati Buratoki	These non-commissioned officers were with Subadar Fateh Sing Newar's detachment when it was cut off during the action November 2nd, 1914. All did exceptionally good work in keeping their men together, and displayed great coolness.

GOORKHAS (THE SIRMOOR RIFLE REGIMENT)

Names.	Reasons.
Jemadar BAHADUR GHALE	All these men were conspicuous in the counter-offensives against the Germans on November 2nd, 1914, and acted as leaders in the charge, and received the Indian Distinguished Service Medal.
Naik TEGBAHADUR GHARTI	
Naik RAMPERSHAD THAPA	
Naik GAMAR SING BURATOKI	
Naik NAIN SING GHARTI	
Naik PADAMDHOJ GURUNG	
L./Naik DALBIR RANA	
L./Naik SHER SING GHALE	
L./Naik KESAR SING GURUNG	
L./Naik BUDHIBAHADUR GURUNG	
Rifleman TULA GURUNG	
Naik RAMPERSHAD THAPA	
Rifleman MOGAN SING GURUNG	
Rifleman KUNBIR THAPA	
Rifleman PREM SING THAPA	
Naik PADAMDHOJ GURUNG, I.O.M.	These men stayed with the Connaught Rangers through the night of November 2nd-3rd, 1914, and displayed great gallantry throughout the fighting that day.
Naik PATIRAM THAPA, I.D.S.M.	
L./Naik LILARAM THAPA	
L./Naik BARUA SING GURUNG	
Rifleman PREM SING THAPA	
Rifleman KALU GURUNG, I.D.S.M.	
Havildar SARABJIT GURUNG	For invaluable work done as scouts, frequently in most dangerous circumstances.
Naik NAR SING GURUNG	
L./Naik BUDH SING GURUNG	
2265 Rifleman TULA GURUNG, I.O.M.	In the trench they were occupying a "minenwerfer" shell had buried a man alive. These two riflemen set to work to dig him out, and saved him, although the shells were bursting close around them.
1959 Rifleman BHAGATBAHADUR GURUNG, I.O.M.	
1628 Havildar BHAG SING THAPA, I.D.S.M.	Both non-commissioned officers of No. 2 Company, which occupied the left section of the 2nd Goorkha trenches when the Germans broke into them on December 20th, 1914. These two men at the exposed end of their trench held the ground with their men, preventing any further progress of the enemy along the trench. They held this point with the Germans on two sides of them until ordered to retire by Captain Bethell on the 21st.
1517 Havildar BHIMBAHADUR THAPA, I.D.S.M.	
1971 L./Naik KHAMBA SING GURUNG	For good work generally on December 20th, 1914, when the Germans had broken into our trenches.
1775 L./Naik ATTAR SING GURUNG	These men showed great presence of mind and coolness when their trench was being shelled by "minenwerfer" on December 20th, 1914, at once manning their loopholes and keeping up a steady fire on the enemy until ordered to evacuate the trench.
2493 Rifleman DHANBIR GURUNG	
1599 Rifleman UJIR SING GURUNG, I.O.M.	
1029 Rifleman NATHA SING GURUNG	
1398 Havildar CHANDAN SING GURUNG	For good work done daily in the trenches when in charge of telephones.
2329 L./Naik AMAR SING PUN, I.D.S.M.	For good work done daily in scouting.

Names.	Reasons.
4024 Rifleman Manjit Gurung, I.O.M.	For conspicuous gallantry on March 10th, 1915. His Company was lying in the open preparatory to attack, having left the trenches behind the Des Layes River, and had crossed to the other side. He heard of a wounded non-commissioned officer, and later, when the attack was cancelled and retirement ordered, he found and carried the wounded man back across the river under heavy fire.
3266 Rifleman Jagtia Pun, I.O.M.	For conspicuous gallantry on March 11th, 1915. His Company Commander was severely wounded while the Company was lying in the open preparatory to attack. This rifleman bound up the Goorkha officer and carried him back across the river under heavy fire.
2515 Rifleman Hastabir Roka, I.O.M.	Though wounded in the arm on March 10th, 1915, while bringing up machine-gun ammunition, he continued to carry the boxes across ground swept by machine-gun fire and brought them to the fire trench.
1599 L./Naik Ujir Sing Gurung, I.O.M. 2447 Rifleman Partiman Gurung, I.O.M.	While their Company was temporarily held up by heavy machine-gun fire on March 10th, 1915, these two men attended to a badly wounded man and carried him to a sheltered spot. Later, when the retirement took place, they searched in the dark for the wounded man and carried him in safely.
1959 L./Naik Bhagatbahadur Gurung, I.O.M.	On March 10th, 1915, he dashed from the trench in face of heavy enfilading machine-gun fire and carried in a wounded man. He has already received the "Order of Merit."
4267 Rifleman Ranbahadur Gurung, I.D.S.M. 3791 Rifleman Jit Sing Gurung, I.D.S.M.	These two men risked their lives twice to succour wounded men lying in the open between the fire and support trenches. The ground was enfiladed by machine-gun fire.
2438 Rifleman Dilu Pun, I.D.S.M. 2014 Rifleman Thorong Gurung, I.D.S.M.	For bringing in wounded men from a position exposed to heavy fire on March 10th, 1915.
3741 Rifleman Narbhopal Thapa, I.D.S.M.	Risked his life to succour a wounded officer of the 4th Seaforths, March 10th, 1915, who was lying out behind the fire trench.
3184 Havildar Sarabjit Gurung, I.D.S.M.	Has done repeatedly good scouting work, often at great risk, throughout the campaign. His name has already once been submitted.
1957 Naik Bambahadur Gurung, I.O.M. 2693 Rifleman Anarupe Rana, I.O.M.	These two men had on May 10th, 1915, reached a point within 25 yards of the German trenches, but were forced to withdraw owing to our own shell fire. Later in the day, when the Black Watch repeated the attack, a man of that regiment lay out in the open wounded about 40 yards from us. The man was crying for help, and both these men, although under heavy shell fire, went out and carried him under cover.
3222 Havildar Jangbir Thapa ... 2621 Rifleman Narbahadur Gurung 4814 Rifleman Randhoj Limbu ... 2032 Rifleman Harkbir Thapa ... 501 Rifleman Dirbahadur Khattri	Conspicuous gallantry in the attack of the German trenches on May 10th, 1915. These men, with the exception of two others, were the sole survivors of their platoon. Though exposed to heavy machine-gun fire and with their unit depleted, they made most determined efforts to reach the hostile trenches, and were only held up 30 yards from them by our own shells. All were awarded the I.D.S.M.
2025 Naik Amer Sing Pun, I.O.M.	This non-commissioned officer is in charge of the Battalion scouts and is a fearless leader. While in the front trenches he was over his parapet most nights, and his bold scouting has been of the greatest value to the Battalion. Due to his example and work, the spirit of his men is very high in spite of constant danger. He has already won the Distinguished Service Medal.

GOORKHAS (THE SIRMOOR RIFLE REGIMENT)

Names.	Reasons.
1819 Havildar DILBAHADUR RANA, I.D.S.M.	On June 15th, 1915, while the Battalion was subjected to heavy "minenwerfer" fire which completely destroyed part of our parapet, this non-commissioned officer fearlessly carried messages to the telephone, and several times the bombs fell close to him. In spite of this, he displayed remarkable qualities of coolness and bravery under fire, and is deserving of recognition.
1278 BASHIRAM SHARMA (*Sub-Assistant Surgeon, 2nd Class*)	While with this Battalion has worked strenuously and well. In the actions round Neuve Chapelle, and on May 9th, 1915, he showed fine qualities under shell fire. He is deserving of recognition.
Subadar GAMER SING BURA, I.D.S.M., 1914 ... Subadar BAG SING THAPA, I.D.S.M., 1914 ... Subadar BHIMBAHADUR THAPA, I.D.S.M., 1914 Subadar BAHADUR GHALE, Despatches, 1919 ... Subadar GAMER SING GURUNG, Despatches, 1914 Jemadar BOMBAHADUR GURUNG, I.O.M., 1915 ... Jemadar JUDHIA SARKI, I.D.S.M., 1915 ... ... Jemadar RAMPERSHAD THAPA, I.D.S.M., 1914 ... Jemadar AMER SING PUN, I.D.S.M., 1914 ... Jemadar AIMAN THAPA, Despatches, 1914 ... Jemadar SHERBAHADUR GURUNG, M.S.M., 1918 ... Jemadar BASKER GURUNG, M.S.M., 1918 ... Jemadar HASTABIR GURUNG, M.S.M., 1918 ... Jemadar SHAMSHER BOHRA, M.S.M., 1918 ... Havildar Major TULA GURUNG, I.O.M., 1915 ... Havildar 2896 JAGIA RANA, I.O.M., 1915 ... ... Havildar 2447 PARTIMAN GURUNG, I.O.M., 1915 ... Havildar 2153 SHER SING GHALE, I.D.S.M., 1914 Havildar 1935 DHANRAJ GURUNG, I.D.S.M., 1919 Havildar 2132 HARAKBIR GHARTI, M.S.M., 1918 ... Havildar 2189 TULBIR GURUNG, M.S.M., 1918 ... Havildar 2246 GAMER SING GURUNG, M.S.M., 1918 Naik 2554 SARU GURUNG, M.S.M., 1918 ... ... L./Naik 1958 BHAGATBAHADUR GURUNG, I.O.M., 1914 L./Naik 4166 GAGAN SING THAPA, Despatches, 1919 L./Naik 2582 GOPAL PUN, M.S.M., 1918 ... ... L./Naik SETIA GURUNG, M.S.M., 1918	These Goorkha officers, non-commissioned officers, and men were all rewarded or mentioned in despatches for sterling good service in France and on the North-West Frontier of India between 1914 and 1919.
Jemadar HOSHIAR SING RANA ... ... Havildar 812 GANGARAM LOHAR ... ... Havildar 1389 RAM SING NEWAR ... ... L./Naik 3966 DALBAHADUR GURUNG	These received the Meritorious Service Medal for valuable work in India during the war.

Names.	Reasons.
Major J. E. Cruickshank Captain N. J. Hind Lieutenant H. Green (I.A.R.O.) Lieutenant G. H. Woollcombe Subadar Bahadur Ghale Subadar Gamer Sing Gurung 3677 Havildar Bhanu Gurung 1935 Havildar Dhanraj Gurung 2090 Havildar Gajbir Thapa 2346 Havildar Gamer Sing Gurung 1803 Havildar Lilambar Gurung 4166 L./Naik Gagan Sing Thapa 4176 L./Naik Ude Bura 2403 L./Naik Dhanraj Gurung 2944 Rifleman Hira Sing Newar	These officers, non-commissioned officers, and men were "mentioned" for excellent work done in Waziristhan, 1918-1919.

LIST OF OFFICERS AND MEN OF THE 1/2ND KING EDWARD'S OWN GOORKHAS MENTIONED AND AWARDED DECORATIONS FOR GOOD SERVICES AND GALLANTRY IN MESOPOTAMIA AND NORTH PERSIA, 1916-1921

Lieut.-Colonel E. H. Sweet, C.M.G., D.S.O.	Mentioned in despatches in 1917 and 1919 for excellent services in Mesopotamia and North Persia; D.S.O., 1917; and C.M.G., 1919.
Major A. Dallas Smith, M.C.	For excellent work in North Persia, 1917-1920, during which period he held several independent commands.
Captain P. A. R. Pritchard	This officer's work was consistently good throughout 1916 until seriously wounded on February 24th, 1917. After Major Nicholl's death on March 8th, 1916, he was in command of the Battalion till Lieutenant-Colonel Sweet arrived. His gallantry in the actions of February 3rd and 24th, 1917, was most marked (wounded).
Captain G. M. McCleverty, D.S.O., M.C.	This officer was Adjutant in the successful attack on February 3rd, 1917, and had only taken over this duty when Captain Marsh was killed the previous day. He did most sterling work in reorganizing the three lines of trenches which had been carried in the assault, showing absolute disregard of danger. It was largely due to his efforts in stimulating the men to extra exertion that when the Turkish counter-attacks came we were able to repel them. He was wounded in France on November 2nd, 1914, and again on March 10th, 1915, and was mentioned in despatches. Again :— Captain McCleverty commanded two strong companies in North Persia during 1918 with greatest success. They were in action on several occasions against Kuchik Khan's force, and he distinguished himself in the attack on Resht, when his action saved the British Consulate there.
Major E. Ridgeway, C.I.E.	For excellent work and organization of regimental communications during the fighting in early February, 1917. (Killed.)

GOORKHAS (THE SIRMOOR RIFLE REGIMENT)

Names.	Reasons.
Captain H. F. F. MARSH, M.C.	For gallantry on March 8th, 1916. (Wounded; killed February 1st, 1917.)
Captain R. D. BUCKNALL	For gallantry in North Persia during 1918-1920. (Wounded.)
Captain W. G. H. GOUGH, M.C.	For excellent work in 1916. (Wounded at bomb practice.)
Captain C. H. WINGFIELD	For efficiency when in charge of the signallers during 1919-20; also for good work as Quartermaster.
Lieutenant SNOW, I.A.R.O.	For sterling work as Quartermaster during 1917-18-19.
Captain A. E. WARHURST	For good work in North Persia during 1918-19-20.
Lieutenant O. DE T. LOVETT	For gallantry in North Persia during 1918-19-20. (Wounded.)
Lieutenant DUNLOP	For gallantry with our bombing parties early February, 1917. (Killed.)
Lieutenant W. S. BAKER, M.C. I.A.R.O.	On February 3rd, 1917, this officer was in command of the Company leading the attack on the right which succeeded in penetrating and holding three lines of Turkish trenches. The command fell to him the previous day, after Major Bruce had been killed. He received a very painful wound before reaching the objective at 10 a.m., but refused to leave his men or cease reorganizing his company until ordered to by the Commanding Officer at 8 p.m. that night. It was undoubtedly due to his excellent and gallant example under trying circumstances that his men were able to repel various counter-attacks.
2/Lieutenant H. TROTTER, M.C., I.A.R.O.	After the unsuccessful attack on the Turkish trenches on February 1st, 1917, this officer accompanied a night patrol and brought back much useful information. The ground moved over was covered with wounded and dead, whom Arabs were robbing. Finding some wounded Sikhs in a nullah, the patrol tried to bring them in, but it was impossible without stretchers. At 3 a.m., when Lieutenant Trotter had given in his report, he guided Captain Marsh and some stretchers to the nullah, and it was here while they were binding up a wounded Sikh that Marsh was fatally wounded. Lieutenant Trotter assisted to dress his wound and took Marsh back to the dressing station. Lieutenant Trotter was seriously wounded on the morning of February 3rd, 1917, when leading his men in the assault.
2/Lieutenant JERRAM, M.C. (I.A.R.O.)	This officer has been in charge of the Battalion scouts, and has done excellent service on many occasions when he penetrated Turkish trenches at great risk and often under fire, bringing back most useful information.
Lieutenant TOOGOOD, D.S.O.	These two officers were the first to effect the landing at No. 3 Ferry during the crossing of the Tigris under heavy fire. The gallantry with which they defended themselves and maintained their position for hours before reinforcements could reach them, was of a very high order.
Lieutenant BAKER, M.C.	
Lieutenant COXE, M.C.	This officer has done excellent service in North Persia when in command of detachments taking part in various encounters with tribesmen and Bolsheviks, and generally displaying soldierly qualities in a high degree.
Subadar Major TULSIRAM GHARTI, O.B.I.	For excellent service during the campaign in Mesopotamia and North Persia, 1916-1920.
Subadar SARABJIT GURUNG, I.O.M., M.C.	This Goorkha officer received the "Indian Order of Merit" for gallantry in France when with our 2nd Battalion. In the assault of February 3rd, 1917, he showed great coolness and courage in the attack when commanding a platoon, later taking command of the Company when the Company Commander was wounded. He was conspicuous where the fire was hottest, and by his example, leadership, and determination to push forward at all costs under very heavy machine-gun fire and in spite of severe losses, inspired his men to emulate him. On reaching the enemy's trenches, he shot two Turks, who first put up their hands and then threw a bomb at him. He was also very conspicuous in supervising preparations for resisting counter-attacks and in getting up supplies of bombs.

Names.	Reasons.
Jemadar DHANBIR SONWAR, I.O.M.	Was on February 3rd, 1917, in command of a platoon on the right flank which advanced along the river bank and took the hostile trench on that side, together with Lieutenant Dunlop, with the Battalion bombers. This platoon was enfiladed by a machine gun on the east bank of the Hai, and suffered severely. When his men began to hesitate he urged them on, leading them into the Turkish trench, which he was the first to enter. He then started to block the trench from the north; and although his work was twice blown down by our own guns causing severe casualties, he urged the men to build the third and final one, which prevented the whole of our right flank from being successfully attacked by the enemy. This was all done on his own initiative, as Lieutenant Dunlop had been killed some while before. He was afterwards severely wounded.
Subadar KARBIR THAPA, I.O.M.	This Goorkha officer was in command of the leading platoon of his company, which he led with great dash in the assault of February 3rd, 1917. Later he was instrumental in assisting to consolidate the position gained. The assault swept over the first Turkish trench, and the Subadar, noticing that this was weakly held on our left, took a party and held the left flank of the trench against a stiff counter-attack. He had previously displayed great gallantry on March 8th, 1916, at the Dujailah Redoubt.
Jemadar LAL SING RANA, I.D.S.M.	On February 3rd and 4th, 1917, after the assault and capture of three lines of Turkish trenches, this officer worked continuously under heavy fire, being the only unwounded officer in his company, and was of the greatest assistance in consolidating the captured position and preparing against counter-attacks. He had also shown gallantry in the battle of the Dujailah Redoubt on March 8th, 1916.
Subadar MANSUR RAI, I.O.M. (*attached from 1st Assam Rifles*)	This officer's help from February 1st, 1917, to after the assault and capture of the Turkish trenches on the 3rd was invaluable. He showed great gallantry throughout these operations. For his services in France with our 2nd Battalion he had received the "Indian Order of Merit," 3rd Class.
3719 Havildar BAHADUR GURUNG, I.D.S.M.	For conspicuous gallantry on February 3rd, 1917, and devotion to duty in working his Lewis gun under very heavy fire, and thus contributing in no small degree to the successful repulse of the Turkish counter-attacks.
3557 Naik NARAIN MAL, I.D.S.M.	For conspicuous gallantry on February 3rd, 1917. A strong Turkish bombing attack developed on the left of his company. Hearing a call for bombs, he took his party out of the trench which he had just cleared and blocked, and went 100 yards across the open under very heavy fire and attacked the advancing Turks. This prompt and gallant action contributed largely to the repulse of the counter-attack.
1531 Naik AMERDHOJ RAI	For conspicuous gallantry on February 3rd, 1917. He twice led parties across the open, exposed to heavy shell and machine-gun fire, to attack the enemy seen to be crowding up their communicating trenches. His gallantry and determination enabled a successful block to be established, and made the enemy chary of venturing up their chief communicating trench, where they were helpless against attacks of this nature.
4814 L./Naik RANDHOJ LIMBU, I.D.S.M.	For conspicuous gallantry and initiative on the night of February 1st-2nd, 1917. He went out volunteering to bring in wounded, and carried in two Sikhs under heavy fire. Finding numbers of Arabs killing and robbing the wounded, he came back for bombs, going out again, when he killed three Arabs and wounded another. While out he discovered that the nullah in continuation of "Worcester Street" was not filled in as reported by aeroplane, but only partially at one end. He returned, reported this, and, taking more bombs, went out again to

GOORKHAS (THE SIRMOOR RIFLE REGIMENT)

4212 L./Naik Puran Sing Gurung, I.D.S.M. — the nullah, driving off marauding Arabs right up to the Turks' first line trench, into which he threw five bombs. The information *re* the nullah was of great value, as it provided a communicating trench for our bombers next day. This man again showed great gallantry in the assault on February 3rd, 1917, continuing to lead his bombers until severely wounded. He had previously been brought to notice for gallantry in France.

For conspicuous gallantry and initiative in the attack on February 3rd, 1917. Seeing that several of the Battalion bombers had been killed and wounded and the Turks were coming up the communicating trench in large numbers, he collected a number of bombs, and, running along the top of the trench in the open, although wounded in the head, he continued bombing the Turks till they broke.

4975 L./Naik Jitbahadur Gurung — For conspicuous gallantry and devotion to duty on February 3rd and 4th, 1917. He was employed as a messenger, and, though wounded early on the 3rd, refused to go back to the dressing-station, and continued to carry messages under heavy fire all that day and the next, until forced to desist from weakness and loss of blood.

4415 L./Naik Kulman Rana
4400 Rifleman Gopi Chand Gurung — For conspicuous gallantry on February 3rd, 1917. While the trench line was being consolidated considerable losses were being caused by a party of Turks still holding on in a "dug-out" 35 yards in front. These two men ran forward under heavy fire, threw bombs at the party, killing some, and then went in and killed the rest with their kookeries.

4848 L./Naik Bahadur Rai, I.D.S.M.
4311 Rifleman Ranbir Thapa, I.D.S.M. — For conspicuous gallantry on the night of February 1st–2nd, 1917. They were collecting Sikh wounded exposed to snipers and Arabs looting the dead and wounded. Again, on the 3rd, they volunteered to go back over the open 150 yards to fetch bombs, and made six journeys, exposed the whole time to heavy shell and machine-gun fire, bringing up fifty or more bombs badly needed in the front line.

3893 Naik Gorea Gurung, I.O.M. — For conspicuous gallantry in the fighting on February 3rd, 1917. This non-commissioned officer was very conspicuous throughout, standing up on the parapet hurling bombs and encouraging his men. On hearing the Battalion on our left (the Devons) shout for bombs to repel a strong Turkish counter-attack at the junction of the two battalions, he collected four or five men, and, running across the open under very heavy fire, attacked the supporting Turks well down their communicating trench, driving back the attackers and cutting off their leading bombers, who surrendered.

3114 Rifleman Chandrabahadur Mal — For conspicuous gallantry on February 3rd, 1917. While our bombers were working up a main communicating trench after the assault he noticed a few Turks in a nullah parallel to it; having no bombs, he dashed forward under heavy fire and attacked them with his kookerie, killing one, wounding two, and taking two prisoners.

1915 Rifleman Dalbahadur Gurung, I.D.S.M. — For conspicuous gallantry during the action of February 3rd, 1917. The party he was with having run out of bombs while clearing the enemy's second-line trench, he went back under heavy fire and collected bombs from killed and wounded men, then advanced down a fire trench alone looking for concealed "dug-outs," of which he found several and killed their occupants.

4325 Rifleman Narbahadur Gurung
4153 L./Naik Man Sing Thapa
4345 Rifleman Bismal Rana
4813 Rifleman Surbir Rana
4631 Rifleman Tahbil Thapa
1319 Naik Narbahadur Limbu
3744 Naik Tulbir Gurung — For conspicuous gallantry on February 3rd, 1917. A party of 14 men were building a forward block on the Hai bank when several of our own shells from across the river fell amongst them, killing and wounding a number of our men. These seven survivors continued building and completed the block, which was twice blown down by shells.

HISTORY OF THE 2ND KING EDWARD'S OWN

Names.	Reasons.
43 Rifleman DILBIR THAPA	For conspicuous gallantry on February 3rd, 1917. He continued to fire his Lewis gun alone after the rest of the team had been killed and wounded, and after the gun had been put out of action by a shrapnel bullet continued to keep up a rapid fire with his rifle. To get a field of fire he was forced the whole time to lie in a very exposed situation on top of the enemy's parados under heavy fire. He remained there until ordered to come down into the trench by his Company Commander.
4991 Rifleman PADAM SING THAPA, I.O.M.	For conspicuous gallantry and devotion to duty on February 3rd, 1917. When engaged in bombing up and blocking the Turkish main communication trench several of our leading men were killed by shell fire, and he was severely wounded. He, however, pushed on with greatest determination, though alone, and succeeded in checking the advancing Turks until he fell severely wounded again by a bomb. His gallant conduct enabled the men behind to complete the forward block before the enemy could reach it.

Subadar Major TULSIRAM GHARTI ...	O.B.I., 2nd Class ; M.C., 1917
Subadar MANJIT GHARTI ...	O.B.I., 2nd Class, 1918
Subadar LACHMAN SING KHATTRIE	I.D.S.M, 1919
Subadar CHAMPA SING GURUNG ...	Despatches
Subadar GUMAN SING GURUNG ...	I.D.S.M., 1919
Subadar AIMAN RANA ...	I.D.S.M., 1918
Subadar TILBIR THAPA ...	I.O.M., 1921
Subadar MANBAHADUR GURUNG ...	I.D.S.M., 1917
Jemadar PERTAB SAHI ...	I.D.S.M., 1916
Jemadar GUMAN SING GURUNG ...	I.D.S.M., 1917
Jemadar NAIN SING THAPA ...	I.D.S.M., 1919
Jemadar NANDBIR THAPA ...	I.D.S.M., 1918
Jemadar DILA SING GURUNG ...	I.D.S.M., 1919
Jemadar HARKA SING GURUNG ...	Despatches
Jemadar GAMBIR SING THAPA ...	Despatches
Jemadar JITBAHADUR GURUNG ...	Despatches
Jemadar RAN SING THAPA ...	I.D.S.M., 1919
Jemadar KARAK SING GURUNG ...	M.S.M., 1918
Jemadar KESHAR SING THAPA ...	M.S.M., 1918
3699 Havildar KESHAR SING RANA ...	I.D.S.M., 1917
3030 Havildar ATIBAL GURUNG ...	Serbian Cross of Karageorge, 1917
4383 Havildar PARSABAHADUR THAPA	I.D.S.M, 1917
4366 Havildar JIWAN SING LOHAR ...	M.S.M., 1918
4348 Havildar BISMAN RANA ...	Despatches
3627 Havildar KAMAN SING GURUNG ...	Despatches
3799 Havildar KHARAK SING GURUNG	Despatches
4021 Havildar RAGBIR SAHI ...	Despatches
3989 Havildar TILAKCHAND GURUNG	I.D.S.M., 1918
2483 Havildar PURAM SING THAPA ...	M.S.M., 1918
1443 Havildar SINGBIR LAMA (A.M.P.)	M.S.M., 1918
3958 Havildar CHATTER SING THAPA	M.S.M., 1919
4143 Havildar PARTA SING GURUNG	I.D.S.M., 1919

All were mentioned for excellent services in Mesopotamia and North Persia, and for which decorations were awarded as shown opposite their names.

GOORKHAS (THE SIRMOOR RIFLE REGIMENT)

3009 Havildar LAL SING RANA	...	Despatches
3381 Havildar LALBAHADUR GURUNG	...	Despatches
3955 Havildar MAN SING THAPA	...	M.S.M., 1920
3757 Havildar PERTAB SING KHATTRIE	...	M.S.M., 1920
3821 Havildar BHANGU SING PUN	...	M.S.M., 1920
3695 Havildar KULEA THAPA	...	I.O.M., 1919
3966 Havildar KUMAN SING GURUNG	...	I.O.M., 1919
4449 Naik BAKHTA GURUNG	...	I.D.S.M., 1917
4791 Naik PADAM SING THAPA	...	I.O.M., 1917; Serbian Silver Medal
4216 Naik RASKER GURUNG	...	Serbian Silver Medal, 1917
199 Naik KALU GHARTI	...	I.D.S.M., 1918
2905 Naik BAKHTIA GURUNG	...	M.S.M., 1919
3975 Naik JITBAHADUR GURUNG	...	I.O.M., 1917
3977 Naik MANBAHADUR PUN	...	M.S.M., 1920
4434 Naik MANBAHADUR GURUNG	...	M.S.M., 1920
4466 L./Naik BHUDIBAL THAPA	...	I.D.S.M., 1918
1695 L./Naik MAKARDHOJ RAI (B.M.P.)	...	I.D.S.M., 1918
248 L./Naik HARDATTA JAISI (A.M.P.)	...	M.S.M., 1918
4042 L./Naik JAIBAHADUR THAPA	...	M.S.M., 1918
2322 L./Naik MANIRAJ GURUNG	...	I.D.S.M., 1918
4407 L./Naik NAR SING GURUNG	...	Despatches
1833 L./Naik BALBIR RAI	...	I.D.S.M., 1918
3555 L./Naik SHERBAHADUR BURA	...	Despatches
1823 L./Naik PARSADMAN RAI (A.M.P.)	...	I.D.S.M., 1919
4362 L./Naik DEB SING THAPA	...	M.S.M., 1920
4487 Rifleman KAMBA SING GURUNG	...	I.D.S.M., 1916; Serbian Gold Medal
1032 Rifleman SHERBAHADUR ALE	...	I.D.S.M., 1918
4535 Rifleman JAGIA GHARTI	...	I.D.S.M., 1918
455 Rifleman KEHAR SING RANA	...	I.D.S.M., 1918
1234 Rifleman SINGBIR THAPA	...	I.D.S.M., 1918
1348 Rifleman BHUDIMAN THAPA (A.M.P.)	...	I.O.M., 1916
1599 Rifleman PARBIR THAPA	...	I.O.M., 1921

APPENDIX B.

Casualty List in Action of the 2nd King Edward's Own Goorkhas in France, Egypt, Waziristhan, Mesopotamia, and North Persia from October, 1914, to June, 1921.

		British Officers.	Goorkha Officers.	Other Ranks.	
2/2nd Goorkhas :—					
France ...	Killed	12	9	144	Died of disease, 37.
	Wounded	4	7	313	Invalided to India, 220 (including 3 B.Os. and 17 G.Os.)
	Died of wounds	3	1	25	Missing, 133.
Egypt ...		—	—	—	—
Marri Expedition	Killed	—	—	1	Died of disease, 1.
	Wounded	—	—	5	
Waziristhan, N.W.F.	Killed	—	—	1	Died of disease, 8.
	Wounded	—	—	3	
1/2nd Goorkhas (attached 2/2nd Goorkhas) :—					
France ...	Killed	2	1	44	Died of disease, 7.
	Wounded	3	2	72	Invalided to India, 47 (including 1 B.O. and 2 G.Os.).
	Died of wounds	—	—	5	
1/2nd Goorkhas :—					
Mesopotamia & North Persia 1916-1921	Killed	8	6	281	Died of disease, 150 (including 1 B.O. and 1 G.O.).
	Wounded	13	14	452	Missing, 42.

The above is from Regimental Returns, and shows a total of casualties in action throughout all operations, 1914 to 1921, of 45 British Officers, 40 Goorkha Officers, 1,521 other ranks, which, with those who died of diseases contracted on, or who were invalided to India from field service during that period, gives a grand total of 50 British Officers, 60 Goorkha Officers, 1,966 other ranks.

APPENDIX C.

DECORATIONS AWARDED TO THE 2ND KING EDWARD'S OWN GOORKHAS FOR SERVICES IN FRANCE, EGYPT, WAZIRISTHAN, MESOPOTAMIA, NORTH PERSIA, 1914-1920.

Honours.	France and Egypt.	Waziristhan.	Mesopotamia and N. Persia.
Companion of the Order of the Bath	3	—	—
Companion of the Order of St. Michael and St. George	4	—	1
Companion of the Indian Empire	2	—	—
Companion of the Star of India	1	—	—
Order of British Empire	3	—	2
Companion of the British Empire	3	—	—
Distinguished Service Order	7	—	4
Bar to same	1	—	—
Military Cross	6	—	13
Belgian Croix de Guerre	1	—	—
Belgian Ordre de la Couronne	1	—	—
Italian Croix de Guerre	1	—	—
Albert Medal	1	—	—
Legion of Honour	2	—	—
Crown of Italy	1	—	—
French Croix de Guerre	2	—	—
Russian Order of St. George	1	—	—
Serbian Order of Karageorge	1	—	1
Serbian Order of White Eagle	1	—	—
Serbian Gold Medal	1	—	1
Serbian Silver Medal	1	—	1
Crown of Siam	1	—	—
Italian Bronze Medal for Valour	—	—	—
Brevet Colonelcy	1	—	—
Brevet Lieutenant-Colonelcy	3	—	—
Indian Order of Merit	14	—	10
Indian Distinguished Service Medal	14	2	28
Indian Meritorious Service Medal	15	—	4
Royal Humane Society	—	1	—

APPENDIX D.

MESSAGES OF CONGRATULATION TO THE 2/2ND KING EDWARD'S OWN GOORKHAS DURING THEIR SERVICES IN FRANCE AND THE NORTH-WEST FRONTIER OF INDIA, 1914-1920.

Copy of a Telephone Message from G.O.C. Meerut Division to G.O.C. 19th (Dehra Doon) Brigade. No. G 169 of 3/11/14 relative to action 2/11/14.

Indian Corps wires begins 129/I.A. of 3rd hearty congratulations 2nd Goorkhas on their distinguished gallantry in action; just what I expected from so fine a Regiment ends.

Divisional Commander has much pleasure in communicating above message to the Battalion AAA and in forwarding the same the Brigadier General Commanding Dehra Doon Brigade is most happy to receive the congratulations of the Indian Corps Commander."

(Signed) J. C. FREELAND, *Captain,*
Staff Captain 19th Infantry Brigade.

From Lieutenant-General C. A. Anderson, C.B., Commanding Meerut Division, to O.C. 2/2nd Goorkhas, through G.O.C. 19th Infantry Brigade.

I desire to express my warm approval and high commendation of the behaviour of the Battalion under your command under the extremely trying circumstances of the afternoon and evening of the 2nd November, and also of the excellent fighting spirit since the day of severe trial which they underwent. I wish also to congratulate you on the manner in which you have commanded the Battalion during the past trying days, and request you will express my approval to your British and Goorkha officers, wishing them all success from me. I mourn with you the gallant comrades you have lost.

(Signed) C. A. ANDERSON, *Lieut.-General.*

H.Q. Indian Corps, 10/11/14, *to O.C. 2/2nd Goorkhas.*

It has grieved me much to learn of the heavy losses in officers and men in your fine Battalion. I hope to relieve you and give your Battalion a short rest from the trenches very soon. I am sure the 2nd Goorkhas will live up to their reputation and add to their name during this war.

(Signed) JAMES WILLCOCKS, *Lieut.-General,*
Commanding Indian Corps.

P.S.—I look to you and your officers to carefully watch any cases of hand wounds and help me to eradicate this grave evil.—J.W.

To O.C. 2nd Goorkhas.

Commanding Meerut Division message begins 20th November the following received from Sir John French AAA please congratulate your Indian troops on their gallant conduct and express my gratitude to them ends AAA please convey above to all ranks AAA For information and necessary action.

From Staff Captain 19th Infantry Brigade, 7/12/14.

Copy of a Letter from General Sir James Willcocks, G.O.C. Indian Army Corps, to Brigadier-General C. W. Jacob, Commanding Dehra Doon Brigade, March 12th, 1915, re the Battle of Neuve Chapelle.

Please convey to all your gallant officers, Goorkha officers, N.C.Os. and men my very hearty thanks and congratulations on their splendid behaviour in the field at Neuve Chapelle. I am indeed fortunate and proud to be associated with such good soldiers, and am confident all ranks are ready for immediate further efforts.

(Signed) JAMES WILLCOCKS, *Lieut.-General.*

General Sir John French's Address to the 2nd Goorkhas and 9th Goorkha Rifles of the Dehra Brigade on his Inspection of them on April 10th, 1915, in France.

Goorkhas, I have come here to meet you to-day in order to congratulate you on your gallant behaviour during the recent attack on Neuve Chapelle. During that fighting you took the Bois du Biez, from which for tactical reasons you were ordered to retire. I know full well if you had not received those orders you would not have retired, but in war occasions of this sort arise. I know that, coming from a warm climate you must have found the winter climate of France very trying, therefore your fine conduct during the winter months is all the more creditable to you. Again I wish to thank you for the good work you have done on all occasions, and I am confident that whenever you are called upon to attack again, you will do so as readily as you did at Neuve Chapelle.

Copy of a Letter from General Sir James Willcocks to Brigadier-General Jacob, Commanding Dehra Doon Brigade, dated May 13th, 1915, re the Action May 9th-10th, 1915.

MY DEAR JACOB,

I must write and tell you with what admiration I followed your gallant Brigade in the recent fighting. You, the Commanding Officer, and troops deserve well of your country, and have added another fine page to the story of the Indian Corps. The Staff worked admirably, and I look on your troops as a great asset in these famous days.

(Signed) JAMES WILLCOCKS, *Lieut.-General.*

Extract from General Jacob's Report on the Battle of Neuve Chapelle.

The Goorkha Battalions (2nd and 9th) had an opportunity of making up for the terrible ordeals they had been through in the earlier days of the war, and they took full advantage of it. Their spirits were high, and nothing could stop their dash.

Copy of a Letter from General Sir Douglas Haig to the First Army on Results of the Battle of Neuve Chapelle, March 9th-10th, 1915.

I desire to express to all ranks of the First Army my great appreciation of the task accomplished by them in the past three days' fighting. The First Army has captured German trenches on a front of 2 miles, including the whole village of Neuve Chapelle and some strongly defended works. Serious losses have been inflicted on the enemy, nearly 2,000 prisoners being in our hands, while his casualties are estimated at over 16,000. The results, however, of the successful actions just fought are not confined to material losses sustained by the enemy. The organization of the German forces from Ypres to south of the La Bassée Canal have been thrown into a state of disorganization. Reinforcements available to oppose the French in the battle taking place at Notre Dame de Lorette or destined for other parts of their line have been drawn into the fighting opposite the First Army, and have been severely handled. The losses sustained by the First Army, though heavy, are fully compensated for by results achieved, which have brought us one step forward in our efforts to end the war.

Copy of Sir Douglas Haig's last paragraph in his Report of the Action of September 25th, 1915.

The General Officer Commanding First Army wishes to express his appreciation of the good work done by all ranks and his gratification at the good progress made by 1st and 4th Corps. Also, although the opposition north of the Canal prevented great progress of the subsidiary attacks, the G.O.C. is very pleased with the manner in which the 1st, 3rd, and Indian Corps carried out the rôle assigned to them of retaining the enemy on their front.

Copy of concluding paragraph in Sir John French's Despatch dated October 15th, 1915, on the Action of September 25th, 1915.

The Indian Corps attacked the Moulin du Piètre, while the 3rd Corps was directed against the trenches at Les Bridoux. These attacks started at daybreak and were at first successful. Later in the day the enemy brought up strong reserves, and after hard fighting and variable fortunes the troops engaged had to reoccupy their original trenches at nightfall. They succeeding, however, admirably in fulfilling the rôle allotted them and in holding large numbers of the enemy away from the main attack.

Copy of H.M. the King's Farewell Message to the Indian Corps on their leaving France, October 25th, 1915.

Officers, N.C.Os., and men of the Indian Corps, more than a year ago I summoned you from India to fight for the safety of my Empire and the honour of my pledged word on the battlefields of Belgium and France. The confidence which I then expressed in your sense of duty, your courage, and chivalry, you have since then nobly justified.

I now require your presence in another field of action, but before you leave France I send my dear and gallant son the Prince of Wales, who has shared with my armies the dangers and hardships of the campaign, to thank you in my name for your services and to express my satisfaction.

British and Indian comrades-in-arms, yours has been a fellowship in toils and hardships, in courage and endurance often against great odds, in deeds nobly done in days of ever-memorable conflict. In a warfare waged under new conditions and in peculiarly trying circumstances you have worthily upheld the honour of the Empire and the great traditions of my army in India.

I have followed your fortunes with deepest interest and watched your gallant actions with pride and satisfaction. I mourn with you the loss of many brave officers and men. Let it be your consolation, as it was their pride, that they freely gave their lives in a just cause for the honour of their Sovereign and the safety of my Empire. They died as gallant soldiers, and I shall ever hold their sacrifice in grateful remembrance.

You leave France with a just pride in honourable deeds already achieved, and with my assured confidence that your proved valour and experience will contribute to further victories in the new fields to which you go.

I pray God to bless and guard you and to bring you back safely when the final victory is won, each to his own home, there to be welcomed with honour among his own people.

GEORGE R.I.

Copy of a Letter received by the Battalion while in Egypt from Major-General C. W. Jacob, late G.O.C. Meerut Division in France, dated November 12th, 1915.

MY DEAR BOILEAU,

I was very sorry to find you and your gallant Battalion had gone when I returned from leave. I should like to have seen you all before you started, and to tell you again how grateful I am for all the good work the 2nd Goorkhas have done in France.

When I look back on what you have been through and the strenuous times you have had both in fighting the Germans and contending with the weather, I realize what sterling good stuff there is in all ranks of your Battalion. You have deserved well of your country, and no Commander could wish to have finer troops.

What gallant fellows you have lost both in officers and men, and what fine examples they were in courage and leading! We have been together now for over a year, and I shall never forget what you all did, what keenness there always was when any hard fighting or work had to be done.

It is owing to such loyal support and the way you have met me half-way when we had extra work to put in, that I have been so fortunate myself in this campaign.

Will you tell your officers and men that I am so sorry not to have seen them to say good-bye, and tell them I wish them all the best of good fortune.

I don't know where your ultimate destination will be, but whatever arduous times you may have before you there is no doubt in my mind that your Battalion will do well and add more to the reputation you have earned so well in France.

I am getting command of another Division out here, but which it is I don't know yet.

With best wishes to you all.

Yours sincerely,
(Signed)   C. W. JACOB.

Letter from the 60th Rifles Aid Society, and Reply.

RIFLEMAN'S AID SOCIETY,
RIFLE DEPOT,
WINCHESTER,
19/2/15.

SIR,

The Vice-Patrons and Executive Committee of this Society desire me to write—as it may be some gratification to your gallant Riflemen in the trenches, little though it be—to say that the sum of £100 has been granted by the King's Royal Rifles Branch of this Society for use in any way you may think best at the time as it is feared there must be some distress in the ranks of your Battalion. I am to assure you that all ranks of the King's Royal Rifles follow with the greatest interest the doings of their sister Regiment, whose Riflemen have proved themselves worthy successors of the heroes of the Mutiny.

We deeply regret the loss of so many valuable and gallant lives both in Officers and Riflemen.

Kindly accept this gift in the spirit in which it is tendered, and it is hoped the friendship of the two Regiments cemented at Delhi may continue for all time.

Messrs. Cox & Co. have remitted the amount through their Indian branch to the Regimental H.Q. at Dehra Doon.

I have the honour to be,
Sir,
Your most obedient servant,
J. W. DANE, *Major (Secretary)*.

IN THE FIELD,
March 3rd, 1915.

To the Secretary,
  Rifleman's Aid Society.

SIR,

I have to thank you for your letter of the 19th February, which has been read to all ranks of the Battalion.

The kind action of the Society in presenting the sum of £100 towards the provident expenses of the Regiment has been deeply appreciated. No better stimulant could have been received by any regiment. Whatever losses we suffer the *esprit de corps* always remains, and with it the honoured friendship of the King's Royal Rifles.

Our one regret is that we are not brigaded with one of your Battalions, so that we could be side by side throughout the war. The men are not fighting for their country, but as Riflemen of the British Army, and to feel that their old comrades of the Mutiny are watching them has given them something else to link them to the cause for which they are fighting.

Please convey to the Society the hearty thanks of every man in the Regiment for its kind gift. I am sending a copy of your letter to the Adjutant of our other Battalion, which unfortunately is not with us here, that they too, may appreciate it as much as we do.

  I have the honour to be,
    Sir,
      Your most obedient servant,
        E. CORSE SCOTT, *Lieut. and Adjutant,*
          2/2nd Goorkhas.

The following letter was received in the end of November, 1914, from Major-General Wylie, formerly Resident in Nepal, asking what gift would be most useful to the men, as the Prime Minister of Nepal was very anxious to do anything he could for the Goorkhas in France:—

  HILL TOP,
    FARNHAM COMMON,
      BUCKS.
        18/11/14.

MY DEAR SIR,

Maharaja Sir Chandra Shumsher Jang, Prime Minister of Nepal, has written to me as an old friend asking if I can find out for him whether there is anything he could send to the Goorkha soldiers in the field which they would appreciate and find useful.

I showed the letter to the India Office, and the opinion there is that the Maharaja has already been so extraordinarily generous in his gifts and donations that we ought not to accept any large amount more from him.

I think, however, the Maharaja would be disappointed if he were not allowed to do something more for the Goorkhas in the field, but as I do not know what they want I am referring the question to you and to the other Commanding Officers of Goorkha Battalions abroad, and shall be very much obliged if you will give me the benefit of your advice and opinion.

Unfortunately the Maharaja has fixed no sum which he would wish to make the limit of his gift, so all I have to go on is the India Office letter saying we should not accept a large amount.

We were all very grieved to read of the heavy losses your Battalion suffered lately, especially in British officers, and trust you are all having a little rest and will soon be ready for work again. With every good wish for the future.

Believe me,
Yours sincerely,
H. WYLIE, *Major-General.*

An amusing but kindly letter was received in late November, 1914, evidently from an admirer of Johnny Goorkha, and with it came a small tin parcel containing four match-boxes, a box of fifty cigarettes, and some paper and envelopes. The letter ran :—

E. FOSTER,
106, STANSTEAD ROAD,
FOREST HILL.
15/11/14.

DEAR GHURKHAS we most heartily thank you for your great services you have rendered to England during this Terrible Trial in which we are placed but not through our seeking ; may God protect you all and give you a safe and speedy return to your homes and beloved ones kindly let me have a little Note.

E. F.

The following courteous letter was received on May 31st, 1915, from Messrs. Pulford and Sons, the regimental tailors, to whom application had been made for a quantity of medal ribbons, which included, besides pre-war medal ribbons, a strip of the 4th Class of the Russian Order of St. George, awarded to our scout leader, Havildar (later Jemadar) Sarabjit Gurung :—

65, ST. JAMES' STREET,
LONDON.
28th May, 1915.

SIR,—

We beg to acknowledge your favour of the 24th inst. and herewith forward ribbons as requested, trusting the same will be found satisfactory. As you are requiring the various ribbons for your men, we should take it as a compliment if you will allow us to offer the same without charge. Trusting this will be to your entire approval.

We are, with respectful compliments,
Your obedient servants,

PULFORD AND SONS.

Address by General Sir Arthur Barrett, G.C.B., K.C.S.I., Commanding the Northern Army at his Inspection of the 2/2nd Goorkhas at Tank (Waziristhan) on January 14th, 1919.

Officers, non-commissioned officers and men of the 2/2nd Goorkhas, I am very glad to have this opportunity of presenting these medals, and I wish for your sakes that they might have been given you by H.M. The King himself, but this was not possible. I must do my best to take his place and tell you what a great name you have made for yourselves in all the hard fighting you have been through, how much you have added to the good name of the fine Regiment to which you belong, and which has now for over 100 years been taking a glorious part in many campaigns in different parts of the world. I can assure you the British Empire is deeply grateful to you for all you have done to help her in her time of great trouble and danger. Your good deeds will never be forgotten. This medal which I now give you is one which I hope you will always be proud to wear, and in times to come it should remain in possession of your families in memory of the gallant services of their forefathers. I congratulate you all most heartily, and wish you all long life and prosperity to enjoy the honours that you have earned and deserved so well.

Special Order of the Day issued by Brigadier-General W. C. Walker, Commanding Lines of Communication, Tank (lately Derajāt Column).

On the departure of the 2/2nd King Edward's Own Goorkhas from the Derajāt area on relief after nearly two years, the last six months of which was on active service, the G.O.C. desires to express his appreciation of the valuable services rendered by the officers, non-commissioned officers, and men of this fine Battalion. Conduct and discipline have been exemplary both in camp and in the field, and all duties have been carried out in so smart and soldierlike a manner as to be a pleasure to all observers. We wish them continued success in the future.

Congratulatory Letters and Telegrams concerning the Operations in Mesopotamia and North Persia.

Telegram from the Commander-in-Chief, India, of April 24th, 1916, to Army Commander :—

" C.-in-C. desires you to express to the troops under Gorringe and Townshend his appreciation of their gallant efforts and tenacious endurance in the face of a brave and determined enemy and under exceptional physical difficulties. He knows they will respond to the next call of their leaders in the same spirit and looks forward to hearing that success will finally crown their endeavours.

The following message from His Majesty the King-Emperor was received May 4th, 1916, by the G.O.C. Tigris Corps for communication to the troops:—

"Although your brave troops have not had the satisfaction of relieving their beleaguered comrades in Kūt, they have, under the able leadership of yourself and subordinate commanders, fought with great gallantry and determination under most trying conditions; the achievement of relief was denied you all by floods and bad weather, and not by the enemy whom you have resolutely pressed back. I have watched your efforts with admiration, and am satisfied that you have done all that was humanly possible, and will continue to do so in future encounters with the enemy."

GEORGE R.I.

Order of the Day, July 10th, 1916, by General Gorringe on leaving the Front.

In handing over command of the 3rd Indian Army Corps, I desire to express to all under my command my warmest thanks for loyal co-operation and assistance which one and all have given me during my tenure of command.

We have had great difficulties to contend with, but these have been tackled in a manly, soldierly manner, and although we were unsuccessful in relieving our comrades in Kūt we may all feel that in any case we did our best, and that we did so was fully recognized, as shown by our King-Emperor in his gracious message.

During the last two months conditions have been continuously trying; shortage of water, cholera, scurvy, etc., all had to be tackled.

In saying good-bye, I wish all the fullest success in future operations, and trust we may serve together again at no distant date. Our comrades in France, and Allies both in Europe and Asia Minor have recently won magnificent successes; when the time comes for your turn I am confident you will all add fresh laurels to those already gained.

Remember that "difficulties were made to be overcome and conquered."

G. F. GORRINGE, *Lieut.-General.*

Copy of Telephone Messages from General Keary, G.O.C. 3rd Division, to Brigadier-General Fowler, Commanding 37th Brigade, re the Operations at Beit Aiessa, 18/4/16.

On the departure of your Brigade from this Division (13th), General Keary directs me to convey to you his thanks for the good work done by it.

And from Corps Commander to 37th Brigade, 19/4/16.

The course of the operations carried out during the past 36 hours round Beit Aiessa, which began at dawn yesterday, were most skilfully and successfully carried out, and good reconnaissances were made over very difficult country. I consider great credit is due to General Keary and this Brigade under his orders.

Copy of Telegram from General Egerton to Brigadier-General Commanding 37th Brigade relative to the Fighting near the Liquorice Factory, 3/2/17.

" Corps Commander wires begins please accept most sincere congratulations on success to-day. Thank your troops from me for their great gallantry both in the assault and in repelling enemy's counter-attacks ends," and Brigade Commander adds to above, " For communication to all ranks, whom I thank for their admirable gallantry and untiring efforts in to-day's success."

Concerning the same action, General Marshall's wire to General Egerton runs :—

" Army Commander telegraphs begins tell 1/4th Devons, 1/2nd Goorkhas and 62nd Punjabis how much I admire not only their excellent work yesterday, but also the splendid spirit which prompted them to ask to be allowed to carry on instead of being relieved ends."

Copy of a Letter from O.C. 36th Sikhs concerning the Action of 1/2/17.

DEAR SWEET,

Just a line to thank your men for all they did in helping to bring our wounded off the field last night. I hear they did splendidly, and can well believe it. I was awfully grieved to hear about poor Bruce and Marsh. Good luck to you all ! I am feeling very broken at the losses in my Regiment.

Yours sincerely,
(Signed) ORLANDO GUNNING.

Copy of Wire from G.O.C. 3rd Corps to Brigade Commander 37th Brigade relative to Operations in Neighbourhood of Kizil Robāt, December, 1917.

" Corps Commander wishes to express to General Maclachlan and Colonel Underhill his satisfaction with the handling of their columns during recent operations ; their co-operation was of definite value in the attainment of our main objectives to our advance on Kirkuk." To above the Brigadier adds : " and I wish to express my best thanks for the cheery way in which the troops worked and marched, their efforts forcing many of the enemy into the net prepared for them."

Brigadier-General Maclachlan, who commanded the 37th Brigade when we were one of its units, had been on leave when the Battalion left his command, and on his return, August 8th, 1918, he sent us a message running :—

"It was with great regret that I heard on return from leave that the 1/2nd Goorkhas had left the Brigade in which they had done such sterling good work on many a hard-fought field. My regret is shared by the rest of the 37th Brigade, who all wish the 1/2nd Goorkhas the best of luck and will always be interested to hear of their future welfare."

On February 23rd, 1918, the following telegram was received by the 37th Brigade from Lieutenant-General Egerton, G.O.C. III Corps (late G.O.C. 14th Division) :—" Here's the best to you all in memory of the Shumrān crossing " while he sent one to our Battalion running, " To the glorious men of the Shumrān and Dahra bend."

Copy of Telegram received by Battalion from G.O.C. 36th Brigade relative to the Operations by Captain McCleverty's Detachments in Operations of June and July, 1918, round Resht.

Heartiest congratulations to Regiment on fine record in Special Order 123 from self and staff.

These operations gave 1 M.C., 2 I.O.Ms., and 7 I.D.S.Ms. to the 1/2nd Goorkhas.

Copy of Letters from Brigadier-General H. B. Champain, Commanding 36th Brigade in North Persia, to all Officers and to the G.O.C. Baghdad relative to Enzeli Incidents, and on his vacating the Command.

RESHT,
25/5/20.

To all Officers.

Before leaving for Kāsvin I wish to thank all officers and men of the Enzeli garrison for the good work they put in there before we were obliged to evacuate.

I am sorry not to have been able to see you all before leaving, for I should like to have explained how it was that we left Enzeli as we did without putting up a fight.

I therefore circulate a copy of a letter written to the G.O.C.-in-Chief which will, I hope, make the matter clear, and I shall be glad if you will make the contents of this known to all ranks.

H. B. CHAMPAIN,
Brigadier-General, 36th Indian Brigade.

To G.O.C., Baghdad, 25/5/20.

SIR,

I have the honour to forward herewith a narrative of the events that took place in Enzeli on Tuesday, May 18th, 1920.

In doing so, I beg to point out that the situation was governed more by political than by military considerations. It had been agreed between H.B.M.'s Minister at

Teheran and myself that in the event of an attack and before opening hostilities with the Bolsheviks I was to attempt to parley with the Commander with a view to prevent embroiling Persia in hostilities.

Bearing this in mind, I acted as I did. Had I not been operating in a neutral country, and had not political considerations been uppermost, I should have opened fire as soon as their ships came within effective range. In that case the result would have been the same, in so far that the Bolsheviks would have captured Enzeli without any doubt owing to their overwhelming superiority in guns. We should no doubt have taken toll of them, but, on the other hand, my force would have been captured.

In accepting the terms offered, the chance that my troops might some day have an opportunity of meeting the enemy on land on more equal terms carried considerable weight.

As regards my dispositions, I would draw your attention to the fact that the coast-line to be defended measures roughly 27 to 30 miles—the coast-line, that is, in the immediate neighbourhood of Enzeli from which passable roads lead inland.

From Chefaroud on the west to beyond Verst 13 on the east a landing can be effected anywhere in small boats. With the force at my disposal I had to concentrate mainly at Enzeli and Kāzian, and in order to try and protect my direct communication with Resht I held a defensive post at Verst 13. To the west I had to content myself with patrolling, and intended, had they effected a landing on that side, to fall back on Resht.

I have no doubt whatever that my dispositions were known in detail by the Bolshevik commander, letters giving such information having been previously intercepted in the post going through to Bāku. As a result, he effected landings on undefended and defended portions of the coast and cut my communications.

The discipline and bearing of the troops under trying circumstances was beyond praise. I would add that I only arrived at Enzeli the evening of 17th May. The defence scheme which I had previously approved had been drawn up by Lieutenant-Colonel Sweet, C.M.G., D.S.O., commanding the 1/2nd Goorkhas, whose loyalty and co-operation have been of the greatest assistance throughout.

I have the honour to be, etc.,

(Signed) H. B. CHAMPAIN, *Brig.-General,*
Commanding 36th Indian Brigade.

The narrative referred to has been embodied in the general history of events at that period.

APPENDIX E.

List of Commanding Officers of the 2nd King Edward's Own Goorkhas from 1911 to 1920, and their Services during the Great War.

L. W. Shakespear, C.B., C.I.E.

On completion of tenure of command of the 2nd Battalion was appointed officiating A.Q.M.G. 7th (Meerut) Division in April, 1911; A.Q.M.G. 6th (Poona) Division in April, 1913, and went with it to Mesopotamia in November, 1914. Present at the Battle of Sahil; the occupation of Basra during November, 1914; the actions at Shaiba, April, 1915; the Second Battle of Kurna and pursuit of Turkish gun-boats, May–June, 1915. Invalided to England for six months. In April, 1916, appointed A.Q.M.G. newly forming 15th Division at Nasiriyeh on the Euphrates; action of As Sahilan, September, 1916. With the 15th Division to Baghdad, March, 1917, and completed service on Staff in September, 1917, returning to Poona. October, 1917, appointed D.I.G. Assam Rifles; Operations connected with the Kukie Rebellion, January to November, 1918. Retired October 2nd, 1921, after over forty-one years' service. Medals for Great War, bar to British General Service medal, C.B., C.I.E., and the Russian Order of St. Stanislaus (2nd Class).

J. Fisher, C.B.

Completed tenure of command of 1st Battalion, and retired November, 1912. On the outbreak of the Great War was attached to the Rifles' Depot at Winchester. In September, 1914, appointed to raise and command the 79th Infantry Brigade near Salisbury, which he trained till April, 1917, when he was sent to France as Town Major and Area Commandant at Locre, near St. Eloi, in the 9th Corps. In April, 1918, was sent to Hazebrouck to clear away civilians owing to German advance. After the Armistice was employed in France demobilizing troops and other duties till April, 1919, when he was demobilized and returned to England with the rank of Brigadier-General and the war medals.

C. de M. Norie, C.B., C.M.G., D.S.O.

Commanded the 2nd Battalion from April 2nd, 1911, to end of December, 1914, and took it to France. Battles of November 2nd and December 20th, 1914, both near Neuve Chapelle. Appointed G.S.O.1 Meerut Division, and took part in the Battles of Neuve Chapelle, March 9th, and of Aubers Ridge, May 9th, 1915. Appointed D.A. and Q.M.G. Indian Corps till September, 1915, when he was given command of the Bareilly Brigade, which took part in the actions north of Neuve Chapelle subsidiary to the Battle of Loos. In November, 1915, officiated in command of the 7th (Meerut) Division, and on the Indian Corps leaving France was sent to Mesopotamia, where he commanded a Brigade in January, 1916. Present at the

Battles of Sheikh Saad, Wadi, Um el Hanna, and Sannayat till 1917, during which period he twice officiated in command of the 7th (Meerut) Division. Led his Brigade in the advance on, and occupation of, Baghdad, March, 1917, and in several actions farther up the Tigris. In May, 1917, was invalided to India and was appointed to command the Poona Brigade in July, 1917, from which he finally retired in September, 1920, with the rank of Major-General. Received a Brevet Colonelcy, C.B., C.M.G., the Serbian Order of the White Eagle, and war medals.

W. Beynon, K.C.I.E., C.B., D.S.O.

Gave up command of the 1st Battalion on November 1st, 1914, on being appointed G.O.C. Nowshera Brigade. In June, 1915, was given command of the Malakhand Movable Column in the Swat Valley; actions of August 29th and October 28th, 1915. Commanded the Mohmand Blockade Force, including minor actions from November 7th, 1916, to February, 1917. On conclusion of these operations, he was appointed to command the South Waziristhan Field Force till August, 1917, when he was given command of the Derajāt Brigade, holding this till May, 1918. The command of the 16th Infantry Division then fell to him, which post he filled till December, 1919. General Sir W. Beynon finally retired from the Service on May 3rd, 1920. He was promoted Major-General on January 1st, 1918, was " mentioned " four times in despatches, and in August, 1917, received the thanks of the Governor-General in Council. Decorations awarded him during this period of service were C.B., C.I.E., K.C.I.E., and the war medals.

E. H. Sweet, C.M.G., D.S.O.

Was Second-in-Command of the 2nd Battalion in France until September 30th, 1915, and was then transferred to command the 2/8th Goorkha Rifles from October 1st, 1915, to March 20th, 1916, in France, Egypt, and India. From April, 1916, to December 31st, 1920, he commanded the 1st Battalion in Mesopotamia and North-West Persia, and was present with it in the actions near Beit Aiessa, the battles of February 1st and 3rd, 1917; the Tigris crossing, February 23rd; the actions at the Diala River and beyond Deltawa; the Battle of Band i Adhaim; actions near Kizil Robāt and in Persia, until November 14th, 1920. During this period, while on leave in England he was attached to the Indian Peace Contingent, July to September, 1919. During January and February, 1921, he commanded the Indian Contingent Camp at Delhi for the Duke of Connaught's visit, and throughout this year was on special duty at Delhi and Simla as organizing secretary for Earl Haig's ex-Services Association. He received the C.M.G., D.S.O., and war medals, was " mentioned " in despatches four times, and retired as Lieutenant-Colonel on January 1st, 1922.

E. R. P. BOILEAU, C.B., C.I.E., C.B.E.

Commanded the 2nd Battalion in France. Present at the Battles of Neuve Chapelle, Bois du Biez, subsidiary actions connected with the Battle of Loos, and served with the Battalion in Egypt and on the North-West Frontier, India. In May, 1917, was appointed Commandant of the Cadet College at Quetta, was Administrative Commandant of the Sibi-Chaman section in the third Afghan War, May to October, 1919, and then became Assistant Military Secretary at Army Headquarters from October, 1919, to June, 1921. He was then appointed Colonel-Commandant 11th Indian Infantry Brigade till he retired in the end of 1922. Decorations—C.B., C.I.E., C.B.E., and war medals.

K. WIGRAM, C.B., C.S.I., C.B.E., D.S.O.

After commanding the 2nd Battalion in 1922, was in March that year appointed to command the Delhi Brigade Area, where he is still on duty (January, 1924). From late 1913 to May, 1915, he was on duty in Simla as G.S.O. 3, 2, and 1 at Army Headquarters, when he was sent to France as G.S.O., and later as B.G.G.S. at Army Headquarters till October, 1918. He was then appointed C.S.O. at Headquarters R.A.F. till the end of the year. From January to end of March, 1919, he was a member of the Bird Committee in England, and returned to India in mid-May, 1919, on appointment to Army Headquarters, Simla. During February and March, 1921, he served on the Imperial Service Troops Committee, and in April, 1921, was sent to England to represent the C.-in-C. India at the Imperial Conference in London till mid-October that year. He was then deputed to attend the Washington Conference as Military Adviser to the Indian Delegate. In mid-January, 1922, he returned to India. Decorations awarded :—C.B., D.S.O., C.B.E., C.S.I., Chevalier of the Legion of Honour, the Crown of Belgium, the Croix de Guerre of Belgium, the Crown of Siam, and war medals.

APPENDIX F.

Services of Officers of the 2nd King Edward's Own Goorkhas who were detached from the Regiment during the War.

Captain A. J. Chope, 1/2nd Goorkhas, was detailed for service with the Bikanir Camel Corps about August 10th, 1914, and served with them in Egypt on the Canal and in Palestine till late December, 1916. He was then sent to India, and served at the Depot till the end of the war, this owing to illness and an operation in England which unfitted him for further active service with the Egyptian Field Force.

He was twice recommended for the D.S.O., which was awarded him in late 1915 for good work, hard reconnaissances, and several minor fights in the neighbourhood of the Canal, and the actions at Bir el Nass and the El Katia north-east of Suez. At the latter he and his detachment of Camelry nearly came to grief through an act of treachery, where a hostile party of Camelry approached waving two white flags, and when fairly close these suddenly opened fire on the Bikanir men. Chope, at once charging home, accounted for most of the Turks and Arabs with them.

When the Prince of Wales made his visit to the Canal, Captain Chope took him for his first ride on a camel into the desert.

Captain Chope was later in 1917 awarded the Order of the Nile, 4th Class, by the Sultan of Egypt for good service in the war.

Captain C. L. N. Newall left the Regiment to join the Flying Corps in 1913, and was with the Air Force at Sitapur, United Provinces, India, when war broke out. He went with that Corps to France, serving there almost throughout the war, where he did splendid work, which was recognized by being "mentioned" in despatches, the award of the decoration of Officer of the Legion of Honour in 1918, followed by that of the Crown of Italy, the C.M.G. in 1919, and the C.B.E. in 1920. While in France he also was awarded the somewhat rare Albert Medal for brave work done in a dangerous fire which broke out in an ammunition dump not far behind the lines where his air squadron was. By his energy and bravery in personally assisting and directing the extinguishing of the fire, a most serious explosion was averted.

In the summer of 1923 Brevet Colonel Newall received the further honour of being made Air A.D.C. to H.M. the King.

Services of Major H. T. Fulton, D.S.O., 2nd King Edward's Own Goorkhas.

Major Fulton, D.S.O., was on leave in his own country (New Zealand) on the outbreak of the Great War, and accepted the appointment of Second-in-Command of the 5th Wellington Regiment on August 5th, 1914, on its being mobilized for the Samoan Expedition. He was shortly afterwards promoted Lieutenant-Colonel in Command of a composite Battalion which sailed with the force for Samoa on

August 14th, 1914. That island was captured from the Germans, and the Battalion returned to New Zealand in March, 1915. The end of this month saw Lieutenant-Colonel Fulton in command of the 4th Reinforcement (two battalions) of the New Zealand Expeditionary Force and training them at Trentham Camp, New Zealand, till October 10th, 1915, when they (now styled the New Zealand Rifle Brigade) sailed for Egypt. There they were encamped at Heliopolis till January 8th, 1916, when the New Zealand Rifle Brigade embarked for Mersa Matruh for operations against the Sennussi, being part of Colonel Braithwayte's Brigade. On the 23rd of that month Lieutenant-Colonel Fulton led his command into action at Bir Shola as part of General Wallace's column, and in mid-February they returned to Alexandria, being camped at Moascar, where on March 1st, 1916, they were joined by two more battalions from New Zealand, and the Rifle Brigade, of which Colonel Fulton was now appointed Brigadier-General, was complete.

Early April, 1916, saw this Brigade in France, where from May to September, 1916, they held a part of the line at Armentières and its vicinity. General Fulton and his Brigade during the first Battle of the Somme were engaged continuously till October 3rd, 1916, when they were sent to hold the line Laventie—Fleurbaix till February, 1917. In January, 1917, Brigadier-General Fulton was mentioned in despatches and received a well-earned C.M.G. From February to June, 1917, he and his men were holding the line Plögstraete Wood—Hill 63—Messines, and were heavily engaged for three days in the Battle of Messines, June 7th-9th, 1917. Thereafter, and till August 30th, 1917, the Rifle Brigade was employed in the operations round Warneton and the Messines sector, followed by the Battle of Passchendaele; but Brigadier-General Fulton, having been invalided to England with bad influenza, had been retained there on duty, so was not present at the latter battle. In May he had been again mentioned in despatches, and in November, 1917, was awarded the Croix de Guerre.

From mid-November, 1917, to March 24th, 1918, Brigadier-General Fulton and the New Zealand Rifle Brigade were holding the Butte de Polygon and Polderhoeck sectors, then the Broodseinde Ridge and vicinity of the Ypres section, when the Second Battle of the Somme, March 26th, 1918, drew them into it at the actions of Hebuterne and Colinscamp, where he was badly wounded on March 28th, succumbing in hospital the following day, to the very great regret of all who served with and under him.

An extract from New Zealand Records states :—" Brigadier-General Fulton, D.S.O., C.M.G., won the highest regard of all ranks by his efficiency and energy. It was the sheer force of character and singleness of purpose of this one man which welded the four battalions of the New Zealand Rifle Brigade into what was really one unit, and produced an efficiency and discipline acknowledged by the Divisional Commander which enabled the Brigade to win a high name for itself on the battlefields of the Somme, at Messines, and many other actions. General Fulton's name will ever be revered in this country by all who knew and served with him."

To perpetuate his memory, the New Zealand Rifle Brigade founded a Scholarship Bursary at his old school—the Otago Boys' High School, at Dunedin—which bears his name.

Major Fulton, 2nd Goorkhas—Prophecy by a Native.

In connection with Major (later Brigadier-General) Fulton's service an incident occurred which is worth recording.

When he and his wife were at an hotel in Simla about 1905 an old native fortune-teller came up, and several people had their future foretold amidst much amusement. On Major Fulton putting out his hand, the old man looked at it and at once said : " At forty-five years old you will command troops and raise your flag in a strange land." Again glancing at the hand, he went on : " And at forty-seven years old you will be a ' burra ' General Sahib." Of course this was greeted with cheers and laughter, and the fortune-teller left.

Now when the Great War started it found Major and Mrs. Fulton on leave in their own country, New Zealand, he being then just forty-five. He was given command of a force of New Zealand troops and sent to Samoa, where he succeeded in ousting the Germans and raised the flag, as that country then came under the English. Later he was sent to Egypt in command of the New Zealand Rifle Brigade, and from there took them to France to take part in the stern struggle of the last year of the war, and where he was killed. He was then almost forty-seven years old ; there was only one man senior to him—viz., General Godley—who commanded the whole of the New Zealand forces, and who, being desirous himself of vacating, it is fairly certain that Brigadier-General Fulton, had he lived, would have succeeded him, thus strangely fulfilling the whole of the old native's prophecy.

SERVICES OF MAJOR D. M. WATT, 1/2ND GOORKHAS.

Major D. M. Watt was in England on the outbreak of the Great War and was at first employed (September to November, 1914) as G.S.O.2 13th Division in England, after which he joined the 2/2nd Goorkhas in France, serving with them as second-in-command and officiating Commandant during the period November, 1914, to March, 1915, being badly wounded in the Second Battle of Neuve Chapelle (March 11th, 1915), and from then on was detached from the Regiment save for a few months with it on the North-West Frontier of India. In May 1915, he served for a short while as G.S.O.2 Colchester Division in England, followed by a year and a half as G.S.O.1 25th Division in England and France, and during which time he also commanded the 1/7th Duke of Wellington's Regiment for seven months. In November, 1916, he was given command of the 145th South Midland Infantry Brigade, with which he served in France and Italy until September, 1918. In December, 1918, he rejoined the 1/2nd Goorkhas at Tank, North-West Frontier, India, as officiating Commandant for a few months, leaving it in June, 1919, for the temporary command of the Abbottabad Brigade from which he finally retired in late 1920. He was "mentioned" in despatches seven times, and gained a Brevet Lieut.-Colonelcy, the D.S.O. and a bar, and the Italian Croce di Guerra during the Great War.

APPENDIX G.

THE REGIMENT'S CHARTER.

A reference to the first volume of the Regimental History gives the wording of this Charter, which gives Dehra Doon Cantonment to the 2nd Goorkhas (at that time only one Battalion existed), their wives and families as their home *in perpetuo*. From 1908 several attempts had been made by high authorities to break through this Charter, and locate other battalions in one or other of our lines when they happened to be vacant, such as when one of our battalions went for a year or so to Chitral or elsewhere. These occasions led naturally to much correspondence and trouble, as the families of the absent unit being left behind in their " home " were subjected to much interference and annoyance by the men of the stranger battalion, culminating in 1918 in some serious trouble. Strong representations being made to Government on the subject with a view to strict maintenance of our Charter and its privileges resulted in the following correspondence, from which it may be hoped the matter is satisfactorily settled for good.

No. 1287/C.R.]

DEHRA DUN,
21st *April*, 1921.

From : THE OFFICER COMMANDING,
    2ND BATTALION 2ND K.E.O. GOORKHAS.
To : THE BRIGADE MAJOR,
    17TH (INDIAN) INFANTRY BRIGADE,
        DEHRA DUN.

SIR,
    With reference to the question of the location of units, other than the 2nd Goorkhas, in the lines of that Regiment during the temporary absence of one or both of its Battalions, I have the honour to submit for your information a copy of the correspondence sanctioning Dehra Dun as the " Home " of the 2nd Goorkhas, and guaranteeing that during the absence of the Regiment the families would be able to remain in quiet occupation of the lines until the Regiment returned.

I also attach a short résumé of the events which led to the grant of this privilege.

2. It is true that when this correspondence took place the 2nd Battalion did not exist. It is also true that, according to the terms of letter No. 424 of 29th June, 1864, the privilege was granted to the 2nd Regiment and not to a single battalion of that Regiment ; and in the same way as the 2nd Battalion automatically inherited the battle honours and traditions of the parent unit, so it also inherited the privileges held by that unit in respect of its " Home." " Esprit de Regiment " has always

been a feature in the education and training of the personnel of the 2nd Goorkhas, and the principle received official recognition before the war by the arrangement adopted in the Army List whereby the officers of both battalions were shown on one list. The events of the last seven years have still further cemented the ties which formerly existed owing to the numerous interchanges which have taken place between the personnel of the two battalions.

3. It isn't as if the men of the Battalion had been warned before leaving for the Frontier of the possibility of the withdrawal of a privilege they have enjoyed for so many years, and which they now regard as a right; nor were they given the opportunity of sending their womenkind to Nepal during their absence in anticipation of such possibility. On the contrary, they regarded the move merely as the fulfilment of the first part of the contract mentioned in para. 4 of letter No. 424 of the 29th June, 1864, in the full confidence that the "Sircar" would, as has been the case hitherto, carry out their portion of the contract in respect of their families.

4. Under existing conditions, owing to the proximity of the bachelor lines to the married lines, it would not be practicable to locate another unit in the former, and at the same time preserve the privacy of the latter; and, judging by the episode which occurred in 1918, when the privacy of the married lines was disturbed by the men of a certain unit who were located in the vicinity, any attempt to locate the men of a unit which had recently returned from Field Service, and which was under orders for disbandment in the existing bachelor lines, would be to court a recurrence of such an episode in an accentuated form.

5. Although in no way wishing to appear selfish or parochial, I feel it my duty, on behalf of the men whose commandant I have the honour to be, to lay these facts before you, and to request that no other unit should be located in the bachelor lines of the 2nd Battalion during the absence of that Battalion.

6. Should be this found to be impracticable in the interests of the Service and owing to the abnormalcy of the situation, I would request that only such units as have already been reduced to cadre may be accommodated in these lines, as such units will be composed of older and more responsible men, who will appreciate the feelings of the absentee husbands to a greater extent than would a collection of youngsters with lots of money and about to be demobilized.

7. I would further request that as early intimation as possible may be given as to the final decision in order that a true and accurate account may be sent to the men as to the arrangements which will be made to protect their families. This I consider of the utmost importance, as otherwise discontent may be created by false rumours.

I am,
Sir,
Your obedient servant,
(Signed)　K. WIGRAM, *Colonel*,
Commanding 2nd Battalion 2nd K.E.O. Goorkhas.

No. 3/20/2/Q.]
Accommodation General.

DEHRA DOON,
30*th April,* 1921.

Copy of a Wire, No. 469 *(Q.A.), dated 29th April,* 1921, *from Updist., Mussoorie, to 17th (Indian) Infantry Brigade.*

469 (Q.A.) Yr 3/20/1/Q of twenty-third AAA District Commander rules that in accordance with the charter granted to the 2/2nd Gurkhas the Bijapore Lines at Dehra Doon be not occupied by any other troops during their absence.

GOORKHAS (THE SIRMOOR RIFLE REGIMENT)

APPENDIX H.

LIST OF ACTIONS AND CASUALTIES SUSTAINED BY THE 2ND KING EDWARD'S OWN GOORKHAS FROM 1911 TO 1921.

Names of Expeditions and Actions and Dates.	Killed.	Wounded.	Missing.
Abor Expedition, 1911-12	3 O.Rs.	7 O.Rs.	—
FRANCE.			
Near Neuve Chapelle, 31/10/14	1 B.O.	4 O.Rs.	—
Near Neuve Chapelle, 2/11/14	7 B.Os. 4 G.Os. 31 O.Rs.	1 B.O. 3 G.Os. 64 O.Rs.	— — 37 O.Rs.
La Quinque Rue, 20/12/14	1 B.O. — 29 O.Rs.	2 B.Os. 4 G.Os. 34 O.Rs.	— 2 G.Os. 60 O.Rs.
Battle of Neuve Chapelle, 10-11/3/15	— 2 G.Os. 17 O.Rs.	2 B.Os. 1 G.O. 41 O.Rs.	1 B.O. — 27 O.Rs.
Battle of Festubert, 9/5/15	4 B.Os. 2 G.Os. 25 O.Rs.	— 2 G.Os. 62 O.Rs.	— — 6 O.Rs.
Battle of Loos, 25/9/15	3 O.Rs.	18 O.Rs.	2 O.Rs.
MINOR AFFAIRS—FRANCE.			
21/11/14	— 3 O.Rs.	1 B.O. 4 O.Rs.	—
8/12/14	1 O.R.	3 O.Rs.	—
14/12/14	—	2 B.Os.	—
1/2/15	—	1 O.R.	—
26/2/15	—	8 O.Rs.	—
10-26/4/15	2 O.Rs.	28 O.Rs.	—
29/5/15	2 O.Rs.	9 O.Rs.	—
23/6/15	—	2 O.Rs.	—
24/6/15	2 O.Rs.	1 O.R.	—
10/8/15	—	1 O.R.	—
29/9/15	—	1 O.R.	—
7/10/15	1 B.O.	3 O.Rs.	—
MESOPOTAMIA.			
Dujailah Redoubt, 8/3/16	3 B.Os. 96 O.Rs.	1 B.O. 108 O.Rs.	—
Near Beit Aiessa, 13-18/4/16	— — 6 O.Rs.	2 B.Os. 3 G.Os. 55 O.Rs.	—
Bomb accident at Twin Canals, 25/4/16	— 1 O.R.	1 B.O. 5 O.Rs.	—
26/5/16	1 O.R.	—	—
Near Kāla Haji Fahān, 28/1/17	—	1 B.O. 10 O.Rs.	—

Names of Expeditions and Actions and Dates.	Killed.	Wounded.	Missing.
MESOPOTAMIA—*continued.*			
Near Kāla Haji Fahān, 1/2/17	{ 2 B.Os. —	1 G.O. 41 O.Rs.	— —
Near Liquorice Factory, 3/2/17	{ 3 B.Os. 2 G.Os. 82 O.Rs.	2 B.Os. 5 G.Os. 197 O.Rs.	— — —
Tigris Crossing and Dahra, 23 and 24/2/17	{ 1 B.O. 3 G.Os. 69 O.Rs.	2 B.Os. 1 G.O. 72 O.Rs.	— — —
Near Nahr Tawila, 12/4/17	—	3 O.Rs.	—
Advance on Deli Abbas, 13/4/17	{ 1 B.O. —	1 G.O. 35 O.Rs.	— —
Band i Adhaim, 30/4/17	War Diary merely states slight casualties		
Resht, early July, 1918	4 O.Rs.	13 O.Rs.	—
Near Kermanshah, July, 1920	{ — —	1 B.O. * 1 O.R.	— —
Tabriz reconnaissance and the Kuflon Kūh action, September, 1918	5 O.Rs.	1 B.O.	—
Enzeli, 18/5/20	2 O.Rs.	6 O.Rs.	—
Menzil, 28/7/20	{ — 2 O.Rs.	1 B.O. 8 O.Rs.	— —
Imām Zādeh Hachem, 23/11/20	2 O.Rs.	2 O.Rs.	—
Near Rudbar, early December, 1920	—	1 B.O.	—
Naglebar, 20/12/20	1 O.R.	1 G.O.	—
Naglebar, 29/12/20	1 O.R.	1 B.O.	—

* Accidentally.

APPENDIX I.

LIST OF INDIAN ARMY RESERVE OFFICERS ATTACHED TO THE 2ND KING EDWARD'S OWN GOORKHAS DURING THE WAR, 1914 TO 1921.

In France, Egypt, and the North-West Frontier, India.

Captain A. S. E. Roberts.
Lieutenant R. H. Burne.
2/Lieutenant C. G. Barker.
2/Lieutenant M. R. K. Jerram.
2/Lieutenant G. Sanderson.
2/Lieutenant Swaine.
2/Lieutenant Helm.
2/Lieutenant F. M. Daly.
2/Lieutenant E. De Brath.
2/Lieutenant G. L. Field.
2/Lieutenant H. Green.

In Mesopotamia and North Persia.

Captain P. A. R. Pritchard.
Lieutenant K. H. Coxe.
Lieutenant M. R. K. Jerram.
Lieutenant C. A. Snow.
Lieutenant V. R. Murray.
Lieutenant J. H. Smith.
Lieutenant H. T. Thomson.
Lieutenant D. A. Oliphant.
Lieutenant H. T. Meredith.
Lieutenant Simmonds.
Lieutenant Macleod.
Lieutenant Sheridan.
Lieutenant Dunlop.
Lieutenant Goodall.
2/Lieutenant Rowbotham.
2/Lieutenant Baker.
2/Lieutenant Miller Hallett.
2/Lieutenant W. L. Tanburne.
2/Lieutenant G. M. Bruce Kerr.
2/Lieutenant Morgan.
2/Lieutenant Harrison.

In all probability certain names have been omitted, which I regret, but the loss of documents at Enzeli has made it difficult to trace all.

APPENDIX J.

The Regimental Ram.

In 1917 various regimental bands were ordered to proceed to Mesopotamia to be attached to divisions in central places : for instance, the 5th Goorkha Rifles' band came to the 15th Division at Baghdad, that of the 2nd Goorkhas to the 14th Division at Baquba, and so on. After playing for Brigadier-General H. Champain one night, he gave our bandsmen some young sheep, one of which the men kept and made a pet of. In course of time he grew into a fine large ram, and followed the 1st Battalion all through Persia, returning with it to Dehra. He had by then become a regimental mascot, and, being an intelligent beast, had picked up various tricks taught him. One of these was for men to tell the ram to go to a spot 50 yards off, where he halted and fronted at the word of command. On the command " Charge," he would lower his head and come like a bullet for the men, one of whom would then sing out " Halt " when the animal was within a few yards of them, on which he at once planted his fore-feet and threw up his head. The 2/2nd Goorkhas went to Delhi on the occasion of the Duke of Connaught's visit in the winter of 1920-21, and with them went the ram. At Rankens he was fitted with a fine ornate scarlet and green " jhūl," and marched past at the head of the band—an ornament to the Regiment and living emblem of its badge, a ram's head, a distinction dating from October 2nd, 1824, at the capture of Koonja Fort, near Roorki.

Another pet of the Battalion to see service in Persia was " Tu Tu," a fine dog belonging to Colonel Sweet. She was one of a litter of puppies left behind in Baghdad by a German officer—her mother an Alsatian wolf-hound, her father a Great Dane. " Tu Tu " was in several actions during the operations in North Persia, and was badly wounded on three occasions—the first time at Enzeli, then was badly hit from an armoured car, and again in early 1921 a Bolshevik bullet bowled her over. She, however, recovered, and is now in Dehra with the Battalion.

APPENDIX K.

LIST OF POLO TOURNAMENTS AND FOOTBALL MATCHES FOR WHICH THE 2ND GOORKHAS ENTERED TEAMS, AND THEIR RESULTS.

Since the early "eighties" polo has been a prominent game at Dehra, in those days the only ground available for it being the "maidan" in front of the Forest School in the Civil Lines. About 1887 the lower half of the 1st Battalion parade ground, till then all rough ground covered with jungle bushes, was cleared and levelled for ceremonial parades, polo, etc., which, being entirely carried out by our own fatigue parties, took a long time to complete.

In 1894 the regimental team, captained by Major Charles Judge (killed at Dargai in 1897), entered for its first tournament, and five years later the 2nd Goorkha Polo Tournament came into being, the title being changed in 1904 to that of the Dehra Doon Tournament.

Increasing prices for good ponies being a difficult matter for small means to overcome, a Regimental Polo Fund was started to which all officers subscribed, and which in 1903 was put firmly on its feet through an endowment by Colonel Wright, D.S.O., Medical Officer of the Regiment, who most kindly gave a sum of Rs4,500, the fund thereafter being styled the "Wright Fund."

Since then the regimental team has played annually in most of the tournaments in the United Provinces and the Punjab, fathered by the capable efforts of Major Ross and Captain Ridgeway (both killed in the Great War), whose knowledge of horsemastership and of polo generally was of the very best.

Round this lower parade ground is also the golf course. Golf was originally started by Lieutenant and Adjutant L. W. Shakespear in 1890 round the area of the 2nd Battalion recruits' parade and rifle range. It was transferred for a few years to the open ground between the Circuit House and 1st Battalion lines, and eventually was laid out about 1900 or 1901 as it is at present.

A list of polo tournaments and results since 1894 is as follows :—

Year.	Where played, and Tournament.	Team.	Results.
November, 1894. Lost	At Meerut. N.W.P. and Oudh Tournament	Capt. Judge Mr. Watson Mr. Home Mr. Wylie	Beaten in two rounds by the 5th Lancers by 6 goals and 1 subsidiary. Won by the R.A.
October, 1899. Won	At Dehra Doon. 2nd Goorkha Polo Tournament	Mr. Ridgeway Mr. Lindsay Mr. Wigram Mr. Boileau	In two rounds beat the South Wales Borderers (2nd team) by 9 goals to 3 goals and 1 subsidiary. In finals beat South Wales Borderers (1st team) by 5 goals and 3 subsidiaries to 4 goals and 2 subsidiaries.

Year.	Where played, and Tournament.	Team.	Results.
February, 1900 Lost	At Meerut. Infantry Tournament (the first Indian Army Regiment to enter for this Cup)	Mr. Ridgeway Mr. Becher Mr. Wigram Mr. Boileau	Beaten in two rounds by the Rifle Brigade by 6 goals and 1 subsidiary to 3 goals. Won by the Rifle Brigade. The *Civil and Military Gazette* reported : " The best game of the Tournament was between the Rifle Brigade and 2nd Goorkhas."
February, 1903. Lost	At Dehra Doon. Challenge Cup	Mr. Ridgeway Mr. Wigram Capt. Ross Mr. Boileau	Beaten in two rounds by the 3rd B.C. by 4 goals and 2 subsidiaries to 3 goals and 2 subsidiaries. Won by 3rd B.C.
February, 1903. Lost	At Lahore. Infantry Tournament	Mr. Ridgeway Mr. Wigram Capt. Ross Mr. Boileau	*1st Round.*—We beat the Somerset Light Infantry by 5 goals and 2 subsidiaries to 1 goal and 1 subsidiary. *2nd Round.*—We beat the Gordons by 4 goals and 2 subsidiaries to 2 goals and 1 subsidiary. *Finals.*—Beaten by the Queen's by 2 goals and 1 subsidiary to 1 goal and 1 subsidiary.
November, 1903 Lost	At Dehra Doon. Challenge Cup	Capt. Watt Major Bradley Mr. Ridgeway Major Watson	*1st Round.*—We beat the Welsh Fusiliers by 6 goals and 1 subsidiary to 6 goals. *2nd Round.*—Beaten by the Rifle Brigade by 9 goals. Tournament won by the I.C.C.
November, 1904. Lost	At Dehra Doon. Polo Tournament	Entered " A " and " B " teams	Both teams beaten in 1st tie by Welsh Fusiliers and Skinner's Horse, latter team winning finals.
February, 1905. Lost	At Meerut. Infantry Tournament	As for Infantry Tournament, 1903	*1st Round.*—We beat Royal Irish Rifles by 7 goals and 6 subsidiaries to 3 subsidiaries. *2nd Round.*—The 60th Rifles beat us by 6 goals and 2 subsidiaries to 1 goal and 1 subsidiary. The 60th Rifles won the Tournament.
October, 1905. Lost	At Dehra Doon. Polo Tournament	As for Infantry Tournament, February, 1905, but with Mr. Bruce instead of Capt. Boileau	*1st Round.*—Beaten by I.C.C. by 9 goals and 1 subsidiary to 3 goals and 3 subsidiaries. I.C.C. won the final.

GOORKHAS (THE SIRMOOR RIFLE REGIMENT)

Year.	Where played, and Tournament.	Team.	Results.
February, 1906. Lost	At Lucknow. Infantry Tournament	Mr. Elles Mr. Barton Capt. Ross Capt. Boileau	*1st Round.*—We beat the Oxfordshire L.I. by 6 goals and 6 subsidiaries to 1 goal and 1 subsidiary. *2nd Round.*—We beat the Somerset L.I. by 2 goals and 1 subsidiary to 1 goal and 1 subsidiary. *3rd Round.*—Durham L.I. beat us by 3 goals and 1 subsidiary to 1 goal. Durham L.I. won the Tournament.
November, 1906. Lost	At Dehra Doon. Polo Tournament	Mr. Barton Capt. Nicholl Capt. Ross Capt. Boileau	*1st Round.*—We beat the 9th G.R. by 5 goals and 1 subsidiary to 1 goal. *2nd Round.*—Rifle Brigade beat us by 3 goals and 3 subsidiaries to 3 goals and 2 subsidiaries. Rifle Brigade won the Tournament.
November, 1907. Lost	At Dehra Doon. Challenge Cup	Mr. Mathew Mr. Fremantle Mr. Barton Capt. Ridgeway	*2nd Round.*—We beat the Cameronians by 5 goals to nil. *Semi-Finals.*—The Rifle Brigade beat us by 8 goals to 3. Rifle Brigade won the Cup.
May, 1907. Lost	At Mussoorie. Polo Tournament	Entered " A " and " B " teams	Lost to 17th Lancers and Mussoorie " A " team respectively in 2nd Round. 17th Lancers won the Tournament.
February, 1908. Lost	At Dehra Doon. Indian Army Tournament	Mr. Mathew Mr. Barton Capt. Ross Capt. Ridgeway	*2nd Round.*—We beat the Guides by 4 goals to 3. *Finals.*—We beat the 22nd Punjabis by 5 goals to nil. This was the first time the I.A.T. Cup was ever brought south of the Indus.
February, 1908. Lost	At Bareilly. Infantry Tournament	Mr. Mathew Mr. Barton Capt. Ross Capt. Ridgeway	*1st Round.*—We beat the South Lancs by 5 goals to nil. *Semi-Finals.*—We beat the Royal Irish Rifles by 6 goals to nil. *Finals.*—The Queen's beat us by 7 goals to nil. The Queen's won the Tournament.
May, 1908. Lost	At Mussoorie. Mussoorie Tournament	Mr. Mathew Mr. Mullaly Capt. Ridgeway	*1st Round.*—We beat the 17th Lancers' subaltern team by 4 goals to 2. *Semi-Finals.*—17th Lancers beat us by 6 goals to 5 (extra time).

Year.	Where played, and Tournament.	Team.	Results.
November, 1908 Lost	At Meerut. Meerut Tournament	Mr. Barton Mr. Mullaly Major Ross Capt. Ridgeway	2nd Round.—King's Dragoon Gds. beat us by 6 goals to 1. Tournament won by 17th Lancers.
January, 1909. Lost	At Dehra Doon. D.D. Tournament	"A" Team: Mr. Mathews Mr. Mullaly Major Ross Capt. Ridgeway "B" Team: Mr. Cruickshank Capt. Blair Mr. Barton Capt. Nicholl	1st Round.—I.C.C. beat our "B" team by 6 goals to nil. Semi-Finals.—Our "A" Team beat the I.C.C. by 6 goals to 4. Finals.—The Rifle Brigade beat our "A" team by 6 goals to 2.
May, 1909. Won	At Mussoorie. Mussoorie Tournament	Mr. Mullaly Capt. Barton Major Ross	1st Round.—We beat the King's Dragoon Guards by 6 goals to 4. Finals.—We beat the 15th Hussars by 11 goals to 1.
February, 1909. Lost	At Bareilly. Infantry Tournament	Mr. Mathew Capt. Barton Major Ross Capt. Ridgeway	The Rifle Brigade beat us by 9 goals to 2.
January, 1910. Won	At Lahore. Indian Army Infantry Tournament.	Mr. Mullaly Capt. Barton Major Ross Capt. Ridgeway	1st Round.—We beat the 26th Punjabis by 6 goals to nil. 2nd Round.—We beat the 53rd Sikhs by 6 goals to 2. Finals.—We beat the 5th Goorkha Rifles by 2 goals to 1.
January, 1910. Won	At Dehra Doon. D.D. Tournament	Capt. Seymour Mr. Cruickshank Mr. Mullaly Mr. Chope	1st Round.—We beat the Gymkhana "A" team by 3 goals to 2. Finals.—We beat the I.C.C. by 3 goals to 2, and won the Tournament.
December, 1910. Lost	At Dehra Doon. D.D. Tournament	Mr. Mathew Mr. Chope Mr. Mullaly Capt. Ridgeway	Beaten by the I.C.C. by 4 goals to nil.
May, 1911. Won	At Mussoorie. Mussoorie Tournament	Mr. Marsh Mr. Lucas Major Ross	We beat the Chakrata team by 9 goals to 4 and won the Tournament.
February, 1912. Lost	At Dehra Doon. D.D. Tournament	Capt. Mathew Mr. Lucas Capt. Barton Major Ross	The King's Dragoon Guards beat us in 1st round by 2 goals to 1.

GOORKHAS (THE SIRMOOR RIFLE REGIMENT)

Year.	Where played, and Tournament.	Team.	Results.
February, 1912. Lost	At Bareilly. Infantry Tournament	Capt. Barton Capt. Mathew Mr. Lucas Major Ross	*1st Round.*—We beat the 60th Rifles by 8 goals to 1. *Semi-Finals.*—Welsh Fusiliers beat us by 6 goals to 1.
May, 1912. Lost	At Mussoorie. Mussoorie Tournament	Mr. Newall Capt. Barton Capt. Chope	The I.C.C. team beat us by 8 goals to 5.
January, 1913. Lost	At Dehra Doon. D.D. Tournament	Mr. Corse Scott Mr. Lucas Capt. Barton Major Ross	*Semi-Final.*—The 18th Hussars beat us by 11 goals to 2.
March, 1913. Lost	At Mussoorie. Mussoorie Tournament	Mr. Saunders Capt. Becher Mr. Lucas	*1st Round.*—We beat the I.C.C. by 7 goals to 2. *2nd Round.*—The 7th Fusiliers beat us by 7 goals to 6.
January, 1914. Lost	At Dehra Doon. D.D. Tournament	Major Becher Capt. Chope Mr. Lucas Major Ross	*2nd Round.*—We beat 9th Goorkha Rifles by 5 goals to nil. *Semi-Finals.*—We beat the Rifle Brigade by 5 goals to 2. *Finals.*—We were beaten by Skinner's Horse by 9 goals to 2.
February, 1914. Won	At Bareilly. Infantry Tournament	Capt. Chope Major Wigram Mr. Lucas Major Ross	*1st Round.*—We beat the 4th Rifle Brigade by 4 goals to nil. *Semi-Finals.*—We beat the 3/60th Rifles by 8 goals to 2. *Finals.*—We beat the 2nd Rifle Brigade by 4 goals to 3 (extra time).
May, 1914 Won	At Mussoorie. Mussoorie Tournament	Mr. Saunders Capt. Bailey Mr. Lucas	We beat the I.C.C. by 14 goals to 6; Dehra Details by 10 goals to 4; Dehra Ramblers by 9 goals to 8.
September, 1916. Lost	At Naini Tal. N.T. Tournament	Capt. Bailey Mr. Hinde Col. Boileau	*1st Round.*—The Canaries beat us by 6 goals to 4 and won the Tournament.
January, 1920. Lost	At Dehra Doon. D.D. Tournament	"A" Team: Capt. Tottenham Capt. Woollcombe Capt. Gough Major Cruickshank "B" Team: Mr. Hutton Capt. McConkey Capt. Toogood Capt. Miller Hallett	*1st Round.*—Our "A" team beat the Dehra Gymkhana by 6 goals to 1. 12th Cavalry beat our "B" team by 6 goals to 4. *2nd Round.*—9th Goorkha Rifles beat our "A" team by 3 goals to 2. *Finals.*—12th Cavalry beat 9th Goorkha Rifles by 12 goals to 2.

Year.	Where played, and Tournament.	Team.	Remarks.
January, 1921. Lost	At Dehra Doon. Radha Mohan Tournament.	Capt. Bain Capt. Woollcombe Capt. Gough Major Cruickshank	*2nd Round.*—Viceroy's Staff beat us by 8 goals to 2. The Seaforths won the Cup.
February, 1921. Lost	At Bareilly. Infantry Tournament	Major Corse Scott Major Woollcombe Capt. Toogood Major Cruickshank	*2nd Round.*—3/60th Rifles beat us by 8 goals to 1. Seaforths winning the Cup.
January, 1922. Lost	At Dehra Doon. D.D. Tournament	Capt. Bucknall Capt. Lovett Capt. Toogood Capt. Wingfield	*2nd Round.*—We beat the Dehra Gymkhana by 3 goals to 2. *Finals.*—12th Cavalry beat us by 8 goals to 2.

RESULTS OF ASSOCIATION FOOTBALL SUCCESSES BY THE REGIMENTAL TEAM.

GARHWAL BRIGADE CUP.

Year.	Teams in Finals.	Winners.	Captains.
1900	2/2nd Goorkhas v. 1/4th Goorkha Rifles	2/2nd Goorkhas, by 1 goal to nil	Lieut. E. Sweet.
1910	1/2nd Goorkhas v. 2/39th Garhwalis	1/2nd Goorkhas, by 3 goals to nil	Lieut. G. M. McCleverty.
1911	1/2nd Goorkhas v. 2/8th Goorkha Rifles	1/2nd Goorkhas, by 4 goals to nil	Lieut. H. F. Marsh.

GOORKHA BRIGADE CUP.

Year.	Teams in Finals.	Winners.	Captains.
1910	1/2nd Goorkhas v. 2/5th Goorkha Rifles	2/5th Goorkha Rifles, by 2 goals to 1	Lieut. G. M. McCleverty.
1911	1/2nd Goorkhas v. 2/6th Goorkha Rifles	1/2nd Goorkhas, by 2 goals to nil	Lieut. H. F. Marsh.

SUCCESSES AT RIFLE MEETINGS OF THE 2ND GOORKHAS SINCE THE WAR.

No. 8 Platoon, "B" Company, 2nd Battalion, won the Cawnpore Woollen Mills Cup, 1920-21; "B" Company, 2nd Battalion, was third in the Commander-in-Chief's Cup, 1921.

Bugle-Major Dhanbahadur Mal won the A.R.A. Championship, Class V, 1921; also the Priestley and the Magdala Medals. He was the best shot in the Indian Army and third best shot in the British and Indian Army.

Naik Makan Sing Gurung was second in the A.R.A. Championship, Class VI, 1921.

APPENDIX L.

Translation from *Lille War Gazette*, March 3rd, 1915. (This was a weekly newspaper, issued by the Germans in Lille, in German.)

N.B.—A copy of this newspaper was found on a German prisoner captured during the recent fighting at Neuve Chapelle. It is of interest as showing the hatred for Great Britain which is being sedulously cultivated in Germany. This hatred is being encouraged and fostered officially by every possible means.

FIRE.

By Lieutenant-Colonel Kaden.

As children many of us have played with it : some of us have seen an outbreak of fire. First a small tongue-like flame appears, it grows into a devastating fury of heat. We out here in the field have seen more than enough of it.

But there is also the fire of joy, of sacred enthusiasm ! It arose from sacrificial altars, from mountain heights of Germany, and lit up the heavens at the time of solstice and whenever the home countries were in danger. This year fires of joy shall flare from the Bismarck Columns throughout the length and breadth of Germany, for on 1st April, just one hundred years ago, our country's greatest son was born. Let us celebrate this event in a manner deep, far-reaching and mighty ! BLOOD AND IRON.

Let every German, man or woman, young or old, find in his heart a Bismarck Column, a pillar of fire, now in these days of storm and stress. Let this fire, enkindled in every German breast, be a fire of joy, of holiest enthusiasm. But let it be terrible, unfettered, let it carry horror and destruction ! Call it HATE ! Let no one come to you with " Love thine enemy !" We all have but one enemy, *England*. How long have we wooed her almost to the point of our own self-abasement. She would none of us, so leave to her the apostles of peace, the " No-War " disciples. The time has passed when we would do homage to everything English—our cousins that were !

" God punish England !" " May He punish her !" This is the greeting that now passes when Germans meet. The fire of this righteous hate is all aglow !

You men of Germany, from East and West, forced to shed your blood in the defence of your home-land through England's infamous envy and hatred of Germany's progress, feed the flame that burns in your souls. We have but one war-cry, " GOD PUNISH ENGLAND !" Hiss this to one another in the trenches, in the charge, hiss as it were the sound of licking flames.

Behold in every dead comrade a sacrifice forced from you by this accursed people. Take ten-fold vengeance for each hero's death !

You German people at home, feed this fire of hate !

You mothers, engrave this in the heart of the babe at your breast !

You thousands of teachers, to whom millions of German children look up with eyes and hearts, teach HATE !—unquenchable HATE !

You homes of German learning, pile up the fuel on this fire! Tell the nation that this hate is not un-German, that it is not poison for our people. Write in letters of fire the name of our bitterest enemy. You guardians of the truth, feed this sacred HATE!

You German fathers, lead your children up the high hills of our home-land, at their feet our dear country bathed in sunshine. Your women and children shall starve; bestial, devilish conception. England wills it! Surely, all that is in you rises against such infamy?

Listen to the ceaseless song of the German forest, behold the fruitful fields like rolling seas, then will your love for this wondrous land find the right words—HATE, unquenchable HATE. Germany, Germany above all!

Let it be inculcated in your children, and it will grow like a land-slide, irresistible, from generation to generation.

You fathers, proclaim it aloud over the billowing fields, that the toiling peasant below may hear you, that the birds of the forest may fly away with the message: into all the land that echoes from German cliffs send it reverberating like the clanging of bells from tower to tower throughout the countryside: " HATE, HATE, the accursed English, HATE "!

You masters, carry the flame to your workshops; axe and hammer will fall the heavier when arms are nerved by this HATE.

You peasants, guard this flame, fan it anew in the hearts of your toilers, that the hand may rest heavy on the plough that throws up the soil of our home-land.

What CARTHAGE was to ROME, ENGLAND is to GERMANY. For ROME as for us it is a question of " to be or not to be." May our people find a faithful mentor like Cato! His " ceterum censeo, Carthaginem esse delendam " for us Germans means:—

"GOD PUNISH ENGLAND."

APPENDIX M.

Note on the Abor Expedition, 1911-12.

That this Expedition, from the point of view of military operations, was more of a disappointment than a success goes without saying, and it received many severe strictures both from officers connected with it and from the Press, chiefly on account of the dilatoriness of the advance, the size of the force, and its consequent expense amounting to some 12 lakhs. Much was expected as a result of these operations, which a high official stigmatized openly as a "contemptible farce, differing only from all others on the North-East Frontier in its colossal expense." Weeks were passed in reaching Rohtang and Kekyar Monying, a bare 40 miles, when small active columns in different directions could have effected far more than two large, slow-moving units hampered by orders tying their hands and obviating the possibility of any activity and initiative.

The *Morning Post's* animadversion on this expedition is interesting as showing governmental methods, and may be quoted.

"With the exception of the survey and exploration part of it, this expedition may fall into the same category as those of earlier days whose lessons had not been learnt, viz., unsatisfactory and practically a failure from a military and punitive point of view. As usual, the advice of those on the spot was ignored as to methods, the 'show' was controlled (one might almost say conducted) by higher authority far from the scenes, and the interests of the civilian and exigencies of Government were once again to outbalance the military, whose original scheme of advancing rapidly and overrunning the country in several small and handy columns was vetoed by a Committee none of whom had been nearer the frontier than Calcutta. On the recommendation of this Committee orders were issued forbidding the use of small columns, stating the force was to run no unnecessary risks. Thus the General Officer Commanding had his hands tied, whether to his content or the reverse is not known, though it might be said here that often it is 'better to have commanded an expedition and failed, than never to have commanded one at all.' Once over the border, the advance was far too slow. Had freer scope been given to initiative and originality of those acquainted with these hills and wild tribes, and had it all been conducted with greater dash and deeper determination, the final punishment of the Abors would have been more adequate."

As it was, the only real punishment such people recognize was not meted out, while the actual murderers of Mr. Williamson and Dr. Gregorson and party, who were given up, were not tried summarily in the field and hung according to their deserts; but were tried later by a civil tribunal, which sentenced them to the Andamans for a period of years, from which in 1920 one or two of them were allowed back to their village. When the expedition withdrew Government decided to leave the tribes to themselves, to have no political dealings with them, and declined to establish the suggested trading and police post at Rohtang which would have tended towards a better feeling between these wild folk and ourselves. A few years later this matter was reconsidered, and the trading post with a hospital, was established, backed by 200 rifles of the 2nd Assam Rifles, disposed at Pasighat, 100 ; at Rohtang, 75 ; and at Yambung, below Kebang village, 25. It was then, however, more or less too late to produce any good effect, for the Abors, finding themselves left alone again, adopted a sullen, truculent demeanour and declined to trade, though they come in occasionally for treatment in the post hospitals.

www.ingramcontent.com/pod-product-compliance
Lightning Source LLC
Chambersburg PA
CBHW080725300426
44114CB00019B/2491